# Communication and Cyberspace

## Social Interaction in an Electronic Environment
### Second Edition

# The Hampton Press Communication Series
## Communication and Public Space
## Gary Gumpert, supervisory editor

Communication and Cyberspace: Social Interaction in an Electronic Environment
(Second Edition)
*Lance Strate, Ron L. Jacobson, and Stephanie B. Gibson (eds.)*

The Huddled Masses:
Communication and Immigration
*Gary Gumpert and Susan J. Drucker (eds.)*

Modernity, Space, and Power:
The American City in Discourse and Practice
*Katharine Kia Tehranian*

Take Me out to the Ballgame:
Communicating Baseball
*Gary Gumpert and Susan J. Drucker (eds.)*

*Voices* in the Street: Exploration in Gender, Media, and Public Space
*Susan J. Drucker and Gary Gumpert (eds.)*

# Communication and Cyberspace

## Social Interaction in an Electronic Environment
### Second Edition

Edited by
**Lance Strate**
**Ron L. Jacobson**
*Fordham University*
**Stephanie B. Gibson**
*University of Baltimore*

HAMPTON PRESS, INC.
CRESSKILL, NEW JERSEY

Printed in the United States of America

**Library of Congress Cataloging-in-Publication Data**

Communication and cyberspace : social interaction in an electronic environment / edited by Lance Strate, Ronald Jacobson, Stephanie B.Gibson.
      p.   cm. -- (The Hampton Press communication series, Communication and public space)
    Includes bibliographical references and index.
    ISBN 1-57273-393-4 (alk. paper) -- ISBN 1-57273-394-2 (pbk.: alk. paper)
      1. Communication--Data processing.  2. Communication and technology.  3. Computer networks.  4. Cybernetics.  5. Social interaction.  6. Virtual reality.  I. Strate, Lance. II. Jacobson, Ronald L., 1956- III. Gibson, Stephanie B.  IV. Series.

P96.D36 C66 2002
302.2'0285--dc21

                               2002068822

Hampton Press, Inc.
23 Broadway
Cresskill, NJ 07626

❖❖❖❖

# Contents

◇◇◇◇

# Acknowledgments

The editors of this book would like to extend their deep and sincere appreciation to Gary Gumpert and Barbara Bernstein for making this project possible, for their confidence in us, and for their support of our efforts.

We would also like to thank the following individuals for their help: Sue Barnes, James Capo, Richard Cutler, Raymond Gozzi, Jr., Nancy Kaplan, Neil Kleinman, Judith Yaross Lee, Roger Musgrave, Christine Nystrom, Everett C. Parker, John M. Phelan, Janet Sternberg, and Edward Wachtel.

Acknowledgments are due to Fordham University's Office of Research for two supporting grants, and to the McGannon Communication Research Center, Fordham University's Department of Communication and Media Studies, and the University of Baltimore's School of English and Communication for more indirect forms of assistance. Special thanks go to the *TINAC* Collective, and to *Girls Just Wanna Have Drums*.

We would like to thank the following individuals for deepening our understanding of communication and cyberspace: Tony L. Arduini, Jr., Eva Berger, Kay Fielden, Michael E. Holmes, John McDaid, Joshua Meyrowitz, Pat O'Hara, Henry Perkinson, Rita Rahoi, Susan Mallon Ross, Amy Sauertieg, Charles J. Stivale, and David Thompson.

We are grateful to Joseph Barrett, Michael B. Beaubien, Margaret Cassidy, Richard H. Cutler, Mark Lipton, and Lizzy Weiss, whose work enriched the first edition of this book, and whose chapters could not be included in this edition for reasons of space, not quality. Their scholarship stands as significant contributions to the literature on communication and cyberspace.

Finally, a special thank you to Barbara, Betty, Benjamin, and Sarah Strate, to Akiko, Brando, and Suki Jacobson, and to Orton, Bear, Cleo, and Percy Gibson for their love and support, and understanding and patience.

❖❖❖

# About the Authors

**Susan B. Barnes** is an Associate Professor at Rochester Institute of Technology in the Communication Department. She is also the editor of *Interpersonal Computing and Technology (IPCT-J)* and the author of *Online Connections: Internet Interpersonal Relationships*.

**James R. Beniger** is an Associate Professor at the University of Southern California's Annenberg School of Communication. He is the author of *The Control Revolution: Technological and Economic Origins of the Information Society*.

**Jay David Bolter** is a Professor in the School of Literature, Communication and Culture at the Georgia Institute of Technology. He is the author of *Turing's Man: Western Culture in the Computer Age* and of *Writing Space: The Computer, Hypertext and the History of Writing*. He is also the co-author of *Remediation: Understanding New Media*, and of the hypertext authoring software program *Storyspace*.

**Frank E.X. Dance** is John Evans University Professor of Human Communication Studies at the University of Denver. A past president of the National Communication Association and the International Communication Association, he is the author, co-author, or editor of 10 books, including *Public Speaking* and *Speaking Your Mind: Private Thinking and Public Speaking*, both with Carol C. Zak-Dance.

**Susan J. Drucker** is an attorney and Associate Professor of Journalism and Mass Media Studies at Hofstra University. She is the co-editor with Robert Cathcart of *American Heroes in a Media Age* and with Gary Gumpert of *Voices in the Street: Gender, Media, and Public Space*, *The Huddled Masses: Communication and Immigration* and *Take Me Out to the*

*Ballgame: Communicating Baseball*. Her primary areas of interest include media law and the impact of laws on social interaction and public space. Her work has appeared in *The New York State Bar Journal*, *Communication Quarterly*, *Communication Theory*, and *Critical Studies in Mass Communication*.

**Stephanie B. Gibson**, one of the co-editors of this anthology, is on the faculty in the School of Communication at the University of Baltimore where she teaches communication theory and hypermedia design. Her major research areas are the relationship between culture and technology, hypermedia and pedagogy, and feminist studies, and she has directed several conferences about interactive media.

**Mark Giese** is an Assistant Professor in the School of Communication at the University of Houston. His research interests include virtual communities and social uses of new electronic communication technologies.

**Gary Gumpert** is Professor Emeritus of Communication Arts and Sciences at Queens College, City University of New York. He is the author of *Talking Tombstones and Other Tales of the Media Age* and has co-edited with Robert Cathcart three editions of *Inter/Media: Interpersonal Communication in the Media World*. He has also co-edited with Sandra Fish *Talking to Strangers: Mediated Therapeutic Communication*, and with Susan Drucker *Voices in the Street: Gender, Media, and Public Space*, *The Huddled Masses: Communication and Immigration* and *Take Me Out to the Ballgame: Communicating Baseball*. His articles have appeared in journals such as *The Quarterly Journal of Speech*, *Critical Studies in Mass Communication*, and *Communication Theory*.

**Chris Hunter** is a doctoral student in the Annenberg School for Communication at the University of Pennsylvania.

**Ron L. Jacobson**, one of the co-editors of this anthology, is Associate Dean of Fordham College and an Associate Professor in the Department of Communication and Media Studies at Fordham University. He is also the author of *Television-Related Cartoons* in *The New Yorker Magazine*, and *Television Research: A Directory of Conceptual Categories, Topic Suggestions and Selected Sources*.

**Neil Kleinman** is Professor of communication and media and Dean of the College of Media and Communication at the University of the Arts, Philadelphia. He is the author of a book on propaganda, *The Dream That Was No More a Dream*, writes and lectures on intellectual property, the digital economy, and the influence of technologies on society. He holds a PhD from the University of Connecticut and a JD from the University of Pennsylvania. Until recently, he was Professor of English and Communication Design at the University of Baltimore, where he was director of the Institute for Language, Technology, and Publications Design, co-director of the School of Communications Design, and director of the university's doctoral program in Communication Design. In 1997, he received the Yale Gordon College's Distinguished Chair for teaching, and in 1998, he received the University of Maryland System Regents Award for Distinguished Teaching.

**Charles Larson** is a Professor in the Department of Communication Studies at Northern Illinois University, and the author of *Persuasion: Reception and Responsibility*. He has published numerous articles and monographs concerning political communication, advertising, dramatism, and the need for community.

**Judith Yaross Lee** is Professor in the rhetoric program in the School of Interpersonal Communication at Ohio University. A historian of American popular culture, she is the author of *Defining "New Yorker" Humor* (2000) and *Garrison Keiller: A Voice of America* (1991).

**Paul Levinson** is Professor of Communication and Media Studies, and Director of Graduate Studies, Master's Program in Communications at Fordham University. He has written eight books and more than 150 scholarly and popular articles on history, philosophy, and future of media, communication, and technology. His most recent books are *The Soft Edge: A Natural History and Future of the Information Revolution* (1997) and *Digital McLuhan: A Guide to the Information Millennium* (1999). His novel, *The Silk Code*, won the Locus Award for the best first science fiction novel of 1999. He founded Connected Education, which began offering courses for graduate-level credit on the Internet in 1985.

**Paul Lippert** is Professor of Speech Communication at East Stroudsburg University. His research interests include cinema studies, orality-literacy theory, and media epistemology.

**Stuart Moulthrop** is an Associate Professor in the School of Communications Design at the University of Baltimore. He is the author of *Victory Garden*, a critically acclaimed electronic fiction, as well as numerous essays on hypertext and new media.

**Camille Paglia** is a scholar and culture critic who is University Professor of Humanities and Media Studies at the University of the Arts in Philadelphia, where she has taught since 1984. She is the author of four books: *Sexual Personae: Art and Decadence from Nefertiti to Emily Dickinson* (1990); *Sex, Art, and American Culture* (1992); *Vamps & Tramps: New Essays* (1994); and *The Birds*, a study of Alfred Hitchcock published in 1998. She is a columnist with the online magazine *Salon,* for which she has written since it was launched in 1995. She has contributed numerous articles on art, literature, popular culture, feminism, and politics to publications around the world, and she has appeared extensively on television and radio in the United States and abroad.

**Terri Toles Patkin** is an Associate Professor in the Department of Communication at Eastern Connecticut State University. Her research interests include organizational communication and telecommunications policy.

**John M. Phelan** is a Professor in the Department of Communication and Media Studies at Fordham University, and former Director of the McGannon Communication Research Center. He is the author of *Apartheid Media: Disinformation and Dissent in South Africa, Disenchantment: Media and Morality in the Media,* and *Mediaworld: Programming the Public.*

**Neil Postman** is University Professor and Chair of the Department of Culture and Communication at New York University. He is the author of over twenty books, including *The End of Education, Technopoly, Amusing Ourselves to Death, The Disappearance of Childhood, Teaching as a Conserving Activity, Crazy Talk, Stupid Talk,* and *Teaching as a Subversive Activity* with Charles Weingartner.

**Douglas Rushkoff** is the author of eight books on media, technology, and culture including *Coercion, Playing the Future, Media Virus,* and *Cyberia.* He teaches media theory at NYU, delivers regular commentaries on NPR's All Things Considered, writes a monthly column syndicated internationally by *The New York Times,* and lectures around the world. He is also a Senior Advisor to the Markle Foundation.

**Lance Strate**, one of the co-editors of this anthology, is an Associate Professor in the Department of Communication and Media Studies at Fordham University. He is co-author, with Neil Postman, Christine Nystrom, and Charles Weingartner, of *Myths, Men, and Beer,* and is currently working on a book on media theory entitled *Understanding Media Ecology.* He is the co-editor of *Critical Studies in Media Commercialism* and of *The Legacy of McLuhan.* He is also the supervisory editor of Hampton Press' Media Ecology Content Area Series.

**Philip A. Thompsen** is an Assistant Professor of Communication at William Jewell College, Liberty, Missouri, and General Manager, KWJC radio. His research interests include computer-mediated communication, human-computer interaction, and new communication technologies. Prior to his career in academia, he was a professional radio announcer for nine years.

**Herbert Zettl** is Professor of Broadcast and Electronic Communication Arts at San Francisco State University. His major research areas are media aesthetics and video production. He has published extensively in both fields. His CD-ROM "Video Producer: A Video Production Lab," developed with the Cooperative Media Group for Wadsworth Publishing Company, has won the Macromedia People's Choice Award for Best Educational Product 1994, the New Media CD-ROM 1995 Gold Medal in the Higher Education category, and Silver Medals in the Continuing Education and Best Use of Video categories.

**Eric Zimmer**, S.J. is a doctoral candidate in the Annenberg School for Communication at the University of Pennsylvania.

✧✧✧✧

# Surveying the Electronic Landscape: An Introduction to *Communication and Cyberspace*

Lance Strate
Ron Jacobson
Stephanie B. Gibson

The title of this book begins with the word *communication* because the book's primary concern is with the processes by which human beings create messages, transfer information, and make meanings; with the ways in which individuals form relationships and create communities; with individuals' capacity to construct identities and realities through discourse. Social interaction never takes place in a vacuum, however, and this anthology is devoted to the new communication contexts made possible by computer technologies. Again, emphasis is on communication as it is mediated by computers, not on computer technology itself. We take the position that computer media, in fact, that all media are best understood not just as means or agencies through which communication takes place, but as environments or scenes in which communication occurs. Thus, in this volume we are specifically concerned with communication in the electronic environment known as *cyberspace*.

## WHAT IS CYBERSPACE?

We realize that the meanings of the term *cyberspace* have evolved and multiplied as it has grown in popularity and diffused through different sectors of society. Although we are especially concerned with cyberspace as a contemporary phenomenon, it is important to acknowledge that the word was coined by author William Gibson (1984), who used it as part of a science fiction scenario in which individuals could directly connect their nervous systems to a global computer network referred to as the *matrix* and experience a form of *virtual reality*:

> The matrix has its roots in primitive arcade games," said the voice-over, "in early graphics programs and military experimentation with cranial jacks." On the Sony, a two-dimensional space war faded behind a forest of mathematically generated ferns, demonstrating the possibilities of logarithmic spirals; cold blue military footage burned through, lab animals wired into test systems, helmets feeding into fire control circuits of tanks and war planes. "Cyberspace. A consensual hallucination experienced daily by billions of legitimate operators, in every nation, by children being taught mathematical concepts . . . A graphic representation of data abstracted from the banks of every computer in the human system. Unthinkable complexity. Lines of light ranged in the nonspace of the mind, clusters and constellations of data. Like city lights, receding." (p. 51)

Gibson's neologism and his vision of the future originate in popular culture, a fact that has prompted some to dismiss the concept of cyberspace. But others have taken the term and the idea seriously, one of the first being architect Michael Benedikt (1991), editor of *Cyberspace: First Steps*; he argues that a "fully developed cyberspace does not yet exist outside of science fiction and the imagination of a few thousand people" (p. 123), but believes that "cyberspace is 'now under construction'" (p. 124). Offering proposals for the design of this cyberspace to come, Benedikt clearly has Gibson's matrix in mind, minus the dystopic elements. He describes his cyberspace as

> a globally networked, computer-sustained, computer-accessed, and computer-generated, multidimensional, artificial, or "virtual" reality. In this reality, to which every computer is a window, seen or heard objects are neither physical nor, necessarily, representations of physical objects but are, rather, in form, character and action, made up of data, of pure information. This information derives in part from the operations of the natural, physical world, but for the most part it derives from the immense traffic of information that constitute human enterprise in science, art, business, and culture. (pp. 122-123)

Benedikt sought to bridge the gap between science fiction and reality, but he situates his cyberspace in the future, and therefore his concept remains hypothetical, unrealized, and unreal. On the other hand, Michael Heim (1993), in *The Metaphysics of Virtual Reality*, connects Gibson's prophecies to today's technologies in the following definition:

The juncture of digital information and human perception, the "matrix" of civilization where banks exchange money (credit) and information seekers navigate layers of data stored and represented in virtual space. Buildings in cyberspace may have more dimensions than physical buildings do, and cyberspace may reflect different laws of existence. It has been said that cyberspace is where you are when you are having a phone conversation or where your ATM money exists. It is where electronic mail travels, and it resembles the Toontown in the movie Roger Rabbit. (p. 150)

Here, Heim implies that we have already entered the cyberspace age; his description brings together Gibson's notion of the visualization of abstract data with more common conceptions of virtual reality. For many (including Benedikt), the terms *virtual reality* (VR) and *cyberspace* are more or less interchangeable, although Heim also refers to the electronic storage and transmission of spoken and written language, and numeric data in his definition of cyberspace. Others, however, use the term in conjunction with *computer-mediated communication* (CMC) and communications through computer networks. For example, in the following passage from *Cyberpunk: Outlaws and Hackers on the Computer Frontier*, Katie Hafner and John Markoff (1992) introduce the word in their description of the experiences of a young hacker accessing mainframe computers through his personal computer and modem:

Being inside a global computer network gave Pengo the same adrenaline rush that playing a video game did, magnified many times over. Once he had entered a computer network, he was no longer playing a game; he was master of real machines performing real tasks. He could be nowhere and everywhere at the same time. From in front of a computer screen, he could open doors and solve problems. He was able to get things. The stuff on the screen wasn't anything more than electrons hitting phosphor, but it was nice to imagine that there really was something there, around the back somewhere. The networks— unconstrained by conventional geographic boundaries—had become a self-contained universe known to a growing number of computer researchers as cyberspace. (p. 150)

Clearly, virtual reality technology is not a factor in this version of cyberspace. This usage, to describe a contemporary communications phenomenon, is attributed to John Perry Barlow, a Grateful Dead lyricist who went on to become a cyberspace pioneer and co-founder (with Mitchell Kapor) of the Electronic Frontier Foundation:

Barlow was the first commentator to adopt novelist William Gibson's striking science-fictional term "cyberspace" as a synonym for the present-day nexus of computer and telecommunications networks. Barlow was insistent that cyberspace should be regarded as a qualitatively new world, a "frontier." According to Barlow, the world of electronic communications, now made visible through the computer screen, could no longer be usefully regarded as just a tangle of high-tech wiring. Instead, it had become a *place*, cyberspace, which demanded a new set of metaphors, a new set of rules and behaviors. The term, as Barlow employed it, struck a useful chord, and the concept of cyberspace was picked up by *Time, Scientific American*, computer police, hackers, and even constitutional scholars. "Cyberspace" now seems likely to become a permanent fixture of the language. (Sterling, 1992, p. 236)

A similar emphasis is found in Howard Rheingold's (1993) definition in *The Virtual Community: Homesteading on the Electronic Frontier:* "the conceptual space where words, human relationships, data, wealth, and power are manifested by people using CMC technology" (p. 5). In this sense, cyberspace is not identical with communication through computer media, but rather is the context in which such communication occurs; nor is it the same as the computer network, but instead is the sense of place created through such networks. From this perspective, cyberspace may be understood as a form of social space, as Allucquere Rosanne Stone (1991) states in her discussion of the term:

> Electronic networks in their myriad kinds, and the mode of interpersonal interaction that they foster, are a new manifestation of a social space that has been better known in its older and more familiar forms in conference calls, communities of letters, and FDR's fireside chats. It can be characterized as "virtual" space—an imaginary locus of interaction created by communal agreement. In its most recent form, concepts like distance, inside/outside, and even the physical body take on new and frequently disturbing meanings. (pp. 83-84)

Stone also suggests here that cyberspace exists only through social interaction; her emphasis on "communal agreement" is reminiscent of W. Gibson's (1984) reference to cyberspace as a "consensual hallucination." This perspective seems to rule out the more basic idea of cyberspace as the "place" where data is "located," as well as the possibilities for intrapersonal communication presented by virtual reality technology.

In summary, we have many different definitions of cyberspace, some viewing it as a fictional construct, others as imaginary but in development, others as real and present. Some equate cyberspace with virtual reality, others with the electronic storage and transmission of information, or with CMC, or with communication over computer networks. Some see cyberspace as an individual conceptual space, others as a product of social interaction. Part of the ambiguity surrounding this word may be related to its novelty, but it is also true that the term acts as a nexus for a variety of different phenomena, such as telecommunications; cybernetics and computer technology; CMC and the Internet; virtual reality and telepresence, hypertext and hypermedia and the World Wide Web; and cyberculture. It is therefore useful to consider each of these phenomena in turn.

## TELECOMMUNICATIONS

Throughout the history of our species, human beings have sought to conquer time and space through speech, art, and architecture, through writing and printing, and through various forms of transportation (Innis, 1951). It was not until the mid-19th century invention of the telegraph, however, that we gained the ability to communicate instantaneously through electronic data transmission. *Telecommunications* continued to evolve and grow with the development of the telephone, radio, and television, and innovations such as cable television, satellite communications, and fax machines. Beyond the development of individual technologies, the most striking trend in contemporary telecommunications is the tendency toward convergence among the various media, a convergence that encompasses the computer as well. Thus, the term *telematics* (from the French *télématique)* was coined to refer to "the merging of computers and microcomputers with major data banks and transmission systems" (Provenzo, 1986, p. 28), while George Gilder (1994) offers *telecomputer* or *teleputer* to refer to the combination of computing, telephone, and television. More recently, the term *cyberspace* has been adopted within telecommunications to emphasize those technologies clustered around computers (and sometimes simply the telephone), and the phrase *information superhighway* or *infobahn* has become a popular way to refer to the continuing convergence of these technologies; the use of cyberspace emphasizes the social and cultural aspects of telecommunications, while the highway metaphor favors the commercial and otherwise utilitarian functions of CMC (Gozzi, 1999; Rheingold, 1993; Strate, 1999). A somewhat more neutral term, *information infrastructure* (both national and global), is also used in this context. In more popular discourse, terms like the *Internet,* the *Net,* the *Web,* or simply *online* are used to refer to these same technologies, as the general public tends to experience cyberspace through the interface of commercial services such as America Online.

Merged with telecommunications technologies, computing facilitates the transmission and storage of large amounts of data, in a variety of formats. Computerized telecommunications made possible experiments in teletext and videotex, the creation of online newspapers and other forms of electronic publishing, and ultimately bulletin board systems and commercial online services. The convergence of the computer with telephone and television technologies has led to new communication environments, from distance learning programs in penal institutions to home shopping networks. Often emphasized is computing's potential to bestow the quality of *interactivity* on mass media previously limited to one-way communication (Brand, 1987; Gilder, 1994; Woolley, 1992). Also highly significant is the computer's ability to store and transmit information in binary code, as a sequence of numbers, making possible *digital media* such as the compact disc; digitized images, sounds, and so on, are easier to store, transmit, and edit than analogic versions, opening the door to new forms of expression and manipulation of content

(Binkley, 1993; Kroker, 1993; Lanham, 1993; Negroponte, 1995; Ritchin, 1990; Woolley, 1992). Moreover, computer technology's ability to control and digitize a variety of forms makes it central to any discussion of *multimedia*, the combination and blending of otherwise discrete media and forms such as still images, video, and text (Cotton & Oliver, 1993; Moody, 1995; Pimentel & Teixeira, 1993; Rickett, 1993; Wachtel, 1978).

Most if not all of the questions and problems that have been associated with telecommunications in the past also apply to cyberspace. For example, economic questions include who pays for and who owns cyberspace, the Internet, or the information superhighway (Branscomb, 1994; Loader, 1997; Rheingold, 1993)? Should it be a public trust or privatized and commercialized; a monopoly, heavily regulated, or open to competition (Critical Arts Ensemble, 1994; Gilder, 1994; Hauben & Hauben, 1997; Smith, 1993)? Who benefits from the technology, and who has access to it (Gandy, 1993; Hill & Hughes, 1998)? Will diverse degrees of access create a digital divide between the information rich and the information poor, the virtual and nonvirtual cyberclasses (Kroker & Weinstein, 1994; H. Schiller, 1996)? What are the effects of replacing an industrial economy with one based on information (Dutton, 1999; Gilder, 1994; D. Schiller, 1999)? What are the consequences of the rise of cybercaptialism and e-business (Dutton, 1999; Gates, 1995, 1999; Rifkin, 2000; Rushkoff, 1999; Swisher, 1998)? Political and legal questions include who regulates cyberspace, and who patrols the information superhighway (Loader, 1997; Lyon & Zureik, 1996; Sterling, 1992)? How will privacy, property rights, and freedom of speech be protected (Branscomb, 1994; Diffie & Landau, 1998; Gandy, 1993; Levinson, 1997; Ludlow, 1996; Lyon & Zureik, 1996)? How will laws be enforced, and cybercrime be punished (Dibbell, 1999; Grabosky & Smith, 1998; Hafner & Markoff, 1992; Ludlow, 1996; Ross, 1991; Sterling, 1992)? How are cyberspace technologies affecting government and politics, and could they be used to foster democratic participation through teledemocracy (Davis, 1999; Dutton, 1999; Gilder, 1994; Hill & Hughes, 1998)? How are they affecting the legal system (Katsh, 1995)? Warfare (DeLanda, 1991)? Social questions include the degree to which cyberspace will substitute for transportation (e.g., home shopping, telework, and teleconferencing; Critical Arts Ensemble, 1994; Dutton, 1999; Gilder, 1994; Mitchell, 1995). What happens to communities and public places as more and more people go online, and what is the nature of the new forms of community formed (Mitchell, 1995)? Is cyberspace creating global community (Dizard, 1997)? Has cyberspace become overly commercialized (Dutton, 1999; Rifkin, 2000)? These are just some of the issues currently being debated.

## CYBERNETICS AND COMPUTER TECHNOLOGY

The term *cyberspace* is clearly based on Norbert Wiener's (1967) neologism, *cybernetics.* Referring to the function of information to control or govern environments, cybernetics is most closely associated with computer technology, but is meant to be applied to a variety of technological, biological, and social systems; certainly, as James Beniger (1986) argued, the development of technologies of control predates the modern computer and the contemporary information society. The computer itself, as a technology for performing numerical calculation, can be traced back to such ancient devices as the abacus, as Janet Sternberg (1991) makes clear, and has a long history of technological development leading up to the advent of the electronic digital computer following World War II (Biro, 1999; Bolter, 1984; Kidwell & Ceruzzi, 1994; Lubar, 1993). Programming through direct manipulation of the computer's wiring, via plugboards, and by batch processing of punched computer cards ("do not bend, fold, spindle, or mutilate") gave way to computer terminals that include video monitors in the 1960s, around the same time that minicomputers were introduced. Further developments during the 1970s include early versions of menu-based *graphic user interfaces* (GUIs) and point-and-click input devices (e.g., "the mouse"), and the marketing of handheld calculators, video games, and microcomputers. The 1980s were characterized by rapid expansion of computer-related industries, and increasing emphasis on networks, supercomputers, and work stations (Kidwell & Ceruzzi, 1994); during the 1990s, there was tremendous growth in all areas of CMC, the Internet, and the World Wide Web, and great interest in cyberspace and virtual reality technologies; also, the quality of portability became particularly popular (e.g., laptop or notebook personal computers, personal digital assistants [PDAs], as well as fax machines, beepers, and cellular and digital telephones).

As computing technologies have developed, so has concern about their nature, their role in society, and their relationship to human beings and culture (see, e.g., Bertman, 1998; Bolter, 1984; Coyne, 1999; Gleick, 1999; Logan, 1997, 2000; Perkinson, 1995; Postman, 1992; Roszak, 1994; Shenk, 1997, 1999; Slouka, 1996; Stoll, 1995; Talbott, 1995; Turkle, 1984, 1995; Weizenbaum, 1976); along with general studies of computers and society, more specific social and cultural aspects of computing that have been studies include artificial intelligence (Dreyfus, 1979; Dreyfus & Dreyfus, 1986; Hofstadter, 1980; Hofstadter & Dennett, 1981; Kurzweil, 1999; Penrose, 1989; Pickard, 1997), artificial life (Leonard, 1997; Levy, 1992), education (Papert, 1980, 1993; Tuman, 1992a, 1992b), news (Harper, 1998), the arts and entertainment (Rushkoff, 1996; Rutsky, 1999; Johnson, 1997; Peterson, 1983; Smith, 1996), word processing (Heim, 1987), and video games (Provenzo, 1991; Rushkoff, 1996; Sudnow, 1983). Critics and proponents of the computer may differ on the positive or negative effects of the technologies, and debate the purposes for which they are or should be used, but by and large they agree that as a machine that is both virtual and universal, there seem to be few limits to the computer's applications and little that is unaffected by it. And projections for the future have just about every sector of human activity revolutionized by computing (Kurzweil, 1999; Pickover, 1994; Robertson, 1998). This of course includes, and has included human communication.

## CMC AND THE INTERNET

Although most often viewed as a tool for performing calculations, processing data, and manipulating symbols, the computer is also an information technology and a medium of communication (see, e.g., Logan, 1997, 2000; Lubar, 1993; Provenzo, 1986). And any form of human–computer interaction can be seen as a form of communication, varying in the degree to which the computer or the user is in control (Chesebro & Bonsall, 1989). Thus, such interactions would include both humans programming computers and computers programming humans (e.g., through educational software, video games, etc.), as well as using computer programs to input, store, search for, manipulate, output, and transmit information. The qualities most closely connected to contemporary CMC, interactive computing and direct human-to-human communication, are dependent on the addition of video technology as a way to display information graphically and allow for much faster feedback than waiting for mechanically produced printouts, and the addition of sufficient computing power and programming to handle multiple users simultaneously:

> The invention of time-sharing computers in the 1960s not only enabled many people to use the same central computer by exchanging commands and results with the computer interactively, it also provided a channel of communication between humans and humans—people on the earliest time-sharing systems built electronic mail systems for sending each other messages. As the time-sharing systems evolved, so did the mail systems. Eventually, what we will send one another over the telecommunication lines will not be restricted to text, but will include voice, images, gestures, facial expressions, virtual objects, cybernetic architectures—everything that contributes to a sense of presence. We will be sending worlds and ways to be in them. The advent of interactive computing and e-mail in the late 1960s was a twin milestone in the making of the Matrix, the network of networks where future cyberspaces will evolve. (Rheingold, 1991, p. 88)

Along with *electronic mail* or *e-mail*, which is asynchronous (messages are stored and need not be read at the time of receipt), early forms of CMC include synchronous *chat* (text exchanged "live" as in a telephone conversation), and computer *bulletin boards* that allow for interchanges among many different users; later variations include the computer conference, the mailing list, discussion list or *listserv*, and the *newsgroup*. Pioneered through time-sharing computers with multiple terminals linked to one mainframe computer, itself a network of sorts, these forms of communication were extended as different computers were linked locally or over distance (e.g., by telephone lines or cable); furthermore, microcomputers could be linked directly to each other in a closed circuit network, or through modem and telephone services to other micros or more powerful mainframe and minicomputers (Abate 1999; Hauben & Hauben, 1997). Thus, the development of the personal computer in the late 1970s has led to a revolution in *interpersonal computing*, leading researchers to study CMC on the interpersonal, group, and organizational communication levels (Barnes, 2001; Chesebro & Bonsall, 1989; Sproull & Kiesler, 1991; also see Gumpert & Cathcart, 1986). Not surprisingly, CMC research is often published through the Internet, notably through the online *Journal of Computer-Mediated Communication*. Apart from scholarly research, a number of memoirs and cyberspace travelogues have been published, documenting personal interaction online, including virtual romance and cybersex (see, e.g., Bennahum, 1998; Booth & Jung, 1996; Dibbell, 1999; Odzer, 1997; Seabrook, 1997).

Cyberspace is most often associated with the interconnections among different computers, with computer networks, and with further interconnections among different networks. The sum total of this network of networks has been referred to as the *Matrix*, the *Net*, and sometimes the *Internet;* this last term also refers to the specific network that has been supported by the U.S. government (see Abate, 1999; Hauben & Hauben, 1997) , as opposed to other networks such as Bitnet, Usenet, and Fidonet. (Whatever the final result of the privatization of the present Internet, and its replacement by more advanced telecommunications technologies, it is likely that the term *Internet*, or at least the shortened form of the *Net* will persist for some time.) Many of the nodes or cyberplaces that make up these networks are computers owned by educational institutions, governments, and corporations. Another significant presence consists of tens of thousands of hobbyists who have set up bulletin board systems (BBSs), some of which have turned commercial; there are also larger commercial services such America Online, which offer home shopping, entertainment, and online reference libraries and news services in addition to CMCs.

Beyond e-mail, the current cyberscape includes Usenet newsgroups, the Internet Relay Chat, and connections to remote computers through Telnet and the World Wide Web. Also accessible are Multi-User Dungeons or Multi-User Dimensions (MUDs), programs or nodes that allow many people to participate in role-playing games, or simply interact in a computer-simulated environment. Moreover, many cyberspace nodes include databases of information that can be accessed and downloaded through File Transfer Protocol (FTP), Gopher, Wide Area Information Servers (WAIS), or the Web. As Anthony Smith (1993) points out, cyberspace retrieves the ancient idea of the Alexandrian library as a storehouse to which people come, reversing the Gutenbergian principle of mass production and distribution (but not necessarily mass communication). Software that aids in the finding and retrieving of data, such as Lycos and AltaVista are attempts to construct electronic librarians or navigators native to cyberspace, whereas many e-mail systems include a software "Postmaster." The projection of agentic status onto these programs is more than anthropomorphism; rather, it reflects ongoing efforts to develop (or evolve—see Levy, 1992) software capable of independent action in the cyberspace environment, software to search and retrieve, perform surveillance and act as a surrogate for us, as well as perform maintenance functions. This effort may well reinvigorate the somewhat moribund state of artificial intelligence and expert systems research. Thus, we may anticipate a near future cyberspace populated by projected "entities" variously known as intelligent agents, software agents, knowbots, electronic personas or epers, or simply bots (Gelernter, 1991; Heim, 1993; Leonard, 1997; Pickover, 1994; Rheingold, 1993).


## VIRTUAL REALITY AND TELEPRESENCE

Of the terms associated with cyberspace, *virtual reality* (VR) has been one of the most compelling (e.g., Biocca, 1992; Hayward & Wollen, 1993; Heim, 1993; Hillis, 1999; Laurel, 1993; Pimentel & Teixeira, 1993; Rheingold, 1991; Woolley, 1992). According to Pimentel and Teixeira (1993) the term *virtual,* in computing

> refers to the essence or effect of something, not the fact. IBM started using the word in the late 1960s to refer to any nonphysical link between processes or machines, such as virtual memory (random-access memory being simulated using disk drives). (p. 288)

Virtual reality, then, is not true, factual reality, but a simulation that gives the effect and essence of reality. The illusion of reality is generated through the computer's interface with its user; computer screens generate an artificial reality, so that we may imagine we are reading an electronic book when in fact we are viewing a video image, and we may feel a sense of presence when communicating over a network or playing a video game, and using joystick or mouse. Virtual reality is generally associated with such interface devices as goggles, data gloves, and body stockings that in theory could both relay information about the individual's movements and position, and convey realistic visual, auditory, and even tactile information to the user; the goal is to create the illusion of immersion in a virtual environment or virtual world. Through VR technology, we would be able to enter into a video game, participate in a film or television program, go to work in a virtual office (Pruitt & Barrett, 1991), take a virtual vacation, and engage in virtual sex. Virtual reality can also serve as a blueprint or prototype (Benedikt, 1991), as a real-time map or "mirror world" of actual reality (Curry, 1998; Gelernter, 1991), or as a way to concretize abstract data as in W. Gibson's (1984) speculative fiction (also see Benedikt, 1991). Projections of VR technologies include simulations produced at a particular site, and *televirtuality,* the transmission of a virtual reality from a distance through convergence with other forms of telecommunications.

Telepresence, the lesser known counterpart of virtual reality, refers to the transmission of the user's "presence" to another location, allowing the user to act from a distance. Anyone issuing commands to a computer system from a remote location may experience a sense of telepresence—related terms include *teleoperation* and *tele-existence.* Telepresence is particularly associated with the remote operation of machines or robots, "telerobotics," and coupled with virtual reality technology would give the user the illusion of actually being present. Through telepresence, individuals may safely engage in high-risk activities in outer space or in nuclear facilities, and in otherwise impossible situations, such as performing microsurgery through miniature robotics. Telepresence may also allow for new forms of safe sex: *telesex* and *teledildonics.*

## HYPERTEXT, HYPERMEDIA, AND THE WORLD WIDE WEB

Whether the VR is a three-dimensional environment or an electronic book, cyberspace transcends conventional notions of dimension, connection, and navigation. The term hypertext, alluding to the higher dimensionality of hyperspace, was coined by programmer Ted Nelson (1987, 1990), although the original vision for this medium is credited to Vannevar Bush (1945); it refers to nonlinear documents where text nodes are linked to other relevant pieces of text, forming a textual network (Berk & Devlin, 1991; Bolter, 1991; Cotton & Oliver, 1993; Delany & Landow, 1991; S. Gibson & Oviedo, 2000; Hawisher & Selfe, 1991; Landow, 1992; Murray, 1997). A node can include any type of text: words, graphics, moving images, sound, or any combination of these, making hypertext a form of multimedia or *hypermedia.* The manner in which hypertext is navigated is by linking text nodes to one or more other text nodes; for instance, a photograph of a Grecian urn can be linked to a paragraph of printed text describing that urn and to a map showing where it was recovered during an archeological dig. Also used as a compositional tool, much has been written about hypertext's impact on theories of writing and on the writing classroom. In its use as a "writing space," as Jay David Bolter (1991) puts it, a number of hypertext novels have been authored, and new forms of fiction and criticism are being created and legitimized. Hypertext, electronic literature, cybertext, and similar permutations call into question the future of the book, and of publishing and libraries (Aarseth, 1997; Molz & Dain, 1999; Nunberg, 1996). Ultimately, hypertext and hypermedia dissolve the differences between texts, book series or encyclopedias, and even libraries, between fiction and gaming (an intermediate form is known as "interactive fiction"), and between texts as objects to be read, and as environments to navigate through (thus, VR can also be viewed as a form of hypermedia). The World Wide Web is based on the application of interface to the Internet. Hence, the ubiquitous identifier of Web addresses, http, stands for "hypertext transfer protocol" and the programming codes used on Web sites, html, stands for "hypertext markup language." Given its textual origins, it is not surprising that the Web, as opposed to chat and mail formats, has more often than not followed publishing formats, from the simple Web page, to more sophisticated forms of electronic publishing; the Web has also been used as a broadcast medium, but the larger framework still tends to be a variation on print media.

One of the key aspects of hypermediated communication has been the developing of useful navigational systems or cybernautics. Without ways to determine how to travel from one text node to another, hypertext can be viewed as a disorganized jumble: a pile of book pages without any sort of organizing pattern. Hypertext authors and programmers have been working to design creative and helpful systems that show relationships among text nodes. The basic goals of navigational systems have been to give readers a way of moving seamlessly through the text without getting lost in hyperspace. This has been accomplished through several navigational devices: leaving a trail showing where the reader has been, showing some paths to other relevant nodes, allowing only readers who have completed certain parts of a text to move on to other parts, and highlighting places where links are available instead of making links invisible. On the Internet, Web browsers such as Mosaic, Netscape, and Internet Explorer are attempts to provide cyberspace with navigational order, albeit one that transcends traditional conceptions of linear direction and the limitations of three dimensions. Despite such devices as search engines and bookmarks, movement through cyberspace has been something less than user-friendly so far. Still, hypermediated interfaces have brought some coherence and clarity to the contemporary cyberscape, which is why they have replace earlier interfaces and devices.

## CYBERCULTURE

Through social interaction in the electronic environment of cyberspace, a new kind of culture has developed, referred to as cyberculture (Dery, 1993; see also Shields, 1996). Included under this heading are the various hacker subcultures, such as the original hardware hackers: unstructured programmers who see programming as an end in itself (Turkle, 1984). According to Steven Levy (1984), the first group of hackers formed in MIT circa 1959, and developed a "hacker ethic" that emphasized complete freedom of information and access to computers, decentralization and antiauthoritarianism, and better living through computing. Much of this was consistent with the counterculture of the 1960s, although the hacker's apolitical tendencies were not (see Roszak, 1994, for further criticism of their "cult of information"). Younger hackers, during the 1970s and 1980s, turned to programming for microcomputers (Levy, 1984), but the label "hacker" has come to be more closely tied with individuals who explore and break into computers and networks, generally through personal computers and modems. Both a counterculture and an underground, sometimes outlaw culture, contemporary hacker culture is seen by some as criminal, by others as unduly persecuted (Hafner & Markoff, 1992; Ross, 1991; Sterling, 1992).

The concept of cyberculture transcends the hacker phenomenon, however, and also refers to the unique culture associated with CMC and online interaction. This includes the emergence of special forms of language and symbols, the development of rituals, conventions, norms, and rules of conduct for CMC, and phenomena such as flaming (hostile communication), spamming (messages that are too long or verbose), and less offensive forms of ranting (Benedikt, 1991; Dery, 1993; Jones, 1995; Rheingold, 1993). Over time a sense of social ties may develop, resulting in what Howard Rheingold (1993) refers to as a "virtual community," also known as an "electronic village" (Dery, 1993) and "cybersociety" (Jones, 1995). Cyberculture is also linked to other forms of counterculture; thus Douglas Rushkoff (1994) uses the term *cyberia* as a variation of cyberspace, but also to point to the associations among hackers, virtual reality pioneers, and members of virtual communities on the one hand, and the various contemporary subcultures associated with smart drugs and psychedelics, New Age mysticism and neopaganism, and raving and other forms of popular music and dance.

There is, of course, a significant connection between cyberculture and the genre of science fiction, in which the term *cyberspace* originated. The style of science fiction produced by William Gibson, Bruce Sterling, and others is referred to as *cyberpunk*, which generally includes an emphasis on electronic technologies, urban decay, and underclass characters (Bukatman, 1993; McCaffery, 1991; Sterling, 1986). More than a literary genre, cyberpunk may also be applied to other forms and media, including film, comics, music, and fashion; it has also be used in conjunction with actual hackers (Hafner & Markoff, 1992). Sometimes interpreted as a critique of capitalism and an oppositional ideological stance, cyberpunk also may be seen as hacker chic, or as a disembodied style that best fits social interaction in cyberspace. Donna Haraway (1991) appropriates the related science fiction concept of the *cyborg*, the cybernetic organism that is half human and half machine, to discuss our relationships to technology (see also Gray, 1995). It should be noted that not all forms of science fiction that deal with cyberspace are considered forms of cyberpunk (e.g., Disney's science fiction film *TRON*, 1982). Cyberpunk itself can be seen as a manifestation of postmodern culture.

The term *postmodern* refers to our own time period, and is generally said to begin sometime after the end of World War II. Postmodern culture is the culture of the age of television and computers, and postmodernist theorists often make direct references to computer technology: Jean-François Lyotard (1984) attributes the postmodern condition in part to computer science; Jean Baudrillard (1983) writes of our present "digitality," while his concepts of simulation and hyperreality seem to correspond to virtual reality (Woolley, 1992); Arthur Kroker (1993; Kroker & Weinstein, 1994) follows up on many of Baudrillard's insights, making their connection to the cyberspace phenomenon more explicit, if no less opaque. Fredric Jameson (1991) sees a correspondence between his notion of postmodernism as the culture of late capitalism and William Gibson's cyberpunk vision of cyberspace (also see Critical Arts Ensemble, 1994). Poster (1990) relates various forms of computing to the poststructuralist notion of the decentering of the self, whereas Gergen (1991) describes a saturated self in relation to symbolic communities such as those formed through computer networks. The notion that new technologies are creating new types of individuals is one reason why the term *cyborg* has come into heavy use as of late, as has such variations as posthuman and transhuman (Dewdney, 1998; Hayles, 1999). Moreover, hypertext theorists see in that form of computer media the concrete realization of much of postmodern, poststructuralist, and critical literary theory (Bolter, 1991; Landow, 1992). Along the same lines, Lanham (1993) connects computer-mediated art to contemporary rhetorical theory (as well as the history of rhetoric), and Heim (1987) argues for the relationship between word processing and Heideggerian phenomenology (also see the somewhat self-indulgent "media philosophy" of Taylor & Saarinen, 1994). Although rooted in the tradition of continental philosophy and critical theory, postmodernism, as Strate (1994) points out, is also derived from the media ecology perspective.

Media ecology refers to the perspective of theorists such as Marshall McLuhan (1962, 1964; McLuhan & Powers, 1989), Harold Innis (1951), Walter Ong (1982), Neil Postman (1979, 1985, 1992), Joshua Meyrowitz (1985), Jay David Bolter (1984, 1991; Bolter & Grusin, 1999), Robert Logan (1997, 2000), and Paul Levinson (1997, 1999). In many ways, cyberspace represents the culmination of McLuhan's arguments about electronic media: that through this extension of our nervous systems we become members of a global village, that we replace individual identity with role playing, and that our forms of perception and our sense of our own bodies are altered (also see Provenzo, 1986; Smith, 1993). It is for this reason that McLuhan has become the Patron Saint of *Wired* magazine, and in general a symbol of the cyberspace age. Similarly, Ong suggests that electronic media continue to transform and technologize the word, extending the process begun with writing and printing; he refers to our present postliterate stage as one of secondary orality. In this respect, we might consider the uses of computer technology for voice transmission, recognition, and synthesis, and the ways in which electronic writing retrieves characteristics of scribal and oral communication and culture (Bolter, 1984, 1991; Heim, 1987; Lanham, 1992; Woolley, 1992). Flaming may therefore be compared to oral culture's agonistic tendencies (Dery, 1993, insightfully compares it to "the dozens"), and spamming to orality's bias towards copiousness and verbosity. Cyberspace also represents an unprecedented integration of analogic (i.e., audiovisual) and digital (i.e., verbal and numeric) forms of communication (Strate, 1994). Meyrowitz's (1985) sociological elaborations of media ecology theory are especially significant here, as cyberspace technologies further contribute to the fact that we have "no sense of place," further increase the general accessibility of information, and further alter the way in which we play our roles. Thus, Meyrowitz's theory coincides with the arguments of postmodernists such as Poster (1990) and Gergen (1991) concerning the decentering of the self. Paul Levinson (1997, 1999) and Robert Logan (1997, 2000), like other media ecologists, analyze computers, cyberspace, and digital media within the context of the history of communication, media, and technology (see also Baron, 2000; Borgman, 1999; Hobart & Schiffman, 1998; Mitchell, 1995; O'Donnell, 1998; Robertson, 1998).

In general, the media ecology perspective suggests that cyberspace technologies not only constitute a site for new cultural formations, but also affect pre-existing elements of culture, situated in other kinds of spaces; more and more we may find mainstream culture mimicking cyberculture in a variety of ways.

So far, we have considered both communication and communication technology. We have examined the *cyber*, but not the *space*. It is easy to take the notion of space for granted, but in fact much of the confusion surrounding the meaning of cyberspace is connected to the ambiguity surrounding the idea of space itself.

## THE SPACES

The concept of space is actually quite complex, and the notion that there is no one single, uniform "thing" called space can be traced back to the late 19th century (Kern, 1983). We are better off, then, making reference to the variety of spaces that can be encountered, beginning with physical space, the space that (theoretically) exists independently of human beings (itself no longer seen as uniform). Physical space is often confused with perceptual space, the impression of space that we obtain through one or a combination of our senses. At best, perceptual space can only correspond to a portion of physical space, and is always subject to error. Also, we tend to equate perceptual space with visual space, but we also experience auditory space, tactile, thermal, and kinesthetic space, and even olfactory space—generally, our perceptual space is based on the interactions of all these senses (Hall, 1966). Another distinction that often goes unacknowledged is that between perceptual space and conceptual space, the sense of space generated within our minds. Conceptual space may include memories of perceptual space, as well as imagined and fictional spaces that have never been perceived. It is the space where plans are made and future actions visualized. It is the realm of the mind's eye, and the place where we look when we turn inward in thought. The relationships among physical, perceptual, and conceptual spaces have been the subject of much debate throughout the centuries, and it is not our intention to enter into that discussion here, merely to note the distinctions. Suffice it to say that these three types form the basis for all other forms of space that we experience.

Edward T. Hall's (1966) investigations into proxemics teach us that human beings have further senses of space based on our interactions with others. There is, for example, a sense of a personal space, the individual's own sense of territoriality, and a sense of a social space, the area that is shared with others; pioneering research on the relationships between communication and social space has been conducted by Gary Gumpert and Susan Drucker (Drucker

& Gumpert, 1991; Gumpert, 1987; Gumpert & Drucker, 1992). Our spaces are further defined through verbal designations such as public or private, sacred or profane, and through physical modifications (i.e., architecture). There are also forms of aesthetic space created through media, including the physical space occupied by an object, the relational space between the item and its audience, the illusionary perceptual space suggested by items such as visual images, and the conceptual space activated in the minds of audience members (Gumpert, 1987; Meyrowitz, 1986; Zettl, 1990). A book, for example, occupies space as a physical object, enters into a spatial relationship with its reader, displays information as words laid out on a page (much as objects may be arranged in a given physical area), and may produce a further experience of space in readers' imaginations through their decoding of its content.

Historically, new media have introduced new notions of space such as writing space and typographic space (Bolter, 1991; Ong, 1982), but never so radically as with the introduction of the electronic media, which eliminate both the need for human presence and for physical transportation: thus, they create new forms of spatial relationships as, for example, it is not entirely clear where your voice is when you talk on the telephone (at your end, at the receiving end, or somewhere in between), and therefore it is not entirely clear where you are (perceptually or conceptually). We might therefore conclude that there is a whole new sense of space created in a telephone conversation, an electronic space (not cyberspace, as some suggest, but a closely related form, telephonic space). Electronic space, then, is divorced from any idea of physical location, which is why Meyrowitz (1985) characterizes it as providing "no sense of place." He goes on to suggest that both spatial situations and media are information systems that provide variable possibilities for transmitting and receiving information, that vary in the accessibility of and barriers to information. In other words, according to Meyrowitz, all forms of space are cybernetic, and therefore all might be referred to as cyberspace. While we support this theoretical position, for reasons of precision we favor limiting the use of the term cyberspace to those forms of electronic space associated with computer technologies.

Furthermore, based on the preceding breakdown of the varieties of space, we might well refer to different types of cyberspace. There is the physical cyberspace of the computer itself, the structure of its chips and circuits, its "architecture." This physical structure determines the possible patterns of electronic flow, and therefore the basic operations of the computer. But there is also a logical cyberspace, including the address space of the computer: "the range of numbers that can be invoked in fetching and storing data" (Bolter, 1984, p. 83). Logical cyberspace incudes the locations where information is stored and processed in memory, and the sectors where it is saved on magnetic and optical media. Physical cyberspace is almost never directly accessed or even conceptualized by programmers, as Bolter explains

This logical space exists in the programmer's mind. . . . The programmer ignores those qualities that have no bearing on his problem (such as the pattern of wires and transistors forming the memory) and is left with the fundamental qualities of electronic space. Logical space is not computer memory freed of its physical limitations, for the corporeality of information in the computer imposes restrictions and offers possibilities that the programmer cannot ignore—rather, it is computer memory reduced to its essence. (p. 84)

Bolter's (1984) description of logical space as "an abstract, geometrical, and mathematical field in which the programmer can build his data structures" (p. 243) has much in common with W. Gibson's (1984) description of a fictional cyberspace based on the visualization of abstract data.

As Rheingold (1991) notes, the evolution of computer technology has been towards putting greater and greater distance between the user and the hardware, thereby reducing or eliminating access to physical cyberspace. Instead, through the development of various interfaces, computers create a perceptual cyberspace, which would include the visual space of the computer monitor, graphic user interfaces, and tactile input devices such as the keyboard, joystick, and mouse. At the same time, our ability to go beyond our perceptions, particularly through computer-mediated verbal communication, results in a form of conceptual cyberspace. Cyberspace is also conceptualized through a variety of metaphors: the "electronic frontier" conceptualizes cyberspace in terms of the natural environment, whereas "information infrastructure" implies a human construction. "Information superhighway" and "infobahn" conceptualize cyberspace as a conduit, a place to pass through, while "virtual community" instead emphasizes the idea of an electronic landscape filled with relatively small, stable dwellings; "electropolis" (Reid, 1992) and "netropolis" (Taylor & Saarinen, 1994) frame cyberspace as a more cosmopolitan locus of human activity. Liquid metaphors are also quite popular, as they emphasize the fact that cyberspace is not physical space, certainly not solid space—it is both liquefied space and liquidated space. This metaphor is present throughout Benedikt's (1991) Cyberspace anthology, especially in Marcos Novak's discussion of "liquid architectures" (pp. 225-254), and in Rheingold's (1991) use of the term cybernautics, and is implicit in the popular phrase, "surfing the Internet" as well as the related notion of "channel surfing" through cable and broadcast television.

Our perceptions and conceptions together make up our experience of cyberspace, and through human–computer interaction or through the use of computing for intrapersonal communication, we generate a kind of personal cyberspace; this includes our sense of territoriality directed at our computer's "desktops" and arrangements of files and directories, our working spaces on mainframe computers, and our senses of self as we "move" through the levels of our computers (and others we may connect to). Through our sense of personal cyberspace, we may be said to merge with the computer and become cyborgs. We also may enter into a shared social cyberspace such as a bulletin board;

generally, those that gain a sense of group membership in a virtual community also develop a sense of responsibility towards the social cyberspace in which it is situated, much as residents of a neighborhood may take responsibility for the area's cleanliness and safety (Rheingold, 1993). Finally, we may further consider aesthetic cyberspace, and the design of human–computer interfaces, an area of particular interest to programmer Brenda Laurel (1990, 1993), who advocates the theater as an aesthetic model. These, then, are the cyberspaces. (See Strate, 1999, for an elaboration on the taxonomy of cyberspace.)

## ABOUT THIS BOOK

It has long been a typographic cliché to inform readers that they can read the chapters in an anthology in any order they please, and it is certainly in keeping with our topic that we welcome you to treat this collection as a database, randomly access its contents, and forge your own hypertextual links. Each medium has its own bias, however, and a printed book works best with a good measure of linearity. We, therefore, have put a great deal of thought and effort into the structure of this book and the sequence of the contributions, so that those in search of a traditional cover-to-cover reading will be rewarded. To this end we have divided the book into four sections, the first of which is devoted to chapters that provide theoretical contexts, broad overviews, and general criticism of computing and cyberspace as communication phenomena. The purpose of Section 1, therefore, is to provide perspectives that allow us to *place* cyberspace. The following three sections are based on the three-part conceptual structure used by architects and designers: form, function, and meaning.

Section 2, based on the idea of function, consists of discussion and research on cybernetworks (e.g., the Internet and the information superhighway) and cyberplaces (e.g., nodes, multi-user dungeons, virtual organizations). Of concern here are the ways in which cyberspace functions as an alternative for traditional locations and forms of transportation, and the consequences of such substitutions; also of interest are the ways in which cyberplaces and cybernetworks differ from their physical counterparts, and how such differences affect cyberspatial interactions. Section 3, based on the idea of form, brings together studies of new senses of space and navigation, or cybernautics. This includes examinations of the idea of virtual reality, and the perception of immersion generated by cyberspace technologies, as well as hypertext and hypermedia as new forms of nonlinear space and new methods of steering through the electronic landscape. Section 4, based on the idea of meaning, consists of examinations of cybercommunication and cyberculture. Among the topics covered are the codes and modes of communication associated with communication in cyberspace, and the new cultural formations, including altered notions of self, the body, and sexuality; relationships, community, and affiliation; and space, time, and reality that arise in this new communication environment.

Each section begins with a brief introduction that helps to identify the relationships among the section's chapters; each chapter has its own introduction, which also points to relationships with chapters in other sections. And we have given the last word, in the form of an epilogue, to Neil Postman, who raises the most basic question of all: Do we really need a cyberspace in the first place? His critical essay challenges us to justify cyberspace on the basis of genuine human needs. Finally, we invite and encourage your responses and feedback. Let us know what you think of the book, and what the book made you think of.

## REFERENCES

Aarseth, E. J. (1997). *Cybertext: Perspectives on ergodic literature.* Baltimore: Johns Hopkins University Press.

Abate, J. (1999). *Inventing the Internet.* Cambridge, MA: MIT Press.

Barnes, S. B. (2001). *Online connections: Internet interpersonal relationships.* Cresskill, NJ: Hampton Press.

Baron, N. S. (2000). *Alphabet to email: How written English evolved and where it's heading.* London: Routledge.

Baudrillard, J. (1983). *Simulations* (P. Foss, P. Patton, & P. Beitchman, Trans.). New York: Semiotext(e).

Benedikt, M. (Ed.). (1991). *Cyberspace: First steps.* Cambridge, MA: MIT Press.

Beniger, J. R. (1986). *The control revolution: Technological and economic origins of the information society.* Cambridge, MA: Harvard University Press.

Bennahum, D. S. (1998). *Extra life: Coming of age in cyberspace.* New York: Basic.

Berk, E., & Devlin, J. (Eds.). (1991). *Hypertext/hypermedia handbook.* New York: McGraw Hill.

Bertman, S. (1998). *Hyperculture: The human cost of speed.* Westport, CT: Praeger.

Binkley, T. (1993). Refiguring culture. In P. Hayward & T. Wollen (Eds.), *Future visions: New technologies of the screen* (pp. 92-122). London: British Film Institute.

Biocca, F. (Ed.). (1992). Virtual reality: A communication perspective [Special issue]. *Journal of Communication, 42*(4).

Biro, G. M. (1999). *Marshall McLuhan meets the millennium bug: The first 100 years of computers, and how we can make it.* Kingston, ON: Uplevel.

Bolter, J. D. (1984). *Turing's man: Western culture in the computer age.* Chapel Hill: University of North Carolina Press.

Bolter, J. D. (1991). *Writing space: The computer, hypertext, and the history of writing.* Hillsdale, NJ: Erlbaum.

Bolter, J. D., & Grusin, R. (1999). *Remediation: Understanding new media.* Cambridge, MA: MIT Press.

Booth, R., & Jung, M. (1996). *Romancing the net.* Rocklin, CA: Prima.

Borgman, A. (1999). *Holding on to reality: The nature of information at the turn of the millennium.* Chicago: University of Chicago Press.

Brand, S. (1987). *The media lab: Inventing the future at MIT.* New York: Viking.

Branscomb, A.W. (1994). *Who owns information? From privacy to public access.* New York: Basic Books.

Bukatman, S. (1993). *Terminal identity: The virtual subject in postmodern science fiction.* Durham, NC: Duke University Press.

Bush, V. (1945, July). As we may think. *Atlantic Monthly,* pp. 106-107.

Chesebro, J.W., & Bonsall, D.G. (1989). *Computer-mediated communication: Human relationships in a computerized world.* Tuscaloosa: University of Alabama Press.

Cotton, B., & Oliver, R. (1993). *Understanding hypermedia: From multimedia to virtual reality.* London: Phaidon.

Coyne, R. (1999). *Technoromaticism: Digital narrative, holism, and the romance of the real.* Cambridge, MA: MIT Press.

Critical Arts Ensemble. (1994). *The electronic disturbance.* Brooklyn, NY: Autonomedia.

Curry, M. R. (1998). *Digital places: Living with geographic information technologies.* London: Routledge.

Davis, R. (1999). *The web of politics: The Internet's impact on the American political system.* New York: Oxford.

DeLanda, M. (1991). *War in the age of intelligent machines.* New York: Swerve Editions.

Delany, P., & Landow, G.P. (Eds.). (1991). *Hypermedia and literacy studies.* Cambridge: MIT Press.

Dery, M. (Ed.). (1993). Flame wars: The discourse of cyberculture [Special issue]. *The South Atlantic Quarterly, 92*(4).

Dewdney, C. (1998). *Last flesh: Life in the transhuman era.* Toronto: HarperCollins.

Dibbell, J. (1999). *My tiny life: Crime and passion in a virtual world.* New York: Owl.

Diffie, W., & Landau, S. (1998). *Privacy on the line: The politics of wiretapping and encryption.* Cambridge, MA: MIT Press.

Dizard, W., Jr. (1997). *Meganet: How the global communications network will connect everyone on earth.* Boulder, CO: Westview.

Dreyfus, H.L. (1979). *What computers can't do: The limits of artificial intelligence* (rev. ed.). New York: Harper Colophon Books.

Dreyfus, H.L., & Dreyfus, S.E. (1986). *Mind over machine.* New York: The Free Press.

Drucker, S.J., & Gumpert, G. (1991). Public space and communication: The zoning of public interaction. *Communication Theory, 1*(4), 294-310.

Dutton, W. H. (1999). *Society on the line: Information politics in the digital age.* New York: Oxford University Press.

Gandy, O.H., Jr. (1993). *The panoptic sort: A political economy of personal information.* Boulder, CO: Westview.

Gates, B. (1995). *The road ahead.* New York: Viking.

Gates, B. (1999). *Business @ the speed of thought: Using a digital nervous system.* New York: Warner.

Gelernter, D. (1991). *Mirror worlds or the day software puts the universe in a shoebox . . . How it will happen and what it will mean.* New York: Oxford University Press.

Gergen, K.J. (1991). *The saturated self.* New York: Basic Books.

Gibson, S. B., & Oviedo, O. O. (Eds.). (2000). *The emerging cyberculture: Literacy, paradigm, and paradox.* Cresskill, NJ: Hampton Press.

Gibson, W. (1984). *Neuromancer.* New York: Ace Books.

Gilder, G. (1994). *Life after television: The coming transformation of media and American life* (rev. ed.). New York: W.W. Norton.

Gozzi, R., Jr. (1999). *The power of metaphor in the age of electronic media.* Cresskill, NJ: Hampton Press.

Grabosky, P. N., & Smith, R. G. (1998). *Crime in the digital age: Controlling telecommunications and cyberspace illegalities.* New Brunswick, NJ: Transaction.

Gray, C.H. (Ed.). (1995). *The cyborg handbook.* New York: Routledge.

Gumpert, G. (1987). *Talking tombstones and other tales of the media age.* New York: Oxford University Press.

Gumpert, G., & Cathcart, R. (1986). *Inter/media: Interpersonal communication in a media world* (3rd ed.). New York: Oxford University Press.

Gumpert, G., & Drucker, S.J. (1992). From the agora to the electronic shopping mall. *Critical Studies in Mass Communication, 9*(2), 186-200.

Hafner, K., & Markoff, J. (1992). *Cyberpunk: Outlaws and hackers on the computer frontier.* New York: Touchstone.

Hall, E.T. (1966). *The hidden dimension.* Garden City, NY: Anchor.

Haraway, D.J. (1991). *Simians, cyborgs, and women: The reinvention of nature.* New York: Routledge.

Harper, C. (1998). *And that's the way it will be: News and information in a digital world.* New York: New York University Press.

Hauben, M., & Hauben, R. (1997). *Netizens: On the history and impact of Usenet and the Internet.* Los Alamitos, CA: IEEE Computer Society.

Hayles, N. K. (1999). *How we became posthuman: Virtual bodies in cybernetics, literature, and informatics.* Chicago: University of Chicago Press.

Hawisher, G.E., & Selfe, C.L. (Eds.). (1991). *Evolving perspectives on computers and composition studies.* Urbana, IL: NCTE Press

Hayward, P., & Wollen, T. (Eds.). (1993). *Future visions: New technologies of the screen.* London: British Film Institute.

Heim, M. (1987). *Electric language: A philosophical study of word processing.* New Haven: Yale University Press.

Heim, M. (1993). *The metaphysics of virtual reality.* New York: Oxford University Press.

Hill, K. A., & Hughes, J. E. (1998). *Cyberpolitics: Citizen activism in the age of the Internet.* Totowa, NJ: Rowman and Littlefield.

Hillis, K. (1999). *Digital sensation: Space, identity, and embodiment in virtual reality.* Minneapolis: University of Minnesota Press.

Hobart, M. E., & Schiffman, Z. S. (1998). *Information ages: Literacy, numeracy, and the computer revolution.* Baltimore: John Hopkins University Press.

Hofstadter, D.R. (1980). *Gödel, Escher, Bach: An eternal golden braid.* New York: Vintage Books.

Hofstadter, D.R., & Dennett, D.C. (Eds.). (1981). *The minds I.* New York: Basic Books.

Innis, H.A. (1951). *The bias of communication.* Toronto: University of Toronto Press.

Jameson, F. (1991). *Postmodernism, or, the cultural logic of late capitalism.* Durham, NC: Duke University Press.

Johnson, S. (1997). *Interface culture: How new technology transforms the way we create and communicate.* San Francisco: HarperEdge.

Jones, S.G. (Ed.). (1995). *Cybersociety: Computer-mediated communication and community.* Thousand Oaks, CA: Sage.

Katsh, M. E. (1995). *Law in a digital world.* New York: Oxford University Press.

Kern, S. (1983). *The culture of time and space, 1880-1918.* Cambridge, MA: Harvard University Press.

Kidwell, P.A., & Ceruzzi, P.E. (1994). *Landmarks in digital computing.* Washington, DC: Smithsonian Institution Press.

Kroker, A. (1993). *Spasm: Virtual reality, android music, and electric flesh.* New York: St. Martin's Press.

Kroker, A., & Weinstein, M.A. (1994). *Data trash: The theory of the virtual class.* New York: St. Martin's Press.

Kurzweil, R. (1999). *The age of spiritual machines: When computers exceed human intelligence.* New York: Viking.

Landow, G.P. (1992). *Hypertext: The convergence of contemporary critical theory and technology.* Baltimore: John Hopkins University Press.

Lanham, R.A. (1993). *The electronic word: Democracy, technology, and the arts.* Chicago: University of Chicago Press.

Laurel, B. (Ed.). (1990). *The art of human-computer interface.* Reading, MA: Addison-Wesley.

Laurel, B. (1993). *Computers as theatre.* Reading, MA: Addison Wesley.

Leonard, A. (1997). *Bots: The origins of new species.* San Francisco: HardWired.

Levinson, P. (1997). *The soft edge: A natural history and future of the information revolution.* London & New York: Routledge.

Levinson, P. (1999). *Digital McLuhan: A guide to the information millennium.* London & New York: Routledge.

Levy, S. (1984). *Hackers: Heroes of the computer revolution.* New York: Dell.

Levy, S. (1992). *Artificial life: A report from the frontier where computers meet biology.* New York: Random House.

Loader, B. D. (Ed.). (1997). *The governance of cyberspace: Politics, technology, and global restructuring.* London: Routledge.

Logan, R. K. (1997). *The fifth language: Learning a living in the computer age.* Toronto: Stoddard.

Logan, R. K. (2000). *The sixth language: Learning a living in the Internet age.* Toronto: Stoddard.

Lubar, S. (1993). *Infoculture: The Smithsonian book of information age inventions.* Boston: Houghton Mifflin.

Ludlow, P. (Ed.). (1996). *High noon on the electronic frontier: Conceptual issues in cyberspace.* Cambridge, MA: MIT Press.

Lyon, D., & Zureik, E. (Eds.). (1996). *Computers, surveillance, & privacy.* Minneapolis: University of Minnesota Press.

Lyotard, J.-F. (1984). *The postmodern condition: A report on knowledge* (G. Bennington & B. Massumi, Trans.). Minneapolis: University of Minnesota Press. (Original work published 1979)

McCaffery, L. (Ed.). (1991). *Storming the reality studio: A casebook of cyberpunk and postmodern fiction.* Durham, NC: Duke University Press.

McLuhan, M. (1962). *The Gutenberg galaxy.* Toronto: University of Toronto Press.

McLuhan, M. (1964). *Understanding media: The extensions of man.* New York: Mentor Books.

McLuhan, M., & Powers, B.R. (1989). *The global village.* New York: Oxford University Press.

Meyrowitz, J. (1985). *No sense of place.* New York: Oxford University Press.

Meyrowitz, J. (1986). Television and interpersonal behavior: Codes of perception and response. In G. Gumpert & R. Cathcart (Eds.), *Inter/media: Interpersonal communication in a media world* (3rd ed.; pp. 253-272). New York: Oxford University Press.

Mitchell, W. J. (1995). *City of bits: Space, place, and the infobahn.* Cambridge, MA: MIT Press.

Molz, K. R., & Dain, P. (1999). *Civic space/cyberspace: The American public library in the information age.* Cambridge, MA: MIT Press.

Moody, F. (1995). *I sing the body electronic: A year with Microsoft on the multimedia frontier.* New York: Viking.

Murray, J. H. (1997). *Hamlet on the holodeck: The future of narrative in cyberspace.* New York: The Free Press.

Negroponte, N. (1995). *Being digital.* New York: Alfred A. Knopf.

Nelson, T.H. (1987). *Computer lib/Dream machines.* Redmond, WA: Tempus Books.

Nelson, T.H. (1990). *Literary machines.* Sausalito, CA: Mindful.

Nunberg, G. (Ed.). (1996). *The future of the book*. Berkeley: University of California Press.

O'Donnell, J. J. (1998). *Avatars of the word: From papyrus to cyberspace*. Cambridge, MA: Harvard University Press.

Odzer, C. (1997). *Virtual spaces: Sex and the cyber citizen*. New York: Berkley.

Ong, W.J. (1982). *Orality and literacy: The technologizing of the word*. New York: Methuen.

Papert, S. (1980). *Mindstorms: Children, computers, and powerful ideas*. New York: Basic Books.

Papert, S. (1993). *The children's machine*. New York: Basic Books.

Penrose, R. (1989). *The emperor's new mind: Concerning computers, minds, and the laws of physics*. New York: Oxford University Press.

Perkinson, H. (1995). *No safety in numbers: How the computer quantified everything and made people risk-aversive*. Cresskill, NJ: Hampton Press.

Peterson, D. (1983). *Genesis II: Creation and recreation with computers*. Reston, VA: Reston.

Pickard, R. (1997). *Affective computing*. Cambridge, MA: MIT Press.

Pickover, C.A. (Ed.). (1994). *Visions of the future: Art, technology and computing in the twenty-first century*. New York: St. Martin's Press.

Pimentel, K., & Teixeira, K. (1993). *Virtual reality: Through the new looking glass*. New York: Intel/Windcrest/McGraw-Hill.

Poster, M. (1990). *The mode of information*. Chicago: University of Chicago Press.

Postman, N. (1979). *Teaching as a conserving activity*. New York: Delacorte.

Postman, N. (1985). *Amusing ourselves to death*. New York: Viking.

Postman, N. (1992). *Technopoly: The surrender of culture to technology*. New York: Alfred A. Knopf.

Provenzo, E.F., Jr. (1986). *Beyond the Gutenberg galaxy*. New York: Teachers College Press.

Provenzo, E.F., Jr. (1991). *Video kids: Making sense of Nintendo*. Cambridge, MA: Harvard University Press.

Pruitt, S., & Barrett, T. (1991). Corporate virtual workspace. In M. Benedikt (Ed.), *Cyberspace: First steps* (pp. 383-409). Cambridge, MA: MIT Press.

Reid, E.M. (1992). Electropolis: Communication and community on internet relay chat. *Intertek, 3*(3), 7-13.

Rheingold, H. (1991). *Virtual reality*. New York: Touchstone.

Rheingold, H. (1993). *The virtual community: Homesteading on the electronic frontier*. Reading, MA: Addison Wesley.

Rickett, F. (1993). Multimedia. In P. Hayward & T. Wollen (Eds.), *Future visions: New technologies of the screen* (pp. 72-91). London: British Film Institute.

Rifkin, J. (2000). *The age of access: The new culture of hypercapitalism where all of life is a paid-for experience*. New York: Jeremy P. Tarcher/Putnam.

Ritchin, F. (1990). *In our own image: The coming revolution in photography*. New York: Aperture.

Robertson, D. S. (1998). *The new renaissance: Computers and the next level of civilization.* New York: Oxford University Press.

Ross, A. (1991). Hacking away at the counterculture. In C. Penley & A. Ross (Eds.), *Technoculture* (pp. 107-134). Minneapolis: University of Minnesota Press.

Roszak, T. (1994). *The cult of information: A neo-Luddite treatise on high-tech, artificial intelligence, and the true art of thinking* (2nd ed.). Berkeley: The University of California Press.

Rushkoff, D. (1994). *Cyberia: Life in the trenches of hyperspace.* New York: HarperCollins.

Rushkoff, D. (1996). *Playing the future: What we can learn from digital kids.* San Francisco: HarperCollins.

Rushkoff, D. (1999). *Coercion : Why we listen to what "they" say.* New York: Riverhead.

Rutsky, R. L. (1999). *High techne: Art and technology from the machine aesthetic to the posthuman.* Minneapolis: University of Minnesota Press.

Schiller, D. (1999). *Digital capitalism: Networking the global market system.* Cambridge, MA: MIT Press.

Schiller, H. (1996). *Information inequality: The deepening social crisis in America.* London: Routledge.

Seabrook, J. (1997). *Deeper: My two year odyssey in cyberspace.* New York: Simon & Schuster.

Shenk, D. (1997). *Data smog: Surviving the information glut.* San Francisco: HarperEdge.

Shenk, D. (1999). *The end of patience: Cautionary notes on the information revolution.* Bloomington: Indiana University Press.

Shields, R. (Ed.). (1996). *Cultures of Internet: Virtual spaces, real histories, living bodies.* London: Sage.

Slouka, M. (1996). *War of the worlds: Cyberspace and the high-tech assault on reality.* New York: Basic.

Smith, A. (1993). *Books to bytes: Knowledge and information in the postmodern era.* London: British Film Institute.

Smith, A. (1996). *Software for the self: Culture and technology.* New York: Oxford University Press.

Sproull, L., & Kiesler, S. (1991). *Connections: New ways of working in the networked organization.* Cambridge, MA: The MIT Press.

Sterling, B. (Ed.). (1986). *Mirrorshades: The cyberpunk anthology.* New York: Arbor House.

Sterling, B. (1992). *The hacker crackdown: Law and disorder on the electronic frontier.* New York: Arbor House.

Sternberg, J. (1991). The abacus: The earliest digital computer and its cultural implications. *New Dimensions in Communications: Proceedings of the 48th Annual New York State Speech Communication Association Convention, 4,* 69-71.

Stoll, C. (1995). *Silicon snake oil: Second thoughts on the information highway.* New York: Doubleday.

Stone, A.R. (1991). Will the real body please stand up? Boundary stories about virtual cultures. In M. Benedikt (Ed.), *Cyberspace: First steps* (pp. 81-118). Cambridge, MA: MIT Press.

Strate, L. (1994). Post(modern)man, Or Neil Postman as a postmodernist. *Etc.: A Review of General Semantics, 51*(2), 159-170.

Strate, L. (1999). The varieties of cyberspace: Problems in definition and delimitation. *Western Journal of Communication, 63*(3), 382-412.

Sudnow, D. (1983). *Pilgrim in the microworld.* New York: Warner.

Swisher, K. (1998). *AOL.COM: How Steve Case beat Bill Gates, nailed the netheads, and made millions in the war for the web.* New York: Times.

Talbott, S. (1995). *The future does not compute.* Sebastopol, CA: O'Reilly & Associates.

Taylor, M.C., & Saarinen, E. (1994). *Imagologies: Media philosophy.* London: Routledge.

Tuman, M.C. (1992a). *Literacy online: The promise (and peril) of reading and writing with computers.* Pittsburg, PA: University of Pittsburg Press.

Tuman, M. C. (1992b). *Word perfect: Literacy in the computer age.* Pittsburg, PA: University of Pittsburg Press.

Turkle, S. (1984). *The second self: Computers and the human spirit.* New York: Simon & Schuster.

Turkle, S. (1995). *Life on the screen: Identity in the age of the Internet.* New York: Simon & Schuster.

Wachtel, E. (1978). Technological cubism: The presentation of space and time in multi-image. *Etc.: A Review of General Semantics, 35*(4), 376-382.

Weizenbaum, J. (1976). *Computer power and human reason.* San Francisco: W.H. Freeman.

Wiener, N. (1967). *The human use of human beings: Cybernetics and society.* Boston, MA: Avon.

Woolley, B. (1992). *Virtual worlds: A journey in hype and hyperreality.* Oxford: Blackwell.

Zettl, H. (1990). *Sight sound motion: Applied media aesthetics* (2nd ed.). Belmont, CA: Wadsworth.

# SECTION *1*

# CYBERSPACE IN PERSPECTIVE: THE THEORETICAL CONTEXT

On one side there is the hype, hoopla, and how-to-oriented discourse of the popular media, the communications industry, and computer hobbyists and professionals. On the other, there is denial, dismissal, and silence. Between the two lies the path we must follow if we are to take cyberspace seriously, to study it as a communication phenomenon. To do so properly requires a grounding of the electronic environment, a framework for contextualizing the topic, a way of providing even cyberspace with a sense of place—placing cyberspace and, possibly, putting it in its place. Thus, the purpose of this section is to provide theoretical and philosophical bases for more specific analyses of cyberspace and to provide links to larger issues in the field of communication.

This section begins with Gary Gumpert and Susan Drucker's exploration of the electronic landscape from the communication and social space perspective. Noting how cyberspace functions as a substitute for public places, they raise questions concerning cyberspace's impact on privacy and law and on social interaction and overall quality of life. Following with a strong critique of the Internet environment, John M. Phelan takes on the utopian fantasies of cyberspace boosters, discussing the social, political, economic, and religious implications of the digital world and the rhetoric that surrounds it. The third chapter by James R. Beniger is concerned with the present and future ownership, control, and exploitation of cyberspace. Arguing that the Internet and the World

Wide Web will probably not continue in its present form indefinitely, he outlines the vulnerabilities of cyberspace to commercialization and outside political control. Whereas Beniger's focus is on control of cyberspace, the very concept of ownership is destabilized in an electronic environment, as Neil Kleinman explains in Chapter 4. Presenting a history of intellectual property rights and copyright law, he emphasizes the problems posed by cyberspace's immaterial nature and its lack of barriers to the flow of information.

The idea of virtual reality is one of the most evocative concepts related to cyberspace. In the section's fifth chapter, Herbert Zettl examines virtual reality (VR) technologies as a medium and art form, discussing the aesthetic, metaphysical, and ethical issues involved in implementing VR systems. Charles U. Larson, in the following chapter, explores virtual reality from a rhetorical perspective. Employing Burke's dramatistic model, he focuses on virtual reality as a virtual scene in which virtual acts are performed. The virtual environments described by Zettl and Larson are a far cry from today's primarily text-based forms of computer-mediated communication, networking, and hypermedia. In Chapter 7, Jay David Bolter considers the conflict between audiovisual modes of communication, such as VR, with their emphasis on sensory experience, and those based on electronic writing and print, which stress rational discourse. Providing a historical and philosophical context, he makes clear the relationship between multimedia and virtual reality and what has been described as the decentering of the subject, the dissolution of the Cartesian ego, or simply changes in the concept of the self.

However much these authors differ in their outlook and method, they all help to clarify the concept of cyberspace, and they all provide theoretical contexts for its study based on communication and related disciplines.

# From Locomotion to Telecommunication, or Paths of Safety, Streets of Gore

Gary Gumpert
Susan J. Drucker

. *As innovations, the technologies of electronic space are intended to function as alternatives to physical location and transportation. In actual use, however, they also function as social environments, as human beings adapt the technologies to fulfill their own needs and desires. Thus cyberspace becomes the setting for social life in which we meet others, form relationships, even hold funerals. Gary Gumpert and Susan J. Drucker take the measure of cyberspace as a social environment, exploring its range and peculiarities. They take the position that, although we may use cyberspace as a substitute for the physical environment, the two are by no means equivalent. Thus laws that are drafted to deal with physical objects and real persons in actual locations may not quite work when applied to the unstable world of electronic transmissions over shifting networks. Common-sense notions such as the distinction between public and private may no longer apply in the microworld of computer-mediated communication. Ultimately, the most important difference between the two environments, according to Gumpert and Drucker, is quality of life; they are concerned not just*

*with what computers and telecommunications can do, but with what they undo.*
*Outside of Section I, further examinations of cyberspace as social and public*
*space can be found in Frank Dance's discussion of the digital divide in Chapter*
*10, and Eric Zimmer and Christopher Hunter's report on sex in cyberspace in*
*Chapter 11; related views on social interaction and relationships are present in*
*Philip Thompsen's research on flaming in Chapter 20, and Susan Barnes's*
*exploration of virtual environments in Chapter 14. Additional discussion of legal*
*issues can be found in Ron Jacobson's piece on cyberspace policy in Chapter 9,*
*and also see Douglas Rushkoff's essay on the commercialization of cyberspace in*
*Chapter 21.*


## PROLOGUE: REVISITING THE PAST


It is potentially a traumatic experience to confront ones' own errors in judgment, careless mistakes, and lack of insight in one's own writing. It is, therefore, our general practice never to return to a chapter once published. On some rare occasions, insightful remarks are discovered, eloquence unearthed, and pleasure derived from the artifacts of a previous age of writing and creation.

Can "From Locomotion to Telecommunication, or Paths of Safety, Streets of Gore" remain unedited and stand on the merits of a 1995 mentality? Has the cyberworld and vision of 1995 remained unchanged or does contemporary reconsideration require modification, re-evaluation, backtracking, or an apology? After a thoughtful examination of the chapter, we came to the conclusion that many of the observations and concerns stand the test of time, that a minute change here and there, some meticulous tweaking and updating, would do little to improve what had been written more than 5 years earlier. On the other hand, there are innovations, developments and unexpected or unaddressed twists that now occupy the forefront of our concerns. The title of the chapter has changed in meaning. Streets of Gore was meant to be a play on words and a reflection of an increasing degree of alienation to the physical environment. The election of 2000 swept Vice President Al Gore out of power and the events of 2001 increased our perception of the streets as filled with gore. The body of this manuscript was written prior to the catastrophic events of September 11, 2001 but it is impossible to discuss the relationship of physical and electronic spaces without reflecting on the implications of a world changed. Although many individuals seek refuge from the risks of the physical world (whether those risks be general or more terrorism oriented), our belief in the values and importance of the physical environment has been strengthened by the recent devastating events. These new directions or nuances are best understood after exploring the original work, so we invite the reader to return to this reconsideration in the epilogue at the end of this chapter.

## Probe I

This co-authoring relationship of scholarship is fragile. It has withstood crises and attack. It survives on productivity and originality. It has an intellectual foundation grounded in the study of the Canons of Communication. But it's time to confess. It is also a research relationship firmly rooted in conspicuous consumption and the psychological reverberation that derives from a deep-seated computer neurosis. It has come to this. We define ourselves by the size of our RAM, the number of megs, the compatibility of our machines and programs, the speed of our trusty steeds, and our concern with the quality of our CD-ROM. It innocently began with a nonthreatening frolic with computer #1, now sitting unused and unwanted in one corner of the memorial library, with a hard card (rather than disk) and its two yawning 5 1/4-inch floppy drives. It sits there alone, unwanted, an outmoded, impotent, former friend, a steady companion who was at our creating, soothing, and offending side for a long period of time. But relationships are ephemeral and we must move on to new friends. Remember bigger and faster is better.

We graduated to a 386 33-meg machine with a 2400-Baud Hayes modem, but it's too slow for the Windows environment in which we now work, and we were about to order a new Pentium 586 machine with a built-in fax/modem (it's awfully inconvenient working with the separate fax machine), CD-ROM (with quality speakers), and tape backup. We were about to order, but became concerned that our high-powered communication research might be threatened by the high-powered divisional flaw of the Pentium chip.

It's media central, the nerve center of the radiating scholarly empire that links us to the riches of the Internet, the chat rooms of America Online, to the Chase Manhattan bank for high-finance transactions, to the local library to check on whether they have a copy of Gumpert's *Talking to Strangers* or Drucker's *American Heroes in a Media Age,* to Prodigy and Zagat's listing and ranking of restaurants around the globe, to Compuserve and Eaasy Sabre for airline schedules and rates, and to the keyboard through which ideas flow and are processed. *But neither of us have ever been in a neighbor's house.*

## Probe II

It was almost the deadline for submitting panels to the Environmental Design conference being held in Boston in Spring 1995. We had four days to get the panel together and send it to the conference organizer. A call to Boston. A friend advised us that the Dean of Architecture would be a good person to have on the panel and sent us his e-mail address. We quickly drafted a letter, and uploaded it to the College computer center. Two days later, in checking on the latest e-mail, we received a reply from the Dean who indicated that the e-mail sent to Boston two days before had caught up with him in Australia. The Dean agreed to participate in the panel—if he were free—and asked us to e-mail his assistant at MIT to check on his commitments. Everything was fine and we sent out the proposal on time, with an exciting group of scholars around the United States—and beyond—who have agreed to participate. *But we don't know our neighbors' names. Sometimes we wish someone were outside so we could talk away our loneliness.*

## Probe III

A working relationship is predicated on ritual. It is influenced by where we work ("Your place or mine?"). Physically we are separated by 2.4 miles—miles that easily dissolve under the circumstances of electronic geography. The internalized path leads from the kitchen, where a pot of tea is delicately brewed, later to be replaced with coffee, to an amble down the steps into the basement corridor, which leads to the study, an environment of books, papers, photographs, collected memorabilia, and a soft black chair from which we enter the rest of the world. The early morning radio companion substantiates that there is an outside, and we sit surrounded by answering machine, facsimile, computer and modem, laser jet printer, and cordless telephone. A right foot hits the switch and our electronics center lights up and, unlike those ancient relatives of old with whom we shared the simple act of locomotion, we cavort and connect as travelers in electronic space. We check the answering machine, which was turned on as we left to run compulsory errands. It's only a matter of 15 minutes, but someone might be crazy enough to call this early. The idea of missing a call is a perverse and alien notion. (More sophisticated, perhaps more important, scholars have trained themselves to screen calls.) The Crosstalk Icon is selected, and the ceremonial sound of computer coupling (do they have sex?) is heard and eventually the necessary passwords are negotiated so that electronic mail that has reached our computer accounts through enigmatic nodes, paths, gateways, and bridges can be processed and figuratively fondled. We reject, reply, forward, upload, download—in a strange boundless environment that is often only located in our imagination and that is described by some as *cyberspace.*

## SPACELESS SPACE AND VIRTUAL ROADS

The term *cyberspace* is attributed to science fiction author William Gibson, who coined the term in his novel *Neuromancer*, "where it names a 21st century virtual dimension, entered into via a neuro-electronic interface, in which the world's data networks unfold before the user as a sensually vivid geography" (Dibbell, 1993, p. 13). It is described by Compuserve as "that nowhere space in the telephone line between you and where all things on-line happen, but it's also the 'room' or other expanse you're not really in when you're visiting any form of virtual reality" ("Cyberspace," 1994, p. 12). The telephone call is a ticket of entrance.

Cyberspace, although not limited to the Internet, is often associated with its most well-known and largest expanse. The Internet is an unbelievably dense global matrix of 46,000 computer networks, 3.2 million host computers, woven together by telephone lines, undersea cables, microwave links, and gigabit fiber-optic pipes. Touching down in 146 countries, linking 25 million to 30 million people and growing by a million users each month, it's doubling in size each year (Internet Society, 1994; Lewis, 1994b). It's a super data highway that carries the freight of the information age—electronic mail, digital video and sound, computer viruses, and more (Markoff, 1993a). There are an estimated 3.2 million computers around the globe today with predictions that the Internet will grow to more than 100 million computers in 5 years (Internet Society, 1994; Lewis, 1994b). There are 21,700 commercial "domains" (the Internet equivalent of storefront addresses) officially registered (Verity & Hof, 1994): "Some companies are . . . laying the groundwork for entirely new ways of doing business—dealing directly with suppliers, industrial customers, and potentially millions of on-line shoppers" (p. 39).

The Internet began in the 1970s as a U.S. Defense Department network called ARPAnet. Slowly, corporations, universities, and information providers phased and dovetailed their networks into the system, agreeing on compatible connecting software (McNichol, 1994). Furthermore, it is the Internet that is a focal point of the electronic data highway featured as a high priority in the Clinton-Gore Administration. Such a system includes digital libraries (making libraries accessible to everyone), database publishing, electronic mail, electronic communities (virtual or nonplace communities that link people with similar interests), software access, weather information, entertainment, and data exchange (Markoff, 1993b).

Progress and technological developments can be terribly exciting. Being able to connect with the outside world from our intellectual dungeon is amazing and helpful, but it is much more difficult to forecast the impact of such developments. It is not our intention to examine the intricacies of the electronic data highway. We are probably not capable of that task, and there are Internet experts who perform such functions well. What we are concerned with is the impact and relationship of such developments with concurrent situations and institutions.

Langdon Winner (1993) wrote an article for the *Chronicle of Higher Education* in which the problem is succinctly stated:

> What most conventional ideas about technology lack is any notion of technological development as a dynamic social and cultural phenomenon. This is not an arcane topic. Every thorough-going history of the building of technological systems points to the same conclusion: Substantial technological innovation involves a reweaving of the fabric of society—a reshaping of some of the roles, rules, relationships, and institutions that make up our ways of living together. (p. B1)

The preceding analysis stresses the complex interrelationships of innovation and states that "the technology is never the sole cause of the changes one sees. But it is often the occasion and catalyst for a thorough redefinition of the operating structures of society and of the daily experiences of people in their work, family, life, and communities" (p. B1). Winner, a professor of political science at Rensselaer Polytechnic Institute, quite astutely uses as an analogy the construction of the national interstate highway system after the Second World War. The system was inspired by a wish to improve commerce, foster social mobility, and bolster national defense. In actual usage, its grid of arteries and ring of roads permanently changed the American social landscape. Among other consequences, the interstate highways amplified a growing split between urban centers and outlying communities, a serious and troublesome split characterized by today's suburbia as compared with the inner cities. As it built physical boundaries between neighborhoods, the highway system modified not only the nation's economy, but our personal relations as well.

With the development of all communication systems prior to the telegraph, the stress was placed on place rather than on the movement of data. The early development of telegraphy was linked to transportation and speed of transmission, but the economic structure of even the telegraph had extraordinary implications. Anthony Rutkowski, executive director of the Internet Society, points out that "at the very earliest telegraph conferences of 1850, there were issues about the additional cost necessary to reach remote places and who should pay. The iteration of the debate is about the Information Superhighway" (quoted in Gerwig, 1994, p. 23). Thus, geographic implosion further redefines rural and urban divisions. About 20% of Americans must pay long distance rates to get on the electronic highway. Although the concept of rural may be defined by the expense of access to the highway, rather than by expanse of land, even some suburban and urban dwellers may find themselves distanced by cost as well.

The spatial relationship of radio was between listener and station, of television between viewer and channel. But the virtual community is a construction existing in our vision and imagination, and it is significant that geographical and architectural terms are the primary metaphors used to describe the emerging electronic environment in which place and location are deemphasized in favor of speed of transmission.

It begins as soon as we turn on the computer. We enter the graphical environment of Windows through which we can access software and connections to data and others. The screen of the computer is converted from an opaque frame to a transparent conduit that leads bits of data out to an amorphous electronic environment. We are linked to bulletin boards, malls, and rooms through ports, highways, exits, gateways, bridges, routers, and nodes.

## SOCIAL LIFE AND SPACELESS RELATIONSHIPS

David Alsberg was a 42-year-old computer programmer. He was standing in a Times Square store when a stray bullet from a nearby robbery attempt instantly killed him. *The New York Times* account does not focus on the all-too-common circumstances of Mr. Alsberg's death, but on the grieving that followed (Lewis, 1994a). The story states that Mr. Alsberg lived in two communities, one being his Astoria neighborhood, where his wife, son, and hundreds of friends came together to mourn his death. The other community in which he lived was "the electric community called Cyberspace" (p. A1). Mr. Alsberg's personal computer friends came together in an online wake in an electronic forum.

In a world where physical contact is impossible, Mr. Alsberg's cyberspace neighbors consoled each other over the senseless loss of a mutual friend. And in their collective grieving, they demonstrated an impulse for togetherness that is as modern as the digital age and as old as humankind. For as more people become citizens of cyberspace, they are forging relationships that many describe as being as rewarding as their face-to-face-friendships (Lewis, 1994a, p. D2)

It is estimated that the population of cyberspace consists of between 30 to 35 million people. *The New York Times* reports that what some might call "artificial intimacy is catching the interest of psychologists and sociologists" (Lewis, 1994a, p. D2). The Alsberg incident links the hostile world of the street with the more secure, nonthreatening, electronic Internet highway of cyberspace. Safety seems to be the primary defining criterion by which individuals choose the spaces in which they work, play, live, and interact.

Not so very long ago our social lives were divided between public and private spaces. (We define such spaces on the basis of access rather than ownership.) We maintained our private relationships in the home, but activities outside the home were important. We learned about events and people. We played and watched others play. We escaped the tyranny of those we love for a moment or two by watching others whom we had not yet met. We conversed with strangers we might not meet again and old companions who were recurring supporting characters in our lives.

Social interaction of both a private and a public nature has entered the realm of electronic space, interaction located in a placeless vacuum in which two or more people can link via telephone or where one or more persons can become involved with the program of a distanced computer (Gumpert & Drucker, 1992). Face-to-face communication in physical space and mediated communication may serve the same purposes but are experienced in very different ways. Every media development alters the availability and nature of traditional private and public places. The newspaper influenced and defined, in part, the barbershop, the village green, and the cafe. The telephone shaped the nature of courtship. Radio altered the experiences of the living room, the car, and the doctor's office. The computer keyboard opens up distant retrievable vistas.

For some, cyberspace alternatives for social interaction are limited by lack of access to electronic connection because of cost, technophobia and/or lack of technical virtuosity. Street life which once beckoned and called has been swept away by the realities of fear and risk. Those who are afraid to go out instead sit alone in rooms, often disconnected from the environment in which they sit.

## REGULATING METAPHORS

It is significant that at a time when we seek refuge from the street, when the highway has been reduced to a connection between hostile zones, as we continue down the path of interiorizing and privatization, that the nomenclature of urban planning and architecture has been transformed into metaphors of cyberspace. Thus, there is a reason for the subtitle of this chapter—"Paths of Safety, Streets of Gore."

The vocabulary surrounding new technologies, new uses for old technologies, and the joinder of multiple media is significant as it not only allows us to talk about a phenomenon, but also shapes the perception of the reality being named. In fact, the words created and metaphors employed function persuasively: "Kenneth Burke has argued that 'naming' is an interpretive act which functions as a guide to action toward that which is named" (Blankenship, 1980, p. 321). Therefore, "the command that one act one way rather than another is 'implicit' in the name" (Burke, 1950, p. 41).

Approached from a dramatistic perspective, we may see these clusters of metaphors as a symbolic reaction to an environment that involves "the use of words by human agents to form attitudes or to induce action in other human agents" (Burke, 1950, p. 41). The adoption of spatial terminology may appear a ready and useful mechanism for making the revolutionary changes of the information age less strange, intimidating, and boundless. Thus, for example, the concept of "broadcasting" can be traced to somewhere between 1760 and 1770, and it originally was an agricultural term used to describe the spreading or the sowing of seeds. To cast the seed broadly became a suitable metaphor to portray the transmission of sound in a manner quite distinct from the prior notion of point-to-point transmission. We now use the term not only to describe a medium of communication, but also the act of making something generally widely known, and sometimes it refers to the indiscriminate act of spreading lies. In this case, we begin to think, perceive, and reshape the world with an agriculturally based, technologically transformed metaphor. Although a few of us may throw seeds into the wind as a romantic gesture, the art of agriculture has also been redefined, and broadcasting is seldom performed by hand in an industry that has left the confines of the small farm for large conglomerate-run outfits. Furthermore, how do you keep them down on the farm when broadcasts have revealed that there are other and more varied fields to sow?

Words are what we make them, but they also make us over. In the case of cyberspace and electronic communication, the matter of metaphor is more than a simplistic linguistic exercise created to keep academics off the street. Very early in the primordial arcane days when strange people plotted the computer future of the world, decisions were made linking our metaphysical souls to the evolving communication philosophy that would emerge out of that mass of blinking, winking, and groaning set of tubes, lights, and valves. When the International Standards Organization adopted an Open System Interconnect reference model (somehow also linked with IBM's Systems Network Architecture) in order to assure compatibility among users, the language of architecture and urban planning had already provided a metaphorical lexicon to guide future development and usage.

Words are what we make them, but they (and what they represent) evolve, dynamically change, and reflect back on their origins. The significance of the landscape orientation of cyberspace is not only that a prior spatial identity has been applied to a nonterritorially defined medium, but that the very process of naming redefines the earlier application. The nomenclature of space, urban planning, and architecture has been transformed into metaphors of cyberspace. Metaphors shape perceptions, expectations, and psychological assumptions, which drive the relationships formed with that which has been named. Spatial metaphors have been transposed from the physical world in which property and ownership are defining principles to the electronic realm of connection. Through application of this metaphor the implications emerge as spatial metaphors become not merely useful tools for making the revolutionary changes of the information age less strange and unsettling, but a ready mechanism through which to manage and regulate the alien phenomenon. So, for instance, the technologies of communications challenge developments in applicable laws governing rights of free expression in such areas as libel,[1] hate speech,[2] and obscenity,[3] as well as rights of privacy and related issues of sexual harassment,[4] and jurisdictional questions. In attempting to keep pace with technological growth, developments in "cyberlaw" have been handled through the application of preexisting legal doctrines, some taken from the pages of property law.

---

[1] *Cubby v. CompuServe Incorporated* (1991) is the sole case to date in which a libel action was reportedly brought against an information service provider. In this case a plaintiff sued CompuServe on the basis of allegedly false and defamatory statements contained in an electronic newsletter available in CompuServe's Journalism Forum; the newsletter was not published by CompuServe, however, but rather by a third party. The court granted CompuServe's motion for summary judgment relying upon CompuServe's actions as distributor, exercising no editorial control and acting as an electronic library.

[2] Hate speech has confronted information providers as an issue which requires attention. The Anti-Defamation League of B'nai B'rith cited anti-Semitic notes sent via e-mail but rejected for public posting by Prodigy as an example of electronically networked hate speech (Miller, 1991; for further discussion, see Leroux, 1991).

[3] Obscenity has received a good deal of attention within the context of cyberspace (Jackson, 1994). One of the most widely noted cases involved the operators of "Amateur Action" electronic bulletin board service who were convicted under the federal law criminalizing transmitting obscene images electronically from California to Tennessee (Landis, 1994).

[4] Santa Rosa Junior College in California was the site of a case in which three students were offended by sexual comments on a computer bulletin board run through the school. Separate male and female bulletin boards were operated prompting the students to allege sexual discrimination. The students brought charges under Title IX of the Civil Rights Act which prohibits sexual discrimination in schools. Further it was found that one female student, Jennifer Branham, had been subjected to sexual harassment in that a hostile educational environment had been created with regard to the posting of the messages. A settlement was reached between the students and the college in the amount of $15,000. The case against the Education Department under Title IX remains open (Lewis, 1994b).

From a legal perspective real property, or physical space, is distinguished by possession and use and enjoyment. The laws of real property and access to that property in order to communicate produce distinct issues determined by whether the public space is publicly or privately owned. Although title to real property is easily identifiable, who owns cyberspace? Bulletin boards have been called the computer-age equivalent of a public forum (Naughton, 1993), but approximately 90% are operated by private individuals or organizations on privately owned computers (Feder, 1991). Many bulletin boards (particularly commercial ventures) are governed by subscription agreements that generally expressly reserve the right to reject messages deemed inappropriate or to terminate the user's privilege to use the board. For example, America Online's Subscriber Agreement "reserves the right, at its sole discretion, to immediately, without Notice, suspend or terminate a Member's access to and use of America Online upon any breach of the Terms of Service."

The laws of privacy represent an area of law that has been more fully developed with regard to electronic, nonphysical spaces of interaction. The evolution of the right to be let alone, or the right to privacy and reasonable expectations of privacy, has regularly been rooted in the nature of a particular geographic location. Fourth and Fifth Amendment rights are involved when considering search and seizure and freedom from self-incrimination associated with places in which there is a reasonable expectation of privacy. Courts have explored these expectations in physical spaces ranging from homes and offices to cars and school lockers (Kamisar, LaFave, & Israel, 1986). It is clear that reasonable expectations of privacy are no longer restricted to the physical spatial realm. Dating back to 1967, the Supreme Court enunciated this point in *Katz v. United States*, at which time the Court found "the emphasis on the nature of a particular targeted area deflected attention from the issue of Fourth Amendment infringement" (p. 351). Justice Steward wrote:

> For the Fourth Amendment protects people not places. What a person knowingly exposes to the public, even in his own home or office, is not a subject of Fourth Amendment protection. . . . But what he seeks to preserve as private even in an area accessible to the public, may be constitutionally protected. (*Katz v. United States*, 1967, p. 351).

One of the most popular types of communication in electronic space is electronic mail, a nearly instantaneous means of exchanging written messages and documents. Is the electronic space involved private? Can one assume no one would open e-mail? The answer to this may be addressed in service agreements with commercial service providers, but additional issues are raised in the university or business setting. Employers often monitor employee's job performance, but the latest twist is to do this via access to employee e-mail. Employers claim they do this for reasons ranging from system maintenance, message routing, and trouble shooting to protection of trade secrets and quality control (Kelly, 1994). According to Joel P. Kelly, writing in the February 1994 *Employment Law Strategist:*

> The tremendous rise in the number of employees who now use this technology, and the increasing ability of management to monitor such use, raise novel legal and ethical issues including: Do employees have a privacy right in their electronic mail communications? Under what circumstances can managers lawfully monitor employees' electronic mail? Is the employees' consent necessary? What facts are necessary to show consent? (p. 831)

Answers? The Electronic Communications Privacy Act of 1986 (ECPA) generally protects e-mail from illegal monitoring and makes it a federal crime to intercept and disclose electronic communications (18 U.S.C. 2510, 1988) punishable by imprisonment for up to five years or a fine of up to $250,000 for an individual and $500,000 for an organization. Individuals who show communications have been intercepted or used in violation of statute can claim actual and punitive damages of up to $100 per day of violation. But the ECPA does not protect privacy of messages sent on internal company electronic mail systems. The law treats such messages as interoffice memos that can be read by authorized employees, supervisors, or systems managers without violating the law. One party to the communication must consent to the monitoring, but the employees' consent can be implied from the circumstances of employment. Employees claim this violates their privacy rights, particularly if the intercepted communication is of a personal nature, but to date the courts have not addressed the right of privacy in the context of employers' monitoring of employee e-mail for legitimate business reasons. Under the Fourth Amendment, courts have even upheld an employer's right to engage in workplace surveillance for legitimate business reasons (*O'Connor v. Ortega*, 1987). There is a developing policy regarding employee expectations of privacy that seems to indicate there is not a reasonable expectation of privacy for company files and business correspondence generated by employees during work time, using company equipment. This extends from physical files and offices to electronic space on e-mail and computer files.

## THE REPERCUSSIONS OF CYBERSPACE ON PHYSICAL SPACE

Each medium leaves its mark by altering our institutions and personal attitudes and values, a concept eloquently embodied in Victor Hugo's *The Hunchback of Notre-Dame*. In that marvelous work the character of the archdeacon boldly states that "the book will kill the church":

> Omitting the detailing of a thousand proofs, and thousand objections to what has been said, we may sum the matter up as follows: That architecture, up to the fifteenth century, was as the chief register of humanity; that during this interval,

no thought of any complexity appeared in the world that was not built as every
religious commandment has its monument; that human nature, in short, had not
thought of importance that it did not write in stone. And why? Because every
idea, whether religious or philosophic, is concerned in being perpetuated. The
idea that has stirred the emotions of one generation desires to affect others, and
to leave its trace behind. . . .

In the fifteenth century, everything underwent a change. Humanity discovered a
means of perpetuating thought more lasting and durable than architecture, and
even simpler and easier. Architecture was dethroned. To the stone letters of
Orpheus are to succeed Gutenberg's letters of lead.
*The book will destroy the church.*

The book unchained the worshipper from dependence on the institution
of the church and created the individual supplicant. Similarly, the computer, at
the apex of media technology, as the trigger of interactivity combining other
media, will redefine not only other and previous media, but the structural
metaphor it has borrowed in order to function. Victor Hugo understood the power
of print to delineate the new spiritual relationship to be found in the church. Few
of us comprehend that the electronic highway is not just an extension of the
turnpike, that it not only co-opts but devalues the domain of public space.

In *Progressive Architecture*, Thomas Fisher (1988), discussing the new
urban design, says: "The city of today is primarily a private city. Most of its open
space, most of its transportation, most of its buildings, indeed most of the forces
that shape it are private" (p. 7). In *The Conscience of the Eye*, sociologist Richard
Sennett (1990) states:

What is characteristic of our city building is to wall off the differences between
people, assuming that these differences are more likely to be mutually
threatening than mutually stimulating. What we make in the urban realm are
therefore bland neutralizing spaces, spaces which remove the threat of social
contact. (p. xiii)

It takes little acumen to understand that our cities are self-destructing.
Suburbia dominates while urban life deteriorates to such an extent that we seek
refuge from the street. Our highways separate rather than connect while
transporting folks from place of work to place of residence, from home to mall,
from outside threat to inside safety.

Although fear and decay threaten and alter the quality of urban life, there
are those of us who continue the quest to rejuvenate the public place, sharing a
romantic notion that there is a need for the opportunity to talk to and touch each
other away from the obligations of office, home, and predetermined programmed
responsibilities, and that the shopping mall does not provide the answer to
isolation. But there is something seductive about electronic communication with
others, and we in the United States have begun to rely on mediated communication
and even to prefer that mode to the old, particularly because it is safe, forgetting

that there are qualitative differences between the two. The mediated functional alternatives that we choose generally occur inside controlled private space.

So we retreat inward where we can control at least some of the threats. No one wants to hand in their facsimile machine, answering machine, telephone, television, CD-ROM, cassette player, radio, beeper, video games, cellular phone, laser discs, VCR, and walkman. No one, in their right mind, seeks to dismantle the electronic highway and its potential store of activities. Ironically, it is the electronic highway (and what it symbolizes) that threatens to dismantle the traditional streets, squares, highways, and communities that once were so important to us.

## EPILOGUE I

Once upon a time, not so many years ago, people could go out into the city lights when the fancy struck them, when they had nothing better to do, when it occurred to them that it might be fun to be with others. Sometimes it was necessary to walk into the street to find out what was happening in the world. They wandered out to the square to talk, to the café to contemplate their lives over a cup of coffee, to the park to stroll among others, to the pub to flirt with those who were there to rush the blood, to the bench where ancient memories reside, to the chess tables to advise and criticize, to the public realm to vanquish loneliness, discuss politics, or simply talk. But it is no longer that time past, and the old and familiar have often become hostile and menacing. We sadly step back and find other possibilities and less threatening opportunities to play and frolic— safely, often alone.

## EPILOGUE II

From the vantage point of time, several observations come to mind.

1. The vocabulary of cyberspace can now be refined with significant adjustments in the conceptualization of issues. In 1995, the terms *cyberspace* and the *Internet* were used interchangeably. What has become clearer is that the Internet is a multimedia transport medium, whereas cyberspace is an environment of communication more capable of modulating or regulating the content placed onto the transport than regulating the transport system itself. But the technology of the "InterNET" impacts on the nature of communication within that environment. The language of the "network" emphasizes the process of connection. The earliest meaning of the term *network* originates around

1560 and referred to any netlike combination of filaments, lines, veins, passages, or the like. Later, the term referred to any network of arteries, for example the sewers under the city, or a system of interrelated buildings, offices, stations found over a large area. And, of course, later, the term was forever linked to a group of radio and television stations connected by wire or microwave relay in order to broadcast the same program (*Random House Dictionary*, 1966). But when did "networking" become remotely synonymous with social interaction? Sometime, not so long ago, "networking" assumed a figurative meaning in referring to the time we spend meeting people who will be useful to our business or ambitions. It comes to mind that we have a handy example of the technological transformation of social interaction. We become involved in programmed, ritualistic hunting expeditions in which we harvest the human crop. Before there were technological networks there were social networks. Today these networks confront one another.

The nature of the relationship of these distinct types of networks, one interpersonally interactional, the other technologically integrational, has significant consequences on our attitudes toward public and private spaces and toward community. The distinction between the *Internet* and *cyberspace* becomes increasingly significant when considering regulations that are resulting in jurisdictional and technologically based confusion. This is reflected in local, national, and international regulatory efforts around the world.

2. The ambiguous identity of the Internet, cyberspace, and its inhabitants has been exacerbated by the convergent nature of this new technology leaving unanswered questions of governance and jurisdiction. When the original chapter was written, regulatory issues were explored in the midst of the confusion of diffusion, or the uncertainty that generally accompanies invention. According to Lawrence Lessig (1999) of the Harvard Law School, the earliest phase of exploring regulatory approaches to the Internet was characterized by the claim that governments could not regulate cyberspace, that cyberspace was essentially and unavoidably, free. Governments could threaten, but behavior could not be controlled. Laws could be passed, but they would be meaningless. The society of this space would be a "fully self-ordering entity" (p.4)

Lessig argues, after 5 years of attempts, some successful, some not, the conceptualization of a lawless frontier has given way to the next phase, a second generation, which sees the future of control of the Internet coming from an alliance of commerce and government that will make the Internet a highly regulable space where behavior is much more tightly controlled than in physical space. He argues the two social forces of commerce and code will come to be the framework of regulations.

Regulation of software and hardware rather than content will make the Internet capable of being regulated. In this regard, the Internet/cyberspace distinction becomes essential in that the code of the architecture of the transport medium of the Internet is regulated, whereas communication and interaction in cyberspace is not directly regulated.

3. The convergent or multifunctionality of communication technologies in general and cyberspace in particular were not as developed when first we considered these new social environments. The convergent nature of a broadband environment in which we glide from medium to medium, in which we move with transparent ease from one function to another, signals not only the impact of technology upon technology but also of technology upon the social nature of community.

This sense of transparency, this permeability of function and medium, is linked to an illusion of transparency that characterizes the broadband and physical environments. Transparency suggests ease, an effortless movement in and between those environments thereby erasing the intrinsic differences between each. And eventually we begin to confuse the distinctiveness, the uniqueness of each domain, the characteristics that define each medium. The convergence of virtual and physical space is occurring with regard to our social networks, community affiliation, and expectation of publicness. The qualitative and experiential differences between virtual and physical have begun to blur, as the borders of each become less apparent and more transparent.

The wiring of existing communities and the design of new communities like Celebration in Florida and Cyberjaya in Malaysia represent new assumptions being made with regard to the relationship of media technology and the social and commercial uses of the built environment. At the beginning of the 21st century the need for safety, security, and control seem to overshadow and outstrip any need for unplanned social stimulation.

4. The search for safety and security has escalated with the denizens of cyberspace seeking to determine when they connect and interact in safety. Yet, much like interaction in physical space, exposure to information or contacts in cyberspace can be filled with risk, spontaneity, serendipity, and undesired connections. Privacy has become one of the most discussed aspects of this new technological environment. But privacy has two facets to it in its linkage to broadband technology. We cherish our privacy. In its name we seek to diminish the uncertainty of the street shifting spontaneous activities into controllable sectors. We seek privacy and avoid public accountability. In the name of privacy and safety, we tolerate surveillance and surrender

the value of privacy held up as so important. At the same time, we are alarmed at invasion of privacy that permeates the cyberworld. U.S. courts are now hearing cases in which they are asked to apply the laws of "stalking" and "The Americans With Disabilities Act" to cyberspace (Kaplan, 1999, 2000). So here we have another sign, another omen, that the functions of cyberspace and physical place (not falling into that trap that cyberspace is not real), that cyberspace either displaces or replaces the activities of physical space. In the name of safety we have actually created another, more pervasive, perhaps more powerful a defining force with regard to our perceptions of public and private spaces—the wired city as a surveillance environment.

Surveillance cameras placed in public places by security forces and police departments and cameras linked for transmission via the Internet represent variations on the increasing complexity of technological connection and public life and illustrate the difficulties in fixing boundaries of publicness and privateness. The technology of communication, while extending our ability to transcend locality also accepts and demands control of the environment. We seek safe serendipity that is increasingly sought online even as that serendipity is designed out of the urban and suburban environment.

After the events of September 11, 2001, the acceptance of sweeping changes in personal privacy protections evidences the metamorphosis of safety issues into security concerns and the public fervor for control and security. On October 26, 2001, President George W. Bush signed the USA Patriot Act, an anti-terrorism law expanding the government's ability to conduct electronic surveillance. The law eases restrictions on intelligence wiretaps, allows for authorization of roving wiretaps, and provides for expanded surveillance of computers and telephones.

Although many of these provisions are set to expire after four years, this authorization of increased surveillance far surpassing previously permitted incursions on personal privacy was passed in near record time, with only one public hearing and little debate.

The Internet has been called the "electronic commons" capable of providing a global meeting place. We believe that the current path shifts the emphasis from communities of place to virtual communities where . entertainment and commerce are divorced from obligation and technological and commercial convergence leads to regulatory convergence divorced from locality.

## REFERENCES

Blankenship, J. (1980). The search for the 1972 Democratic nomination: A metaphorical perspective. In B. Brock & R. Scott (Eds.), *Methods of rhetorical criticism: A twentieth century perspective* (2nd ed., pp. 321-345). Detroit, MI: Wayne State University Press.

Burke, K. (1950). *A rhetoric of motives.* New York: George Brazeller

*Cubby v. CompuServe Incorporated,* 776 F. Supp. 135 (S.D.N.Y, 1991).

Cyberspace. (1994, March). *Compuserve Magazine,* p. 12.

Dibbell, J. (1993, March). Let's get digital: The writer à la modem. *The Voice Literary Supplement,* pp. 13-14.

Feder, B.J. (1991, November 3). Toward defining free speech in the computer age. *The New York Times,* p. D5.

Fisher, T. (1988, March). Editorial. *Progressive Architecture,* p. 7.

Gerwig, K. (1994, November 28). Dealing with the price of rural access to the Internet. *Interactive Age,* pp. 22-23.

Gumpert, G., & Drucker, S.J. (1992). From the agora to the electronic shopping mall. *Critical Studies in Mass Communication, 9*(2), 186-200.

Internet Society. (1994, August 4). *Latest Internet measurements reveal dramatic growth in 1994* [press release].

Jackson, D.S. (1994, July 25). Battle for the soul of Internet. *Time,* pp. 50, 56.

Kamisar, Y., LaFave, W.R., & Israel, J.H. (1986). *Modern criminal procedure* (6th ed.). St. Paul, MN: West.

Kaplan, C.S. (2000, February 18). Lawsuit says web cookies allow illegal stalking, *CyberTimes,* http://www.nytimes.com/library/tech/00/02/cyber/cyberlaw/18law.html.

Kaplan, C.S. (1999, November 12). Is cyberspace a "public accommodation?" *CyberTimes,* http://www.nytimes.com/library/tech/99/11/cyber/cyberlaw/12law.html.

*Katz v. United States,* 389 U.S. 347 (1967).

Kelly, J.P. (1994, February). Whose e-mail is it anyway? In E. Kirsh, L. Rose, & S. Steele (Eds.), *Business and legal aspects of the internet and online services* (pp. 831-834). New York: Law Journal Seminars Press.

Landis, D. (1994, August 9). Regulating porn: Does it compute? *USA Today,* p. D1.

Lessig, L. (1999). *Code and other laws of cyberspace.* New York: Basic Books.

Leroux, C. (1991, October 27). Hate speech enters computer age. *Chicago Tribune,* p. C4.

Lewis, P. (1994a, March, 8). Strangers, not their computers, build a network in a time of grief. *The New York Times,* pp. A1, D2.

Lewis, P. (1994b, June 19). Getting down to business on the Net. *The New York Times,* p. C1.

Markoff, J. (1993a, September 5). The Internet. *The New York Times,* p. 11.

Markoff, J. (1993b, January 24). A key project of Clinton and Gore raises a debate: Public or private? *The New York Times,* pp. 1,6.

McNichol, T. (1994, January 21). Fellow travelers on the info highway. *U.S.A. Weekend,* p. 4.

Miller, M.W. (1991, October 22). Prodigy network defends display of anti-Semitic notes. *Wall Street Journal*, p. B1.

Naughton, E.J. (1993). Is cyberspace a public forum? Computer bulletin boards, free speech, and state action. *The Georgetown Law Journal, 81*, 409-441.

*O'Connor v. Ortega*, 480 U.S. 709 (1987).

*The Random House Dictionary of the English Language*. (1966). New York: Random House.

Sennett, R. (1990). *The conscience of the eye*. New York: Knopf.

Verity, J.W., & Hof, R.D. (1994, November 14). The Internet: How it will change the way you do business. *Business Week*, pp. 38-46.

Winner, L. (1993, August 4). How technology weaves the fabric of society. *The Chronicle of Higher Education*, pp. B1-B3.

18 U.S.C. Sections 2510-2520 (1988).

# CyberWalden:
# The Online Psychology
# of Politics
# and Culture

## John M. Phelan

*That cyberspace, virtua!' reality, the Internet, and the like are hot topics at present is quite clear. Newspapers and magazines now devote special columns and sections to these aspects of computer media and telecommunications; new books promising quick and easy access to the electronic environment abound, commercial services such as America Online and CompuServe are flooded with new members. The hype surrounding cyberspace seems to draw on the self-help genre by promising better living through computing. In this wide-ranging essay, John M. Phelan deflates the utopian fantasies of cyberspace enthusiasts, arguing that the rhetoric of cyberculture misleads us about our own real-world efficacy. As a long-time cybernaut, he sees the Internet as an efficient research tool, but not a substitute for public life and political participation. Placing cyberspace in the larger contexts of cybernetics and broadcasting, he discusses its relationship to secondary orality and the retrieval of religious worldviews. Outside of this section of the book, additional research on the Internet appears in Mark Giese's historical overview in Chapter 8, Ron Jacobson's discussion of contemporary policy issues in Chapter 9, and Eric Zimmer and Christopher Hunter's study of sexual content on the Web in Chapter 11; related critiques of Net culture and politics can be found in Frank Dance's examination of the digital divide in Chapter 10, Camille Paglia's essay on electronic publishing in Chapter 16, and Paul Lippert's examination of the social implications of cyberspace metaphors in Chapter 18, and Douglas Rushkoff's critique of cybercommercialism in Chapter 21. Paul Levinson's arguments concerning online education in Chapter 13 offer an alternate point of view.*

## THE INNER FACE OF INTERFACE

Cyberspace is a new field for old dreams. It is the latest meeting place for both doing things together and trying to figure out, as we never cease to do, where we really are. Where the word comes from will help us to understand where we might be going with it.

Norbert Wiener, the child prodigy and mathematical wizard who formulated the basis for the engineering of "feedback" into so many of the devices we associate with computer-assisted living, from cruise control to the "smart house," gave his pathfinding book, *The Human Use of Human Beings*, the prescient subtitle of *Cybernetics and Society* (1954). Wiener, who had wanted to become a medical doctor, found he was unable to properly slice sections for up-to-standard microscopic slides (an essential task for all medical students in those days). He could not do so, not because he had unsteady hands, but because his vision was very poor. His eureka was to realize that his hand and eye formed a loop of control and adjustment; a feedback loop, he called it, realizing it was an essential component of all activity, because all activity is interactivity (Wiener, 1954). Feedback then began to be consciously engineered into all sorts of devices and was used metaphorically in the social sciences and group psychology. But it is important to note that the essential note of feedback is one of control effect, hence, the term *cybernetics*. The Greek root, guber-, also forms the gov- in government. *Cyber* indicates control effect through interactivity.

This is the essential note of cyberspace: people controlling devices through computers that give them the feeling of feedback as if the devices were parts of their own bodies. The defining characteristic of the later notion of virtual reality is not its visual verisimilitude, but its feedback and its acceptance of our manipulations. We can see a brilliantly realistic HDTV rendering of rainbow populated coral reefs, but we can have the illusion of swimming and catching fish inside the rather crude representations of much lower bit renderings of Virtual Surfing. We just don't witness it, we live in it. That's what makes it more "real" than the admitted greater vividness of HDTV.

Projection of our own body parts into inanimate tools and devices is an essential human experience of feedback because our senses always strive to be transparent. Anyone who drives knows that a sedan "feels" different from a hot sports car because it "responds" more sensitively to our control. The gears translate gas pedal pressure more immediately and delicately to engine rpm's. Transparent tight feedback is a sign of control. The machine is part of us. So, too, in sports: the better the athlete, the less mental distance between her and racquet or golf club. The best athletes transparently project their intentions to the flying tennis or golf ball after they have lost any "real" contact with it. It is like breathing or walking for them. Likewise, great performers so project personality out from the stage that they devour the audience.

Once computers, through video screens, began to give real-time feedback to operators, this sense of feel, of self-projection, inevitably followed. That's one of the main reasons we demand so much more speed from our chips than we need (for most of the programs actually used): the immediacy of the response makes it more transparent, more like a bit of ourselves, and thus greatly enhances our own interior neural net's natural tendency to integrate with the machine. Anne McCaffrey (1969), over 25 years ago, wrote of immense space ships that had handicapped and otherwise helpless human beings hardwired into their central computer control so that the ships could be seen as either enormously bionic humans or wetware-operated hardware.

This neural integration is getting tighter and tighter in cyberspace. Although most of the Net was first accessed through a kind of super DOS hell of maddeningly slow menu selections, arcane command strings, and absurdly unmemorable e-mail addresses, three developments have changed it. First is the growth of friendly GUI (graphic user interfaces) started at Xerox Parc more than 25 years ago, used by Apple, and now coming to the PC world through Windows and its stream of constant upgrades. The exponential explosion of microchip speed and sophistication (Pentium™, Power PC™, and beyond) gives enough speed and power to enhance these GUIs from sort of primitive kindergarten sketches to the more sophisticated graphics of full-motion video. Finally, the building of the so-called Information Superhighway is providing sufficient bandwidth on most links to accommodate such heavy signal loads. Now that the interface philosophy of America Online, Mosaic, and Netscape is teamed up with full access to the Net denied on most commercial services and humanizes the nerdland of TCP/IP and other gateway software, the illusion of being plugged into some kind of world has become harder to resist.

These technologies then enable us to experience control ("cyber-") as a projection of self out of our center, from our wills, into something else. That something else, that field of activity, is space. It is real because it is independent of us, but paradoxically more real because it also responds to us. It has dimensions that are real only because they can be probed. There is no perfect tee-shot without a green to go to.

The sense of projected bodily power onto a field, so readily grasped in sports, is thus naturally best and most easily translated into a game on a screen. From there it is a short reach to make the screen the world or environment for all action. This feature was one of the first to be exploited after video games—the adventure or story world in which the reader became a participant. The game player becomes the role player—but an active one whose moves, as in a game, will certainly affect the outcome of the story. And so the real-time responding screen becomes a field where one's actions produce outcomes and further enhance the metaphor and illusion of control through or in a space—cyberspace. The wedding of two old activities—game playing and vicarious living through fiction—transforms each. Fiction not only becomes interactive, it becomes collaborative, a kind of team sport.

The word *cyberspace* in its roots thus well describes any space that is a field for human effects through environmental interaction. But it has in fact been restricted to a certain type of human effect field—that of computer-mediated electronic tele-effects, most of them in the form of symbol exchange. *Cyberspace* is not unlike *technology* in that respect. Technology properly refers to any human organization of tool use, from chipping flints in the cave to cadcaming microchips in Silicon Valley. But it is almost always presumed to mean high technology of recent vintage. Also like *technology*, *cyberspace* evokes a shared space of common goals, for the human world requires both witness and collaboration, surveillance and competition.

Some years ago, commenting on the seminal work of Innis, McLuhan, Havelock, Ong, and others, I suggested that television and radio, by communicating through what Ong called Secondary Orality, had created a world of Secondary Tribalism (Phelan, 1980). That is, observers and call-ins on broadcast material participated without really being present and had the illusion of social interaction while remaining alone and, in any true political sense, impotent. My point at the time was that what was being touted as a brave new world of possibilities was in many ways a reduction of social life and real political participation to a pale substitute. What was a public, I said in the 1970s, was becoming an audience (Phelan, 1977).

Subsequent studies have borne out this view (Abramson, Arterton, & Orren, 1988; Barnet & Cavanagh, 1994; Chomsky, 1991; Dahlgren & Sparks, 1991; Entman, 1989; Greider, 1992; Herman & Chomsky, 1988; Krugman, 1994). From 1972 to 2000 there has been a steeply rising curve of money and time spent on political campaign media, especially television, and it has directly matched a descending curve of actual political participation (Phelan, 1995). Granted the hopeful presence of PeaceNet, EcoNet, the Electronic Frontier Foundation, and the alleged role of the Internet in getting news out of Iraq, Iran, China, Russia, and Mexico during recent crises, there is overwhelmingly greater evidence of big players and governments gaining Net control the old-fashioned way: by buying it and licensing it. Governments have more direct methods of control: the Clinton Administration has proposed the Clipper chip—a preinstalled opening for the U.S. Feds to tap all communications, however encrypted. The Saudis, more traditionally, have already outlawed all private satellite downlinks and are putting their oceans of cash into a totally government-controlled wired Islam.

This dramatic conflict of empowerment hope in the face of disenfranchising reality is being played again, it seems, by telecomputed MUDs (Multi-User Dungeons[= fantasies]/Dimensions) and MUSES (Multi-User Simulated Environments). Imaginatively, the Markle Foundation has funded Maxis to develop *SimHealth* as a device to educate the masses about the complexities of national healthcare policy; let's hope it helps. But we already have the dispiriting paradox of our real inner cities and suburbs sinking into a Grimpen Mire (the grim foggy bog haunted by the Baskervilles' hound) of actual ungovernability, as more and more bright people score brilliantly on *SimCity*. If real politics has degenerated into image management, who needs to bother with the real thing?

So we see the paradox of cyberspace, which enhances the illusion of images as reality because we can move and change the images and thus are deluded into thinking we are effective in the real world (Phelan 1984, 1988).

Having noted that for the overwhelming majority of Net users and Web surfers the experience of being wired to the world is more passive than it seems and that the social interaction is more pallid than touted, we cannot ignore that for activists and entrepreneurs, politicians and salesmen, investment bankers and day-traders and many other risk-takers, world shakers, and the occasional shakedown artist, the Net is being explosively exploited as the tool of savvy choice for mobilizing money from investors, votes for candidates, protests from activists, sales to customers, and just about anything else desirable from or for any precise target available. This very effective and diverse minority of users is surely changing both the world of business and of consumerism (buying a car is more of an informed choice over the Web and selling one is becoming more effective through Net outreach). Mainstream party politics and its growing plurality of grassroots critics are simultaneously being empowered by use of the Net.

As an activist in the middle 1990s, I observed the enormous reach and power of the Net to mobilize support for the renewal of the Nuclear Test Ban Treaty and its draw of live bodies from all over the world to the UN where it was debated. The surprising and surprisingly well-informed protests in Seattle at the 1999 meeting of the World Trade Organization and the later summit of the super-rich in Davos, Switzerland, could not have occurred as they did without prior wire mobilization. As a teacher, I am now very happily dependent on e-mail and digitized texts from all the libraries of the world to send timely (and inescapably available) instructions and information to my students and to receive their requests at any time of the day for aid in understanding specific material shared at a distance. It is hard for the dog to eat the term paper when it is electronically distributed to multiple hard disks. And electronic editing has taken much of the drudgery out of correcting and re-doing texts for professor and student.

As this is written, there is a growing battle between the enthusiasts for decentralized open-ended access to and use of the Net and the large corporate players who seek greater control over its every aspect, from content to infrastructure, in order to maximize profits and monopolize markets. The early 2000 merger of Sprint and WorldComm, for instance, would put 50% of the World Wide Web backbone into a single corporate hand, threatening the established practice of "peering"—the toll-free sharing of switching and transmission facilities among infrastructure "peers." More and more Web pages are cluttered with dancing, singing, and wildly waving advertisements.

It is far too early to even guess whether the democratic promise of the Net will be betrayed as was that of radio and television (McChesney, 1999).

## CYBERCELLS

In his trademark bizarre irony, Franz Kafka (1987) once wrote a letter to his betrothed imploring her to give up such obsessive correspondence with him, referring to a previous request in his last letter sent two hours earlier. I note that the ever-resourceful cyberworld has an online self-help usergroup for those who feel they are addicted to being online.

So a few fall a bit too deeply into the WELL, as one pioneering gathering place of disembodied scripts substituting for living presences was called. It affords not only a shared place of imagined story, as in MUDs, but an ongoing real-time conversation with a large number of globally scattered participants (IRC—Interactive Relay Chat).

What accounts for the stunning popularity of going online?

There is the magic of mysterious connection with the enchanted distant—something felt by youngsters in the 1920s (like young Richard Feynman in Brooklyn), who manipulated the old crystal sets under the blankets when they were supposed to be asleep, pulling in signals from ships at sea and from dance bands in Cleveland. There is the desperate need for contact among the marooned, like ham radio operators in snowbound Alaska or isolated islanders in the Pacific. Some of those obsessively hooked by Electropolis, as it has been called, are undoubtedly of this stripe. But there are not enough socially uneasy adolescents or cutoff adults to account for the wild popularity of surfing the Web.

Not ignoring that over one-fourth of all American households have but a single occupant (not a misprint!), and taking due account that more and more people flit from one workplace to another because there are far fewer long-term employments, I think a catalytic ingredient in the online explosion is the growing number of adults who, either in an office or increasingly at home, work in front of a monitor screen all day. Like it or not, it is their workplace: a relentlessly no-nonsense workplace with no water cooler, no stair landings, no snack room, no commuting buddies in car pools, trains, or even elevators.

Just as those glued to their television sets for six or seven hours a night reasonably prefer sets with PIP (picture in picture), which lets one see the action of more than one channel at once to enhance surfing (at the loss of coherence, if you value *that*), so, too, do workers chained to computer monitors for eight or more hours a day naturally prefer to have a large screen with 16 million possible shades and hues of color, with a number of programs opened at once. This affords the equivalent of a room with a view, a corner office, lots of windows to look through with all sorts of action going on. If one can wave to friends out the window, even talk to them and get answers back, so much the better. That the window can see as far as Japan or Tahiti is a thrilling bonus. Distance apart, cyberspace is a humanizing device for creating a kind of ersatz office/pub/common room/public square area for those deprived, rather cruelly, of one or more versions of the real thing. There are friendly conversations in bars, and then there are those who observe scripted conversations at Cheers. If you can't get to the former, you can at least, as it were, enter the set and talk back: CyberCheers.

A poignant note sounded by those engrossed in threading through cybertalk is how they are forced to use words to substitute for all the other physical cues of face-to-face conversations and IRL (in real life) settings—no mood music, no roaring sports fans, no candlelight, nor disco strobes. They thus have resorted to typographic signals such as :-) (a smiley, look at it sideways). This is seen as an achievement, and in a way of course it is. But it is stated in a context of reinventing the wheel. Shakespeare, who didn't have special effects to create battle scenes or regal pageantry or mysterious moors to put on high-tech stages, instead put words in auditing ears, the listeners, the *audi*ence.

All creative writers are liberated as well as confined by words. Joyce managed to create an entire inner world as well as to evoke everyday Dublin only with words. Using words to create worlds is what literature does: It requires great skill, it has standards, it is richly varied, it is available without a connect fee, it can be taught; with great effort and talent you can learn to do it, or at least appreciate it. Like reading a musical score, reading literature requires not only education, but some sensitivity training, a developed sense of nuance. These powers must be brought to the keyboard. However long one's days and nights in the blue glare of the screen, one cannot reach in and pull them out.

None of these rejections of thoughtless infomania and Net nuttiness is meant or felt to come from any Olympian height. Because the schools have imitated the old media in embracing marketing—reaching the most at the lowest cost for the highest possible price—one can see that young people, desperate for stimulation, gladly flee from the therapy-over-learning classroom to happily cruise on the Net, in the not unreasonable hope they might meet somebody more interesting.

I am on the Net, and I have been using various parts of it for the last fourteen years. It is a remarkably efficient tool for tracking down bibliographic references and vetted research citations. When I can get an on-the-spot report of a riot in *The* [Johannesberg] *Star* over the Net, it sure does beat driving two hours to the Sterling Memorial Library at Yale to get a day-old copy of the paper at best. But, like Samuel Florman (1994), who fears that "flights through cyberspace, however energizing they may be for the imagination, may weaken the objective rationality needed to do good engineering," I agree with Alan Cromer that the formal linear thinking needed to do science "goes against the grain of traditional human thinking, which is associative and subjective" (p. 65).

Not just science, but literary and other studies, assuredly associative and serendipitous, are also largely linear. Literature is linear. We are led down a path by a master, a wizard, a sorcerer. He leads us to a wider world than we might ever know otherwise, and we are permanently changed. One used to hear that Vietnam was still awaiting its novelist; meaning that the tangled confused hypertext of millions of disparate defeats and small victories, lies, and photo-ops and press conferences make no emotional sense until some Tolstoy can lead us through the emotional and factual jungle to a deeper truth.

In this broader cultural context, cyberspace can in some ways be a step backwards. True, it enables us to do some things better than we can do in libraries; it can substitute for a laboratory if we don't have one; it can get us to resources we might not otherwise find. But it is no substitute for guided linear thinking, friendship, travel, or learning the craft of writing or the equally daunting task of critical reading of demanding texts. Although cyberspace can be a place to go and get things to use, a place to ask questions and give answers, it is not a world of primary experience (Searle, 1998).

From this perspective, the tendency of some observers to reify an immense collection of unevenly useful databases and switched telecommunications links into a world where one "navigates" suggests a return to an earlier worldview long associated with primary orality and its well-attested affinity for religion.

## BACK TO THE FUTURE

Over the centuries there has been a basic human desire for some kind of invisible mental or spiritual atmosphere that connects in some mystic way all the minds and hearts of mankind. Although often allied with religion (Christianity's "Mystical Body"), this yearning goes back at least as far as the pre-Socratics and their preoccupation with the One and the Many. For the medieval schoolmen mining the classic philosophers (not the Bible), there was the Agent Intellect, that part of the mind that enabled it to apprehend essences. A power within each individual mind, it nevertheless existed by sharing in one Great Agent Intellect, that was a kind of animating soul of the world. Hegel, much later, spoke of the *Geist*, not only of the *Zeit* but of the *Welt* (Kaufmann, 1966; Olson, 1992). In post-war France and later the rest of Europe and America, Teilhard de Chardin brought these ideas back for a while by resurrecting the Greek notion of *nous* (the conceiving and communicating mind—opposed to *pneuma*, the animating spirit) and speaking of the global *noosphere* (Teilhard, 1959). In more recent years we have the newly fashionable "Gaia hypothesis" that the planet Earth has a kind of intrinsic ecosystem soul that keeps it in balance.

More than a decade after Teilhard's phrase "everything that rises must converge" had been on English-speaking lips, the debut of Telstar, the first of a shining silver constellation of communications satellites, established a quotidian engineering footing of sorts for the grand mystic vision. Further developments in the real world of affairs increasingly bolstered this originally airy notion of "convergence." The space program and the stunning pictures of Earth, at first grainy black-and-white shadows of the great shapes familiar from maps, gave further impetus to the idea of convergence, of one world.

In less exalted terms, international trade and marketing abetted a growing trend toward a common popular culture of advertising, film, blockbuster books, and top tunes. The World's Fairs in Brussels, New York, Osaka, and Seattle, marching with the development of mass jet travel the world over, accelerated the internationalization of leisure pursuits and fashion through the 1960s and 1970s. Finally, the explosion to satellite communications in the 1980s matched in the most recent years with fiber-optic switching systems and computer processing of cash, words, images, and data—the internetting of global consciousness—has swept up most human endeavors from local names and habitations into the global context of international trademarks, common credit cards, shared diets, world-class athletics, and intercontinental rock concert tours.

Nowhere is this more true than in the spectacularly converging field of communications technologies, communications corporations, software standards, and their correlative hardware open architectures. In technology, we have phones that show pictures, computers that listen, keyboards that paint. We have books on tape and on disc, movies zipping along not only close to the speed of light, but encoded in the form of light. Not only do Japanese manufacturers of TV sets and VCR's own rock stars and movie vaults, but Apple and IBM have collaborated with Motorola in creating a new generation of microchip. Microsoft, still firmly on the desktop, is moving into the cable boxes atop televisions. Mainframes, long identified with monolithic, isolated, and hierarchical megacorporations, have given way to PCs, which in turn have formed local area networks, patched into wide area networks, using netware newly rendered interchangeable. The new arrangements have forced smart work on both management and labor. Editors have access to little more information that lights up the screens of the rest of the newsroom. The shopfloors of Toyota and Chrysler alike bristle with interfaces demanding decisions, once reserved for supervisors, from line workers.

In fact, the ubiquity of by now well-established world pop culture, world finance, world trade, and world tourism into one headless network has made the very idea of convergence so commonplace that we cannot see clearly the microstitching in the seemingly seamless garment. Like a Mandlebrot set, the picture of the whole diverges from the tiny iterations of detail, but yet depends on them. If we miss the trees, we will be lost in the forest.

So a paradoxical merging of quite old and hoary concepts with modern industrial developments have informed the current enthusiasms and misconceptions about cyberspace (defined by Gibson as "consensual hallucination"). These influences are nowhere more evident than in the tendency of many otherwise hardheaded writers to describe cyberspace as "nonphysical." Everyone is aware that without computers, silicon, copper, plastic, fossil fuel for energy production, and many other humbly tangible physical things, the Net could not be constituted nor even exist. But many forget that those magnetic or photonic ons and offs are physical, just as the electromagnetic waveforms of analog broadcasting are physical, although it must be granted their physicality is tenuous relative to the colossal freight of meaning they incrementally embody.

So deeming the content of cyberspace "nonphysical" presumably is thought to indicate that messages, designs, or commands—in short, language itself and the entire symbol world—are meaningless without the interpretations of minds "plugged in" to the Net. But in this sense, of course, all human action is "nonphysical," from sex and singing to tea parties and rock concerts. Flesh, soundwaves, tea sets, and megaboom boxes are all just substrates that permit cultural and symbolic nets to have somewhere to land. But somehow many take typing on a screen as less material than whispering in a lover's ear. There is an irony here in that many take the headless mass of interconnected computer neurons as some sort of world soul and personify "it," just when many scientists (Crick, 1994) and philosophers (Dennett, 1992) forthrightly pronounce that there is no mind, no soul, only neurons within each individual. Neurons may be organized in the brain, but there is no organization ordering the brain.

Are the positivist scientists out of sync with the latest intellectual fashion? Do all those formerly hard heads; once wired, go soft? Have the souls of Christianity and the tutelary spirits of wind, water, and sacred grove once invoked by pagan Greece and Rome come back as software and information, which never diminish however often they are used?

Stay tuned.

## REFERENCES

Abramson, J.B., Arterton, F.C., & Orren, G.R. (1988). *The electronic commonwealth: The impact of new media technologies on democratic politics.* New York: Basic Books.

Barnet, R.J., & Cavanagh, J. (1994). *Global dreams: Imperial corporations and the new world order.* New York: Simon & Shuster.

Chomsky, N. (1991). *Deterring democracy.* London: Verso.

Crick, F. (1994). *The astonishing hypothesis: The scientific search for the soul.* New York: Macmillan.

Dahlgren, P., & Sparks, C. (1991). *Communication and citizenship: Journalism and the public sphere.* London: Routledge.

Dennett, D. (1992). *Consciousness explained.* Boston: Little, Brown.

Entman, R.M. (1989). *Democracy without citizens: Media and the decay of American politics.* New York: Oxford University Press.

Florman, S.C. (1994). The humane engineer. *Technology Review, 97,* 65.

Greider, W. (1992). *Who will tell the people? The betrayal of American democracy.* New York: Simon & Shuster.

Herman, E.S., & Chomsky, N. (1988). *Manufacturing consent: The political economy of the mass media.* New York: Pantheon.

Kafka, F. (1987). *Letters to Felice Bauer* (E. Heller & J. Born, Eds.). New York: Schocken.

Kaufmann, W. (1966). *Hegel: Reinterpretation, texts and commentary.* London: Weidenfeld & Nicolson.

Krugman, P. (1994). *Peddling prosperity: Economic sense and nonsense in an age of diminished expectations.* New York: Norton.

McCaffrey, A. (1969). *The ship that sang.* New York: Walker.

McChesney, R. W. (1999). *Rich media, poor democracy: Communication politics in dubious times.* Chicago: University of Illinois Press.

Olson, A.M. (1992). *Hegel and the spirit: Philosophy as pneumatology.* Princeton, NJ: Princeton University Press.

Phelan, J.M. (1977). *Mediaworld: Programming the public.* New York: Continuum Books.

Phelan, J.M. (1980). *Disenchantment: Meaning and morality in the media.* New York: Hastings House.

Phelan, J.M. (1984). Surfaces in the mediaworld of political fashion. *Media Development, 31,* 12-13.

Phelan, J.M. (1988). Communing in isolation. *Critical Studies in Mass Communication, 5,* 347-351.

Phelan, J.M. (1995). "Media". In P.A.B. Clarke & A. Linzey (Eds.), *Dictionary of ethics, theology and society* (pp. 150-155). London: Routledge.

Searle, U.R. (1998). *Mind, language, and society: Philosophy in the real world.* New York: Basic Books.

Teilhard de Chardin, P. (1959). *The phenomenon of man.* New York: Harper & Brothers.

Wiener, N. (1954). *The human use of human beings: Cybernetics and society.* Boston: Houghton Mifflin.

# 3

# Who Shall Control
# Cyberspace?

## James R. Beniger

*The "cyber" in cyberspace would seem to imply a controlled space, and yet the contemporary Internet-dominated electronic landscape is commonly characterized as decentralized, bottom-up, and anarchistic. Pioneers and homesteaders on the electronic frontier take pride in the egalitarian nature of cyberculture and seek to preserve the delicate balance of this technological ecosystem. It is not a closed system, however, as James R. Beniger makes clear in this essay. Situating cyberculture firmly within our larger social system, and using the impact of the computer on the U.S. Postal Service as an analogy, he argues that the cyberspace environment is an attractive and relatively easy target for commercial and political exploitation. As cyberspace becomes an increasingly contested terrain, Beniger foresees continuing change and rationalization of the Internet and its successors. In other sections of this book, further discussion of the sociological, political, and economic context of cyberspace can be found in Mark Giese's history of the Internet in Chapter 8, and Ron Jacobson's discussion of contemporary policy issues in Chapter 9, and Douglas Rushkoff's examination of the commercialization of cyberspace in Chapter 21. Additional consideration of the topic of control appears in Lance Strate's exploration of cybertime in Chapter 22.*

Harvard Yard, like many American campuses, is crisscrossed by a web of concrete walks and asphalt paths. As new buildings open, both on campus and off, and popular courses move from one part of the university to another, the resulting shifts in Harvard's pedestrian traffic are recorded in new footpaths cutting across the various lawns of the Yard. Even after winter snows have covered the grass, the new paths endure as narrow trails of slush or ice. Each spring, as the melting snows give way to now muddy trails, where grass is unlikely to return without help, Harvard does not attempt to reseed—it simply paves over all the new paths chosen by sufficient pluralities of feet (so that we might imagine Harvard Yard approaching an entirely paved lot as time approaches infinity). In choosing to act in this way, Harvard has eschewed top-down control in favor of a bottom-up variety, forsaking the centralized control of the landscape architect in favor of decentralized control by emergent popular habits.

Cyberspace, born in the late 1970s on the world's first computer network, the U.S. Defense Department's ARPAnet, has grown much like the network of paved walks and paths in Harvard Yard. Despite initial attempts by the Defense Department to suppress what began as a virtual community of science fiction fans, the voices for bottom-up control eventually prevailed. The first citizens of cyberspace were allowed to make and enforce their own rules, bottom up, with relatively little centralized control. Two decades later, cyberspace continues to flourish in this way, not by design but by accretion—more like a coral reef than a product of RAND Corporation engineering. As Howard Rheingold (1993) describes the process:

> Biological imagery is often more appropriate [than are spatial imagery and a sense of place] to describe the way cyberculture changes. In terms of the way the whole system is propagating and evolving, think of cyberspace as a social petri dish, the Net as the agar medium, and virtual communities, in all their diversity, as the colonies of microorganisms that grow in petri dishes. Each of the small colonies of microorganisms—the communities on the Net—is a social experiment that nobody planned but that is happening nevertheless. (p. 6)

A similar view, although one closer to the level of human experience, is that of Michael Benedikt (1991), who characterizes cyberspace as "a common mental geography, built, in turn, by consensus and revolution, canon and experiment" (p. 2). As such, cyberspace continues to emerge, bottom up, its control also largely emergent from the social interactions of millions of independent individuals. This is much as the paved network of Harvard Yard emerges, from many individual and independent actions—in reaction to top-down, centrally controlled physical changes—as recorded by countless independent actors.

## CONCEPTUAL SPACE

Unlike Harvard Yard's web of paths, cyberspace is not only a physical space. Although it is easy to see the entire network of paths in the Yard, it would be impossible ever to see cyberspace. The point is made by James Gleick (1994), who describes the Net as in no sense a physical entity: "It isn't a thing; it isn't an entity; it isn't an organization. No one owns it; no one runs it. It is simply Everyone's Computers, Connected" (p. 57).

In other words, cyberspace consists not only of material things like people and their artifacts (computers, modems, telephone lines, etc.); it also has two major nonmaterial components: relationships among individuals, and the cybercultural contents of their heads—the sense of belonging to cyberspace, and of what that might mean. Taken together, these three components—material, relational, and cognitive—constitute not only cyberspace itself, but what is often called "culture" more generally. In at least the ethnographic sense, that is, all human cultures can be seen as consisting of a material culture (tangible artifacts), a symbolic or relational culture (widely shared information), and a cognitive culture (less widely shared meanings that more directly influence the behavior of a particular individual). To make such distinctions is not to deny, of course, that all three components or levels must ultimately be manifest in some material form. For information, however, the material component is usually irrelevant to cultural control; for cognitive culture, the material level is entirely transparent.

That cyberspace might be subsumed by precisely these three levels of culture is echoed by Rheingold (1993), who formally defines *cyberspace* as "the conceptual space where words, human relationships, data, wealth, and power are manifested by people using CMC [computer-mediated communications] technology" (p. 5). As such, cyberspace is not a society unto itself as much as a proper subset of the larger society, a socioconceptual space that is shared—in greater or lesser degree—by all members of that subset and space. This does make cyberspace a true and distinct human culture, however, in that—as a conceptual space—it tends to organize the social production and reproduction of sense, consciousness, and meaning among its members.

In the foreseeable future, at least, the culture of cyberspace will remain a subculture of various more traditional human cultures. As its continuing development approaches the unreachable physical boundary of all information in all places at all times, however, cyberspace will become a more embracing culture, less a semiconscious artifact opposed to nature and more like nature itself—an entirely unconscious, virtual world that might eventually begin to constitute its own reality. Therefore cyberspace would approach Benedikt's (1991) description of "a place, one place, limitless; entered equally from a basement in Vancouver, a boat in Port-au-Prince, a cab in New York, a garage in Texas City, an apartment in Rome, an office in Hong Kong, a bar in Kyoto, a cafe in Kinshasa, a laboratory on the Moon" (p. 1).

## CONTROL

Of all the known means for controlling human societies, none has proved more effective—in the long run—than the least centralized means of all: face-to-face communication in small, persisting, and intimate groups. Human societies first emerged, throughout the world, by just such means of distributed control. Such control still characterizes the societies least touched by or most resistant to change; it accounts for the common modern perception of small towns and tightly knit social groups as stultifying (whatever their other advantages).

If these earliest of social structures, still the vast majority of all those in recorded history, can be taken as prototypical, nothing has had a greater impact on human societies than the various technological innovations—beginning with the earliest infrastructures of transportation and communication—for increasingly centralized and mass social control. Viewed in modern terms of information processing and communication, the major result of such innovations has been a shift in control from individual programming (socialization) and interpersonal communication to more centralized processing and mass communication. Centralized information processing began with hierarchy, formal organization, and bureaucracy; centralized control developed with road systems and technologies for navigation (Beniger, 1986).

From these anthropological and historical perspectives, the emergence of cyberspace, in only the past 20 years, might be seen as the single greatest reversal in human history of the trend to centralized social control. Cyberspace's unrivaled impact stems more from the relative suddenness of its appearance, however, than from the nature of control on the Net. Throughout history, the trend to more centralized means of mass control has been continually countered by innovations—analogous in form to the infrastructure of cyberspace—to technologize and rationalize interpersonal communication and distributed control: the postal system, an infrastructure for personal world travel, the telegraph and telephone systems, two-way radio, and facsimile (fax) transmission, among many others. Cyberspace, at least to the extent that it depends on point-to-point communication among individuals, is only the latest in this succession of innovations that have countered the larger historical trend to mass communication and centralized control.

For those who would control vast populations, if only in relatively small ways, the growth of cyberspace does present an immediate setback, as well as the promise of even greater control in the near future. For those of you who might want to preserve the decentralized and interpersonal nature of cyberspace, consider: No such infrastructure or medium has ever resisted application to mass persuasion and control. Point-to-point telegraphic communication almost immediately produced the world's first mass newspapers. Radio is not only two-way, but used to reach audiences of millions around the world. Postal systems built to support the interpersonal exchange of letters have now been largely given over to mass mailings. Computers have begun to replace boiler room operations as the chief means of transforming the American telephone system into a mass medium, as have 800 and 900 numbers. New technologies now enable the mass production of personalized fax communication. Even face-to-face conversation can give way to shouting to crowds.

What might keep cyberspace, as we know it today, from a similar fate? Probably nothing. Struggles for centralized control of cyberspace, and between those who would centralize or decentralize its control, have already begun. The rest of this chapter attempts—based on the histories of the other innovations most similar to cyberspace—to outline some of what is likely to come.

## VULNERABILITIES

For those who seek to advertise, politic, persuade, or otherwise control large populations, cyberspace presents two attractive features: First, because cyberspace has the feel (and currently the tradition) of interpersonal communication, it would well serve to conceal the inherently impersonal (and thus less persuasive) aspects of mass communication. Second, because almost all of its communication is inherently accessible, retrievable, and machine readable by virtually anyone, cyberspace would itself foster unprecedented mass processing to support centralized control.

Underlying these two vulnerabilities to centralized control is the essential tradeoff between the range and effectiveness of control of human behavior through persuasion, whether rational or irrational, conscious or unconscious. Our behavior is most affected by those we care most about or see most often: loved ones, friends, coworkers, neighbors—the same people whose behavior most affects us. Seeing and caring about are inherently limited activities; however, we simply cannot personally care about, or regularly visit with, the vast multitudes. To affect the behavior of thousands or even millions of people, we might, for example, publish a letter in a newspaper, but its effects—because the communication is obviously not personal—will usually be slight. Hence the tradeoff: We might have great range or great effectiveness of communication, but very rarely both, at least not with the same message.

Another reason why mass communication is limited in its effects, apart from this tradeoff, is that mass communication is usually one-way. Even the most powerful weapon will be useless in attempting to control someone to whom we cannot communicate, or whose behavior we cannot monitor; two-way communication will prove no less essential for control than the weapon itself. The only reason why mass communication can control human behavior at all is that the sheer numbers of targets can compensate for even the slightest probabilities of success: We know some small percentage will be affected by our message, but not which individuals will be, nor why. Two-way communication is much better than one-way, at least for controlling human behavior, because the effect of any one message can be monitored and responded to in a subsequent message.

A third reason why mass communication is limited in its effects is that it is neither interactive nor purposively iterative. The potential for any means of communication to control increases with the number of iterations of messages sent and responses monitored; however, a reasonable substitute for the monitoring of individual behavior is prior knowledge relevant to predicting that behavior. One reason why our loved ones and friends can so readily affect our behavior, for example, is that they know us so well. Among those who would control large populations, a large databank of prior knowledge, plus the capability to compare current behavior to the desired one and to respond accordingly, through many iterations, are both highly prized.

It ought to be clear by now why someone might want to hijack cyberspace for purposes of mass persuasion and control. Cyberspace presents the possibility, unprecedented in past technologies, to transcend the tradeoff between range and effectiveness in control of human behavior. Because the new technology is inherently interactive, and the tradition of its use still largely interpersonal, the very context of cyberspace would help to conceal the impersonal nature of mass communication, much as, for example, the interactive nature of Joseph Weizenbaum's (1976) ELIZA psychotherapy program helped to obscure its own impersonal nature. Mass communication to cyberspace could also be two-way, not only because each individual might respond to a given message, but also because the Net behavior of all individuals—following any given message or iteration—could be monitored and responded to, individually, toward a particular goal.

In short, mass communication to cyberspace might be based on large databases of the prior Net activity of each individual, driven by massive processing power, and even guided by artificial intelligence systems for persuasive behavior, now well understood by social psychologists. For all these reasons, as well as those mentioned earlier, the possibilities for effective control of a large population via cyberspace appear unmatched by those of any other existing means (at least of comparably large-scale and minimal coercion). Even without its considerable vulnerabilities to mass control, however, the cyberspace population, because of its demographics of age, education, and income (among others), would still rank among the most attractive to advertisers, marketers, and politicians alike, mostly because of the considerable influence this population has over others not yet part of cyberspace.

Discouraging as this assessment might seem, for those who would wish to preserve cyberspace as we find it today, the more important point is not that mass control via cyberspace will succeed, but that it will be tried. The attempts alone, successful or not, will greatly alter—probably irretrievably—the nature of life in cyberspace.

## THE POSTAL MODEL

Lest this seem like so much science fictional extrapolation, if not outright paranoia, a real-life case study appears to be in order. None seems more applicable to cyberspace than that of the U.S. Postal Service, an ancient and for centuries highly interpersonal messaging network that—over roughly the period of cyberspace's existence—has been largely transformed into a computer-processable mass medium for advertisers, politicians, and other mass mailers.

The U.S. Postal Service remained a 19th-century bureaucracy, one that relied on antiquated mail-processing methods such as "pigeonhole" sorting, as late as 1957, when it installed its first automatic letter sorter—a five-position Dutch machine that could sort mail to only 300 different destinations. Today, 40 years later, after adopting optical character readers (1965), bar-code sorters (1982), and the 9-digit ZIP code (1983), the Postal System has become a computerized, highly targetable channel into every American household. In parallel to these developments, a major database marketing industry, which includes geodemographic targeting of mass mailings using census block statistics, ZIP codes, and postal carrier routes, has sprung up around the Postal System.

The Claritas company of Alexandria, VA, for example, links national address and telephone lists to neighborhood units with an average size of only 340 households. By means of the growing wealth of information collected on these units (Claritas routinely links to more than two dozen different databases), mass mailing and telephoning can be highly personalized, not only by name but by housing value, social status and mobility, purchase and credit behavior, and media preferences, among many other variables.

A fleeting hint of what might await cyberspace arrived in the mailbox at my house as early as 1986. I had then just moved from the East Coast to the West and did not yet know any of my new neighbors. The outside of the envelope, obviously a mass mailing promoting some contest, read "One in six will win," along with the computer-printed names of my family and the five other families who then lived on either side of us and across the street. So welcome did I feel, suddenly learning the names of my new neighbors, that I actually forgot—for just an instant—that this highly personalized communal intelligence had come not from a new acquaintance on my block, but from a machine several thousand miles away. It is by elaborating on just such impulses that mass communication masks itself as interpersonal.

Despite the sophistication of such highly computerized marketing applications, however, they exploit a messaging system that—like cyberspace—did not develop with them in mind. ZIP codes, for example, owe their origin to the postal zoning system (for which ZIP represented a "Zoning Improvement Plan") begun in 124 major city post offices in 1943 to save labor in letter sorting under wartime shortages. Only through modern computing power, unanticipated even when five-digit ZIP codes were adopted in 1963, could the database marketing industry have begun to transform the Postal System into the processable and targetable mass medium that it is today. With the data banks and processing power of the modern marketing industry, any informational system—including cyberspace—would seem grist for its mill. If this industry can so effectively exploit the U.S. Postal System, which ultimately still relies on hand-delivered pieces of paper, think of what designs it might have—and intelligently so—on cyberspace.

## WHAT LIES AHEAD

What lies ahead for cyberspace? If the recent examples of the American postal and telephone systems can serve as models, cyberspace—a rather disorganized if not chaotic phenomenon by modern standards of communication, marketing, and control—is overdue to be rationalized. Although rationalization has a variety of meanings in such contexts, the essential idea is that control of anything can be increased by decreasing the amount of its information that requires processing (Beniger, 1976, chap. 1). Cyberspace, it would seem, is about to experience rationalization of its content if not its organization, from without if not from within.

Because this chapter has now reached the point of speculation about the future, always a hazardous enterprise, let me simply list (in no particular order) some of the things that others, judging by their past behavior, might have in store for cyberspace.

1. *Massive operations for downloading and mining the cyberslush and reorganizing it according to user IDs.* Nothing can be sold to cyberspace as a whole, nor much to the various universities and commercial gateway systems that make up the Net. Although many of the virtual communities found in cyberspace might well present commercial possibilities, the real gold lies at the lowest hierarchical level: the millions of individual citizens of cyberspace. Each one's immediately processable record of past behavior on the Net will afford unprecedented support for efforts to persuade, influence, and control her or him.

2. *High-speed, programmable mailers to individual accounts on the Net.* Rather than merely posting messages to listservers, newsgroups, or other mass media already part of cyberspace, with all of the limitations inherent in any such form of mass communication, marketers will exploit programmable technologies capable of delivering unique messages, personalized by means of already existing data sets, to each individual account—and at rapid rates.

3. *New database marketing industries based on various data sets linked by inference to individual accounts.* From my own user ID, it is easy to infer both my last name and my university. Using only these two data points, there is virtually no limit to the data that might be linked to my individual account and, via that, to my past and future activity on the Net.

4. *Greater standardization of Net account formats.* Although this is hardly necessary, and indeed would take much of the fun out of record linking, such fun costs both time and money—hence, a likely push for greater standardization.

5. *Trafficking in specialized lists of user IDs.* These would certainly include lists of the most affluent and the most gullible, and those most likely to

purchase certain products or to support certain causes. Such lists are highly prized for marketing in other media; why should it be any different in cyberspace?

6. *Detailed psychological profiles of individuals based on their past inputs to the Net.* Only processing and storage capabilities will limit the extent to which marketers can dredge the cybersludge and sort by individual accounts. Imagine how much easier it would be to influence the behavior of individuals whose total activity in cyberspace you had analyzed, via artificial intelligence, to produce their psychological profiles (and perhaps also to tailor messages of maximum likely effectiveness for each of them as individuals).

7. *Word-of-mouth campaigns via individuals determined, based on their past Net behavior, to be most likely to spread rumors and gossip.* Anyone with experience in cyberspace could undoubtedly nominate a few likely candidates; marketers' algorithms will find those most likely to be effective. Word-of-mouth campaigns, positive as well as negative, have long proven effective, especially for particular types of products (e.g., political candidates as affected by the "dirty tricks" of whispering campaigns).

8. *Individual accounts run by software "persuaders" that are the modern natural-language processing equivalent of the ELIZA system.* Weizenbaum (1976) reported that even his secretary, who had watched him work on ELIZA for many months, and surely knew it to be merely a computer program, became hooked on it "after only a few interchanges." Are the citizens of cyberspace likely to find a modern version of ELIZA any less convincing as a personal pen pal on the Net?

## WHO WILL PREVAIL?

Already the memories of what cyberspace once was, in its earliest days, have begun to fade. The vast majority of those in cyberspace today have no personal knowledge of these early times. If some of the changes forecast here seem incredible to imagine in cyberspace today, this may be—at least in part—because they will come about in a future in which memories of today's cyberspace have also faded.

Increasingly cyberspace has become polarized into two distinct classes: those who value the experience of cyberspace as inherently good, as an end in itself; and those who see cyberspace as merely one means to other quite specific ends, which might range from the making of an honest profit to various types of criminal behavior. A growing problem of cyberspace, one that afflicts all human societies that transcend face-to-face communication in small, persisting, and intimate groups, is the need to accommodate both those who value sociality as an end itself, and those who see it as but a means to other more personal ends— ends about which they might also disagree among themselves. In this way modernism has brought a certain loss to our collective innocence.

Recent battles over the control of cyberspace have centered on the protection of free expression, something that certainly cannot be overvalued.

Completely free expression, however, includes the expression of those who value cyberspace as only a means and those whose expression might be in the feverish pursuit of ends radically different from our own. Free expression might also include expression by a few individuals backed by many employees, much computing power and expertise, and the unabashed intention to turn cyberspace to their own profit.

To preserve cyberspace as it is today is vastly easier than to preserve the basic freedoms of every one of its citizens equally. To do otherwise might be to provoke a cybernetic version of a civil war, not at all far-fetched if cyberspace is indeed a true subculture of human society. Seen in this way, the answer to our initial question becomes clear: Who will control cyberspace? Most likely those who will control society at large.

## REFERENCES

Benedikt, M. (1991). Introduction. In M. Benedikt (Ed.), *Cyberspace: First steps* (pp. 1-25). Cambridge, MA: MIT Press.

Beniger, J. R. (1986). *The control revolution: Technological and economic origins of the information society.* Cambridge, MA: Harvard University Press.

Gleick, J. (1994, May 1). The information future: Out of control. *New York Times Magazine*, pp. 54-57.

Rheingold, H. (1993). *The virtual community: Homesteading on the electronic frontier.* Reading, MA: Addison-Wesley.

Weizenbaum, J. (1976). *Computer power and human reason: From judgment to calculation.* San Francisco: Freeman.

# 4

# Striking a Balance: Access and Control Copyright, Property, and Technology

## Neil Kleinman

*Cyberspace is clearly a contested terrain, as early hacker subcultures emphasized complete freedom of information, whereas entrepreneurs and capitalists are increasingly seeking to colonize and capitalize on cyberspace through the extension of preexisting notions of property. But how can anyone own anything in an environment characterized by electronic flux? The notion of intellectual property provides a precedent, but as Neil Kleinman argues here, it is based on the physicality and fixity of the printed text. Providing a broad historical overview of the development of the concepts of ownership, property rights, and copyright, he discusses the complex economic, political, and legal factors that have resulted in our current notions of intellectual property, and the ways in which cyberspatial phenomena such as electronic publishing are undermining them. The conclusion, with an eye toward the brewing storm, offers suggestions for managing the approaching chaos brought about by the new digital mode of access. Aside from this section of the book, further study of the legal, regulatory, and economic issues of cyberspace appear in Ron Jacobson's discussion of the Information Superhighway in Chapter 9, Frank Dance's overview of the digital divide controversy in Chapter 10, and Eric Zimmer and Christopher Hunter's discussion of the First Amendment implications of pornography on the Web in Chapter 11. Other views on electronic publishing and related forms can be found in Stuart*

*Moulthrop's exploration of the future of the book in Chapter 15, Camille Paglia's discussion of the online magazine Salon in Chapter 16, and Stephanie Gibson's overview of hypertext in Chapter 17. Douglas Rushkoff in Chapter 21 offers an alternative view on cybercapitalism.*

> *Who's going to own the new electronic frontier? asked the squatter.*
> *Who owned the last frontier? replied the cattle baron.*

## METAPHORS

We need to be careful about the way we describe the world. It can become that way. That's true in philosophy and true also in law. We explain ourselves using a metaphoric language, and the metaphors we use take us in unique directions. Nowhere do we see this more clearly than when we try to understand the impact of the web and digital media on the new electronic environment we are creating. Alternatively, we call this new space the *Electronic Frontier*, the *Information Highway*, or *Cyberspace*, to give only a few of its names. Each one of these carries a different message, paints a different picture of the terrain, and presents a different case for the issues that are at stake.

The *Electronic Frontier* suggests a time prior to law and order, when the pioneers, homesteaders and the cattle baron all still had an opportunity to claim pieces of the territory. There's free land to be gotten, and for those who use this metaphor, the informing principle is that *information wants to be free*. The metaphor carries, however, a dark prediction, based on history: Nothing remains free, and we should expect that to be true in the digital age. So its message, finally, is anarchistic. What's left for those who want freedom is the role of the outlaw who must move further "out" to the edges of the frontier to escape the laws of "society."

What's interesting about this metaphor is that it is a story about metaphor-makers. (One could call it a "meta-metaphor.") To make its point, it is a narrative that presents a space peopled with heroes and villains, a human space with people engaged in conflict. As a story, it doesn't make any difference whether the freedom fighter (call him Linus Torvalds of Linux) or the cattleman (call him Bill Gates of Microsoft) wins. What does matter is the drama. On the frontier, the story is what counts. Content is king.

The *Information Highway* suggests that the network that connects us is more important than what is moving on the road. Here, access to the highway, speed, regulating traffic is what is important—not the products being moved. Those who use this metaphor—legislators, politicians, and publishers—focus for the most part on ownership of the roads—the means of distribution—rather than on the product or the content being created. This metaphor takes into account a principle of the "new economics"—that those owning the tollgates and the on/off ramps will determine the price of information, not those manufacturing the goods.

What we're asked to focus on is the impersonal infrastructure. It's the architecture and the grandeur of the interchanges, not the drama, that we are to appreciate. Not surprisingly for a metaphor shaped by politicians, this description presents the roadway itself as king. (Those who take this metaphor seriously might do well to invest in Cisco Systems, the builder of Internet routers, switches, hubs, and servers.)

*Cyberspace* suggests a universe of "wormholes" and feedback loops where both the user and creator are one and learn from each other. The emphasis here is on the ability to navigate, to find meaning by exploring. Those who believe that the new digital medium is an "environment"—a place to live in, to play in, and to explore—will find this metaphor appealing (Shapiro & Varian, 1999). It is more holistic than the others and presents an ecological view of information and those who work with it, and it also presents a different economic assumption. Value is the result of a combined effort—the efforts of those who steer us through the chaos and the efforts of those who are users of that information. The "creator" of information is secondary, so too is the "information" and the system that distributes it. In cyberspace, relationships are more complex: the dance, the dancers, and the "orchestra" are all equally important. In cyberspace, the navigator and the voyager share the throne. (Those who find this metaphor appealing should be attracted to web sites like Yahoo! or search engines like Google.com.)

One of my purposes in this chapter is to determine which of these three stories is the best descriptor of events, and I do that in the conclusion. I have another purpose, however. I suggest that what these three stories have in common is as important as what distinguishes them. Although each of them gives a very different spin to the meaning of information, ownership, property, and how we price it, they all are sketched out in terms of "real property"—public and private lands, property lines, highways, and even space. My other purpose in this chapter is to show how the idea of property found in these metaphors has played itself out in our attitudes toward intellectual property in general and digital property in particular.

Today, the battle for ownership is, of course, being fought in a much less "real" space than we associate with traditional "real estate" and the physical space of the frontier. It's being fought in the space reserved for creations of the imagination—the legal terrain of intellectual property and the copyright law developed to protect it. What I intend to show is that, despite the rather abstract nature of intellectual property, copyright law has been defined by its ability to make concrete, tangible and fixed those things (i.e., the expression of "ideas") that are normally transitory and sometimes quite ephemeral (Harpold, 2000).

So there is no doubt in the argument I develop here, let me come now to my conclusions. The principles underlying intellectual property are the result of a print-based technology—the printing press. They succeed because the press was able to create fixed and tangible products that shared characteristics of real property. Even as new communication technologies evolved—radio, photography, movies, and television—the logic of intellectual property was easily extended to cover these new forms of expression. But the advent of the Web and digital technology has made it more difficult to extend the print-based assumptions of intellectual property law. Difficult, of course, but not impossible.

What is more interesting, perhaps more perplexing, is that in the context of a digital environment, the principles of copyright law are being subverted even as they are being extended. What made eminent sense both from a public policy and an economic perspective—that copyright law could be shaped to provide a public benefit by stimulating new content at the same time that it rewarded the creators of that content—is now debatable.

## THE ISSUE

The underlying question is whether electronic media has so changed the nature of publication that a too broad and expansive application of copyright law now denies the public useful access to information by creating excessively high barriers of entry. If it does, the copyright law will have been turned against itself since the purpose of copyright protection has always been to promote "broad public availability" (*Twentieth Century Music Corp. v. Aiken,* 1975) of both works of science and imagination.

Through the mid-20th century, the intent of the law was pretty clear—to create a copyright law that balanced two interests: the need to keep the marketplace unregulated and the need to stimulate enterprise (Lessig, 1999). As the authors of the House Report accompanying the 1909 Copyright Act explained,

> The enactment of copyright legislation by Congress under the terms of the Constitution is not based upon any natural right that the author has in his writings. . . . [T]he policy is believed to be for the benefit of the great body of people, in that it will stimulate writing and invention to give some bonus to authors and inventors. . . . Congress must consider . . . two questions: First, how much will the legislation stimulate the producer and so benefit the public, and, second, how much will the monopoly granted be detrimental to the public? (Committee on the Judiciary, House Report, 1909, pp.10-11)

How to strike the right balance is less obvious. The question cannot be answered in the abstract, nor does the same balance work for all works of intellectual property. Some have a longer shelf life than others do. The same balance may not work for all media. In some cases, a monopoly in a media creates a consolidation of information in the hands of too few.

In fact, the relation of access on one side to monopoly on the other has been a matter of considerable discussion. For some time, economists have argued that a careful balance between the scope of copyright protection and its duration (i.e., a "limited monopoly") can best serve the principle of useful access (Breyer, 1970; Chafee, 1945; Kaplan, 1966). What economists have argued is that there is a way to maintain public access and, at the same time, provide incentives to those who produce new work: To do so, we need to decide how much to include in a monopoly and decide on how long to allow the monopoly to last.

The economic assumptions can be summarized in the following way. In the extreme, a broad, generous, and total copyright system that lasted indefinitely would provide a maximum incentive to producers because it would guarantee them complete control over their work and the ability to charge monopoly royalties for it. Under such a system, the public would, of course, be denied access to copyrighted material in both the present and the future except on terms prescribed by the copyright owner. In the other extreme, a limited copyright system that lasted for a relatively short period of time would provide the public with easy and cheap access to the work but would offer few incentives to producers (Braunstein, Fischer, Ordover, & Baumol, 1977; Breslow, Ferguson, & Haverkamp, 1977; Breyer, 1970).

To reconcile the public's and the producers' conflicting interests, one can fashion one of two systems: (a) limited protection combined with a rather extended period of protection or (b) broaden protection combined with a more limited period of protection. Under the first approach, producers trade limited protection for a longer period in which they are free to charge monopoly prices on the aspects of the work they do control. In this way, producers have a long time to make their profit although what they own is carefully constrained. Under the second approach, producers trade a longer period of copyright for total control of what is copyrighted, hence gaining higher rewards. In this way, producers have only a limited period in which to take advantage of a very extensive and powerful monopoly.

If you want to give absolute control over some material but still want to make it available to the public, the argument goes, you should limit absolute control to a short time, or you should limit what can be controlled and extend the time it can be controlled.

## WHAT'S GONE WRONG?

The electronic media make this balancing act—between duration and scope—difficult to maintain. The nature of the new technology makes it hard to limit the scope of what might be covered. In systems that do not distinguish between each stage of information processing, like those found in electronic networks, a broad application of copyright protection creates a particularly acute problem: The public price must be calculated on the basis of a series of incremental costs that can far exceed the one time cost we pay for the printed version of the information. (Those who buy a book pay only once but are able to read and re-read the book as often as they'd like, as well as being free to share it with a friend. On the other hand, those who use information drawn from an online source may be charged multiple times for a number of different uses ranging from the charge to access the material, to download it, to display and manipulate it, to distribute and share it.)

At the same time, new media material—software, data, or multimedia—often suffers from an overly long copyright protection when compared to the useful life of the material (Baumol, 1977; Braunstein, 1981). In the case of computer software or databased information, for example, their average useful life is something less than 3 years (Gleick, 1993; Kleinman, 1993; Post, 1983). The rate of change and obsolescence may be even faster. According to "Moore's Law," the processing power of computers doubles every 18 months, which means that the software written for these systems becomes outdated about once every year and a half (Downes & Mui, 1998). Meanwhile, the current law protects all copyrightable material for the lifetime of the author plus an additional 70 years or 90 years if the holder is a corporation (Copyright Act of 1976, as amended, 17 U.S.C. Sec. 302a-c). Who will want to buy software competitively priced a generation from now when its usefulness had long since ended?

> [I]t is of little significance to the public at large what happens to works that have no commercial value at the end of the term. Few will wish to use them. Such works will not be exploited in as variety of editions, recordings, productions or the like. It is the works which still have commercial value which should fall into the public domain as soon as the constitutional purpose has been achieved [that is, to provide an incentive to production by assuring an economic return to writers and distributors . . . for it is the works which still have commercial value from which the public will benefit in the form of more numerous and varied editions, recordings and productions. (Guinan, 1957, p. 80)

To extend the copyright beyond a useful term is to give the copyright holder a defacto monopoly over the information. This seems obvious, but there is no evidence that either a concern for scope or duration is being taken into account in the application of copyright law.

My aim in this chapter is to make two basic (and essentially political) points: First, that it will be hard to regulate intellectual property in a digital environment through the copyright scheme as we now have it and, second, that, even if it were easy, it would be wrong. It would, in fact, be destructive of the very rationale that is used to justify copyright law.

## THE DEBATE

Intellectual property is not a self-evident proposition. Although its origins can be found as early as the 16th century, as law it began less than 300 years ago. By then, printing was becoming a fact of life: It was the way in which the State defined itself and the way in which the public educated and entertained itself (Bettig, 1996; Kaplan, 1967; Katsh, 1989; Lanham, 1993; Morris, 1963; Patterson, 1968; Steinberg, 1996).

Three hundred years is not a long history as histories go, and, as I suggest, it is possible that copyright law as we know it won't get much older. That doesn't mean, of course, that we won't find a lot of legislators, courts, lawyers, and critics stretching legal precepts to keep the old law working. The authors of the Department of Commerce (1995) White Paper wrote just a few years ago that "[e]xisting copyright law needs only the fine tuning that technological advances necessitate, in order to maintain the balance of the law in the face of onrushing technology" (Working Group, 1995, p. 17). Nevertheless, since the late 1980s, there has been an intense debate between those arguing that the old law needs only a bit of adjustment and those who believe the exercise is futile and wrongheaded (Barlow, 1994; Bettig, 1996; Brand, 1987; Gleick, 2000; Lanham, 1993, p. 274; Lessig, 1999; Wolf, 1994).

If nothing else does, this debate should remind us that we are at a classic point in the evolution of technology and ideas, and, therefore, it is a good time to think about what we've taken for granted (Boyle, 1996; Lessig, 1999). With the current contradictions before us, we can see more clearly the cracks in the mirror. As a result, we just might be able to understand the delicate relationship that develops between principles and laws on one hand and technologies on the other (Kleinman, 1993).

## PROPERTY AND CONSTITUTIONAL VALUES

The thread of "property," woven throughout both liberal and conservative thought, is now characteristic of our "modern" sensibility. Rights we now take to be fundamental in areas that would seem to have little or nothing to do with property—free speech, abortion, product liability, to name a few—draw their meaning from concepts imbedded in real property law. What they all share is an attitude towards control and ownership. What they all reflect is a treatment that makes everything into a form of property. Our bodies, our selves, our ideas—each in turn is subject to analysis as though it were real property.

Property is a question of control, access, and ownership. What many commentators remind us is that the evolution of the net and the digital media have opened up, once again, a question we can never quite seem to settle: the balance between the amount of "control" we will accept and the amount of "freedom" we can afford. In his recent book, *Code and Other Laws of Cyberspace*, Lessig (1999) presents the dilemma nicely.

> Will *cyberspace* promise privacy or access? Will it preserve a space for free speech? Will it facilitate free and open trade? These are choices of substantive value . . .
>
> Theorists of cyberspace have been talking about these questions since its birth. But as a culture, we are just beginning to get it. We are just beginning to see why *the architecture of the space matters*—in particular, why the *ownership* of that architecture matters. *If the code of cyberspace is owned . . . it can be controlled; if it is not owned, control is much more difficult.* The lack of ownership, the absence of property, the inability to direct how ideas will be used—in a word, the presence of a commons—is key to limiting, or checking, certain forms of governmental control. (p. 7, italics added.)

There is no glib answer to the question of control and freedom (Lessig, 1999). Too much freedom creates a dysfunctional system in which none of us can organize our lives, our businesses, and our relationships in a predictable way. Conversely, too much control creates an oppressive environment in which our autonomy as individuals is hidden, if not lost.

Our current fixation on matters of control and ownership wasn't always so, although it has been central to the debate of this Republic and can be found in the language of our Constitution. But, even that debate is relatively modern. It has only been since the late Middle Ages that questions of ownership and control have defined the issue, expressed in the question—What can we own? It's the question raised by the farmer who opposes the spread of housing developments in his rural community. It's the question raised by the woman who supports abortions—and raised also by the woman who opposes them. For each, the first step is to mark out the boundary lines of property, the boundary that defines what is "ours."

Printing helps to do the same thing to ideas. It makes intellectual property tangible, even when it is invisible. Within the tangible, fixed space of a printed product, we have learned how to lay out the field, plow, plant, and harvest. It is here we show our ability to control ideas, shape them, make them public, and it is here that we claim our rights (Kleinman, 2000). Although this chapter focuses on the way in which copyright law and the idea of property are bound together and are unraveling, by no means do I want to suggest that the issues of ownership, control, access, and support for the creative enterprise are limited to a discussion of copyright.

In fact, across a broad range of areas in the law—constitutional, tort, contract, and property—post-Medieval legal principles force us to one conclusion: that "[t]he dichotomy between personal liberties and property rights is a false one," as Justice Stewart wrote (*Lynch v. Household Finance Corp.*, 1972). "Property does not have rights. People have rights. . . . In fact, a fundamental interdependence exists between the personal right to liberty and the personal right in property. Neither could have meaning without the other. That rights in property are basic civil rights has long been recognized." It does not require much embroidery to find in this language, the language of the Fourth Amendment, an argument for a woman's right to abortion—the right to control one's body as "property" that the State should have no ready access to (*Roe v. Wade*, 1973).

In the same way, the notion of property rights serves to underpin our explanations of freedom of speech. Often in a discussion of the right to free speech, we treat language and ideas as though they were commodities, to be traded and exchanged as property in a free market. Belief is best reached, wrote Justice Holmes, "by free trade in ideas—the best test of truth is the power of the thought to get itself accepted in the competition of the market" (*Abrams v. United States*, 1919). What Justice Holmes describes is a marketplace in which fair competition takes responsibility out of the hands of the producer. The "buyer," not the maker, decides what is of value. The maker and the seller have only one responsibility: to produce. It is a powerful and appealing metaphor (Tribe, 1978) because it is consistent with our commercial sensibilities, but we lose something by accepting it. We lose the idea that there is an intimate and important relationship between what we say and who we are (Arendt, 1959). Free speech—our treasured ideal—seems to become little more than a commodity that is traded, bought and sold, along with all the other commercial objects in the marketplace.

As free speech and privacy grow out of our commitments to property, so too does copyright law. The same elements are in play—ownership, property, and marketplace valuation.

## THE RIGHTS OF OWNERSHIP IN REAL PROPERTY

As Justice Stewart explains, "property does not have rights. People have rights." So what are the rights we have as owners of real property? In a classic exposition, Karl Renner (1947) wrote:

> The right of ownership . . . is a person's all-embracing legal power over a tangible object. As far as the object is concerned, ownership is a universal institution: all corporeal things, even, land, can be objects of ownership if they are recognized as such by the law and are not by special provision put [outside of commerce]. Ownership is equally universal with regard to the subject. Everybody has an equal capacity for ownership, and he may own property of every description. These are the norms which are characteristic of this institution. (cited in Tigar, 1977, p. 197)

Renner's formula tells us a good bit. To be an owner, we must have legal power over a "thing." We'll find that that's the point of most law and judicial opinion interpreting property rights: to identify the tangible object that law allows a property owner to control. In the discussion that follows, I return frequently to that notion—the search for a tangible object protected under the law. It is central to any discussion of property generally and critical to understanding intellectual property specifically. If we cannot find a way to treat something as "a tangible object," we cannot control it, and if we cannot control it, we cannot own it.

## GETTING CONTROL OF THE IDEA

### Property and Technology

Property, real or intellectual, exists only when we can determine its boundaries and are able to point to them and the property they surround. For the last 300 years, it did not seem particularly hard to find property lines for the creations of our imagination nor to make ideas into property. The technology of printing allowed us to fix more than boundaries. It persuaded us that meaning was the result of the way an idea was displayed on a page or in a book—how an idea looked, what surrounded it, how it was organized with other ideas, how it was indexed, catalogued, or stored (Kleinman, 2000).

"Typography," wrote McLuhan (1962), "tended to alter language from a means of perception and exploration to a portable commodity" (p. 161). He was right. The effect was to manufacture a visual and spatial domain for ideas. In this space, we became peddlers carrying "objects of art" on our backs, trading and selling ideas as we found buyers for them. It was this space that we called "the marketplace of ideas" and adopted economic regulations like those embodied in copyright laws to protect what was being sold.

Print made our debates very tangible, very concrete, and very physical. As a result, print made it easier for us to place ideas and their expression in the marketplace where, like other manufactured products, they could be sold (Ong, 1971). This commodification of ideas, framed for a consumer market, is only another version of technology at work.

In printing we can see a process invented, like many other technologies, that was intended to standardize behavior and to make predictable the product being made—its size, shape, quantity, and quality. The invention of the mechanical plow, for instance, meant that the art of being a farmer was a bit more regularized, a farmer needed to know less in order to plant a straight furrow, and he didn't need to be quite as strong (Giedion, 1948). As a result, others who were less experienced, less skilled, and less strong could replace the "expert" farmer. At the same time that the plow "standardized" the farmer, it standardized the product: the furrows were identical, the yield of an acre more predictable, and even the quality of the produce, more predictable.

In this example (and any number of other "technologies" we might look to), we can see the similarity between the technology of the plow and that of the printing press. Like the plow, the technology of printing is also based on an ability to rationalize a process and to quantify—quantify both those engaged in the process and the thing being produced. The printing press standardized the book and the pressman. Every book in a print run looked the same, and every pressman followed the same routine to produce the books.

What the technology of printing accomplished was to make ideas "seem" as though they were commodities—items that could be inventoried and counted. In fact, what the press accomplished was to make the form of an idea—its tangible and physical representation—into the tangible property that an owner controlled. It was of course nothing more than a shell game because the tangible property (a book or a magazine or broadside) was only the outer form of something much more ephemeral. Nevertheless, once we focused on this outer shell, the fixed expression of an idea in a medium, we were able to treat ideas as quantifiable commodities. What's more they had a predictable shape, which meant that the "owner" could more easily distinguish the "real" commodity—his or her real property—from its imitation, and therefore he or she could more easily argue claim of ownership.

These principles of a "fixed," "predictable," and "tangible" shape serve as the foundations for contemporary copyright law. "Copyright protection subsists," the law states, "in original works of authorship fixed in any tangible medium of expression" (Copyright Act of 1976 as amended, 17 U.S.C. Sec 102a). The problem we now face is that we can't easily find fixed, predictable, and tangible shapes, which means that it is much more difficult to apply copyright principles (Bolter, 1991).

## The Problem

One would think that the ingenuity of lawyers and businessmen would be able to find a way to fix even the most fluid entity into a tangible form. Certainly they've gone pretty far. In a recent case, Jeff Bezos, founder of *Amazon.com,* the online bookstore, applied for and received a patent for a service he offered his customers: the ability to order a book online using one click that incorporated both the billing information (the credit number and mailing address on file) and the items being ordered. As those familiar with the case remarked, Bezos had managed to patent a business strategy (Gleick, 2000). How did he manage that? The technology of the computer helped.

> The computer is the universal machine almost by definition, machine-of-all trades, capable of accomplishing or simulating just about any task that can be logically defined. . . . Take any real-world procedure or activity; transfer it to cyberspace; and now we have an activity that seems both new and technological.
>
>                          . . . .
>
> "Anything that can be done in hardware can be done in software," says one examiner. "We're not using gears; we're using some other mechanism, some other means." But they are machines without substance—incorporeal machines, machines made of imagination and "logic" and "bits." (Gleick, 2000, p. 47)

What's happening here is the power of a technology to make something rather insubstantial (a way of doing business) into a facsimile of a machine. What could be more tangible?

Despite the craft of Bezos and others, this new technology also creates real problems for those who wish to protect their products under copyright law. The best way to understand why this is so is to look again at the reasons for copyright. In a nutshell, the digital media destroys the distinction that printing makes between the producer/publisher and the reader. With that distinction gone, the purposes for copyright are confused and difficult to satisfy.

Printing made possible a great number of identical copies. For that reason, it became important for publishers to define the extent of their property right over things that might be identical, especially when two or more publishers were producing an indistinguishable product (Morris, 1963).

It was the need to protect these commodities from unfair competition, that is, unfair duplication, that gave rise to the principle of copyright (Kaplan, 1966). Early copyright therefore had a rather practical and limited purpose: to protect the interests of the printer/publisher by giving him the exclusive right to publish a work and to control the number of copies in circulation of the work he had published (Patterson, 1968, p. 9).

The publisher's competitor, the counterfeiter who would copy what the original publisher had produced, had a simple goal—to produce copies that he might distribute at a profit. The counterfeiter did not "use" the work in any conventional sense since the work he "copied" passed through him directly to the reading public. On the other hand, the public had goals other than profit. It used it—read it, studied it, memorized it, commented on it, and consumed it. It's this question of "use" that distinguished the producer, whether publisher or counterfeiter, from the reading public.

Given this separation of producer and reader, it is easy to understand the rights the original producer might want. And it is relatively easy to distinguish between the counterfeiters and the public audience. Counterfeiters were the ones who produced multiples of a book and then distributed and sold them to audiences. Audiences, on the other hand, consisted of individuals who took up a book—one at a time—so they could read it.

In this digital age, it is difficult to distinguish between "counterfeiters" and "consumers, between those who produce works and those who use them. The consumer now takes on many of the functions of the counterfeiter. He must, perforce, copy information in order to store it. He must copy it if he is to manipulate it, and he must display it if he is to use it. Arguably each of these acts—copying, manipulating information, and displaying it—infringes the exclusive rights in copyrighted works granted the owner of copyright (Copyright Act of 1976 as amended, 17. U.S.C. Sec 106). The principles of "property" right are consequently more difficult to apply when the forms of expression are not anchored in permanent commodities.

In an electronic age, the work promises to disappear, leaving the public only with images of work which it can see but not possess, view but not use, and receive but not keep (Harpold, 2000), unless it is willing to pay an additional fee for the privilege of continuing use. At minimum, the public is not clear what it is getting. Similarly, copyright owners find it difficult to distinguish the authorized counterfeits from the unauthorized ones.

We can see that copyright was fashioned to put two absolutes in tandem without mixing them together—the right of control and the right of access. The publisher had the right of control, and the audience had the right of access. The production system and that which was produced, that is the printing press and the publication, remained in the hands of the publisher, while the reading public only got access and control of one printed copy, which they could not duplicate, under pain of law. But what happens when control and access are intermingled, when the reader cannot gain access without acquiring some level of control? That's the problem—or at least one of the problems—which those who publish in the new media must face.

## THERE'S A PLACE FOR EVERYTHING

Let's understand that copyright, as an extension of property rights, has its place and serves important economic functions. It is necessary to appreciate these functions if we're to understand why they may not be useful or adequate in an economic environment in which electronic media promise to dominate. A few examples should illustrate the multiple purposes copyright can serve. What I hope will be clear from the outside is that most of the values I am highlighting here have little to do with protecting the interests of the individual creator of an original work. To be sure, copyright does provide an incentive to the artist and the publisher to invest time and money and talent in creating a new work generally. Nevertheless, the value of copyright is its ability to promote the creation of work. When it cannot do that, even if it enriches writers and publishers, it is not serving its function.

### The Scribe: Resource Development

Ownership is one of the ways we encourage the growth of resources. Promising it helps us persuade others to invest time, energy, and money. In return, we ask the farmer, as the metaphor goes, to sink his roots into the soil, take the time to plow, sow, and harvest, and continue each year to manage the property. That principle holds true in book publishing as it does in farming.

On the other hand, when there are few resources to begin with, ownership may restrict the development of new resources. To determine what strategy works best, it's important to look careful at the resources that are available (what's the raw material?); to understand the investment that's required (is it time, money, or skill?); and to appreciate the size of the marketplace and the competitive forces in it (what are the barriers to entry?).

We can see this kind of calculation at work in the period before printing when books were the result of the copyist's craft. Before Gutenberg, the investment required of the copyist was limited and of short duration. The rate of return was: one man, one "book" at a time, and 3 months or more to make it (Eisenstein, 1983). Ownership was of little concern because new content was not a resource that needed to be developed. The standard books that copyists worked on were the "good books" and the classical texts, and it was these that they reproduced. A copyist did not need new works because the demand of the market was still limited to those older texts. At the same time, the completed book he'd copied had an immediate exchange value. He made what he could from his labor, and the "author," for his part, could not expect to make much out of such a limited production system (Bettig, 1996; Morris, 1963).

Not only could the author not expect to make much from his work, the work itself was valued not because it was new or "original" but because it was "old," a part of a tradition—a classic that had been passed down. (Authors sometimes quite deliberately hid their "contributions" to a text by pretending that they were merely following the text rather than adding original work to it (Woodmansee & Jaszi, 1994).

This attitude toward publication could be understood to be an extension of religious doctrine. From the point of the religious and the pious, literature might be said to be "a fund of man's knowledge, rather than belonging to its individual authors" (cited in Katsh, 1989, p. 172). Knowledge was a common field, open to anyone who wished to use it. This view satisfied both a social need and a social incentive. "To copy and circulate another man's book [was] regarded as a meritorious action in the age of manuscript" (cited in McLuhan, 1962, p. 87) because it maintained sacred texts and passed them along to the next generation.

We can see that in the pre-print culture, there was an economic value to be found in copying, which argued against creating barriers to the act of copying. Free use and the right to copy—in fact, the duty to copy—balanced the economies of scarcity. What little there was went further if shared. This is the communal economics of the poor, which we often find in those who have little and must share what they acquire merely to have enough. (Scarcity does not necessarily lead to an economic structure based on barriers and enclosures. Have-nots have more to gain by sharing than by controlling their little pieces of property—a principle also to be found in the experimental and start-up businesses that can be found on the early Web.)

Scarcity creates an open economy and tends to eliminate barriers. By doing this, it makes a limited commodity available to a wider audience. The rule in these circumstances is: When information is scarce, we devise systems to promote copying so that access to information is easier. The Church promoted such a system by making the role of scribe a religious devotion (Katsh, 1988, p. 173). A tax of the kind imposed by copyright would have limited the spread of information and the propagation of the faith. What were needed were more copies of Aquinas and Augustine, not fewer.

## Feudal Land: Relationships and Service

If the purpose of a economy is to promote service relationships, as some suspect is the case in an information economy (Drucker, 1993; Hagel & Armstrong, 1997; Kelly, 1998), modern principles of ownership and property may be less effective ways to achieve that end. An alternative economic model, which suggests a working model for the current economy, evolved during the Middle Ages. It is based on relationships and obligations.

Feudal property land was not owned. In the legal language of the time, "the grantee takes the land and holds it 'of' the grantor" (Tigar, 1977, p. 196). In fact, it could not be "owned." It was held in trust (Lopez, 1976). If it could not be owned, it could not be sold, and it was not. Its value flowed from something other than that which a marketplace provides.

The purpose of feudal property was to establish relationships among those who gave it, those who took it, and those who used it. Property defined the society, the structure, the duties men owed each other, and the responsibilities they had to their superiors and inferiors. According to R. H. Tawney (1926),

> [Property's] raison d'etre [in the feudal system] is not only income, but service. It is to secure its owner such means, and no more than such means, as may enable him to perform those duties whether labor on the land, or labor in government, which are involved in particular status which he holds in the system. (cited in Tigar, 1977, pp. 196-197)

In such a world, both social and economic forms were tightly integrated. The land they lived on identified people and defined the roles they played. The land defined what they could be; what they could do; how they must act; and what their duties to others must be. And these definitions were true for both the high and low born, for the knight and the peasant.

The system encouraged community. The land within each economic unit was managed with the needs of the whole in mind. What was grown, used, and saved was the result of a delicate calculus that took into account a mix of promises, responsibilities, and duties that all the members of the community—from the top to the bottom—owed each other. Financial motives, even when present were subdued and certainly never brazen. As Tawney (1926) puts it, "He who exploits his property with a single eye to its economic possibilities at once perverts its very essence and destroys his own moral title, for he has 'every man's living and does no man's duty'" (cited in Tigar, 1977, p. 197).

The medieval man's attitude towards real property is not dissimilar from his attitude toward intellectual "property." A text, like land, was to be shared. More importantly, both text and land were to be held in trust for the next generation of users, whether readers or tenants. The value of both was determined by the ability of each to promote use and clarify relations as well as to establish bonds of common belief.

The rule we can draw here is: In a pre-capital economy, efficiency requires that we learn to maximize the ways in which we use the same object as well as the ways in which we increase the number of links between people.

## The Commons: Control, Access, and Production

What we see in these examples is the way in which the idea of property can be used to increase productivity or to decrease it. In all these cases, what is being regulated is "control" and "access" in order to promote a socially desirable good. In some instances, access was restricted as a way of developing a resource or maintaining the value of what's been produced. In other instances, access was left open as a way of promoting the development of a new product or an important resource. One final example—that of the English Commons—can help to explain the delicate balance between open and closed access.

Before the 16th century, much land in England was held in common. The nobility and the squires had their grand estates, but the English farmer had access to land too. He could use the land "owned" by his village. It was this right of access and use of common land that gave many a servant the opportunity to improve his condition. With access to the commons, a man might do a bit of farming, hunting, and graze his few animals. His profits from that activity provided him with an opportunity to move one step up the social and economic ladder without the initial investment of capital required of an owner (Hammond & Hammond, 1948; Mingay, 1968). By providing access, the commons was a useful economic mechanism: it relieved the social pressure created by an emerging middle class who sought access to property as a way of establishing independence.

Nevertheless, appealing as the idea of common land might have been as an economic pressure valve, the commons was in crisis. Land controlled by many was the responsibility of no one, and this was the case for the English commons. It was threatened by the anarchy of too much access and too few with assigned duties. The tragedy of the commons was that no one would take responsibility for it when they used it. It became unproductive. Sheep left to graze devoured the countryside. Hunting, uncontrolled, threatened the stock.

To protect the land, as well as to stabilize the economy and the social order, the English began to enclose the common lands, and the land that had "belonged" to many became the private property of a few. Despite the political and economic consequences to the tenant farmers and the emerging middle class, the benefits of enclosure became apparent. "Fencing permitted controlled experimentation on improving yields of both crops and animals, as well as helping to limit the spread of disease by wandering animals" (Burke, 1985, p. 166).

The practical effect of the enclosure laws was to make land into a factory for the efficient production of farm goods. A flock of sheep could be treated as nothing more than "raw" material—to be reared, tended, and sheared. The wool produced could then be easily gathered and sorted to be made into cloth, all within the close confines of a well-defined and well-regulated enclosure (Tigar, 1977, p. 205).

The efficiency of the enclosure was paralleled by similar efficiency in manufacturing—and for the same reasons. As Peter Drucker (1993) commented, the industrial revolution, which happened about the same time as the enclosure of the commons, "required concentration of production, that is, the shift to the factory. Knowledge could not be applied in tens of thousands of small individual workshops and in the cottage industries of the rural village. It required concentration of production under one roof" (p. 29). Both the farmer who took advantage of the enclosure laws and the proto-industrialist found profit in controlling space and managing what takes place in that space.

What's to be learned from this kind of consolidation? In an early capital economy, profit requires efficiency in the means of production. To achieve this, we bring the means of production together under one roof so that the thing being created can be more easily controlled, organized, refined, and sold.

For many of the same reasons, a similar form of consolidation and concentration took place among early printers and publishers. They pulled together writers, editors, printers under one roof, creating a role of "publisher" that gave them far more control over what was being produced than had been possible under the decentralized scribal tradition (Eisenstein 1983; Steinberg, 1996).

## RULES AND SPECULATIONS

There's a lot to be learned from these stories of scribes, feudal estates, and the English commons. They explain why, at certain economic times, barriers are lowered so that ownership and control are minimal and why, at other times, barriers are raised. Perhaps most interestingly, they help to explain what is now happening in the "new economy" that's been introduced with the advent of digital media. We hear arguments that seem remarkably similar to those used in the pre-capitalist, feudal economy. We hear demands for open access to information and related arguments about free software, open source software or open code (Lessig, 1999) that sound a good deal like those for property based on open access or service relationships (Kelly, 1998; Peters, 1987).

Some preliminary questions we might ask include the following:

1. Is the need for content so great that our attitudes toward content have now switched from a need to protect content to a need to promote more copying, as was true in the scribal culture? If that's the case, we may find that copyright is a less valuable, less functionally necessary, structure. (Incentives may change, of course, without our conscious planning and deliberate acts on our part. Schemes atrophy because they no longer serve a useful purpose. Without realizing it, we may be witnessing a slow demise of copyright law simply because it does not serve a useful purpose.)

2. Have the economics changed so that what the market demands (and will pay for) are services and relationships, rather than products? Given the short, useful life of much software, the consumer may now be wondering why she should pay full price (a monopoly price) for a product that has such a limited use. If that's so, we'll find that the scheme we evolve will increasingly be centered on the "sale" of relationships and services, rather than on the sale of products.

3. Is scarcity now a central concern in the marketplace? Do the start-up entrepreneurs, the have-nots, the third-world and developing countries, and the broadened base of entry-level users require a more open and accessible economic model? If that's the case, we can imagine a drift towards an open commons with its low barriers of entry and open use.

It is perhaps too much to say that the new media will return us to an agrarian economy based on the commons and a medieval economy defined by relationships. Nevertheless, there are sufficient similarities between what came before and what is happening now to suggest that we are in a "pre-capitalist" economy. If in fact we are changing the nature of our economy and our assumptions about economy value, we will also need to change our view of copyright and the purposes it serves.

The question we should first ask, though, is whether it is good economic policy to lower the barriers so ownership and control are minimal. We should conclude that the barriers should be lowered only if we believe that we need more content, more information, more access to information for the have-nots and start-ups. If on the other hand, we conclude that we do not need to promote the development of scarce resources, we might decide to raise the barriers, limit access, or make access more expensive.

### Pre-Capitalist and Post-Capitalists Economies

If we do decide to lower the barrier, we shall be creating a "post-capitalist" economy that looks something like a "pre-capitalist" one. If that's the case, it's useful to recall now the differences between pre-capitalist and capitalist attitudes toward property and to sketch out what a post-capitalist approach to value might be, especially as we see these attitudes worked out in copyright.

*Service Versus Commodities.* The pre-print culture was a service-based society in which property defined and established relationships (Johnson, 1981; Le Goff, 1990; Tigar, 1977; Tuchman, 1978). In contrast, print created a consumer market based on the notion that ideas could be sold as though they were commodities (Kleinman, 2000; Ong, 1971). A post-print culture, like its pre-print predecessor, may also be based upon service although there will be efforts (perhaps successful) to redefine the service it provides as a commodity (Hagel & Armstrong, 1997).

*Duties Versus Transactions.* In a pre-print society, the right to control carries (or needs to carry) additional responsibilities—the duty to protect the integrity of the work and maintain its value. In a print culture, the link between control and responsibilities became less evident and less important and was replaced by the economic logic of transactions (Braudel, 1982; Tigar, 1977). The shape of a post-print society may depend on whether it maintains its fascination with the idea of a commodity-based, free marketplace or whether it abandons that logic and moves toward a value-based community in which language, action, and product are all forms of self-representation (Lessig, 1999).

*An Open Economy Versus a Closed Economy.* Scarcity creates an open economy and tends to eliminate barriers. In this way, it makes a limited commodity available to a wider audience. The pre-print society had fuzzy property lines while, in contrast, a print economy has a clearly defined set of property boundaries. By controlling access, those who owned intellectual property were in a position to regulate the size of the audience and the price of access. The question now before us is how "open" and accessible should information be. The copyright debate of the next decade will be centered on exactly this question: Should the structure of intellectual property tilt to support the have-nots (i.e., start-ups and those in the scarcity economy) or should it continue to establish property rights which, for the most part, already belong to those who are established in the information society?

*The Principle of Scarcity.* When information is scarce, we devise systems to promote copying so that access to information is easier. "Start-up" cultures, like "start-up" businesses, are likely to lower—or wish to see lowered—the barriers that control access to information because they understand that low barriers stimulate the economic growth of start-ups and have-nots. More "mature" cultures, like more mature businesses, are more likely to want to raise the barriers of control because they recognize that higher barriers protect the economic value of those with substantial investments in information and technology.

*Community Versus the Product.* Efficiency requires that we learn to maximize the ways in which we use the same object as well as the ways in which we increase the number of links between people. In a pre-print economy, efficiency took into account the way in which a community produced more with less. In the print economy, efficiency emphasized the product rather than the community in which the product was created. In a post-print society, it is likely that the emphasis will return to finding ways to create economically effective links between people and information (Drucker, 1993; Hagel & Armstrong, 1997).

*Production Versus Distribution.* Profit requires efficiency in the means of production. To achieve this, the means of production are often brought together under one roof so that the thing being created can be controlled, organized, refined, and sold (Drucker, 1993). In a pre-print culture, efficiency was defined by the effectiveness of relationships. In a print economy, it was defined by the effectiveness of the technology used to produce a product. In a post-print society, the question will be whether a centralization of effort or a decentralization of work will achieve the kind of economic efficiency we desire (Rifkin, 1995). What does seem clear is that efficiency will no longer be defined by controlling "the means of production" but instead will be defined by controlling "the means of distribution," that is, by controlling the media and the networks that distribute media content.

In many ways, the movement from an economy that emphasized "the means of production" to one that now emphasizes "the means of distribution" ushers in both a "post-capitalist" economy and a "post-Marxist" economy. In Marxist terms, the means of production were the paramount tool of capitalists since they were the tools that created products and shaped the lives of the working class (Samuelson, 1973). Now that the emphasis is on distribution, we should expect a displacement that de-emphasizes production, while perhaps redefining what it means to be in the working class.

## MAKING LAW: BALANCING BENEFITS

I have argued that the idea for copyright is based on our notions of property and property rights as they grow out of ideas about owning physical and tangible space. I have also argued that there is place for copyright but that it's becoming difficult to apply when production and consumption are intermingled as they do in new media (Tapscott, 1996). Finally, I have argued that new media makes a mess out of the delicate balance between the scope of copyright (what's protected) and the duration of copyright (how long it's protected). The digital Web-based technology triggers questions of copyright each time a work is displayed, distributed, stored or manipulated, and the technology protects materials long after their useful life is ended.

Difficult as they may seem, technical problems and technological limits should never be the justification for doing or not doing something. We can figure out how to shape the world to reflect our values if we can only figure out what our values are.

One question we'll need to answer is whether our economy depends on setting low (or lower) barriers of entry and easier rights to access. Although there is contradictory evidence about where the dividing line between access and control should be (Lessig, 1999), what is becoming clear is that there is a "wrong" answer. The wrong answer is to extend the scope of copyright so that it protects a work in every medium, in every storage system, in every form, now available or yet to be created, while, at the same time extending, the duration of the copyright beyond the useful life of the thing being protected. Extending copyright in both time and scope will amount to granting a perpetual monopoly on the intellectual property, discourse, and substance of our society to a very few. It is not clear why we should want to do this.

It is certainly clear that the writers of the Constitution did not want to grant a perpetual monopoly. They allowed for monopolies in intellectual property but limited their duration (U.S. Const., Art. I, Sec. 8, Cl. 8). The Constitution is explicit: "secur[e] for limited Times to Authors and Inventors the exclusive Right to their respective Writings and Discoveries." If they'd had a mind to, the authors of the Constitution need not have limited the duration of copyright. They could have made it continuous and without limit, but they did not.

They recognized that broad and continuous copyrights vest absolute control over intellectual material in copyright holders, allowing them to set price and the terms for access. As one British legal historian observed, more than 150 years ago, "copyright is a monopoly, and produces all the effects which the general voice of mankind attributes to monopoly. The effect of monopoly generally is to make articles scare, to make them dear, and to make them bad" (cited in Bettig, 1996, p. 104). It is for this reason that so many economists and legal historians have contended that copyright is, at best, a necessary evil (Bettig, 1996; Braunstein, 1981; Breyer, 1970; Chafee, 1945; Kaplan, 1967.) The reason why even the most skeptical critics of copyright ultimately supported it—even if grudgingly—is that they perceived it to have a certain social utility. For it to work, however, demands a balance between the incentives required of those who create and the needs of those who use what has been created (Bettig, 1996).

There is a good rule of thumb we can use to work out this balance. We should be interested in whether the copyright scheme we embrace assures a predictable net increase of information at a cost related to its social value or usefulness. The question, as economists have observed, is whether "each potential extension of copyright power contribute[s] more to consumer welfare by stimulating the production and dissemination of new information than it costs in terms of availability of the presently existing stock and in increasing the cost of creating more information for the future" (Breslow et al., 1977, p. 7).

There is a lesson in this juggling act of property rights, equities, public good and private incentives, which we would do well to keep in mind. The elements of the balance were constructed by understanding the special nature of intellectual property in a primarily print environment. At the core of the law is an understanding that "ideas" can be made tangible, can become commodities, can be cordoned off and then later opened up for the public to use. These elements—tangibility, fixity in time, and scope—are among the very elements drained of meaning in digital systems. The tension between access and control increases under the ambiguities of the digital medium. The open market is at risk when the time-value of information grows increasingly shorter. We have to understand that the special nature of intellectual property changes as the technological environment changes.

As we exit the more material space created by print, we enter a space in which objects, as well as ideas, are no longer fixed in tangible forms. There are consequences in the marketplace. Here are some tentative conclusions that can be drawn.

1. *Copyright won't work for practical reasons.* It is simply too easy to copy, too difficult to police those who copy, and nearly impossible to detect when "old," already copyrighted material has been combined with "new" material to create another work (Brand, 1987).

2. *Copyright won't work for technical reasons.* The application of copyright law assumes that one can identify "authorship," establish "originality," determine when a work is "fixed in any tangible medium of expression," and agree on when a work has been "copied" (Copyright Act of 1976 as amended, 17 U.S.C. Sec. 102a). These are concepts that are beginning to make less and less sense in the context of digital expression and electronic publishing.

3. *Copyright won't work for economic reasons.* It distorts the marketplace because it leads to increased monopolization of information by fewer producers and distributors of information, and monopoly is at odds with our principled commitment to free marketplace competition.

4. *Copyright won't work for structural reasons.* In an electronic culture, it mitigates against a dynamic economy—one that is organized for "constant change," "innovation," and "creative destruction." As many economists now argue, in a world economy based on information as the primary resource, a dynamic economy is what we shall require (Drucker, 1993, pp. 57-62). In the new economy, current copyright protection may be the anchor in the water that slows us down.

In short, electronic publishing is changing the nature of the marketplace and will in turn change the nature of most of these elements—ownership, authorship, the value we give to structure and form, the price we set for access, and so on. In a digital universe, the tangible object disappears, and control of the means of production becomes far less important than control of the means of distribution.

## CONCLUSIONS

### So Who's Winning?

We are not powerless although we have every reason to be pessimistic. As the Amazon case demonstrates, we are inclined to push the rights of property into every corner and crevice of cyberspace, even when it is not reasonable to do so. One recent example shows how passionately we work to extend the boundaries of copyright property even when we should know better.

If it is hard to police the copyright property we own once it's circulating on the information highway; if it is hard to distinguish the counterfeit from the original, what's to be done? Those who worry about such things appear to have concluded that it is probably a waste of time to figure out ways to extend copyright. Instead they are now trying to find ways to control the space in which copyrighted work is stored. Recently, Congress did exactly that. It enacted The Digital Millennium Copyright Act of 1998 (DMCA) and included a provision, the "anticircumvention provision" (17 U.S.C. Sec. 1201). Its purpose is to prohibit the manufacture or sale of devices (or services) that allow us to circumvent technologies intended to protect copyrighted material. As a commentator observed, "liability under the DMCA does not depend upon whether the use of the copyrighted material is improper. The only question under the DMCA is whether the tools allow a person to get around the protection system" (Lessig, 2000, online).

The effect of this provision is that one can have a "locked box" in which material resides that readers have every right to use. The issue is not, though, what we use and whether it is legal to use it. Rather the issue is whether we have "broken into" the box. It's the tool that's protected (or the tool that's subject to criminal proceedings), not the content.

> The DMCA . . . reaches more broadly than copyright law, and here then is the emerging conflict. . . . Before an act of use can constitute a copyright violation, the court must consider whether the use, in the context, is fair [use].
>
> But the DMCA admits no such limitation. The question the anticircumvention provision asks is simply whether the copy protection can be avoided. Therefore, code that cracks a protection device is criminal under the DMCA even if the use of the copyrighted material that the code enables would be fair use. (Lessig, 2000, online)

What is noteworthy in this legislation is that it prohibits unauthorized access to a work even if the work is itself not copyrighted or if we might reasonably use it under the fair use doctrine. Congress has apparently decided that if it cannot protect content, it can outlaw the burglar's tools. Here is a victory for the construction trade, the road builders who design the information highway, regulate the infrastructure, and create systems of access and distribution.

### Extending the Highway

There have been, of course, a feverish number of mergers and acquisitions in the last few years that have brought together conduit and content—publishing houses, networks, cable companies, and the Internet. One rather heroic example that illustrates the shifting landscape is Time Warner. In 1989, Time Inc merged with Warner Communications. In 1996, it merged with Turner Broadcasting. In 1998, Warner established a distribution agreement (a virtual merger) with the cable company TCI. In January of 2000, it announced plans to merge with AOL (Miller, 1996; Okrent, 2000).

Although the mergers of Time Warner might suggest that content and conduit are equally important, some suggest that the mergers are essentially a way of getting control of a distribution network that combines all media. George

Gilder (1994), for example, contends that the new economic model is merely to control the conduit (e.g., the means of distribution) because it is there that the marketplace will function best. Marketplace economics will be to make each conduit so attractive that subscribers will wish to use it. As a result, the conduit/cable/information network will run as much information as it can to attract a large audience. The Time Warner merger with AOL certainly suggests that the distribution system is central to the story of who is going to control the intellectual property and discussion of the current century.

If we are in doubt about who is winning—is it those who live on the frontier where information is free; those who navigate in cyberspace where information navigators and users collaborate; or those owning the information highway?—we need only look to the record of the stock market. In mid-April 2000, Cisco passed Microsoft as the world's most "valuable" firm with a market value of $550 billion (Greenfeld, 2000). Cisco is the Internet road builder, the maker of the routers, switchers, and related hardware that move information across the Internet. Microsoft is the old king—the great content provider of the electronic frontier who made its fortune by promoting the use of their manufacturing systems (MS-DOS, Windows, and Word). For the moment, at least, the road builders seem to be winning (Berenson, 2000; Greenfeld, 2000). It's in an understanding of this—the infrastructure is most important—that has informed the DMCA and the explosive growth of companies like Cisco, Yahoo!, Sun Microsystems, and Netscape. (It is an understanding of the value of the highway that also motivated Microsoft to launch itself on the Internet and push to make its Internet browser the primary gateway of choice.)

The struggle with copyright ownership and protection could be yesterday's battle—nearly irrelevant but still one we fight. Like so many cold warriors, we busy ourselves fighting today's campaigns with an eye to yesterday's defeats. If we are interested in preserving access and promoting new innovations, we need to turn our attention to the new landscape, asking what access will mean when both law and ownership restrict control of the information highway. In the meantime, we need to re-think our notions about copyright and the purposes that it was meant to serve. Its purposes may be worthy, but the way we achieve them in a digital environment may not be.

## How Can We Protect Our Social Interests?

We do have some alternatives. If we do wish to protect copyrightable works without creating barriers to access, we can do so, but we shall need to rework the copyright system, keeping the following principles in mind:

1. The primary purpose of copyright law is to benefit society, not to benefit the copyright owner. The constitutional grant of a "limited monopoly" must be taken to mean exactly that—a privilege bestowed

out of social necessity to stimulate invention and creativity but granted somewhat grudgingly by society as a means to an end—the public welfare.
2. Decentralized access and decentralized personal use of information is critical to social interests. Intellectual property "rights" should be assessed on the basis of whether they produce more information in the hands of more people. When they do not, the "rights" should be curtailed.
3. The statutory monopoly created by the copyright law, especially as applied to electronic media, blesses an anticompetitive spirit that encourages inefficiency and engenders a concentration of economic power and social control.
4. Copyright protection should be for a limited duration or should require that the applicant satisfy more rigorous standards: that the work promotes a significant social purpose that justifies an extended monopoly.

For those who wish protection, access that is too easy is an invitation to piracy. For those who wish easy access or, at least, inexpensive access, protection that is too strict raises the specter of monopoly and a restricted or expensive public dialogue. If we must pay each time we wish to read the news, study U.S. history, or read those basic primers that help us learn to read, write, and do math, we may find that some of us are excluded because we cannot come up with the price of admission. Who will pay for those too poor to pay for themselves?

## Alternatives

From a merely technical point of view, it does look like a digital culture will force us to rethink what we mean by such commonplaces as ownership, originality, authorship, and a "free" access to ideas. But we can't stop there. Those questions of definition are basically conservative ones. How can we adapt present law and its principles to the new technology (Lessig, 1999)? We must go further, trying to take control over the technology. What kind of economy and workplace do we want. This is the hard question since it assumes that we can control both the technology and the economy.

One way to figure out what's going on is to take some cues from the past. It is easy enough when talking about copyright and property to think only in material terms. What do I own? What will it cost me to get this material? These are useful questions, but they divert us from more interesting questions. Earlier, I argued that the principle of copyright is bound up in certain post-medieval notions about property that lead us to treat ideas as commodities. This was only possible when ideas and language (like land itself) had been shorn of self-defining roles. In a commodities marketplace, one no longer thinks of property or language as carrying duties, defining relationships, expressing responsibilities.

Rather they are items given value only because they can be traded, and because of that, our current notions about copyright become plausible and self-evident.

In the electronic space that we are entering, such transactions may be less evident. The question then should be what kind of system do we now need. Another way of saying this: what kinds of economic and social "values" do we want to create or preserve?

We might wish to maintain a transactional marketplace—one in which commodities are sold. If so, we shall have to work out a strategy that makes more "permanent," "finite," and "tangible," electronic images that are now not permanent, finite, and tangible. Once we've concluded that that is the value system we wish, we shall, no doubt, find a strategy that works. We need to take some of our clues for a structure from the past—the way we enclosed the commons to enhance control and efficiency and made feudal property into real estate to free up land so it could be invested like capital in an economic expansion.

On the other hand, especially if we focus on the plight of the economic "have-nots" and the requirements of economic "start-ups," we might wish to build a system based on access, similar to the open commons or to the scarcity economy of the scribal culture, both of which promoted distribution of old and new learning and assisted the development of scarce resource. (Currently the structure of Internet has many similarities to the open commons. It was designed to encourage access, promote sharing and the exchange of skills and ideas, Kapor, 1993.) Or we might want a scheme like that found in the feudal system— one in which "property" was inextricably interwoven with ideas of service owed to those who use the land.

## Other Schemes

What might such an alternative scheme look like? If, for example, we wished to emphasize ideas of services and the relationships between intellectual property and those who use it, we might dramatically reduce the duration of the copyright. To stay in the market—ahead of competition—the publisher would need to provide incentives to potential buyers. Especially in the case of publishers of software or databases, the limited life of their product creates opportunity for the sale of revisions. Publishers have other ways of bonding their products to potential buyers. They can offer support (800 numbers, manuals, and discounted upgrades) as ways of "selling" service and selling their products.

The economics of software publishing would support this shift. Service is a commodity that cannot be infringed on, and operating manuals and documentation are easily protected under conventional copyright principles. According to some calculations, only 6% to 13% of the price of software can be attributed to its manufacture and revision. On the other hand, documentation accounts for 35% to 40% of the price, and service accounts for 2% to 4%. About 50% of the price can be attributed to marketing, packaging, promotion, and advertising (Beyers & Halcrow, 1984; Garber, 1992).

How might we protect the author? First we should understand that copyright quite often creates an illusion, which weakens the bargaining position of most authors—rather than strengthening it. Authors bargain for the sale of their manuscripts on the expectation of royalties received over their lifetime. It is a fantasy that authors have and which the publishing contract reinforces. Publishers determine the value of a book in the marketplace almost completely—by how much they are willing to invest in advertising, in distribution, and by how long he is willing to keep the book in circulation. Finally, perhaps not surprisingly, copyrights are for the most part the property of corporation, not of individual authors, and the revenue from them goes to the corporate owner. (In a study undertaken by the Copyright Office as part of the process leading to enactment of the 1976 Copyright Act [Blaisdell, 1959], it was determined that 85% of all revenues generated by copyrightable material was earned by corporate creators or their employees. There's every reason to assume that the percentage of corporate ownership has increased over the last 30 years.) Quite possibly, given the limited return most authors receive for their work under copyright law, they should learn to bargain more wisely and negotiate a clearer contract for labor done and would learn this if the copyright scheme were dramatically constrained.

If we wish to stimulate more authors and more work, there are stratagems to do so. To strengthen the hand of the author in negotiating with the publisher, we might require that copyright be granted only to human beings, thereby eliminating corporate copyright. We might rework the tax code so that authors are entitled to deductions and depreciations similar to those we give businesses and investors. We might take the approach of Ireland, which exempts the income of all authors from taxation.

\* \* \*

Our laws are not developed to protect authors or to promote service, no matter what we say to rationalize it (Mobilio, 1994). We have not yet re-fashioned the property lines of intellectual property because we would still like to try to keep it a commodity.

The point is that a discussion of copyright is not merely a legal argument, nor for that matter, an economic one. It reflects a view of language, culture, and the relationships we mean to have with each other. It is this we have to work through.

What we know—or at least, what we are beginning to feel—is that we've entered a new age where most conventions (be they legal or economic) no longer seem to apply and are not easily rationalized. Still, most of us live and work in an industrial economy, and it is the metaphor of that economy and space that still applies and the one we must try to understand before we move on.

## REFERENCES

*Abrams v. United States,* 250 U.S. 616 (1919).

Arendt, H. (1959). *The human condition.* New York: Doubleday.

Baumol, W. J. (1977). Testimony. *Transcript of CONTU meeting No. 15* (NTIS No. PB-271 326, July 1977).

Barlow, J. P. (1994, March). The economics of ideas: A framework for rethinking patents and copyrights in the Digital Age. *Wired,* pp. 84-90, 126-129.

Bettig, R. (1996). *Copyright culture: The political economy of intellectual property.* Boulder, CO: Westview Press.

Berenson, A. (2000, April 23). Seeking solid ground amid falling bodies. *The New York Times,* pp. BU1, BU6-BU8.

Beyers, C., & Halcrow, A. (1984, March). What's behind the price of software? *Interface Age, 59,* 61-63.

Blaisdell, W. (1959). *Size of the copyright industries.* Cong. Senate Subcommittee on Patents, Trademarks, and Copyrights of the Senate Comm. On the Judiciary, 86th Cong., 1st Sess. Study No. 2. Washington, DC: U.S. Government Printing Office.

Bolter, J.D. (1991). *Writing space: The computer, hypertext, and the history of writing.* Hillsdale, NJ: Erlbaum.

Boyle, J. (1996). *Shamans, software, spleens: Law and the construction of the information society.* Boston: Harvard University Press.

Brand, S. (1987). *The media lab: Inventing the future at MIT.* New York: Penguin Books.

Braudel, F. (1982). *The wheels of commerce* (S. Reynolds, Trans.). New York: Harper & Row. (Vol. 2, *Civilization & capitalism: 15th-18th Century.* 3 vols. 1981-84).

Braunstein,Y.M. (1981). The functioning of information markets. In H. A. Shaw (Ed.), *Issues in information policy* (pp. 57-74). Washington, DC: National Telecommunications and Information Administration.

Braunstein, Y.M., Fischer, D.M., Ordover, J.A., & Baumol, W.J. (1977). *Economics of property rights as applied to computer software and data bases* (rev. ed.). Springfield, VA: National Technical Information Services.

Breslow, M., Ferguson, A.R., & Haverkamp, L. (1977). *An analysis of computer and photocopying copyright issues from the point of view of the general public and the ultimate consumer.* Springfield, VA: National Technical Information Services.

Breyer, S. (1970). The uneasy case for copyright: A study of copyright in books, photocopies, and computer programs. *Harvard Law Review, 84,* 281-351.

Burke, J. (1985). *The day the universe changed.* Boston: Little, Brown.

Chafee, Z. (1945) Reflections on the law of copyright. *Columbia University Law Review, 503,* 506-511.

Committee on the Judiciary, U. S. House of Representatives. (1909). *Report on the Copyright Act of 1909.* 60th Cong., 2nd Sess. (House Report No. 2222). Washington, DC: U.S. Government Printing Office.

Copyright Act of 1976, as amended, 17 U.S.C. Sects. 102, 106, 302 (1976).

Digital Millennium Copyright Act of 1998. 17 U.S.C. Sect. 1201 (1998).

Downes, L., & Mui, C. (1998). *Unleashing the killer app: Digital strategies for market dominance.* Boston: Harvard Business School Press.

Drucker, P. (1993). *Post-capitalist society.* New York: HarperCollins.

Eisenstein, E. (1983). *The printing revolution in early modern Europe.* New York: Cambridge University Press.

Garber, R. (1992, August 31). The end of the shoestring. *Forbes*, p. 74.

Giedion, S. (1948). *Mechanization takes command.* New York: Oxford University Press.

Gilder, G. (1994, June 6). Telecosm: Washington's bogeymen. *Forbes ASAP* (Tech. Supp.), pp. 115-116, 118-124.

Gleick, J. (1993, May 16). The telephone transformed into almost everything. *New York Times Magazine*, pp. 26-29, 50, 53-56, 62, 64.

Gleick, J. (2000, March 12). Patently absurd. *New York Times Magazine*, pp. 44-49.

Greenfeld, K.T. (2000), The network effect. *Time Magazine, 155*, 47-48.

Guinan, J., Jr. (1957). *Duration of copyright.* Studies prepared for the Subcommittee on Patents,Trademarks, and Copyrights of the Senate Comm. on the Judiciary, 86th Cong., 2nd Sess. (Study No. 30). Washington, DC: U.S. Government Printing Office.

Hagel, J., III, & Armstrong, A.G. (1997). *NetGain.* Boston: Harvard Business School Press.

Hammond, J.L., & Hammond, B. (1948). *The village labourer.* London: Longmans, Green.

Harpold, T. (2000). The misfortunes of digital text. In S. Gibson & O. Oviedo (Eds.), *The emerging cyberculture* (pp. 129-149). Cresskill, NJ: Hampton Press.

Johnson, M. (1981). *The Borgias.* New York: Holt, Rinehart & Winston.

Kaplan, B. (1966). *An unhurried view of copyright.* New York: Columbia University Press.

Kapor, M. (1993, July/August). Where is the digital highway really heading? *Wired*, pp. 53-59, 94.

Katsh, M.E. (1989). *The electronic media and the transformation of law.* New York: Oxford University Press.

Kelly, K. (1998). *New rules for the new economy.* New York: Viking Press.

Kleinman, N. (1993). Mr. Bloom meets an electronic fox—The canon in the age of a new technology. *Readerly/Writerly Texts, 1*, 15-38.

Kleinman, N. (2000). The Gutenberg promise. In S. Gibson & O. Oviedo (Eds.), *The emerging cyberculture* (pp. 61-96). Cresskill, NJ: Hampton Press.

Lanham, R. (1993). *The electronic text..* Chicago: University of Chicago Press.

Le Goff, J. (1990). *Your money or your life* (P. Ranum, Trans.) New York: Zone Books.

Lessig, L. (1999). *Code and other laws of cyberspace.* New York: Basic Books.

Lessig, L. (2000, April 3). Battling censorsware. *The Standard* http://www.thestand.com/article/display/1.1151.13533.00.html (April 5, 2000).

Lopez, R.S. (1976). *The commercial revolution of the middle ages, 950-1350.* New York: Cambridge University Press.

*Lynch v. Household Finance Corp.,* 405 U.S. 538 (1972).

McLuhan, M. (1962). *The Gutenberg galaxy.* Toronto: University of Toronto Press.

Miller, M. (1996). Free the media. *The Nation, 262,* 9-15, 23-27.

Mingay, G.E. (1968). *Enclosure and the small farmer in the age of the industrial revolution.* London: Macmillan.

Mobilio, A. (1994, October). Inside publishing—publish and retain your copyright or perish. *Lingua Franca,* pp. 17-19.

Morris, T.B. (1963). The origins of the statute of Anne. *ASCAP Copyright Law Symposium, 12,* 222-260.

Okrent, D. (2000). Happily ever after? *Time, 155,* pp. 39-43.

Ong, W.J. (1971). *Rhetoric, romance, and technology.* Ithaca, NY: Cornell University Press.

Patterson, L.R. (1968). *Copyright in historical perspective.* Nashville, TN: Vanderbilt University Press.

Peters, T. (1987). *Thriving on chaos: Handbook for a management revolution.* New York: Knopf.

Post, D.W. (1983). Data communications: Online information industry's influence begins to spread. *Interface Age, 22,* 157.

*Roe v. Wade,* 410 U.S. 113 (1973).

Rifkin, J. (1995). *The end of work.* New York: G. P. Putnam.

Samuelson, P.A. (1973). *Economics.* New York: McGraw-Hill.

Shapiro, C., & Varian H.R. (1999). *Information rules.* Boston: Harvard Business School Press.

Steinberg, S. H. (1996). *Five hundred years of printing* (J. Trevitt, rev. ed.). New Castle, DE: Oak Knoll Press.

Tapscott, D. (1996). *The digital economy.* New York: McGraw-Hill.

Tigar, M. (1977). *Law and the rise of capitalism.* New York: Monthly Review Press.

Tribe, L. H. (1978). *American constitutional law.* Mineola, NY: The Foundation Press.

Tuchman, B. (1978). *A distant mirror: The calamitous 14th century.* New York: Random House.

*Twentieth Century Music Corp. v. Aiken,* 422 U.S. 151 (1975).

Wolf, G. (1994). Who owns the law? *Wired, 98,* 100-101, 138-139.

Woodmansee, M., & Jaszi, P. (Eds.). (1994). *The construction of authorship.* Durham: Duke University Press.

Working Group on Intellectual Property Rights. (1995, September). *Intellectual property and the national information infrastructure* ["White Paper"] Washington, DC: U.S. Patent and Trademark Office.

✧✧✧✧ 5

# Back to Plato's Cave:
# Virtual Reality

## Herbert Zettl

*Virtual reality (VR) has been described as "postsymbolic," implying an experience that is virtually mediated. Herbert Zettl here provides a very different perspective on VR, viewing it as an art form that can be analyzed in terms of aesthetics and as a medium that can be compared and contrasted with other media such as the photograph, the motion picture, and television. He also considers the philosophical implications of VR and the ethical dimension of human action and interaction in cyberspace, an aspect of the electronic environment ignored by many. In other sections of this book, further discussion of virtual reality can be found in Terri Toles Patkin's human factors approach to the virtual organization in Chapter 12, Sue Barnes's exploration of virtual ecology in Chapter 14, Paul Lippert's study of cyberspace and the cinema in Chapter 18, and Lance Strate's piece on cybertime in Chapter 22.*

Insert the CD-ROM. Click on Plato. Choose "Republic" and double click on Book VII. A picture of Socrates appears, in the stereotypical Greek attire, commenting and, as usual, asking questions:[1]

---

[1]The quotes are taken from Allan Bloom's (1968) translation of Plato's *Republic*. Bloom entitles his translation "The Republic of Plato." I have documented Plato's quotes with the customary numbers and letters as they appear in Plato's text, followed by the page number of Bloom's translation.

"Next then," I said, "make an image of our nature in its education and want of education, likening it to a condition of the following kind. See human beings as though they were in an underground cave-like dwelling with its entrance, a long one, open to the light across the whole width of the cave. They are in it from childhood with their legs and necks in bonds so that they are fixed, seeing only the front of them, unable because of the bond to turn their heads all the way around. Their light is from a fire burning far above and behind them. Between the fire and the prisoners there is . . . a wall, built like the partitions [proscenium] puppet handlers set in front of the human beings [audience] and over which they show the puppets.". . . "Then also see along this wall human beings carrying all sorts of artifacts, which project above the wall, and statues of men and other animals wrought from stone, wood, and every kind of material; as is to be expected, some of the carriers utter sounds while others are silent." [514a-c; p. 193] . . . "They are like us," I said. "For in the first place, do you suppose such men would have seen anything of themselves and one another other than the shadows cast by the fire on the side of the cave facing them?" [515a, p. 193] . . . "And what about the things that are carried by? Isn't it the same with them?" . . . "If they were able to discuss things with one another, don't you believe that they would hold that they are naming these things going by before them that they see?" . . . "And what if the prison also had an echo from the side facing them? Whenever one of the men passing by happens to utter a sound, do you suppose they would believe that anything other than the passing shadow was uttering the sound?"

"No, by Zeus . . ." [515b, p. 194]

"Then, most certainly," . . . "such men would hold that the truth is nothing but the truth of shadows of artificial things." [515c, p. 194]

Plato has Socrates explain what would happen if one of the men were finally released, asked to stand up and turn to look into the light. He—the prisoner—would be dazzled by the light and unable at first to make out the things that caused the shadows. Even when told and shown that the things that caused the shadows are "nearer to what *is*" [emphasis in original] and that the shadows were "silly nothings," "he'd be at a loss and believe that what was seen before was truer than what is now shown" [515d, p. 194]. Eventually, his eyes adjust to the bright light of enlightenment and he feels pity for his fellow prisoners. He intends to share his experiences with them and goes back to the cave "to sit in the same seat" [516e, p. 195]. But now, in the dim light, he has become inept in discerning the shadows as accurately as his fellow prisoners, who now bestow honors and prizes for those who "are sharpest in making out the things that go by" [516d, p. 195]. And "wouldn't he be the source of laughter, and wouldn't it be said that he went up and came back with his eyes corrupted, and that it's not even worth trying to go up?" [517a, p. 196].

Click on Exit. Socrates dissolves into some Greek columns.

Have we not picked the wrong CD-ROM? No, definitely not. Although Plato wrote his Republic quite some time ago—at about 380 B.C.—he is talking about virtual reality. His cave analogy could have been written today as an appropriate and penetrating discourse describing our new synthetic world of shadows, an artificial environment that we so proudly call virtual reality. In fact, we hail virtual reality as a supreme technical achievement without, perhaps, realizing that we are returning to Plato's cave in order to become perceptual prisoners. Just as the prisoners in Plato's cave, we willingly restrict our vision by putting on a helmet that displays only a world of shadows, and limit our motion by being tethered by a thick cable to the computer. Plato's analogy, which seems uncomfortably close to our immersion into virtual reality, also directs us to take a look at the prisoners, who, "like us" [515a, p. 193] are fascinated with the shadow world. What I would like to do, therefore, is to examine in some detail how we perceive the new world of shadows and why we seem to feel so comfortable in our high-tech cave.[2]

## THE PROBLEM

The problem, then, is twofold: to examine the aesthetics of virtual reality's visual and aural images, and to comment on some of the major ethical issues of virtual reality. This is a tall order because both subject areas are as amorphous as they are complex. I feel a little like St. Augustine, who more than 1,600 years ago (397A.D.) wrestled in his *Confessions* with the definition of time: "What then is time? If no one asks me, I know: if I wish to explain it to one that asketh, I know not: yet I say boldly that I know" (397/1961, p. 194).

Specifically, the brief analysis of the aesthetics of virtual reality includes three approaches: (a) a media-aesthetic or phenomenological one, (b) an ontological one, and (c) an ethical one. In the media-aesthetic approach, which ordinarily includes the five fields of light and color, two-dimensional space, three-dimensional space, time motion, and sound (Zettl, 1999), I concentrate only on some three-dimensional points, the perception of motion, and the role of sound in virtual reality. In the ontological approach, I attempt to show how virtual reality images differ structurally from other forms of mediated reality, such as the lens-generated two-dimensional imagery of the common photographic arts: still photos, television, and film. Such structural differences have an important, though less than obvious, impact on how we can use the various media most effectively. In the ethical approach, I simply raise some questions about our potential behavior in a basically amoral computer-generated environment. I am especially concerned about the freedom of choice within the deterministic parameters of computer-programmed virtual reality and the potential existential

---

[2]There are, of course, other studies that use Plato's cave analogy to highlight modern media or media practices. For example, Jay Newman (1989) uses Plato's cave as the philosophical basis for defining the nature and value of journalism. F.M. Cornford (1941) mentions that a modern Plato would certainly compare the cave to the shadows of the cinema.

dilemma of decision making in an environment that offers a virtual sanctuary in which choices bear no consequences.

Even at the risk of offending some readers or appearing too pedantic, I would like to define some terms. I do so in order to avoid any misunderstandings of what I mean and to keep the discussion on track:

1. *Reality.* In the aesthetic discussion, I mean by reality simply the actual environment in which we operate and the actual events we experience. In the Kantian sense (Kant, 1787/1956) I refer to phenomena, not noumena (Ding an sich ).

2. *Virtual reality.* A computer-generated three-dimensional image and stereo sound that displays events (objects and environments) and that is interactive with the user. In this case, interactivity means that we change from mere observers or viewers to event participants. As such, we exercise some control over the event display.

3. *Media Aesthetics.* By media aesthetics, I do not mean the traditional study of beauty, form, and emotional response, but rather the study of fundamental image elements (light, space, time-motion, and sound) and how a specific medium—in our case, the computer display—uses these elements to produce specific perceptual responses (Zettl, 1999). I do not include in this discussion the haptic one, which deals with the sense of touch, although there are various efforts underway to integrate tactile sensations in the virtual reality experience (*Time*, 1993; Vingelman, 1993).[3]

4. *Ontology.* I use ontology as the branch of metaphysics that deals with the study of the ultimate nature of things (Audi, 1995). My ontological efforts are limited to the description and thinking about the inherent structural properties of things and events, and how one thing is essentially different from another.

## MEDIA AESTHETIC ANALYSIS

My media-aesthetic analysis is limited to some aspects of three-dimensional representation, the simulation of motion, and the spatial aspects of sound.

### Three-Dimensional Representation

We can witness a dramatic development of representing three-dimensional space on a two-dimensional surface from the time the Greek painter Zeuxis began

---

[3] *Time* (February 8, 1993) reports on the possibility of virtual sex, during which we would wear a tight body suit that transmits the erotic tickles of a virtual interactive lover. Vingelman (1993) reports on a similar development.

adding attached shadows to his painting of grapes to when the Renaissance painters and architects perfected and applied sophisticated rules of linear perspective. But nothing much has happened since that time. There is relatively little difference between the three-dimensional techniques used by Leonardo da Vinci and those by Edward Hopper, such trompe l'oeil artists as William Harnell and Peto, or the three-dimensional renderings of computer graphics. All of them use such Renaissance techniques as overlapping planes, relative size, height in plane, linear and aerial perspective, and cast and attached shadows.[4] The only real difference is that today the painter's brush has been replaced by the programmer's algorithms, and that virtual reality relies more on the mimetic vocabulary of the photographic image than eye-perceived space.

New is the ease and speed with which we can change the image in light and color, contour, and topology. Depending on the sophistication of the taxonomy of geometric transformations, we can manipulate lens-generated images as well as synthesize a great many points of view and degrees of distortions with the computer's virtual camera (Mitchell, 1992). More so, contrary to film and television, in which the change of point of view has been decided a priori and fixed in the editing room, in virtual reality such shifts in point of view are, at least to a certain extent, in the control of the user. For example, when I tilt my head up, I may see in a virtual reality (VR) display a mountain from below, and when I tilt my head down, I see the mountain from above. By turning my head I can see the landscape next to the mountain. These shifts in point of view lead to a continuity that approximates our rapid, yet smooth, cutting when scanning the landscape with our eyes. Nevertheless, such viewpoints are still limited and determined by the relative sophistication of the computer program.

## Motion

Regardless of whether the virtual reality display is nonimmersive or immersive, users do not normally move about in virtual space, but are activating the movement of the screen display through limited hand and head movements from a fixed place. When manipulating nonimmersive virtual environments, we usually watch a three-dimensional screen image, very much like a three-dimensional movie, and change the screen environment through a joystick or computer mouse. Immersive environments are watched and activated through stereo video monitors inside a helmet and a glove that contains various activating sensors. In both cases, we *watch* rather than enter the displayed environment. The problem is that our kinesthetic sensations and our automatic processing of the figure/ground relationships will not make us feel as though we were actually moving through space, but rather leads to our perceiving virtual space move past us.

---

[4]Paul Messaris (1994) makes a case for different depth cues, which, however, do not render the traditional ones (as developed by Renaissance artists and confirmed by perception psychologists) invalid.

## Kinesthesia and the Figure/Ground Principle

The kinesthetic problem is that when I move through actual space, I am aware of my movement and my change of position relative to the environment. I am doing the moving, not the environment, barring earthquakes. In actual space, the environment is being moved through; it is not passing us by. This is why subjective camera scenes rarely, if ever, make us feel as though we are part of the action. Seeing the tips of skis on the bottom of the picture frame with snow rushing past and the horizonline tilting one way or the other does not even approximate the sensation of racing down a steep slope. Even a more gentle movement, such as walking through our living room, is hardly duplicated by the subjective camera that makes the same moves. All we really experience is to see the living room moving on the screen or, at best, a continuous change of points of view of the living room. Our control of viewpoint in interactive VR displays does not make us less aware of the sensation that it is the display that is doing the moving, and not we.

Why, then, are some of the VR displays more convincing than others? For example, the landing strip rushing by in a flight simulator, or the street curving and moving past us in a driving simulation seems to be much more "real" and convincing than the snow rushing by in the downhill skiing simulation. A closer look at the figure/ground principle will help to deal with this problem.

As we all know, the figure/ground principle basically states that we tend to perceive the figure as doing the moving against a more stable ground (Arnheim, 1974; Goldstein, 1999; Rock, 1984). Furthermore, we tend to organize the visual field and, in our case, motion, into hierarchic relationships of figure and ground. As Karl Duncker (1929) points out, we always seek as ground the most approximate framework surrounding the figure. When sitting in an airplane, we take the airplane as the more stable ground. We are the figure and the airplane the ground. We seem to hold on to this perceptual security blanket even if the airplane banks in a turn. We tend to perceive the earth as doing the tilting, rather than the plane. When watching the airplane from the ground, however, it becomes the figure and the earth the ground. We properly perceive, therefore, the airplane doing the tilting. This hierarchic figure/ground relationship is directly applicable to our participation in the VR display.

When we ski down a slope, we are in motion and kinesthetically aware of this motion. We are the figure and the slope the ground. We know and feel that we are skiing downhill and that the slope is not rushing uphill past us. However, when watching a subjective camera display of the downhill skiing, we are basically at rest, even if we can control the display speed and point of view through some computer sensor device. Our ground is not the computer display, but the chair or room in which we are sitting. Even if the complex visual display succeeds in temporarily reversing our figure/ground perception, kinesthetically we remain *in loco* and at rest. And we are very much aware of it (Gibson, 1986).

What about the simulation of landing an airplane or driving a car? Even in a relatively unsophisticated video arcade display of a car race from the driver's point of view, we seem to be more immersed in the display and more ready to act as an event participant rather than observer. I think that the reason for this acceptance is that when piloting a plane or driving a car, we are at rest. We sit in the plane or car seat and literally see the runway or the street curves rushing toward us. Although in actuality we are still aware that it is the plane or car that is doing the moving rather than the runway or the street, we nevertheless are kinesthetically *in loco,* with the cockpit or car interior being the most approximate ground. Perceptually, therefore, we may more readily switch from the actual windshield display to the computer-generated display of the "moving street." In cases in which the immersive VR environment allows us to walk through it rather than merely observe it, the figure/ground relationship will probably approach more our normal experience. However, the problem remains that we still see the ground move even if we are aware of actually walking through the virtual environment (Goldstein, 1999).

## Sound

As in movies and television, sound plays an important part in orienting and immersing us in the virtual reality environment. As we remember, Plato's puppeteers also relied quite heavily on sound in order to make the prisoners believe they were witnessing the real world instead of shadows. In virtual reality displays, we should expect an equally effective audio–video relationship, a picture–sound synergy whereby the three-dimensional visual fidelity is matched by an equally convincing three-dimensional sound environment.

At first glance, we should think that the visual stereo display may best be complemented by stereo sound. However, in practice, stereo sound discloses some serious shortcomings in being truly three dimensional. The problem is that traditional stereo sound best defines the x-axis dimension, as evidenced by the traditional pan pots that move the sound laterally from left to right or vice versa. Even if we perceive the stereo sound from the "sweet spot," the perfect place where the two channels mix into a third "phantom channel," we still don't get the impression that the sound is zooming along the z-axis (the depth dimension), toward or away from us. But the very point of a visual stereo image is that it emphasizes the z-axis extension toward the viewer—a virtual depth illusion that seems to catapult the object not only up to the screen, but through it into the viewer's lap (Zettl, 1999). Traditional stereo sound simply cannot match such a z-axis extension.

Surround sound, such as the 5.1 surround sound system, fares somewhat better in creating a three-dimensional sound space. It adds an actual third front channel and extends x-axis sound articulation at the sides. It also uses two sound channels behind the observer-listener that carry mostly ambient sounds that come from behind. Still another back speaker (the .1 element in the

5.1 system) envelopes the listener with low frequency sounds that often get lost in other sound systems (Alten, 1999). Yet, even when listening to this sound system in an optimal listening position, it cannot match the dramatic z-axis extension of the visual virtual reality display.

So far, the best system seems to be binaural sound that is picked up by two microphones stuck in a dummy head's "ears" (Alten, 1999). When played back through headphones, binaural sound is capable of defining with some degree of accuracy the lateral as well as the z-axis (depth) positions of the sound source relative to the observer-listener. For example, if in our driving simulation we see an oncoming car, we can greatly enhance virtual space by having the car's sound rather soft and "far" when it is seen in an extreme long shot, but having it get louder and "closer" as the car approaches (moves to a close-up), become loudest when it is just about to pass us (our z-axis position), then pass us and fade in back of us at the opposite end of the stereo z-axis projection. There are computer programs being developed that can model human localization of sound with fair accuracy (Alten, 1994). Such programs are intended to facilitate the perceptual illusion that the shadows are actually doing the talking, especially when they are moving toward and away from us.

## ONTOLOGICAL ANALYSIS

I am sure that Plato would have preferred the VR display to his cave analogy in trying to explain the real, and that Kant (1787/1956) would have welcomed it in his efforts to explain his transcendental aesthetics and the difference between phenomena and noumena. But they would have certainly pointed out that even the term *virtual reality* presents an interesting metaphysical paradox. If we assume that all perception is basically virtual, that is, dependent on the conscious perception of objects, what then differentiates the real world from the VR display? Because this chapter is not intended as a platform for metaphysical debate, my "reality" comments are limited to a brief analysis of the structural differences between lens-generated and computer-generated space.

### Analytic and Synthetic Images

There is a rather subtle, yet important structural difference between the lens-generated and computer-generated images. Whereas the lens-generated images are basically analytical, the computer-generated images are synthetic. This means that the lens-generated images are always reflective and interpretative of the segments of reality they select (Bazin, 1967; Kracauer, 1960; Savedoff, 1992), whereas the computer-generated images are always medium-manufactured. We could also say that the lens-generated image is basically deductive, in which optical portions are snatched from a larger landscape event, and computer images are basically inductive, that is, built up from a great variety of pixels as controlled by numbers. Compared to the linear, analog nature of lens-generated images, computer graphics are nonlinear and modular in nature. The lens produces an instant and faithful light image of the object or event it sees, regardless of what the event may be. The computer image, on the other hand, must build its world, painstakingly bit by bit, through a series of elaborate algorithms. In practice this means that the whole world is instantly available to the lens, but that the computer-generated images of virtual reality still depend on what object and event modules have been developed for the graphics palette of the computer artist. Not even a decade ago, Lev Manovich (1992) lamented that "the photographic simulation of 'real scenes' is impossible on a practical level as the techniques available to commercial animators only cover very particular phenomena of visual reality" (p. 14). The computer-generated films *Toy Story* and *Toy Story 2* certainly prove otherwise.

Even then, the computerized images, especially in their various manifestations of the VR display, can be amazingly crude. They appear more than occasionally cartoon-like, and remind us of painting by numbers (which, indeed, they are). Only the most sophisticated systems produce images that go beyond the video-arcade variety. But here we probably need a reorientation of what computer-generated visual images ought to look like. So far, the ultimate goal of computer graphics is paradoxically not to simulate the real environment, but the lens-generated one. Many computer programs have various photographic distortions built into them, such as forced linear perspective (which imitates the perspective created by a wide-angle lens), aerial perspective (which drastically reduces the depth of field in order to show only a limited portion of the z-axis in focus), z-axis compression (which simulates the view through a telephoto lens), z-axis stretching (which simulates the view through a wide-angle lens), and zoom effects (which moves the event toward or away from the observer). Such distortions are definitely not part of our normal perception.

The ontological question here is not whether virtual reality should imitate the lens-generated or eye-perceived environment, but rather what aesthetic parameters and codes are structurally appropriate and unique to this new medium. After all, artificial realities need not, as Krueger (1990) mentions, "conform to physical reality any more than our homes mirror the outside environment" (p. 422). This is, I think, where HDTV (high-definition television) is going wrong. Instead of capitalizing on its own unique attributes, such as the high-resolution image and real-time layering of effects, it tries to mimic the movies.

## VIRTUAL REALITY AND ETHICS

One of Plato's main points in the cave analogy is the risk we take when being exposed to the real world, and whether we would not feel more comfortable remaining in the world of shadows, a world in which we can construct our own safe society with its own games, such as bestowing honors and prizes on the one who can best identify the shape of the shadows and recall the order of their appearance. Plato has the prisoners question the wisdom of leaving the cave only to have one's "eyes corrupted" [517a, p. 196]. In fact, there might be a strenuous objection to such exposure to the world of reality and freedom: "And if they [the prisoners] were somehow to get their hands on and kill the man who attempts to release and lead up [the prisoners to the sun-drenched entrance of the cave], wouldn't they kill him?" "No doubt about it" [517a, p. 196]. Even if we do not react quite so violently toward those who help us understand reality, enlightenment is always accompanied by anxiety and discomfort. The ethical question I would like to raise here is whether our desire to return to the cave of virtual reality is not motivated, at least to some extent, by a basic yearning for irresponsibility, a yearning for not being held accountable for our decisions. Such a morally neutral environment can have negative as well as positive perspectives.

One of the highly practical functions of virtual reality is that it can let us see things that are ordinarily hidden from our view. For instance, a sophisticated VR display can give a medical student an unprecedented view of various organs in a human body, and let the student see how they function under normal and pathological conditions. With the simple movement of the computer mouse, the student can shift them about and look inside them, and even operate on them without ever touching a human being, dead or alive. A mistake in operating procedures may cause an angry computer beep or, at most, a crash. But it will certainly not jeopardize anyone's life. Similarly, flying or driving simulators render even serious mistakes harmless. There is no risk of getting, or having anyone, hurt even when participating in rather aggressive VR games.

However, there is a darker side to such graphic and seemingly harmless VR displays. Today, we have games on the drawing board and already on the market that offer the participants the opportunity to engage in extreme human behavior, such as mutilation, rape, and even murder. In a way, virtual reality provides a perfect existential world, in which we can exercise free will and make any number of decisions, however extreme, without the Kierkegaardian "dizziness of freedom" and the underlying anxiety of accountability (Kaufmann, 1956, p. 17). In effect, we are operating in an amoral environment, an environment free of threats or reprisals, whose virtual character liberates us from feeling any form of existential angst when making choices. After all, we are no longer interacting with real people in a real world, but with synthetic objects and subjects in a virtual environment. Shapiro and McDonald (1992) are quite right when asking whether we should "feel guilty about committing adultery" (p. 106) in virtual reality. The synthetic world of virtual reality seems to promise us not so much how to exercise control over our environment, but rather how to escape from it (Pasqualoni, 1993).

There are other potential problems when we see virtual reality in a postmodern existentialist context. One is the matter of the extent, rather than the consequences, of free choice. Even if the various electronic sensors that extend our nervous system respond to our choices and make the environment change according to where we look and how we gesture, our choices are not free but essentially deterministic. They are, after all, decisively limited by the parameters and algorithms of the computer program, very much like the number and kind of objects that were used to create the shadows in Plato's cave. As such, our decisions will inevitably be based on pseudochoices.

Another area of concern is the experience of extreme human behavior. When Sophocles and Shakespeare show us the tragic consequences of making the wrong choices, we may experience some kind of catharsis (at least, so Aristotle tells us), because we, as an audience, remain firmly rooted in the traditions and mores of a regulated society. But when operating in the neutral asocial environment of virtual reality, we may quite willingly shed our conscience and reinforce basic instinct instead of seeking a liberating catharsis. We may ask whether, as Shapiro and McDonald (1992) claim, "the user's memory of entering the VR environment can serve as a cue that the VR experience is not real" (p. 106). Couldn't there be instances when we will get so caught up in the VR event that we do not remember switching from the real to the virtual world? In any case, will we be able to transfer with ease and without psychological difficulty our responsibility-free actions of the VR environment to the real world in which we are held accountable again for what we do? Or will we eventually suffer some kind of psychosis similar to that of war veterans who, for the act of killing, are declared heroes in one environment and murderers in another?

Finally, we might also ask if or how long we may derive satisfaction and pleasure from eating fruit that is no longer forbidden. Will we be able to remain competitive in an environment that advocates total and angstless freedom of choice? Is there a danger, as Pasqualoni (1993) asks, that repressive political regimes may one day use virtual reality to silence dissidents by immersing them in this limitless world? Or will we, sooner or later, have to establish a new ethical framework for virtual reality with a new value system by which our choices can be scrutinized and judged as good or bad? Will we then have to establish a virtual police, a virtual court system, virtual jails, and perhaps even virtual executions?

## CONCLUSION

I do not want to give the impression that I am pessimistic about virtual reality. On the contrary, I feel that this new cybernetic development is not just another information pollutant, but a significant step forward that gives us a chance to shake loose from our perceptual complacency, to see our world with new eyes, to seek the really real, and to rediscover the value of genuine human relationships. So far, the philosophers are of more help in understanding this new phenomenon than are the social scientists, who have done little to help us elucidate cyberspace or to show us its vast potential and liabilities. The burden is clearly on us, the communication scholars and media artists, to study virtual reality and to guide its course with intelligence, prudence, and sympathy.

# REFERENCES

Alten, S.R. (1999). *Audio in media* (5th ed.). Belmont, CA: Wadsworth.

Arnheim, R. (1974). *Art and visual perception. The new version.* Berkeley: University of California Press.

Audi, R. (Ed.). (1995). *The Cambridge dictionary of philosophy.* Cambridge, MA: Cambridge University Press.

Augustine, St. (1961). *The confessions of Saint Augustine* (E.B. Pusey, Trans.). New York: Collier Books. (Original work published 397 A.D.)

Bazin, A. (1967–1971). *What is cinema?* (2 vols.; H. Gray, Trans.). Berkeley: University of California Press.

Bloom, A. (1968). *The republic of Plato.* New York: Basic Books.

Duncker, K. (1929). Über induzierte Bewegung [About induced motion]. *Psychologische Forschung, 12,* 180-259.

Gibson, J.J. (1986). *The ecological approach to visual perception.* Hillsdale, NJ: Erlbaum.

Goldstein, E.B. (1999). *Sensation and perception* (5th ed.). Belmont, CA: Wadsworth.

Kant, I. (1956). *Kritik der reinen Vernunft* [Critique of pure reason]. Hamburg: Felix Meiner Verlag. (Original work published 1787)

Kaufmann, W. (Ed.). (1956). *Existentialism from Dostoevsky to Sartre.* New York: Meridian Books.

Kracauer, S. (1960). *Theory of film: The redemption of physical reality.* New York: Oxford University Press.

Krueger, M.W. (1990). Videoplace and the interface of the future. In B. Laurel (Ed.), *The art of human-computer interface design* (pp. 417-422). Reading, MA: Addison-Wesley.

Manovich, L. (1992, September). Synthetic realism. *Afterimage,* pp. 12-16.

Messaris, P. (1994). *Visual literacy: Image, mind, and reality.* Boulder, CO: Westview Press.

Mitchell, W.J. (1992). *The reconfigured eye.* Cambridge, MA: MIT Press.

Newman, J. (1989). *The journalist in Plato's cave.* Cranbury, NJ: Associated University Presses.

Pasqualoni, M. (1993, November). *Virtual reality review.* Paper presented at a seminar on media aesthetics and production theory at the Broadcast and Electronic Communication Arts Department, San Francisco State University.

Plato. (1941). *Republic* (R.M. Cornford, Trans.) London: Oxford University Press.

Plato. (1974). *Republic* (G.M.A. Grube, Trans.). Indianapolis: Hackett. (Original work published ca. 380 B.C.)

Rock, I. (1984). *Perception.* New York: Scientific American Library.

St. Augustine. (1961). *The confessions of Saint Augustine* (E.B. Pusey, Trans.). New York: Collier Books. (Original work published 397 A.D).

Savedoff, B.E. (1992). Transforming images: Photographs of representations. *The Journal of Aesthetics and Art Criticism, 50,* 93-106.

Shapiro, M.A., & McDonald, D.G. (1992). I'm not a real doctor, but I play one in virtual reality. *Journal of Communication, 42*(4), 94-114.

*Time.* (1993, February 8).

Vingelman, L. (1993, September-October). S.O.M.A. Sexual orientation manipulation application. *Virtual Reality News*, pp. 16-17.

Zettl, H. (1999). *Sight sound motion: Applied media aesthetics* (3rd ed.). Belmont, CA: Wadsworth.

# 6

# Dramatism and Virtual Reality: Implications and Predictions

## Charles U. Larson

*When understood as an art form and as a medium, virtual reality (VR) also becomes open to rhetorical criticism. Thus, Charles U. Larson draws on Kenneth Burke's dramatistic method to better understand how virtual reality functions as a form of rhetoric; in this, his approach parallels software designer Brenda Laurel's use of Aristotle's* Poetics *to argue for the theatrical nature of computing and VR programming. For Larson, the central characteristics of virtual reality are the virtual act as performed in the virtual scene; also of interest is his focus on intrapersonal communication. In addition to considering the rhetoric of virtuality, he argues that Burkean dramatism is itself affected by the new technologies of cyberspace. Apart from Section 1, other studies that utilize different approaches to VR include Terri Toles Patkin's human factors perspective in Chapter 12, Sue Barnes's exploration of virtual ecology in Chapter 14, and Paul Lippert's commentary on VR in the cinema in Chapter 18; additionally, a rhetorical analysis of e-mail by Judith Yaross Lee can be found in Chapter 19, and Frank Dance discusses the relationship between online communication and speech in Chapter 10. Douglas Rushkoff's essay on information warfare in Chapter 21 offers an interesting alternative to the dramatistic perspective on persuasion.*

### VIRTUAL REALITY: THEN, NOW, AND WHEN

From a conceptual perspective, virtual reality (VR) was "invented" by Aldous Huxley in his classic *Brave New World*, in which the citizenry entertained itself by going to the "Feelies." Feelies were an advanced form of the movies except that they engaged all of the five senses, not just seeing and hearing. Viewers entered a booth, and after planting their hands and fingers on an electronic contact board, experienced sensations identical to whatever was being depicted—eating, fighting, or making love—as if it were "really" happening to them at that moment in the privacy of their individual feelie booth. It is difficult to imagine what a feelie experience would be like, but touchstones to help us imagine one might be the "wrap-around" films displayed in the China and Canada pavilions at Epcot/Disney World, the virtual reality walk down a French street now integrated with the France pavilion at Epcot, the "virtual haircut" one can get from Mickey Mouse at MGM studios, and Alfred Hitchcock's 3-D version of *The Birds* at Universal Studios in Orlando.

In 1984, William Gibson first used the term *cyberspace* in his best-selling science fiction novel, *Neuromancer*, and since then the concept has captured the interest of the electronic game industry, the Pentagon, the pornography industry, and others. Underwritten to varying degrees by all of them, the search began for the technologies to create cyberspace, or virtual reality (Levy, 1992). The concept has various labels including *cyberspace, virtual reality, virtual environment, fake-space*, and the oxymoronic *artificial reality*. One of the Pentagon's interests in virtual reality was trying to determine how it could be used in training pilots, much in the way the old "Link" trainers were used for flight training in the past, and indeed the Air Force used the technology in Operation Desert Storm to permit pilots to "rehearse" their sorties. The electronic game industry quickly saw the potential of the medium to augment video "battle" games. Most of the publicly known advances in developing the technologies that might interface to form virtual reality emerged in the game industry, including high-definition television, digital audio and video, CD-ROM, interactive television, computer graphics, holograms, and laser imaging to name a few. The pornography industry is already marketing CD-ROM materials that employ VR technology—interactive conversations, full-motion live actor video, and a variety of others to titillate porn users.

In his introduction to the special VR issue of *The Journal of Communication*, Frank Biocca (1992) noted that, in 1941, a new and fully functional medium was being introduced, but "few [could] predict the significant influence of this new gadget with the odd name 'television'" (p. 5). Its potential went largely unrecognized by the general public, merchandisers, or social critics until more than a decade later. Today, we understand the enormous potential of television to radically alter society, but, like people in the 1940s, we remain skeptical of the claims made by VR evangelists for various uses of the medium. They cite such uses as being employed to train surgeons who can "practice" operations on virtual reality, correcting "mistakes" as they go, and only then perform the resulting "perfect" operation using computerized laser "knives" and magnetic imaging. This raises interesting questions such as what would constitute "malpractice" in such a case. Another possible use of VR technology is "virtual retailing." Charles Madigan (1993) uses the clothing industry as an example. In this use, consumers discuss their clothing needs with a designer—Ralph Lauren, for example—via a lifesize, 3-D, high-definition television screen. Ralph then suggests that they try on "virtual clothing," seeing how it fits and feels, and then make a "virtual purchase" by placing an order via phone or interactive television. Other suggested uses include invisible "virtual" computer keyboards, "virtual driving lessons," "virtual vacations" around the world (what happens to the tourist industry around the world?), "virtual sex" alternately referred to as *cybersex, cyborgasm,* and *teledildonics* by VR advocates (will this reduce STDs, rape, abuse, etc.?), and "virtual community."

Critics of virtual reality warn of a potentially overwhelming information age, and they wonder how many hours of the day people will want to spend in virtual reality, on the computer, with television, on the phone, and using other technologies that are bound to emerge with the growth of the medium (Ditlea, 1990, 1992; Madigan, 1993). A central concern here is that, whereas other media like television, film, or even the personal computer rely to some degree on interactivity and involve some sense of community (i.e., we watch films in audiences, we "cheer" for the home team on television, and we have begun to "link up" with others using computer networks), virtual reality almost by definition limits the sense of community that accompanied earlier media.

One could think of virtual reality as the ultimate in *intra*personal communication (i.e., the interaction occurs between person, machine image, and one's own central nervous system) and thus is potentially capable of driving Western humanity further inward in the 21st century. Additionally, virtual reality calls into question the very concept of authenticity and what is subjective, objective, social, individual, or personal reality. Virtual reality also raises serious issues regarding our social order such as concern over the degree to which humans might vegetate their lives away playing in a virtual amusement park, never engaging in productive efforts. Another concern is how virtual reality might displace workers who refuse to or cannot learn to use the new medium and its related technologies and "like farriers in towns where there are no longer any horses . . . [become] 'technopeasants' who cannot cope with change" (Madigan, 1993, p. 16).

Moral issues include the right to enslave robots, the use of virtual reality as a tool for propaganda, and whether individuals will be held accountable for the actions they engage in while experiencing the medium. For example, if one commits adultery, theft, assault, battery, or even murder while using virtual reality, under what laws or codes of conduct (if any) are their behaviors to be judged? As Frank Biocca (1992) also notes, the new technology has many implications for the nature of communication research, and he urges researchers to consider at least six general areas for VR communication research, including research on the diffusion of VR technology. For example, will it follow the traditional flow from innovator and early adopter on down to late adopters and laggards? And if so, will it create a "virtual class structure" (especially given its probable price as was the case with early television and personal computer technology)? Another question might relate to the degree to which VR technology will be diffused into varying applications such as medicine, engineering, sports, travel, marketing, and, of course, various forms of VR "entertainment" technologies. He also suggests that because of its three-dimensional feature, virtual reality will probably result in as immense alterations in human communication as did the shift from still to moving pictures and will likely yield its separate semiotics and semiotic codes if Eco is correct about all forms of communication being but separate semiotica (Biocca, 1992, p. 11). Another area for communication research to explore in the face of virtual reality is its likely effects on interpersonal communication and cooperation: What are the implications of VR networks, work spaces, bulletin boards, and education? With its easy access code, virtual reality has immense potential to impact these kinds of questions. Another research area for potential exploration that may be impacted by virtual reality and its implications is, as noted earlier, rhetorical criticism.

## VIRTUAL REALITY AND THE PENTAD

It is possible, then, to speculate about how virtual reality can and does impact dramatistic theory and research, especially as articulated by Kenneth Burke (1969) in his "Terms of Dramatism." In his introduction to the five key terms in *A Grammar of Motives*, Burke noted,

> Any complete statement about motives will offer *some kind* of answers to these five questions: what was done (*act*) when or where it was done (*scene*), who did it (*agent*), how he did it (*agency*), and why (*purpose*) . . . in pondering matters of human motivation, one can simplify the subject by this pentad of key terms which are understandable almost at a glance. They need never to be abandoned since all statements that assign motives can be shown to arise out of them and to terminate in them. (pp. xv-xvi; emphasis in original)

Numerous pieces of insightful and valuable communication research have resulted from and validate Burke's confidence in his key terms and their ability to explain human motivation. As Gozzi and Haynes (1992; Gozzi, 1993) argue, television has significantly implanted the metaphor of the drama into everyday life—especially for those who cannot remember life without television. For these persons the dramatic metaphor and the terms of the pentad seem natural, logical, and obvious as Burke implies.

Enter virtual reality. It potentially alters the way we all think about, define, and apply these five key terms. *Act* becomes "virtual act" or an act that "almost" occurs. Likewise with the other terms of the pentad—*scene* becomes a "virtual scene" or an "almost" scene; *agent* loses some of its identity to "virtual agent," *purpose* is transformed into "virtual purpose," and *agency* to "virtual agency." Within the context of virtual reality, let us explore in more detailed analysis two of Burke's key terms—*act* and *scene.*

## VIRTUAL ACT

The *act* that occurs in virtual reality is rarely shared or in Burke's (1969) words "'addressed' to some person or to some advantage" (p. xvii). The virtual act is a private affair, never externally enacted. Thus, in virtual reality, acts never "really" occur in the same way Burke envisioned—virtual acts are innately private and intrapersonal just as other nonoccurring acts (e.g., dreams and fantasies) never "really" occur and, for the most part, remain unaddressed to any audience other than the self. Instead, such nonoccurring acts become totally internalized, both within the VR device and within the brain of the virtual interactant. However, although virtual acts never really occur in the objective world (except in the computer print-outs that sometimes accompany virtual battle games), they surely seem to occur in the subjective "reality" of the VR user's central nervous system. In virtual reality, Burke's term *act* thus becomes "agentified" by the VR participants who act to turn their gaze and who use the glove or joystick to shoot enemies on the video screen. It is the agent's psyche, nerve endings, and past history that make any given virtual event possible. The relationship between act and agent in virtual reality mirrors the two paradoxical meanings for the word *cleave*. In one use *to cleave* means "to adhere closely; to stick; to cling" and in the alternate definition *to cleave* means "to split asunder; to divide." In virtual reality, act and agent are impossible to cleave, yet are always cloven.

Not to worry—in his discussion of the pentad and the ambiguity that arises out of distinctions (such as the terms of the pentad), Burke (1969) tells us that such distinctions:

> Arise out of a great central liquid where all is merged. . . . Let one of these distinctions return to its source, and in this alchemic center it may be remade . . . whereat it may be again thrown forth as a new crust, a different distinction. So that A may become non-A. . . . And so with our five terms. . . . Their participation in a common ground makes for transformability. (p. xix)

Because of the nature of the VR medium, what Burke calls "a merger" between act and agent is accomplished. But what about the scene in which this merger occurs?

## VIRTUAL SCENE

Burke (1969) describes *scene* as the "setting" or "background" (including time place and occasion) and seems to take a proscenium perspective in most of his examples. The viewer always remains outside the scene looking in through the fourth wall. For example, he observed that:

> From the motivational point of view, there is implicit in the quality of the scene the quality of the action that is to take place within it. . . . Thus when the curtain rises to disclose a given stage-set, this stage-set contains, simultaneously implicitly all that the narrative is to draw out as a sequence explicitly. Or, if you will, the stage set contains the action *ambiguously* . . . and in the course of the play's development, this ambiguity is converted into a corresponding *articulasy*. (p. 7; emphasis in original)

In virtual reality, the scenes—video battles, airplane cockpits, hospital operating rooms, driving lessons, or love nests—never fully appear to VR interactants because the interactants are not on the outside looking in as in a proscenium theater—they are on the inside looking *around*. The interactants must turn their heads and gaze beyond the fourth wall and around its limits to observe not only the wings, but the entire theater, including the grand circle, the various balconies, the back of the house, and even the exits. By doing so, they locate places, enemies, lovers, events, occupations, and so on, and choose to interact with them or not. Thus, the scene in virtual reality is greatly expanded and always incomplete; it is a "virtual scene" or (like an inexpensive turkey)—a scene with "parts missing." The "virtual scene" also always remains in flux; it changes in the parts observed and their affects as well as in the parts unobserved and their implied but unrealized affects. Both sets of affects depend on where the interactants choose to turn their heads. In its present manifestations, the scene for virtual reality consists not only of the VR device being used or the settings depicted on the screen, in the cockpit, or via the viewing helmet, but as internally perceived by the interactant. In that sense, like the virtual act, the virtual scene becomes "agentified" or merged with the agent. As Burke (1969) observes: "It is a principle of drama that the nature of acts and agents should be consistent with the nature of the scene . . . [and that] . . . the scene is a fit 'container' for the act" (p. 3), and that "scene is to act as implicit is to explicit" (p. 7).

To Burke, the scene implies motivation as well—the setting beckons the agent to action, inviting him or her to enter it and follow their own motivations and courses of action. Burke exemplifies this motivational aspect of the scene in a reference to Hamlet's temptation to follow the ghost of his murdered father. Horatio articulates that motivation when he warns Hamlet, using scenic motivations apparent in his words:

> What if it tempt you toward the flood my lord,
> Or to the dreadful summit of the cliff
> That beetles o'er his base into the sea,
> and there assume some other horrible form,
> Which might deprive your sovereignty of reason,
> And draw you into madness. Think of it;
> The very place puts toys of desperation
> Without more motive, into every brain
> That looks so many fathoms to the sea
> And hears it roar beneath. (p. 6)

Burke (1969) hypothesizes that Horatio fears that "the shear natural surroundings might be enough to provide a man with a motive for an act as desperate and absolute as suicide" (p. 6). However, motivation and action are not synonymous. In objective reality, the agent *must choose* to act and follow or not to follow the paths implicit in the scene. In virtual reality, the interactant *must decide* to look left, look right, zoom in, zoom out, or remain static, and the results of his or her decisions determine an infinite web of potential and subsequent paths to follow—any and all of them determined by their agentification for good or evil: "The agent is the author of his acts which are descended from him, being good progeny if he is good, or bad progeny if he is bad, wise progeny if he is wise, silly progeny if he is silly" (Burke, 1969, p. 16).

Unlike live theater or mediated dramas in print or on electronic media, the agentified scene in the mind of the of VR audience member takes at least partial control of the scene on the VR screen and manipulates it to some degree for his or her purposes using the agency of VR technology. Burke (1969) seems to have anticipated the quicksilver nature of virtual reality as transformed into individual sensation and experience to produce a "virtual drama." He reminds us that:

> There is of course, a circular possibility in the terms. If an agent acts in keeping with his nature as agent (act-agent ratio), he may change the nature of the scene accordingly (scene-act ratio), and thereby establish a state of unity between himself and his world (scene-agent ratio). Or the scene may call for a certain kind of act, which makes for a corresponding kind of agent, thereby likening agent to scene. Or our act may change us and our scene, producing a mutual conformity. Such would be the Edenic paradigm, applicable if we were capable of total acts that produce total transformations. In reality we are capable of but partial acts, acts that but partially represent us and that produce but partial transformations. Indeed, if all the ratios were adjusted to one another with perfect Edenic symmetry, they would be immutable in one unending "moment." (p. 19)

## IMPLICATIONS AND PREDICTIONS

A number of implications emerge from this discussion of virtual reality and its potential effects on dramatism, especially as articulated by Kenneth Burke (1969) and elsewhere. For example, virtual reality transforms all of the elements of the pentad and their ratios to some degree. These transformations arise out of the fact that virtual reality is rarely "addressed" to an "audience" with the hope of gaining some "advantage." Instead, virtual reality, as presently envisioned, internalizes the concept of the audience; only one person experiences a given virtual event in a given one-time "program." In this sense, virtual reality is the ultimate in intrapersonal communication (i.e., the communication only occurs once and then only with oneself and using VR technology), and the "drama" only really occurs in the central nervous system of a single individual.

Another implication of virtual reality for dramatism is that it calls the concept of authenticity into question and merges subjective, objective, and social reality by redefining parts of the scene. For example, the definition of time and its passage are important elements of "scene." We might ask such questions as: Does the setting occur in your time? My time? In society's time? Or in Burke's unending moment—a scene that is always and never "really" occurring? We all experience Burke's unending moment or the phenomenon of having "time fly" at some time or another. Think about what happens to time when we are absorbed with composing and revising on a word processor. Hours slip by like minutes and minutes like seconds. The same compression of time occurs while reading a gripping novel or when one's vacation "suddenly slipped away." Contrast that sensation with what we experience while sitting through a boring lecture or working at a boring task. Here the time seems to drag out forever, and repeatedly looking at the clock only seems to slow its passage even further. What kind of sense of time flow will exist in future versions of virtual reality? The medium, when perfected, will probably resemble the computer experience more than the boring lecture or task. The medium will make "time fly" because it captivates its interactants by involving all five senses allowing the audience to engage in "virtual participation." Virtual participation resembles the interactive films where the audience chooses the direction of the story by selecting from among several "routes" or "paths" for the characters or plot to follow. Thus, it affects the pace of a particular drama's chronology, and depending on the path(s) selected, all five terms of dramatism become transformed in some way. One concern over the effects of virtual participation is that, like the computer, its elements are totally internal and intrapersonal. Virtual reality has the potential to further drive Western culture inward in ways similar to those wrought by both literacy and electronic technology. They forced us to internalize significant portions of daily life and resulted in the interiorization of self-perception.

Another implication, also pointed out by Gozzi (1993), is that virtual reality reinforces a powerful metaphor that has fascinated humans for millenia and that has served as an organizational device for explaining human actions— that drama resembles life. With increasing audience involvement with and within the dramas depicted via virtual reality, the already powerful metaphor of drama as life becomes even more central to our explanations of motivation. The distinction between fantasy and reality become mores blurred as VR interactants become scene, players, and audience in a "virtual drama " that results in captivating intrapersonal dramas reminiscent of Ionesco's "Six Characters in Search of an Author," except this time the plot is "in spades."

Biocca's analog of the impact of television technology on individual and social life provides us with a useful lodestone in anticipating the potential effects of virtual reality as presently envisioned. That analog taken together with the facts that the technologies needed to produce high fidelity, sophisticated, and multisensory versions of virtual reality already exist hints at much. As Madigan (1993) points out: "Information technology is moving so rapidly, developing so exponentially, that no one knows quite where it will lead" (p. 16). A major obstacle, however, lies in the development of high-definition television with enough lines of resolution and enough pixels per line to deliver multisensory information capable of producing not only a sophisticated film experiences, but realistic holograms, digital/dolby sound, as well as realistic odors, tastes, and feelings. And the solutions to these problems will necessitate more powerful and infinitely faster computers. We need to keep in mind though that the technology to produce the primitive versions of today's virtual reality appeared on the scene only a few years ago, and new and improved versions are being developed. Other technologies are also rapidly improving (e.g., hologramatic three-dimensional microchips capable of increasing storage, graphic fidelity, and speeding up the computing process by several factors). And we need to remember that the first international conference on virtual reality occurred only recently. Perhaps we should bear in mind the words of Neil Postman:

> We are a culture consuming itself with information and many of us do not even wonder how to control it. . . . We proceed under the assumption that information is our friend. . . . It is only now beginning to be understood that cultures may also suffer grievously from information glut, information without meaning and information without control mechanisms. (cited in Madigan, 1993, p. 30)

The probabilities are awesome; the possibilities mind-boggling.

## REFERENCES

Biocca, F. (1992). Communication within virtual reality: Creating a space for research. *Journal of Communication, 42*, 5-22.

Burke, K. (1969). *A grammar of motives.* Berkeley: University of California Press.

Ditlea, S. (1990, August 6). Grand illusion—coming soon, to your home . . . artificial reality. *New York Magazine*, pp. 27-34.

Ditlea, S. (1992, October). Virtual reality virtually here. *Hemisphere*, pp. 26-27.

Gozzi, R., Jr. (1993, November). *Ten propositions about dramatism in an age of electric drama.* Unpublished conference paper, Speech Communication Association Conference, Miami Beach, FL.

Gozzi, R., Jr., & Haynes, W.L. (1992). Electric media and electric epistemology: Empathy at a distance. *Critical Studies in Mass Communication, 9*, 217-228.

Levy, M.R. (1992). Editor's note. *Journal of Communication, 42*, 3-4.

Madigan, C.M. (1993, May 2). Going with the flow: It's sink or drown as computers overwhelm us with a rising tide of information. *Chicago Tribune Magazine*, pp. 14-16, 20, 30.

# 7

# Virtual Reality and the Redefinition of Self

## Jay David Bolter

*The conflict between word and image is as old as the Ten Commandments of Moses, and is present in current discussions of cyberspace. On the one hand, computer programming, word processing, hypertext, and computer-mediated communication remains largely text-based; on the other hand, there is much interest in and anticipation concerning graphic user interfaces and Web design, sound synthesis and recognition, multimedia applications, and virtual reality. In this chapter, Jay David Bolter discusses this opposition as it exists in electronic environments and its connection to philosophical arguments concerning reasoning versus sensory experience. Noting that our conceptions of the self are related to our interactions with communications media, he examines the way in which multimedia and virtual reality technologies further the 20th-century tendency to repudiate Descartes's text-based notions of ego and body grounded in discursive reasoning, in favor of a new subjectivity based on nonlinguistic visual perception. In Sections 2, 3, and 4, further discussion of cyberspace and the self appears in Sue Barnes's ecological explorations in Chapter 14 and Lance Strate's piece on cybertime in Chapter 22. Notions of textuality are taken up again in Stuart Moulthrop's consideration of the future of the book in Chapter 15, Camille Paglia's piece on online publishing in Chaper 16, Stephanie Gibson's profile of hypertext in the classroom in Chapter 17, and Judith Yaross Lee's research on the oral, literate, and iconic codes of e-mail in Chapter 19.*

It seems clear that in the coming years two- and three-dimensional graphics will play an increasingly important role in electronic representation and communication. Cyberspace is a graphic space, and the role of prose, of discursive written communication, in cyberspace is problematic. It is not only that prose will have to share this new space with other modes of communication, but the legitimacy of prose is called into question. The growing cultural importance of graphics technology seems to be undermining the power of prose to convey and convince. Enthusiasts for cyberspace tend to subscribe to what Murray Krieger (1992) in another context has called the "desire for the natural sign." They believe that a virtual environment rendered in immersive, three-dimensional graphics makes possible unmediated (natural) communication. Written communication, which is mediated by arbitrary signs, then becomes unnecessary.

If our culture does move away from discursive communication into graphic electronic environments, our cultural definition of self will be affected. Writing in general and print technology in particular have contributed to a series of related definitions of self in the period from the Renaissance to the 20th century: The self has been regarded as an autonomous ego, as the author of the text that constitutes one's mental life. Virtual reality and cyberspace suggest a different definition. The self is no longer constructed as an autonomous, authorial voice; it becomes instead a wandering eye that occupies various perspectives, one after another. This virtual eye knows what it knows not through a capacity for abstract reasoning, but rather through empathy, through the sharing of the "point of view" of the object of knowledge.

## TEXT IN MULTIMEDIA

Computer-controlled multimedia programs might be positioned at the near edge of cyberspace. The term multimedia is often eschewed both by computer scientists and by cybernauts because it smacks of kiosks and other business applications. Nevertheless, multimedia applications, especially information kiosks and training programs, are like other programs in cyberspace in the sense that they use text sparingly, if not grudgingly. A typical multimedia application relies for its rhetorical effect principally on video and graphics and secondarily on sound. Words are used most often as captions for graphics or to identify buttons. Like the label on an icon in a desktop interface, the text on a button is as much operational as referential. The words function as a magic formula: When the user clicks on the words, he or she calls forth some other graphic or video. In other cases, text in multimedia is confined to rectangles and used to communicate only what cannot be pictured easily. Multimedia designers consider it an admission of failure to clutter the screen with blocks of text. The worst criticism one can make of a multimedia system is to call it a mere "page turner," a set of texts that the user examines one after another—in other words, the electronic equivalent of a printed book.

Educational multimedia cannot dispense with text as easily as business applications, but even here the strategy is to displace and marginalize the text. A good example is provided by IBM's showcase hypermedia application called "Ulysses," produced in the late 1980s (AND Communication, 1990). The "Ulysses" in question is the poem by Tennyson, and the application is meant to demonstrate how point-and-click hypermedia can be used to teach English literature. The student can click on words and obtain a dictionary definition, an historical explanation, or a critical interpretation. Whenever possible, the linked material is delivered not as alphabetic text, but as video or audio. If the user asks for a critical explanation of a passage, he or she receives a videotaped interview with a literary critic. If he or she wants a summary of the Trojan War, the system presents a short and very well-produced video—the kind of production one sees on public television. A disembodied narrator explains the war while the screen shows mythological figures on Greek vases or in modern European paintings. The text of Tennyson's poem itself is always available in a window, but the user can also choose to have the poem read to him or her by one of a numbers of actors. In fact, the actors offer dramatic performances rather than mere readings. The user can elect to hear the actor's voice while still viewing Tennyson's text. In this case, a wire frame jumps from word to word as the actor declaims, presumably so that semiliterate users will know what word is being pronounced. The system also supplies video of some of the actors performing the poem as if it were a monologue in a play. In general, the goal of the "Ulysses" program seems to be to pull the user away from the text itself and to replace the text as a network of signs with visual or aural experiences.

What happens in the "Ulysses" program might be called the "breakout of the sensory." Images and sound jump out and displace the verbal text, as if the prose can no longer support the process of meaning by itself. This process of displacement is itself made visible: A video window opens up and competes with the text window for the reader's attention. Tennyson's poem is transformed into a series of video clips, as if these were its semiotic elements. The breakout of the sensory is characteristic of multimedia presentation systems in general, as static graphics and video muscle the verbal text into marginal positions on the screen.

## TEXT AND THE INTERNET

For many enthusiasts, multimedia is not a legitimate prototype for cyberspace; they are more likely to regard the Internet as the prototype. In contrast to multimedia, on the Internet verbal text still plays an important role. Electronic mail and newsgroups remain the most widely used applications, and in their generic forms these applications are purely textual. However, it is not likely that they will remain so, as the technology improves for transmitting graphics and audio over the network. Furthermore, even in their purely textual form, e-mail and newsgroups are beginning to show signs of the breakout of the visual.

One of the peculiar characteristics of writing for e-mail and newsgroups is the use of ASCII characters to form iconic faces. For example, the sequence :-) represents a smiling face and adds some ironic nuance to the previous sentence or paragraph. Such icons, or emoticons, are meant to put the verbal text in context: The writer tries to enforce a univocal interpretation on prose that is otherwise open to many interpretations. The desire to contextualize in this way shows that the implicit model is not written or printed text at all, but face-to-face conversation or perhaps conversation on the telephone. Handwritten letters and especially printed prose have always faced the problem of decontextualization. However, at least in Western writing in the last several hundred years, these difficulties have not led to the development of icons designed to fix authorial intent. With a few important exceptions, such as Sterne, modern Western writers have depended entirely on the prose itself in order to manipulate their own and their readers' perspectives. Often, writers have exploited decontextualization to produce texts that are open to several interpretative strategies. The use of icons in e-mail and newsgroups suggests that contemporary electronic writers are not interested in the distancing and ambiguity that prose offers. Instead they want to give their prose a single voice and if possible a face.

As the Internet evolves, it seems likely that synchronous and asynchronous video will replace e-mail for many purposes, precisely because video offers the users the presence and the apparent univocality that prose cannot. The lure of presence will easily be strong enough to overcome the objection often made about videotelephones: that users do not always want to be seen. On the other hand, text need not vanish from electronic communication: Many kinds of documents may continue to be transmitted. Documents may be appended to and sent along with video messages, just as they are appended to ASCII electronic mail today.

Another important manifestation of text on the Internet is the text-based virtual environment called MUD (and its variations, MOO, MUSE, MUSH, and so on). It has often been noted that MUDs (Multi-User Dungeons) and their predecessors, the interactive adventure games, have much in common with hypertextual fiction. However, MUDs seldom employ the techniques of distancing and self-reference found in mature hypertextual fictions such as *afternoon* (Joyce, 1987) and *Victory Garden* (Moulthrop, 1992). But these fictions are interactive verbal texts, in which the reader follows electronic links from screen to screen and so constructs the text in the act of reading. In *afternoon, Victory Garden*, and other similar works, the reader is repeatedly made aware of the artificial character of reading and writing fiction. MUDs function more simply. They embody the naive assumption of perspicacity: that to read a descriptive or narrative text is to look through a window onto another world. With current network technology, a MUD is an example of the classical rhetorical device of *ekphrasis,* the elaborate description in prose or poetry of a striking object or scene. What is unusual is the collaborative character of the ekphrasis. Many writers may work together to create the world, often a building or built environment with a specialized area devoted to each activity. These same and other users then occupy the rooms synchronously and asynchronously, leaving behind their textual traces. In a typical MUD, a user adopts a persona, consisting of a name (say, Luke Skywalker or Madonna) and set of characteristics. He or she can then enter the MUD and travel from room to room. If the writer types a sentence in quotation marks, that sentence is broadcast as his or her utterance to the other characters in the same room. That is, every other user sees on his or her screen: "Luke Skywalker says: '. . .'" The user's typed sentence becomes dialogue in a collective fiction: Each user becomes a textually realized character, and the other characters respond to the text he or she generates.

To participate in a MUD is to accept the illusion of the natural sign, the notion that there can be a simple denotative relationship between a verbal text and a perceived world. Because they accept the illusion of the natural sign, MUDs may be stories, but they are not novels. In a novel, especially in a modern novel (e.g., Conrad, Woolf, Joyce), the reader moves back and forth between an awareness of the text as text and the forgetful act of losing him- or herself in the story. The text is not only a window onto another world; it is also a rhetorical structure of allusions and references. The reader oscillates between looking *at* the textual structure and looking *through* it. Most MUDs do not function in this way: They do not set up an oscillation between rhetorical awareness and forgetfulness. They do not ask their users to look *at* the text, but only to look *through* the text to the world that is being described. There are some notable exceptions—MUDs that do seek to set up this oscillatory relationship between the text and its apparent reference.

The typical MUD is an heroic attempt to recreate in prose what its users would prefer to be a sensory experience. For most users the words only get in the way. Anyone who watches participants in MUDs can see the intense involvement that such participation can require. Repetitive stress syndrome is a vocational hazard among MUD users, as they seek to sustain the rhythms of the visual and auditory illusion entirely in typed prose. So, like e-mail and newsgroups, MUDs seem destined to become video experiences, as soon as Internet technology can support this change. MUDs will then be multiuser, networked virtual realities. And just as with single-user virtual reality, textual communication may be more or less abandoned in this shift. (For a discussion of the distinction between looking at and looking through, see Lanham, 1993. For a further discussion of the illusion of the natural sign in electronic communication see Bolter, in press.)

## TEXT IN VIRTUAL REALITY

Most virtual worlds consist almost entirely of graphic objects: Text is limited to a few words used as labels. In some more interesting cases, the software offers menus that float in virtual space. There is a technical reason for the absence of text. Many head-mounted displays (in which small display screens are mounted over the eyes) cannot make text legible. Users still complain about the readability of text on conventional CRTs, but conventional screens are much easier to read than the current generation of virtual reality (VR) displays. On the other hand, the resolution of head-mounted displays continues to improve. Ultimately, the problem of entering text may prove more intractable than the problem of reading it. Users can hardly be expected to type on a virtual keyboard while wearing one or more datagloves. Speech recognition would be an obvious solution: The user could then dictate into a microphone, and the computer would translate and display the text. However, speech recognition software will not apparently achieve the needed accuracy in the foreseeable future. (For a realistic assessment of speech recognition, see Rudnicky, Hauptman, & Lee, 1994.)

Part of the difficulty of representing text in virtual reality is that software developers have not concentrated on this problem. Instead, both the engineering research and the cultural promotion of virtual reality have focused on giving the user a sense of direct, perceptual (above all, visual) participation. Typical VR applications in telepresence and simulation require little or no verbal information. There is the tacit assumption that perceptual presence can replace words, or indeed symbolic representation altogether. The developer Jaron Lanier has made this assumption explicit. He claims that virtual reality can usher in an era of "postsymbolic" communication, an era in which people show each other what they mean through natural signs (Bolter, 1991). Explicitly for Lanier and tacitly for many others, virtual reality is the realm in which the arbitrariness of the sign can be eliminated. So, in virtual reality we do not see visual elements in the process of breaking out of the text, as we do in multimedia. The visual has already broken free and replaced text altogether. Text is not hiding behind the virtual scene. It is absent, and its absence does not leave behind even a poststructuralist trace.

## THE ELECTRONIC REDEFINITION OF SELF

Our quick survey suggests that alphabetic text is not faring well in early manifestations of cyberspace. It is under challenge by graphic techniques in a way that was not true during the centuries of print. Graphics have played a role in printed books since the 15th century (see Eisenstein, 1979). But with some important exceptions, such as atlases, printed books have firmly asserted the primacy of alphabetic text. Printed books *contain* illustrations; they *are* texts. And they are texts of a certain kind: They define a writing space that is stable and monumental. As our culture moves toward a greater reliance on electronic graphic presentation, the qualities of printed prose are being displaced or marginalized. It seems very unlikely that alphabetic writing itself can be wholly replaced by graphics, but graphic presentation will clearly take over some of the cultural work that is still done by the alphabet. Above all, the graphic rendering of electronic space may well affect the definitions or constructions of self in our culture.

The importance of writing in the cultural definition of self has long been noted (see, e.g., Ong, 1982). In the past several hundred years, Western definitions have been influenced by alphabetic writing in general and by print technology in particular. The printed, prose self has been a complicated creature, modulated by many cultural currents and by various innovations in the technology of printing. For example, the invention of the stream-driven press and mechanical printing in the 19th century made possible the mass-circulation newspaper and the serialized novel with their new constructions of self. Two of the most influential constructions of self in the age of print have been the Cartesian ego and the Kantian subject. In both cases, there was an insistence on the autonomy of the individual and a radical separation between subject and object. In both, the visual and sensual aspects of human nature were subordinated to the faculty of reason. In Descartes's version the subordination was absolute, but even in Kant's version reason could reach beyond the human senses to understand the a priori conditions that made empirical knowledge possible. I concentrate on Descartes below because among the Anglo-American writers he seems to get more of the blame than Kant. (Kant has received more attention from continental writers, especially through Heidegger and those influenced by him, such as Derrida, and through the Frankfurt School and those in its tradition, such as Habermas.)

The Cartesian definition of self was by no means created by the technology of print. However, print technology did offer a writing space in which this definition could flourish. Print emphasized and rewarded the individuality and uniqueness of the author. And in subordinating images to words, print technology encouraged a rhetoric in which abstraction was privileged at the expense of the senses and sensory information. On the other hand, printed versions of the self have been under attack by philosophers and theorists for much of the 20th century, even while our culture was still in the industrial age of printing, although radio and television were already having an impact. The arrival of fully electronic technology does not alone explain the growing dissatisfaction with the notion of the enlightened, autonomous Cartesian ego. But once again this new technology of representation is playing a role in the redefinition of self: It reenforces other popular and elite pressures to replace the autonomous ego as a cultural ideal.

Electronic technology is helping to change the communicative balance between word and image in our media. It calls for a new relationship between (arbitrary) symbolic representation and perceptual presentation. Electronic technology fosters the return of iconic writing and the reemergence of the perceptual out of prose. It is the breakout of the visual that leads to new constructions of the self. In *The Electronic Word*, Richard Lanham (1993) analyzes the shifting balance between the verbal and visual in this period of computer-mediated communcation (see particularly Chap. 1 & 2). Lanham agrees with others that the computer disrupts and destabilizes linear text, but he points out that this destabilization has been a feature of the visual arts throughout the 20th century. The "digital aesthetic" predates the digital computer itself. I would add that this digital aesthetic and the destabilization of text make less attractive to our culture the self defined in printed prose from the Renaissance to the 20th century. Kenneth Gergen (1991) has argued that a "postmodern" definition of the self is emerging, a self that is fragmented, empathetic, and anti-Cartesian: "Technologies of social saturation" are responsible. Gergen includes electronic telecommunication as one technology that is dismantling the traditional (Romantic and modern) definitions of self. Some of Gergen's technologies (railroad, automobile, airplane) simply accelerate the pace in which we propel ourselves around the world. More important, I think, are such technologies as radio, television, print, and the computer, which are means of representation and self-presentation. They are media for presenting ourselves to ourselves and to others, and as such they invite a definition or redefinition of the self.

## PERSPECTIVE AND THE SELF

Electronic technology offers two distinct sets of tools for presentation and representation: tools for writing, and tools for visualization and sensory presentation. The computer and attendant technologies call forth both a new writing space and a new perceptual space. (For more on this distinction and its consequences, see Bolter, 1993, 1994.) Each of these new spaces in turn fosters a different construction of self.

Word processing, numerical and textual databases, (verbal) electronic mail and newsgroups, and hypertext constitute a new writing space. Electronic writing, particularly hypertext, challenges some of the qualities of the printed or handwritten self. The self in electronic writing space is no longer the relatively permanent and univocal figure of the printed page. The electronic self is instead unstable and polyvocal. However, like all earlier writing technologies, electronic writing remains the manipulation of arbitrary networks of signs, so that the hypertextual self is still a written self (Bolter, 1991). The relationships among the author, text, and reader are more complex in hypertext, but the notions of author, reader, and textual mediation remain. Hypertexts are polyvocal, but the notion of voice remains (and can be exploited in hypertextual fictions such as *afternoon* and *Victory Garden*). Hypertext is the writing technology that best realizes the strategies of poststructural literary theory, and so, like poststructural literary theory, hypertext insists on retaining and exploiting the referential ambiguity of the sign. (For more on hypertext and literary theory, see Landow, 1992.)

Computer animation and video, particularly three-dimensional, immersive graphics or virtual reality, are not tools for writing because they are not tools for manipulating systems of arbitrary signs. Instead of a writing space, the computer as graphics engine constructs a new perceptual space. Virtual reality is the most impressive, although not the most practical or widely used, application of computer graphics, and it can serve as a paradigm for the electronic space of perception. Virtual reality belongs in the tradition that begins at least as early as perspective painting in the Italian Renaissance and includes photography, cinema, and television. Like these earlier examples, virtual reality is a technology of illusion, whose purpose is to convince the viewer that he or she is occupying the same visual space as the objects in view. The key innovation is that virtual reality gives the viewer control of his or her own spatial perspective. Illusionistic art since the Italian Renaissance often sought to provide a consistent, linear perspective, but that perspective was necessarily static, determined by the artist. The Italian Renaissance's definition of art depended on the artist's ability to manipulate the viewer's perspective for dramatic purposes (see the contrast between Dutch and Italian art in Albers, 1983). In conventional photography, the viewer's perspective is not as easily manipulated, but it is still constrained by the placement of the camera. Film and television set the perspective in motion; not only could images move in front of the camera, but the camera itself could move. But this motion is determined by the director and editor of the film or video. It is only with virtual reality that the user can have substantial visual control of the scene.

Anne Balsamo (1993) describes virtual reality as a new version of the filmic eye:

> In most programs, a user experiences VR through a disembodied gaze—a floating moving 'perspective'—that mimes the movement of a disembodied camera eye. This is a familiar aspect of what may be called a filmic phenomenology where the camera simulates the movement of a perspective that rarely includes a self-referential visual inspection of the body as the vehicle of that perspective. (p. 126)

An important difference between traditional cinema and virtual reality is that virtual reality enables the viewer to control the placement and duration of each "shot." Just as in electronic hypertext the reader becomes the author, in virtual reality the viewer becomes the painter or the film director. This shift of control enables the viewer to explore the virtual space as he or she will. The ability to change perspective becomes the way to learn about the space. As Balsamo (1993) puts it, in virtual reality the filmic "perspective" becomes the locus of sense knowledge. In fact, perspective becomes the locus of all knowledge because in a virtual world there is nothing to be known apart from the senses. With its filmic eye, virtual reality necessarily construes knowledge as sense perception, not as intelligence of the abstract or the a priori. The virtual traveler defines what he or she knows as what he or she can see and therefore "interact" with.

The eye can be construed as the most abstract and abstracting of the senses. It is so construed by many postmodern writers, as Martin Jay (1988) points out. This construction in fact associates Cartesian rationality with the Renaissance notion of perspective: Jay refers to "Cartesian perspectivalism" in which an "ahistorical, disinterested disembodied subject" claims to know the world by gazing at it from afar (p. 10). But this construction can be turned around. Vision can be construed as involving the viewer in the world and also as a means of reducing the abstract to the visible. For Descartes (as for Plato long before him), sight was ultimately tied to the body. We recall that in his *Meditations* Descartes considered the possibility that everything he saw (as well as heard or felt) was the product of an evil deceiver. To achieve real knowledge, he proposed to withdraw entirely from the realm of perception. He concluded that sense perception itself was derivative from reason rather than the reverse.

> I now know that even bodies are not strictly perceived by the sense or the faculty of imagination but by the intellect alone, and that this perception derives not from their being touched or seen but from their being understood; and in view of this I know plainly that I can achieve an easier and more evident perception of my own mind than of anything else. (Descartes, 1986, p. 22)

## DENYING DESCARTES

No one in the VR community can share Descartes's distrust of the senses. The virtual traveler sees and interacts with bodies, not minds, and must be inclined to deny the traditional hierarchy in which we *are* minds and merely *have* bodies. (This was, by the way, an appropriate hierarchy in an age of printed texts, which are words and merely contain graphics.) Marcos Novak (1991), an architect and VR enthusiast writes:

> The trajectory of Western thought has been one moving from the concrete to the abstract, from the body to the mind; recent thought, however, has been pressing upon us the frailty of that Cartesian distinction. The mind is the property of the body, and lives and dies with it. Everywhere we turn we see signs of this recognition, and cyberspace, in its literal placement of the body in spaces invented by the mind, is located directly upon this blurring boundary, this fault. (p. 227)

This rhetoric places virtual reality in another important tradition: the 20th-century tradition of anti-Cartesianism that reaches from Wittgenstein and Heidegger through Ryle and Rorty to the poststructuralists and various postmodernists. All these have attacked the dichotomy of mind and body, the rigid division of subject and object. It is hard to find a trend of 20th-century thought that does not begin from a tacit or explicit denial of Cartesianism. In a recent article Katherine Hayles (1993) summarizes one important strategy for denial. She describes what Bourdieu and others advocate as "embodied knowledge":

> To look at thought in this way [as Bourdieu does] is to turn Descartes upside down. The central premise is not that the cogitating mind can be certain only of its ability to be present to itself, but rather that the body exists in space and time and through its interaction with the environment defines the parameters within which the cogitating mind can arrive at its "certainties," which not coincidentally almost never include the fundamental homologies generating the boundaries of thought. What counts as knowledge is also radically revised, for conscious thought becomes as it were the epiphenomenon corresponding to the phenomenal body the body provides. . . . Whereas causal thinking that Descartes admired in geometry and sought to emulate in philosophy erases context by abstracting experience into generalized patterns, embodiment and especially vision create context by forging connections between instantiated action and environmental conditions. Marking a turn from foundation to flux, embodiment redefines the role and importance of context to human cognition. (pp. 160-161)

This strategy certainly turns Descartes upside down. We have only to recall his famous rejection of the body to realize the gulf that separates Descartes from his modern and postmodern critics:

> I will now shut my eyes, stop my ears, and withdraw all my senses. I will eliminate from my thoughts all images of bodily things, or rather, since this is hardly possible, I will regard all such images as vacuous, false and worthless. I will converse with myself and scrutinize myself more deeply; and in this way I will attempt to achieve, little by little, a more intimate knowledge of myself. (Descartes, 1986, p. 24)

Now, if the Cartesian rejection of images were the path to true knowledge, then true knowledge could certainly not be found in the lenses of a head-mounted display. Virtual reality is the technology for turning Descartes upside down. Its wandering filmic eye reduces all abstraction to a series of visual perspectives. What it offers in place of causal thinking is precisely that faculty of imagination (making images) that Descartes disparages. The goal of virtual reality is not rational certainty; it is rather the ability of the individual to empathize through imagining. When Jaron Lanier was asked to characterize this new technology, he pointed to new possibilities for emotional involvement. Wearing a VR helmet, "You can visit the world of the dinosaur, then become a Tyrannosaurus. Not only can you see DNA, you can experience what it's like to be a molecule" (Ditlea, 1989, p. 92). So even a molecule can be known through empathy; the symbol systems of mathematics and physics can be left aside.

Knowledge is a matter of perspective, and so the virtual self is defined through perspective. VR specialist, Meredith Bricken (1991), elaborates on this theme:

You don't need a body; you can be a floating point of view. You can be the mad
hatter or you can be the teapot; you can move back and forth to the rhythm of a
song. You can be a tiny droplet in the rain or in the river; you can be what you
thought you ought to be all along. You can switch your point of view to an object
or a process or another person's point of view in the other person's world.
Assuming multiple perspectives is a powerful capacity; only after young children
are developmentally ready to understand that each person sees from a different
perspective can they learn to relate to others in an empathetic way. (p. 372)

Putting Novak, Lanier, and Bricken together, we can see the notion of
self that virtual reality and cyberspace promote. The key is to experience the
world as others do, not to retire from the distractions of the world to discover
oneself as a thinking agent. And instead of asserting its identity over against the
world, the virtual self repeatedly denies its own identity, its separateness from
others and from the world. It does not learn by scientific study in a subject-object
relationship, but by identification and empathy.

In all these ways, virtual reality seems to support the modern and
postmodern rejection of Cartesian or Enlightened thought. However, Hayles
herself remains suspicious. For her the proper alternative to Descartes's
decontextualized reason is an embodied knowledge that virtual reality cannot
achieve. Virtual reality threatens to detach the user from his or her body—as, for
example, Bricken seems to suggest earlier—and such detachment sounds
dangerously Cartesian. Allucquere Roseanne Stone (1991) shares this concern:
"Cyberspace developers foresee a time when they will be able to forget about the
body. But it is important to remember that virtual community originates in, and
must return to, the physical. . . . Forgetting about the body is an old Cartesian
trick" (p. 113). Balsamo (1993) too is troubled: "What is of interest to me in my
encounter with virtual reality is the way that the repression of the body is
technologically naturalized" (p. 126).

From various feminist perspectives, virtual reality is still too Cartesian.
The sense of sight is not adequate to give the user a feeling of complete
embodiment. On the other hand, such embodiment remains the ultimate goal for
many VR specialists. They have designed entire body suits that will allow the user
to manipulate an image of her whole body, not merely her hand. There has also
been serious work on "haptic feedback," so that a joystick or eventually a glove
can simulate the resistence appropriate to the object that the user is trying to
move in virtual space. The fact that the typical virtual interface consists of a
disembodied eye is in part an artifact of the current stage of technical
development. Enthusiasts for virtual reality may sometimes sound, as Bricken
does earlier, as if they wanted to get rid of the bodies. Yet theirs is still a rhetoric
of the body; they do not really have an alternative to offer. Consider, for example,
Randal Walser's prediction:

More than any mechanism yet invented, [cyberspace] will change what humans
perceive themselves to be, at a very fundamental and personal level. In

cyberspace, there is no need to move about in a body like the one you possess in physical reality. You may feel more comfortable, at first, with a body like your "own" but as you conduct more of your life and affairs in cyberspace your conditioned notion of a unique and immutable body will give way to a far more liberated notion of "body" as something quite disposable and, generally, limited. You will find that some bodies work best in some situations while others work best in others. The ability to radically and compellingly change one's body-image is bound to have a deep psychological effect, calling into question just what you consider yourself to be. (cited in Rheingold, 1991, p. 191)

Walser is no Cartesian; he is not denying the importance of the body in defining the self. For him, the importance of the body is precisely the reason why virtual reality will have its great impact. Virtual reality will change our conception of our bodies. Our notion of self will change because we will now be dynamic or unstable bodies. The wandering perspective of virtual reality may not be sufficiently tactile for feminist theory, but it can only define itself in terms of visible bodies in visible space.

Contemporary theorists are diffident about virtual reality, yet they share important assumptions with the VR and computer graphics technologists. Both the assumptions and the diffidence can be found, for example, in the complex rhetoric of Donna Haraway (1991), in such influential essays on "A Manifesto for Cyborgs: Science, Technology and Socialist Feminism in the 1980s" and "The Biopolitics of Postmodern Bodies: Determinations of Self and Other in Immune System Discourse." Haraway's "cyborg" seems to be both a technological monster and a figure of revolutionary potential. Haraway's rhetoric, too, seems to be an ambivalent reaction to the breakout of the visual. Her prose is highly wrought and almost brutally sensual, but it is at the same time full of postmodern jargon and strategies of self-reference and abstraction. Haraway's neologism "cyborg," which derives from "cybernetic" and reminds us of "cyberspace," shows how contemporary theorists are in fact forging a common language with virtual reality enthusiasts.

In virtual reality, the Cartesian ego is dissipated as completely as any postmodern theorist could wish. In fact, if it ever reached the degree of perfection suggested by its proponents, virtual reality would be the perfect technological expression of Descartes's malicious deceiver. It would offer to Descartes's eyes a world that looked completely natural, responded to his movements, and yet bore no correspondence to nature. It was the possibility of a malicious deceiver that led Descartes to cut himself off from every source of sense evidence that might be contaminated. By contrast, virtual reality offers the user nowhere to withdraw to. This is no Cartesian center that is immune to perceptual context. The self in virtual reality is all context. And feminist theorists, poststructuralists, and it seems everyone else (except perhaps a few Thomists and the remaining followers of Ayn Rand) agree that any plausible definition of self must now deny Cartesian detachment and rely exclusively on knowledge obtained in context and through the senses.

## VIRTUAL SILENCE

The self constructed in virtual reality differs in many ways from the constructions of writing or print. Perhaps the fundamental difference is the absence of voice in the virtual self. Like many others, I have referred to the "rhetoric" of electronic media, but this phrase is a catachresis, at least when applied to computer graphics technologies. Computer graphics may be understood as the denial of rhetoric, just as it may be the denial of discursive communication in general. "Rhetoric" comes from a Greek root that means to speak, and virtual reality is utterly silent. It has no rhetorical voice, nor does the addition of sound in virtual space give it one. It is not even silent in the way the printed prose is silent, for in print the silence is accompanied by the trace of the voice that was explored by Derrida and other poststructuralists. Virtual reality and other graphic manifestations of cyberspace substitute sight for sound. And for this reason, unlike MUDs, graphic virtual environments constitutes the inversion of the figure of ekphrasis. For ekphrasis subordinates perception to language; virtual reality subordinates language to visual perception.

Virtual reality denies any construction of self as a linguistic entity. In the space of virtual reality, the Enlightened ego, which was in large part a linguistic entity, is destabilized and ultimately dissolves. The dissolution is more complete and less ambiguous than that accomplished by Derrida, or for that matter by Heidegger and Wittgenstein. Those philosophers were still working inside the textual tradition, ultimately within the same writing space as Descartes. They are all philosophers of print. Virtual space is the abnegation of the space of personal cognition that Descartes envisioned. That space was pure ego, abstracted from the visual and the sensual. Virtual space, cyberspace, is one of pure, if utterly artificial, sense perception.

## REFERENCES

Albers, S. (1983). *The art of describing: Dutch art in the seventeenth century.* Chicago: University of Chicago Press.

AND Communication. (1990). Ulysses and beyond: Knowledge prototype system [computer software]. Presented by J.E. Dezell, "Restructuring Education Through Technology," at IBM Schools Executive Conference, February 2, 1990, Palm Springs CA [videotape].

Balsamo, A. (1993). The virtual body in cyberspace. In J. Rothschild (Ed.), *Research in philosophy and technology: Vol. 13: Technology and feminism* (pp. 119-139). Greenwich, CT: JAI Press.

Bolter, J.D. (1991). *Writing space: The computer, hypertext, and the history of writing.* Hillsdale, NJ: Erlbaum.

Bolter, J.D. (1993). Writing on the world: The role of symbolic communication in graphic computer environments. In *Proceedings of SIGDOC '93*. New York: ACM.

Bolter, J.D. (1994, April). Authors and readers in an age of electronic texts. In B. Sutton (Ed.), *Literary Texts in an Electronic Age: Scholarly Implications for Library Services: Proceedings of the 31st Annual Clinic on Library Applications of Data Processing*. Urbana: University of Illinois Press.

Bolter, J.D. (in press). Virtual reality, ekphrasis and the future of the book. In *Proceedings of "The Future of the Book" Conference* (pp. 7-19).

Bricken, M. (1991). Virtual worlds: No interface to design. In M. Benedikt (Ed.), *Cyberspace: First steps* (pp. 363-382). Cambridge, MA: MIT Press.

Descartes, R. (1986). *Meditations on first philosophy with selections from the objections and replies* (J. Cottingham, Trans.). Cambridge: Cambridge University Press.

Ditlea, S. (1989). Another world: Inside artificial reality. *PC Computing, 2*(11), 90-99, 102.

Eisenstein, E. (1979). *The printing press as an agent of change* (2 vols.). Cambridge: Cambridge University Press.

Gergen, K.J. (1991). *The saturated self: Dilemmas of identity in contemporary life*. New York: HarperCollins.

Haraway, D. (1991). *Simians, cyborgs, and women: The reinvention of nature*. New York: Routledge.

Hayles, N.K. (1993). The materiality of informatics. *Configurations, 1*(1), 147-170.

Jay, M. (1988). Scopic regimes of modernity. In H. Foster (Ed.), *Vision and visuality* (pp. 3-23). Seattle: Bay Press.

Joyce, M. (1987). *afternoon, a story* [computer software]. Watertown, MA: Eastgate Systems.

Krieger, M. (1992). *Ekphrasis: The illusion of the natural sign*. Baltimore: Johns Hopkins University Press.

Landow, G. (1992). *Hypertext: The convergence of contemporary critical theory and technology*. Baltimore: Johns Hopkins University Press.

Lanham, R. (1993). *The electronic word: Democracy, technology and the arts*. Chicago: University of Chicago Press.

Moulthrop, S. (1992). *Victory garden* [computer software]. Watertown, MA: Eastgate Systems.

Novak, M. (1991). Liquid architectures in cyberspace. In M. Benedikt (Ed.), *Cyberspace: First steps* (pp. 225-254). Cambridge, MA: MIT Press.

Ong, W.J. (1982). *Orality and literacy*. New York: Methuen.

Rheingold, H. (1991). *Virtual reality*. New York: Simon and Shuster.

Rudnicky, A.I., Hauptman A.G., & Lee, K.-F. (1994, March). Survey of current speech technology. *Communications of the ACM, 37*(3), 52-57.

Stone, A.R. (1991). Will the real body please stand up? In M. Benedikt (Ed.), *Cyberspace: First steps* (pp. 81-118). Cambridge, MA: MIT Press.

# SECTION 2

# FUNCTION: CYBERNETWORKS AND CYBERPLACES AS ALTERNATIVES TO PHYSICAL LOCATION AND TRANSPORTATION

Face-to-face interaction in real, physical space is the primary mode of human communication. The technologies of telecommunication and computer-mediated communication are meant to function as substitutes and extensions of the primary mode, providing new ways of disseminating information, sharing meaning, and congregating and communing. Used as a functional alternative to a place or a set of places, these technologies give rise to the electronic equivalent to space. This includes all computer networks, from local area networks to the Internet and the information superhighway. These cybernetworks are in turn made up of nodes, *cyberplaces*, such as virtual offices, schools and stores, and other electronic versions of traditional locations; computer conferences, discussion groups, and other electronic versions of face-to-face gatherings; electronic mailboxes, bulletin boards, and cyberspace versions of actual installations; and entirely new cyberlocales such as MUDs (Multi-User Dungeons) and Web sites.

This section begins with Mark Giese offering an overview of the history of the Internet, which is generally acknowledged as the "Main Street" of contemporary cyberspace. The chapter examines the technical innovations, institutional foundations, and cultures of the U.S. Department of Defense and the Academy that led to the configuration of the Internet today. Giese discusses the significant role of the Internet in framing the debate on the "information superhighway." Ronald Jacobson's piece picks up where Giese leaves off in the second chapter in this section, considering present and future plans and policy for the "infobahn." He critically explores corporate interests, the National Telecommunications and Information Administration proposal for an advanced National Information Infrastructure, and public interest concerns. Most significantly, Jacobson raises important questions concerning such issues as access and the impact on older forms of public institutional space.

Focusing in on the specific issue of the digital divide, Frank Dance discusses the problem of separating people into the information rich and the information poor based on the uneven distribution of computer technology. While noting the importance of access to information sources, Dance argues that the more important consequences of the digital divide are social ones that occur because a communication gap is created. In the fourth chapter, Eric Zimmer and Christopher Hunter report on research they have conducted on the sexual content of the World Wide Web. Concluding that popular reports that the Internet is a risky place are quite exaggerated, they discuss the implications of these findings in light of the First Amendment.

Turning from the general notion of cyberspace networks to more specific cyberplaces, in this section's fifth chapter, Terri Toles Patkin focuses on the virtual organization, reviewing research related to human factors in developing virtual reality simulations. Emphasizing its educational function, she describes a desktop virtual environment and identifies elements important for a successful implementaiton of the simulation. Paul Levinson also takes up the subject of education in the next chapter, discussing the potential and the problems relating to online learning. Drawing on his own experiences as the founder of a nonprofit distance education provider, he discusses the implications of replacing physical schools with cyberspace classrooms.

# 8

# From ARPAnet to the Internet: A Cultural Clash and Its Implications in Framing the Debate on the Information Superhighway

## Mark Giese

*Guides to the Internet abound, but few offer more than a cursory sense of its history. In this chapter, Mark Giese discusses its origins in the Department of Defenses's ARPAnet (Advanced Research Projects Agency network), and the subsequent creation by computer scientists of the tangential USENET NEWS. The chapter covers both the technical innovations and the institutional foundations of the Department of Defense and the Academy that led to the configuration the Internet has today. Giese explores the consequences of the inevitable cultural clash between the Department of Defense, guided by it sense of mission in the name of national security, and university computer scientists, influenced by the hacker ethic of the free flow of information. He argues that this prehistory of the Internet and its evolution is important to understanding the current discourse that is framing the debate on the national information infrastructure, also known as the "Information Superhighway." Additional discussion of the Internet and its political context in other sections of this book can be found in Gary Gumpert and Susan J. Drucker's overview of cyberspace as social space in Chapter 1, in John M. Phelan's critical essay in Chapter 2, and James R. Beniger's exploration of the issue of control in Chapter 3; also see Paul Lippert's comments on cyberspace metaphors in Chapter 18, and Douglas Rushkoff's take on the commercial exploitation of the electronic media environment in Chapter 21.*

The concept of a national information superhighway has been around for more than a decade, but with the installation of the Clinton Administration, the rhetoric on the subject exploded. There are several reasons for this, some of a technical nature and some of a social one. On the technical side, the so-called convergence of computer, telecommunication, and broadcast technologies has much to do with this increased awareness of the topic. These technologies are converging into a single integrated complex that will allow access to a wide range of information in as many formats as exist today. This means that, according to the rhetoric, an individual will be able to access anything from online databases to the latest movie from his or her couch. Television is becoming interactive. The viewer may be able to pick from several different camera angles of a sporting event, or, upon seeing a commercial for a product of interest, be able to query the universal box in the living room for more information. According to television ads by the phone companies and cable networks, a brave new world of communications is dawning.

The dawn of this new communications age is made possible by several technical innovations in the still separate communications and computer industries. Among them are fiber-optic cables that afford a quantum leap in capacity over traditional copper and coaxial cables, new compression algorithms that make it possible to squeeze ever more data into the existing copper and coaxial networks, and software packages that make navigating through this sea of data intuitive and natural.

On the social side, there is a growing feeling that the postindustrial age of information has arrived at last and that failure to foster the technologies that make it possible may precipitate a national decline in the global trading arena. There are also speculations that this convergence of technologies will lead to a more participatory democracy. Balancing that optimistic view are those who increasingly argue that these technologies will allow corporate and governmental agencies to invade the private lives of their employees and citizens, thus violating tenets of freedom of speech and the rights of privacy. There are also those who ask questions about the quality of content typified by the question: "500 channels of what?" echoing Bruce Springsteen's lament—"57 channels and nuthin's on."

The metaphor of the superhighway is apropos on three levels. First, it is appropriate on the level of technical achievement in which the building of the information infrastructure is in many ways analogous in cost and engineering to the construction of the Interstate highway system. Second, it also may be analogous in that the construction of the Information Superhighway has the same potential for social transformation that the Interstate highway system had. And third, its original impetus was provided by the military for reasons of national security. In addition, just as the Interstate system was looked on as a more efficient replacement to the network of state highways and two-lane back roads, the Information Superhighway is looked on as a major improvement on an already existing web of computer networks. That web of networks is known commonly as the Internet. The purpose of this chapter is to examine what the Internet is and how it came into being. What was its intended use? How did it grow, and how is it used now? The answers to these questions might be useful in understanding how the Information Superhighway should be structured and how it might be used.

## THE INTERNET TODAY

What is the Internet? Briefly, it is a network of computer networks. In the early 1990s, it connected thousands of smaller networks, almost 1.5 million host computers, and 21 million users worldwide (Rutkowski et al., 1993). During a 2-week period in late April 1993, "87,000 people at 30,000 different USENET sites[1] posted about 26,000 articles per day to 4902 groups" (Hauben, 1993, p. 17). Traffic during this 2-week period totaled 65 megabytes. More than 364,000 individual articles were posted" (Hauben, 1993, p. 17). USENET comprises one of the social aspect of the Internet. It is composed of thousands of topic-oriented "conversations" ranging from electronic want ads to discussions of sex, "Star Trek," or recovery from child abuse. Total traffic is much higher: "3.4 gigabits per second, or, in the popularized measurement, more than three encyclopedias' worth of text a second" (Stix, 1993, p. 102). These statistics are all from mid- to late 1993, but tracking the traffic volume of the Internet is complicated by the fact that it has and continues to have an annual growth rate of 124% (Rutkowski et al., 1993). Seven years later, in 2000, there were 81.4 million hosts and more than 304 million users worldwide with the United States and Canada representing the majority with approximately 136 million users (http://netsizer.com). There are now more than 17,000 USENET newsgroups up from around 5,000 in 1993 (http://liszt.com/news). In 1993, the World Wide Web was nascent. Mathew Grey of MIT estimated that by 1996 (the latest date for which figures are available) there were more than 650,000 Web sites with 62% of those represented by the now almost ubiquitous ".com" domain (http://www.mit.edu/people/mkgrey/net/). Growth continues to be exponential.

This swelling stream of electronic data accommodates not only the relatively minuscule trickle of social conversations—less than 20% of the traffic (Rutkowski et al., 1993)—but also an enormous amount of information related to the original purpose of the network—the facilitation of research, commerce, and governance. William Gibson (1984) coined the term *cyberspace* and described it as a "consensual hallucination" (p. 5). In the decade since the publication of *Neuromancer*, Gibson's vision of a tech noire future, a global network of computers, linked co-equally, has become a reality. The emergence of this global

---

[1]*USENET sites* refers, in geographical terms that are typical of discussions of the Internet, to the topic-specific discussion groups that can be accessed via the computer network. A specific site refers to a specific topic rather than an actual place. These spatial terms are common in discussion about the Internet despite the fact that space and distance, in the traditional sense, are not particularly relevant.

information network has gradually taken shape over the past 30 years and holds both the promise of McLuhan's "global village" and the threat of Gibson's darker vision of transnational capitalism run amok.

## GENESIS: THE EARLY RATIONALE AND
## CONCEPTUALIZATION OF ARPANET

The first wide area network (WAN) was developed under the direction of the Department of Defense Advanced Research Projects Agency (ARPA). The rationale behind the development of the ARPAnet (Advanced Research Projects Agency network) was the Defense Department's concern for maintaining the military's ability to communicate in the face of the destruction of one or more key links in the chain of command that might happen during a nuclear engagement. The major design constraint in the face of this threat was to create a communications system that was nonhierarchical and geographically dispersed. The rationale underpinning the research and its connection with the military was stated in 1962, in the report "On Distributed Communications" by Paul Baran:

> The report proposes a communication system where there would be no obvious central command and control point, but all surviving points would be able to reestablish contact in the event of an attack on any one point. Thus damage to a part would not destroy the whole and its effect on the whole would be minimized. (cited in Hauben, 1993, p. 3)

It is interesting to note here that the driving rationale behind the initial work on the construction of a redundant and highly connective computer network was essentially the same as the one behind the construction of the interstate highway system—national security. Unlike the interstate system, however, the engineering problem was fundamentally different. The interstate highway system was fundamentally a hardware problem—one of building physical structures. The construction of ARPAnet was essentially a software problem—how to connect and get different kinds of computers to "talk" to one another.

The key technical solution that made the Internet possible was derived independently by several researchers: Baran at Rand, Donald Davies in the United Kingdom, and Larry Roberts at MIT. The concept was called *packet switching*. Packet switching entails breaking a message up into several equally sized "packets," with each packet containing the address of the recipient. The packets could be sent separately and reassembled at their destination. The breakthrough concept in this idea was that each packet could be routed independently of the other packets. In this manner each packet could be sent along the most efficient route available at the moment and reassembled when all had reached their destination (Hart, Reed, & Bar, 1992).

Packet switching was easy to implement on a network that was composed of terminals made by the same manufacturer. The problem was that the Department of Defense wanted to implement the concept on a network composed of widely dissimilar computers and terminals. Getting different kinds of computers to "talk" to one another was a thornier problem. It was solved by Vinton Cerf and Robert Kahn, who together came up with the "gateway" concept. This concept allowed packet switching to be accomplished between different networks despite the fact that they used different-sized packets and worked at different speeds. This gateway concept led to a software package known as TCP/IP (Transmission Control Protocol/Interconnection Protocol). Hart et al. (1992) explain the benefits of this software package:

> Thanks to its robustness, adaptability and relative simplicity TCP/IP has become the de facto world standard for interconnecting networks. The gateway concept makes TCP/IP particularly useful for people who wanted to interconnect computers and networks manufactured by different companies. Thus TCP/IP pioneered what is now called the "open systems" approach. (p. 671)

The TCP/IP suite of protocols solved one of the technical problems that stood in the way of constructing wide area networks (WANs), and in 1969 ARPAnet was launched with four nodes. A node on this network was a mainframe computer, typically at a university computer science department, that was capable of addressing, sending, and receiving the electronic packets. Each node might have several "dumb" terminals connected to it capable of displaying output or sending input to the mainframe. By 1971, the network had expanded to 23 nodes and by 1977 grew to 111 nodes (Hart et al., 1992). Almost from the very beginning ARPAnet began to grow geometrically. Demand seems to always have exceeded capacity in the case of first ARPAnet and then the Internet. Unlike the "if we build it, they will come" rhetoric that has dominated the cable and telephone industries' responses to questions about how broadband networks will be used and who will use them, the question for the builders and operators of WANs from ARPAnet to the Internet as it is today has been how to meet traffic demands that seem to have always exceeded capacity despite heroic efforts to increase it. The question has always been: "How can we make the pipe bigger?" not "How will we fill this pipe?" or "Who will use it?" This exponential growth in demand is ironic given the fact that originally the ARPAnet was intended to be restricted exclusively to defense agencies and defense contractors.

Another interesting irony in this open systems approach to the problem of maintaining the military communications system is that an organization known for its rigid centralized, hierarchical organization and its dependency on secrecy was forced into a solution that ultimately went against the ingrained nature of that organization. Despite the Department of Defense's institutional imperative to restrict access, the original ARPAnet grew. There were several factors that contributed to this phenomenal growth. The first, already discussed, was the simplicity and elegance of the technical solution: the TCP/IP protocol suite. It should be noted here that, whereas the protocols were flexible and simple, the arrival at this solution was a time-consuming process that took several years. The problem of getting computers from the same manufacturer to talk to one another was relatively simple. This involved the production of interface message processors (IMPs). IMPs were built for the first nodes by Bolt, Beranek, and Newman under a contract awarded by ARPA in 1969. These specialized processors served well during the period when the number of nodes on the network was relatively small. However, as the ARPAnet grew, it became increasingly difficult and expensive to supply specialized hardware to each node. In addition, the Department of Defense wanted to incorporate satellite and packet radio transmission, as well as dedicated telephone lines, in the delivery system. It was under this new impetus that Vinton Cerf and Robert Kahn developed the gateway concept.

Concurrently with the development and implementation of this gateway concept, the process of debugging the protocol suite took place as a collaborative process among the scientists working at each of the nodes (Hart et al., 1992). This debugging process could only be done on an actual network (Hauben, 1993). Two important factors worked to foster the early growth of the ARPAnet. The first was that an actual network was needed in order to perfect the TCP/IP protocol suite, as well as a cooperative effort by researchers at different nodes in order to successfully debug the system. This cooperative effort fostered discussion of problems and solutions on the network and gave rise to online discussion groups. These discussion groups, in the form of the thousands of topic-specific USENET newsgroups, have become a permanent feature of the Internet.

A second factor that contributed to the growth of the Internet had little to do with finding solutions to the technical problems for the Department of Defense. This second factor can only be described as a clash of cultures. This clash of cultures was between the defense establishment—centralized, hierarchical, rigid, and secretive by nature—and the members of the academic community the Defense Department called on to find solutions to the problem. As already discussed, the design conceptualization of the computer network was one that was, at its very roots, antithetical to the organization it was to be built for and used by. "Open systems" architecture by its very nature goes against the organizational imperatives of the Defense Department. The threat to this institution from the enormous destructive power of nuclear weapons demanded precautions to protect its strategic secrets, its centralized command and control system, and its hierarchical organization. Paradoxically, the only precaution that could be effective called for a nonhierarchical, decentralized, and essentially egalitarian solution.

The computer network, much like the interstate highway system, was to be constructed and maintained by the government. Unlike the interstate highway system though, in the beginning it was never intended for public use. Use was to be subsidized and restricted to an elite group: "Access to the ARPAnet was limited to defense agencies and defense contractors. Within that group the heaviest use of the ARPAnet was by computer scientists" (Hart et al., 1992, p. 670). The question begged by the original conception of the network is: How did the network escape the umbrella of its highly secretive and powerful progenitor—the Defense Department?

The answer resides in a combination of factors that involve the interaction of large social institutions in a given historical context. One factor that played a very important role in this "coming out" is the rather odd coalition of two institutions that had very different internal social tenets—the defense establishment and the academic research community. This cultural clash is made explicit by Steven Levy in *Hackers* (1984), a book that documents the early days of computer programming and the now-stereotypical image of computer "geeks." A basic tenet of the hacker ethic was the free flow of information. A corollary to that axiom was a basic distrust of bureaucracy:

> The best way to promote a free flow of information is to have an open system. Bureaucracies, whether corporate, government or university, are flawed systems, dangerous in that they cannot accommodate the exploratory impulse of true hackers. Bureaucrats hide behind arbitrary rules: they invoke those rules to consolidate power, and perceive the constructive impulse of hackers as a threat. (p. 41)

These basic conflicts in worldviews were resolved, at least on the side of those involved in the early development of computer science and the network, by what Levy terms "willful blindness." This blindness was difficult to maintain in the milieu of the late 1960s. The antiwar movement worked to point out these conflicts, but largely failed.

One can imagine that the military might have viewed the conflict somewhat differently. The task must have seemed much like trying to direct the efforts of a group of deliberately willful but extremely bright children. In the end, the military lost this contest of wills. Perhaps a contest of wills is a less accurate description than one of a gradual subversion of the intended purpose of the network. Taylor has admitted diverting Defense Department funds from "mission-oriented" projects to more "pure science" and research-oriented efforts during those years (Levy, 1984, p. 131). Here cultural tenets of a particular institution are reflected and reproduced through a particular individual's action in an institution and cultural setting that held contradictory tenets and institutional imperatives. These particular actions set the stage for the way the culture of the Internet developed.

## ESCAPE: THE DEMILITARIZATION OF THE INTERNET

ARPAnet could not survive what might be called an almost genetic ideological tenet of the "hacker ethic": the free flow of information. "The challenge which ARPAnet could not handle, and which led to its demise, was to expand access beyond the community of defense agencies and defense contractors" (Hart et al., 1992, p. 671). The turning point in the growth of the Internet was the advent of USENET NEWS in 1979—a "poor man's ARPAnet" (Hauben, 1993, p. 14). USENET NEWS was the result of the effort of computer scientists that were excluded from ARPAnet to provide themselves with a similar computer network. Beginning in Berkeley, they constructed a network that was separate but touched the ARPAnet tangentially. USENET NEWS was the beginning of what is now known as the Internet, and its birth can be traced to the cultural conflicts between the Department of Defense and the community of computer scientists that was responsible for the construction of the ARPAnet.

One symptom of these cultural conflicts was the proliferation of discussion groups. This was due, in part, to the fact that those responsible for the construction of the network initially did not look at it as a medium of communication specifically, but rather conceptualized it as a "tool." During this 1960s period in the development of computer technology, mainframe computers were the only type available. Microcomputers, minicomputers, and desktops were not available, and mainframes were extremely expensive and difficult to acquire. They were used for solving intractable mathematical problems—number crunching. The network was seen as a way to share scarce and expensive resources. However, it was the interconnection, the communication aspect of the network, coupled with the collegial culture of the research community that soon made the network something more than a research tool.

Two major factors played a large role in the expansion of the closely held military network, ARPAnet, as a command and control tool for the military to what has been described as an ad-hoc network (Stix, 1993), commonly known as the Internet. The first is the cultural tenets held by the people who built the network, indicated by Levy (1984) in *Hackers*. The second is the nature of the economic forces that provided the initial funding for ARPAnet. These two factors combined to produce some unanticipated results. One of those results was evident almost from the beginning: "The two most widely used applications on the ARPAnet were electronic mail and remote login services" (Hart et al., 1992, p. 670).

The speed and reliability of e-mail soon spawned what could only be termed "unauthorized communication" on the network. This was made possible by software that made "mailing lists" possible. Mailing lists were a convenient way for researchers to have an ongoing conversation with many people. Essentially a mailing list sends a note to everyone on the list so that one can easily make comments and review feedback from everyone on the list. The original purpose of these mailing lists was to facilitate communication about specific research projects, but tangential conversations quickly sprang up. One was a mailing list with the title "sf-lovers"; it discussed a topic near and dear to many of the researchers' hearts—science fiction. These tangential conversations were tolerated as part of the accommodations that were made between the institutional cultures of the military "clients" and the computer scientist "suppliers." Although documentation is lacking, it is easy to speculate that from the military point of view they were harmless, used few resources, and provided a way to let their unpredictable charges blow off steam. From the other side of the cultural divide they were probably looked at in much the same way: It was easy, it was fun, and it was free—a well-deserved perk.

The clash of the two cultures was directly responsible for the expansion of the network. On one side there was the cultural imperative of the military to hold its assets closely. On the other side, researchers began to resent the exclusivity of access that prevented them from participating. USENET NEWS was the response:

> Usenet News was available to all who were interested as long as they had access to the Unix operating system. And posting and participating in the network was available at no cost besides what the college paid for equipment and the telephone calls to receive or send Netnews. Therefore, the joys and challenge of being a participant in the creation of the ever-expanding network was available via Usenet News to those without political or financial connections—to the common folk of the computer science community. (Hauben, 1993, p. 15)

Like the interstate highway system, ARPAnet's primary purpose was to strengthen national security; however, unlike the highway system, ARPAnet had never been intended to provide access to the general public. Computer scientists not connected to the defense establishment must have felt like eager motorists denied access to a new freeway. USENET NEWS was an end-run around that kind of military exclusivity. In essence, they built their own freeway parallel to the one reserved for military use. Interconnection of the two networks began in 1979. Berkeley had acquired an ARPA contract to supply the Unix operating system to ARPAnet. Already on the ARPAnet, Berkeley joined USENET. This initial joint connection brought into stark relief the sense of exclusion among the non-defense-connected members of the computer science community—between the "haves" of the ARPAnet and the "have-nots" of the USENET. Stephen Daniel notes this division: "It was initially very hard to contribute to those [ARPAnet] lists, and when you did you were more likely to get a response to your return address than to the content of your letter. It definitely felt second-class to be in read-only mode unable to post comments to the mailing list on human-nets and sf-lovers" (cited in Hauben, 1993, p. 15). This shows the sense of resentment felt by those excluded from ARPAnet, but also documents the peripheral and unauthorized nature of some of the mailing lists that had sprung up on ARPAnet. This began the transformation of the conceptualization of the network from a "tool" to a medium for social interaction.

A second major factor in the growth of the Internet had to do with the economics of the network. From the beginning, demand for access to the network and actual traffic has outpaced the network's ability to handle the load. A major reason for this is that users almost never pay for access nor do they pay the cost of their individual messages on the network. Eugene Miya recalls what can only be called the emotional aspect of this method of financing the network and lends credibility to the sense of resentment and exclusion felt by the founders of USENET NEWS that was fostered by the way it was financed:

> ARPA was the sugardaddy of computer science. Some very bright people were given some money, freedom, and had a lot of vision. I think the early ARPAnet was kind of a wondrous neat place, sort of a golden era. You could get into other people's machines with a minimum of hassle (someone else paid the bills). (cited in Hauben, 1993, p. 9)

This points not only to the impact of the government's subsidization of the network on the user, but also provides an implicit view of the clash between the cultural imperatives of the two institutional forces most responsible for the implementation of the early network. An interesting point to note about the advent of USENET NEWS is that its founders were able to maintain, at least from the end-users' standpoint, a financing structure that shielded them from the direct costs of the expansion of the network. These costs were borne by their institutions rather than the individuals using the network.

Despite the fact that ARPAnet was not decommissioned until 1990, replaced by the National Science Foundation Network (NSFNET), the advent of USENET marked the beginning of the end of the military's control of the computer network that was to grow into the Internet. The Internet continues to grow at an exponential pace. This phenomenal growth has been and continues to be fueled by the "free" nature of the original ARPAnet and its first successor, USENET. The Internet is free both in the intellectual sense, because it fosters a diversity of communication among a wide variety of users, and in the financial sense because the vast majority of users are shielded from the direct cost of implementing and maintaining the network. The Internet's intellectual freedom stems from the legacy of the hacker ethic—the free flow of information—the major cultural tenet of the builders of the network. The financial "freedom" stems from the legacy of subsidization of the original ARPAnet by the Defense establishment and the ability of those involved in wresting control of the network away from the military to transfer the ongoing costs of implementation and maintenance to the institutions (largely academic) they worked for rather than to the individuals who use Internet. These twin legacies of freedom have the potential to play a large role in shaping the national information infrastructure.

## EXPANSION: THE ROLE OF THE INTERNET IN FRAMING THE DEBATE ON THE INFORMATION SUPERHIGHWAY INFRASTRUCTURE

The cultural and economic factors that engendered the original construction of what has now grown to a worldwide computer network are changing again. The advent of USENET NEWS was the beginning of a rapid and exponential growth in the life of the computer network. Rapid expansion has brought the attention of private enterprise, notably the telecommunications industry, and has awakened the realization of the industry to a potentially huge new market. The cultural clash between the military and the academic community, surprisingly, was resolved in favor of the academic community. This is, in part, due to both the fact that the network was built by the academic community and subverted almost from the very beginning from the purposes of its commissioners—the military. The subversion and victory coupled with new technological developments and the popularity of this new medium of communication has set the stage for another clash of institutional cultures whose outcome is by no means obvious.

This debate has been framed in economic terms that stem directly from the cultural imperatives of both institutions and can be seen in a brief comparison. The telephone network because of the historical moment of its advent and the social institution of private enterprise within which it grew in its early days has always been perceived as a pay-as-you-go and for-profit enterprise by its users. On the other hand, and also stemming from a particular historical moment, users of the Internet have always been shielded from the costs of using it. In the beginning they were paid for directly by the military establishment, now, while construction costs are still largely financed by the government, user costs such as processing costs, data storage costs, and connect charges are still subsidized by the institutions that the users are members of, principally institutions for research and higher education.

In 1993, Rutkowwski noted, "Most of the registered internets today already are commercial entities. And most of the growth today of internets and the Internet is dramatically commercial" (p. 20). There has been a flood-tide of commercialization characterized by the growing ubiquity of the term *e-commerce.* In hindsight it seems almost inevitable. How far this trend will go and what effect it has on the shape of the national information infrastructure remains to be seen. However, there are factors in play that give rise to the hope that the chaotic diversity of the Internet as it is today will not be completely obscured by the profit motives of the large commercial interests who are the most vociferous proponents of the Information Superhighway. One of the biggest factors may simply be the existence of the Internet and its present constituency. Bruce Sterling (1992) makes a strong argument for this in the last chapter of his book, *The Hacker Crackdown,* citing the organization of the Electronic Frontier Foundation as an exemplar.

A comparison of the computer network as it exists today (essentially in its infancy) and the rise of the telephone network may be useful in understanding how the debate on the information infrastructure has been framed. There are several interesting parallels as well as some interesting divergences. In the beginning, both the phone network and the computer network were restricted to social elites. In the case of the telephone network that elite was the economically privileged. Use was restricted to businesses and the rich upper class. This was due, in large part, to the cost of the technology and the commercial nature of the enterprise. Because the telephone company had an organizational imperative to acquire capital—make a profit—it catered to those users who could afford to finance its technological innovation. In the case of the computer network, as we have seen, the elite class that was cultivated was intellectual rather than economic. Once again this was due in large part to the nature of the way the construction of the network was financed. Because the organizational imperative was different—in this case, national security rather than profit—the cost of development was directed by the military and financed by the taxing authority of the national government.

At the social level, the uses the two networks were put to were originally restricted as well. The diffusion of telephone technology and its use in a social and communal mode was surprising to its enabling institution. Sidney Aronson (1977) noted that "company officials were still somewhat influenced by the concepts that governed the telegraph industry; they saw that medium primarily as an aid to commerce and had given little priority to social telegraphy" (p. 26). The same is true about the advent of discussion groups not related to computer science problems or the construction of the computer network. Both the telephone company and the Defense Department envisioned communication networks that were "strictly business," when in reality both networks were put to more communal and social uses. Although the move to more social uses was unanticipated to both institutions, the motivating forces for that move were different. In the case of the telephone, it was the need by the phone company to expand a market and increase profits. In the case of the computer network, it was largely driven by the users themselves.

From a technical standpoint, the initial conceptualizations of the two networks were driven by differing institutional economic imperatives. The technologies that engendered the telephone network were originally thought of as having no particular use. It was looked on as a novelty. William Orton, head of Western Union, dismissed the new invention as an "electrical toy" when presented with the opportunity to buy the patent for a mere $100,000 (Aronson, 1977).

Conversely the initial conceptualization of the computer network was closely envisioned and narrowly defined to solve a specific strategic military problem. Although Bell and his financial backers searched for a commercial use for an invention whose use was not immediately obvious, the Defense Department had no intention of putting the technical innovations that made the computer network possible to commercial use. In fact, that possible option was probably one that was actively discouraged in Defense circles due to security considerations. Yet, despite this lack of vision on the parts of both establishing institutions, the social uses of both networks have come to play a large role in the constitution of these networks.

It is perhaps this common convergence to a set of social rather than business uses of the two networks that sets the stage for the coming debate about the nature of the information infrastructure, despite the fact that this point of convergence was arrived at from two different directions. Any complex social agglomeration is composed of many specialized subgroupings of people and institutions. These internal constituencies may have competing and conflicting purposes over particular issues and resources as well as across differing political milieu and time. Alfonso Molina (1989) notes how these internal institutional conflicts play out in the definition of what he calls institutional raison d'être:

Ways and means vary not only for different social forces and historical periods, but also for different institutions within the same social force. This flexibility implies the existence of particular interests which constitute the practical expression of social forces' overriding interests. Particular interests thus relate to the more ordinary, daily activities of institutions and people. They are informed by the overriding interests of social forces, but also by other factors such as economic and political pressures, organizational traditions of institutions, and also the personalities, ambitions and visions of individuals working and making decisions in the particular institutions. (pp. 3-4)

Examples abound in the world of communications—the battle over Paramount Communications has been characterized as a battle of egos between the two principles, Sumner Redstone and Barry Diller. This is an example of the bitter competition that may arise within a particular social institution. During ARPAnet's formative years, Robert Taylor redirected funds from mission-oriented projects to pure research projects. Both examples point to the interplay between institutional imperatives and the institutional social constraints operating on individuals and, conversely, how particular individuals may affect the social milieu and raison d'être of the institutions they work within. The cultural clash between the defense establishment and the academy is an example of inter-institutional competition. In the case of ARPAnet and the early development of the Internet, this competition seems to have been resolved more or less in favor of the more libertarian conceptual model of the academy. However, the very success of the Internet and its phenomenal growth has brought the social institution of private enterprise into this institutional social dynamic. The way individuals within particular institutions articulate the institution's raison d'être plays an important role in how issues are framed. Although the raison d'être of the business community is not the same as that of the defense establishment, it still has many points of possible conflict and competition with the academy. In the case of the debate on the Information Superhighway, both cable baron, John Malone, and key executives in the telephone industry, notably Ray Smith of Bell Atlantic, framed the debate in narrow, self-serving economic terms centering on what applications to provide and how much the public might pay for particular applications.

This narrow economic view was the one used for both the telephone network and the cable networks. It worked well because, in both cases, neither technology had developed a constituency. In the case of the Internet, a large and growing constituency already exists and, more importantly, this constituency's cultural tenets are in direct conflict with those of the business interests intent on developing the Information Superhighway. With the rise of the debate on the

Information Superhighway, there will be a continued debate on who will control the highway and access to it. The outcome of this debate may hinge directly on and determine the cultural configuration of the Internet.

The key difference in the historical moment of the rise of the telephone network and that of the rise of the Internet is that, in the early days of the developing telephone system, there were no institutions that could compete with the private enterprise model of that development. In the case of the Internet, it was allowed to develop a substantial constituency before the private sector challenged the economic model it has been based on. That constituency, as has been noted, has grown accustomed to the "freedom" of the Internet in both the economic and intellectual sense. In addition, that constituency is growing at a phenomenal pace and has well-known and powerful advocates such as Mitch Kapor, founder of both Lotus Software and the Electronic Frontier Foundation, which provides a powerful public voice for the cultural tenets of the Internet with its legacy in the hacker ethic. This provides a base for strong opposition to the commercialization of cyberspace.

Despite this cultural legacy of freedom, the phenomenal growth of the Internet has brought to the forefront even in academic circles the realization that there are substantial economic costs associated with maintaining the computer web that has grown up over the past 30 years. David Wilson (1993) notes that the way Internet services and connections are paid for have much to do with the freedom, in the intellectual sense, that is a hallmark of the Internet:

> One of the keys to understanding why colleges and universities make their computers available to the public is the fact that it doesn't really cost them anything. The computer servers are always on. Cycles can be thought of as amount of time a computer is on. "You've got all these clock cycles on a computer, and once they're gone they're gone forever, so you might as well have somebody get some good out of them," says John P. Doyle, assistant law librarian at Washington and Lee University Library. (p. A18)

This indicates that, even at the institutional level, the costs associated with the growth and maintenance of the Internet are diffused and indirect. Once the investment in computer hardware is made, there is little additional cost associated with making access to the Internet available to a wide range of people. However, with the explosive growth of the Internet, new investments in infrastructure will be needed, and it is unclear whether institutions of higher education will be either willing or fiscally capable of subsidizing the construction and maintenance of additional infrastructure. This opens the door for the private sector to impose a direct pricing structure that does not hide the cost of network usage from the end-user.

If the Information Superhighway is based, as many of the commercial interests involved want it to be, on a model similar to the telephone system, the costs associated with access to the data stream that is the Internet would skyrocket. This usage-based rate structure is one that is widely accepted in many areas of the telecommunications industry, most prominently the telephone and the cable sectors. A key component to this pricing strategy is what Vincent Mosco (1989) calls "the commodification of information" and is a key step in the construction of an economic model that allows the commercialization of a product that is intangible and has been traditionally hard to measure: "According to this view, information possesses unique characteristics that distinguish it from other resources, preeminently, that information is non-depletable. It can be used, but not used up" (p. 23). This conceptualization of information as a resource puts it in the same realm as minerals or other natural resources and like other resources open to development and exploitation. Mosco notes that in an electronic age information has been increasingly commodified. This comodification has and will continue to be problematic because of the nondepletable nature of information and because there is a fundamental difference between *information* as a resource, whose value is variable to different people and over time, and *data*, which are measured in volume and can therefore be priced based on usage. This commodification is not new but has accelerated with the advent of electronic telecommunications technologies that allow precise and quantified measurements of a commodity that traditionally has been difficult to measure in terms of value. What these electronic technologies have done is to make data measurable in terms of volume and time—bits, bytes, and minutes. This makes information as a resource subject to rate making on the same basis as other raw materials. This sets up a conflict between the giants of the telecommunications industry and the primary users. In effect the industry wants to have the privilege of charging for a commodity that to this point has been free. Given the exisisting Internet community's strong affinity for the cultural tenets of the hacker ethic, epitomized by the phrase, "information wants to be free," and the indirect finacing method that has been employed for infrastructure construction to this point, this is somewhat akin to telling them that there are plans to charge them for the air they breathe.

Another powerful model private enterprise is using as a template for the construction of the Information Superhighway is a "free" system as well. It is the broadcast or mass media model. Over-the-air broadcasting in America is also based on a method of paying for the products and services available that shields the end-users from direct costs. This method of financing the system is directly connected to the nature of the technology. Broadcasting lends itself to a top-down, one-to-many method of operation. Advertising pays for the content directly, but the end-users ultimately pay for the system through higher prices added to products and services due to the cost of advertising.

Two factors here may work to subvert the kind of culture that has grown up on the network. The first is the way commercial interests in the Information Superhighway are using the broadcast business model as a template. This model has a very restricted conceptualization of the interactive features of the superhighway. Commercial interests tend to visualize interactivity as a way for couch potatoes to order up movies on a pay-per-view basis or to inquire further about products they might see advertised by requesting a brochure or a more elaborate video description of a product through their remote control. One of the most interesting facets of the Internet has been the way individuals have used it to make connections with other like-minded individuals or groups rather than restricting their communication to "authorized" uses. A major concern in this area is that commercial interests may attempt to restrict the interactivity of the superhighway to a passive consummerist mode that is much like the broadcast model. Although this may seem difficult or a remote possibility, Howard Rheingold (1993) documents how one of the most high-profile commercial services, Prodigy, attempted to do this. As a commercial business, Prodigy began their service to sell information services such as banking, stock transactions, and airline reservations, but offered e-mail for free as an added benefit. The commercial services languished while the e-mail service flourished. And, like its much larger cousin, the Internet, free-ranging discussions sprang up, some of which involved topics and comments (specifically antisemitic comments) that Prodigy deemed harmful to its commercial services. Prodigy responded first by monitoring and then censoring customers' e-mail; and then, when the users made an end-run on this tactic by turning provisions of the Electronic Communications Privacy Act of 1986 to their advantage by forming mailing lists, Prodigy retaliated by curtailing e-mail privileges and increasing fees (Rheingold, 1993).

The second, and perhaps more ominous, factor is the way commercial interests intend to use the two-way flow of information to perform what Oscar Gandy (1993) has called the "panoptic sort." This is the practice of commercial interests gathering, collating, and processing information about individuals in order to target markets more precisely. Many businesses already routinely gather and sort information about their customer's lives and buying habits by monitoring credit card purchases and other electronic trails of information that individuals leave in the course of leading their lives in the age of information. The technology of the Information Superhighway provides a quantum leap in the ability of large commercial interests to invade the privacy of individuals surreptitiously. But this information gathering is more complex than described because it encompasses a struggle by commercial interests to restrict individual access to particular types of information that they can be charged for while, at the same time, increasing their ability to control their use of personal information incidentally gathered in these commercial transactions for additional commercial purposes. In effect, the thrust of these maneuvers is an attempt to narrow individuals' uses of the Internet to consumerist purposes rather than social or political purposes. Both these factors can be connected to Molina's (1989) articulation of organizational raison d'être and have historical precedents. Witness Aronson's documentation of Bell executives' failure to envision the social use of the telephone that developed because they were tied to the conceptual template of the way telegraphy was already being used as a model for the telephone business.

This points to the importance of how the debate on the National Information Infrastructure should be framed. There are good arguments on both sides of this conflict. An important ideological tenet of our society has been the importance of the freedom of expression and a lively and free "marketplace of ideas." Equally important has been the commercial and capitalistic nature of our economic structure. The resolution of these institutional contradictions and conflicts will have an important impact on the nature of our culture and social institutions as we move into the twenty-first century and the rhetoric about the information society becomes social reality. Important social issues and concerns that are most often expressed in the phrase "information rich" and "information poor" need to be resolved in an equitable manner that preserves both the economic vitality of the society and the intellectual diversity. Issues that revolve around intellectual property rights, copyright, and universal access need to be resolved in a way that protects economic interests without jeopardizing freedom of expression and access to information that is not based strictly on an ability to pay.

There seems little doubt that metering of information on the computer network will become a reality. What remains to be seen is to what extent this privatization and metering will be allowed to go. There is some hope that there will be an effort to limit this trend. The first indicator of hope is the very explosiveness of the growth of use on the Internet. To this point, the Internet has been self-regulating and egalitarian within the limits of the technological access. The cultural legacy of the hacker ethic—the free flow of information—is promulgated to new members of the electronic community as they enter. This will provide, at least for a time, an ever-growing base of opposition to the kind of commodification that Mosco (1989) fears. Many members of the Internet community share his fears. The second indicator of hope is the military's historic failure to contain and control the use of ARPAnet. This stems from two factors: the technological simplicity of the TCP/IP suite of communication protocols, and the network's initial conceptualization as a decentralized and flexible communication tool. Marvin (1988) seems to feel that the very nature of communication may have a causal relationship to this institutional failure to maintain control by one of our society's most powerful social institutions: "New media embody the possibility that accustomed orders are in jeopardy, since communication is a particular kind of interaction that actively seeks variety. No matter how firmly custom or instrumentality may appear to organize or contain it, it carries the seeds of its own subversion" (p. 8). The historical precedent of the way the social use of the telephone developed coupled with its parallel in the Internet may provide a reminder to those who wish to force computer-mediated communication into a commercial mold based on a mass media model. The examples of both the telephone and the Internet seem to indicate that, if given an opportunity, people will choose to communicate interactively with each other, rather than attend exclusively to mass-mediated, one-to-many products as commercial interests might prefer.

It is perhaps fitting that the term *cyberspace* is a geographic or topographic metaphor. This geographic element seems to capture many of the issues inherent in Mosco's (1989) sense of information as a resource. It also harks back to the days of the Wild West in that many of the issues at the forefront of the debate about the Information Superhighway seem to echo the issues those early settlers faced. David Ronfeldt (1991) makes this geographical notion of colonization explicit:

> Still another analogy views it [cyberspace] as a frontier that virtually exists and beckons for exploration, colonization and development. In this view, different "cyberspace colonies" will be (indeed, they already are being) carved out by many different kinds of actors, many of them initially misfits and adventurers from ordinary society. As colonies get established and grow, they may be expected to develop different forms of government, citizenship, and property rights. (pp. 35-36)

Ronfeldt's geographical conceptualization of cyberspace shares something in common with Mosco's (1989) definition of information as a resource. Virtual real estate, unlike its physical counterpart, seems to have the ability to expand. Like the nondepletable nature of information, cyberspace has no known natural limits—cyberspace expands as information grows. This will be important to remember as players square off in what might constitute a virtual range war between the "mountain men" and "prospectors" of the Internet and the "sodbusters" and "railroaders" of the telecommunications industry who want to fence the frontier in. There should be room in cyberspace for an unprecedented range of diversity. The cultural legacy of the Internet has established both a precedent for that diversity and a large number of proponents. Although the rhetoric of the Information Superhighway framed the debate in a more constricted and limited vision, the outcome of the debate is still in doubt. Current controversies sparked by music reproduction and music-sharing software like mp3, Napster, and Gnutella indicate strong cultural tendencies running counter to the trend by commercial interests to conceptualize the Internet and the World Wide Web as one more one-to-many mass medium whose sole purpose is to commodify content and exploit consumers. Will cyberspace indeed become a "pay-per society" as Mosco suggests? There is hope that the raucous and colorful diversity that is the Internet today will continue to grow and provide a model for future development.

## REFERENCES

Aronson, S.H. (1977). Bell's electrical toy: What's the use? The sociology of early telephone usage. In I. de Sola Pool (Ed.), *The social impact of the telephone* (pp. 15-39). Cambridge, MA: The MIT Press.

Gandy, O.H., Jr. (1993). *The panoptic sort: A political economy of personal information.* Boulder, CO: Westview Press.

Gibson, W. (1984). *Neuromancer.* New York: Ace Books.

Hart, J.A., Reed, R.E., & Bar, F. (1992, November ). The building of the Internet: Implications for the future of broadband networks. *Telecommunications Policy, 16*(8), 666-689.

Hauben, R. (1993, June). *The development of the international computer network: From ARPAnet to Usenet News (On the nourishment or impediment of the NET.Commonwealth).* Paper presented at "Europe in Turmoil: Communication and Democracy in Civil Society," a conference of the International Association for Mass Communication Research, Dublin, Ireland.

Levy, S. (1984). *Hackers: The heroes of the computer revolution.* New York: Bantam.

Marvin, C. (1988). *When old technologies were new: Thinking about electric communication in the late nineteenth century.* New York: Oxford University Press.

Molina, A.H. (1989). *The social bias of the microelectronic revolution.* Edinburgh: Edinburgh University Press.

Mosco, V. (1989). *The pay-per society: Computers and communication in the age of information.* Toronto: Garamond Press.

Rheingold, H. (1993). *The virtual community: Homesteading on the electronic frontier.* Reading, MA: Addison-Wesley.

Ronfeldt, D. (1991). *Cyberocracy, cyberspace, and cyberology: Political effects of the information revolution.* Santa Monica, CA: RAND Corporation.

Rutkowski, A. M., et al. (1993). Who's "on line" with whom: The new global internetworking business, from computer bulletin boards to national infostructure. In C.S. Gregory (Ed.), *Telegeography: Global telecommunications traffic statistics & commentary* (pp. 8-17). Washington, DC: Telegeography Inc.

Sterling, B. (1992). *The hacker crackdown: Law and disorder on the electronic frontier.* New York: Bantam.

Stix, G. (1993, August). Domesticating cyberspace. *Scientific American, 269*(2), 100-110.

Wilson, D.L. (1993, July 28). Electronic riches are free on the Internet, but some worry about the consequences. *The Chronicle of Higher Education,* pp. A18-A21.

✧✧✧✧ *9*

# "Are They Building an Off-Ramp in My Neighborhood?" and Other Questions Concerning Public Interest in and Access to the Information Superhighway

## Ron L. Jacobson

*Cyberspace was once a contested site, with different segments of society staking their claims in what may well have been the greatest "land grab" since the closing of the frontier. The competing interests included big business; local, state, and national governments; institutions such as universities and hospitals; computer professionals and hobbyists; and the general public. In this chapter, Ron Jacobson reviews and updates competing visions and concerns about the emerging National Information Infrastructure, juxtaposing corporate commercial interests in the information superhighway with the National Telecommunications and Information Administration (NTIA) proposal for an advanced National Information Infrastructure. Several public interest questions are posed, including: Who will benefit most from the proposed telecommunications infrastructure, and what will constitute basic service on this information highway? In raising these and other questions, the author calls for a wider public debate to consider the political, economic, social, cultural, and ethical implications of our changing communications infrastructure. Beyond Section 2, additional examination of issues, policy, and law can be found Gary Gumpert and Susan J. Drucker's*

161

*comments on cyberlaw in Chapter 1, John M. Phelan's critique of Internet hype in*
*Chapter 2, James R. Beniger's essay on the control of cyberspace in Chapter 3,*
*and Neil Kleinman's exploration of property rights in Chapter 4; see also Paul*
*Lippert's arguments concerning social class in Chapter 18, and Douglas*
*Rushkoff's essay on information warfare in cyberspace in Chapter 21.*

When this article was first published in 1996, the convergence of the computer
with telephone and television technologies was frequently conceptualized as the
*Information Superhighway*, a popular metaphor for the building of a National
Information Infrastructure (NII) made up of seamless communications
networks, databases, and consumer electronics. Stand-up comedian Paul
Rodriquez used to tell his audience that he's heard all this great talk about an
Information Superhighway, but he's pretty sure "they're not building an off-
ramp in *my neighborhood.*" The information highway, Rodriquez continued, is
"just another place where I can get pulled off and frisked." Rodriquez's humor
was entertaining, but, more than that, it was social commentary that critically
pointed to the inevitable human gap between our aims and achievements, our
ideals and performance. Rodriquez raised significant public access and privacy
concerns about emerging electronic forms of social interaction as he implicitly
posed a key question: "In which directions will the much-heralded Information
Superhighway go?"

The answer to this question in 1996 depended on whom you were
asking. Individuals and groups, often with divergent interests and purposes,
envision different social worlds evolving from new interactive, multimedia
environments. Those groups included, among others, the telecommunications
companies, federal government, public interest groups, and users. The purpose
of this chapter is to review and update corporate, government, and public interest
visions and concerns about the emerging telecommunications environments, and
to raise questions for further discussion and debate.

## CORPORATE VISIONS

The public continues to be sold idealized images of the future, as some corporate
visionaries speak of the Internet almost as if it were the way to enlightenment.
Corporate interests would have us believe that the knowledge of the world will
soon be available at our fingertips and that the consequences of this information
revolution will be wholly positive, as if an injection of new technology is the
panacea for our social problems. Corporate interests are largely to blame for this
hype, which is unprecedented in the history of new technologies.

Indeed, the Internet, fueled by the World Wide Web, became big business in
the closing years of the 20th century. According to the AIM Funds Annual Report,
the Internet economy in 1998 generated approximately $300 billion in the United

States, outpacing the energy sector ($223 billion) and closing in on the auto industry ($350 billion). In 1999, Jeff Bezos, founder of Amazon.com, was named *Time Magazine*'s Man of the Year (despite the fact that his company had yet to show a net profit). During the January 2000 Super Bowl, Internet companies accounted for close to half the advertisers on the broadcast, during which a 30-second spot sold for more than $2 million. However, by the end of 2000, the Internet economy had cooled off considerably.

Electronic commerce will again begin to grow, especially upon resolution of issues concerning privacy, consumer protection, security/reliability, and intellectual property protection. Such growth also begs for some kind of legal framework to cover additional issues such as electronic contracts, digital signatures, taxation, tariffs, and jurisdiction. Additionally, some participants in the Internet economy are looking to the federal government for the policy parameters within which they can continue to expand. The government remains an important participant in building the infrastructure for future electronic commerce in areas such as standards development, opening markets abroad, and especially telecommunications policy.

What the Internet is really about is the transformation of information and knowledge rather than its growth. The public sphere is shrinking as indicated by signs such as libraries losing their funding; more information, including government data, being distributed through private commercial vendors; and blatantly commercial services like Channel One in the public schools. The late Herb Schiller (cited in Ruggiero & Sahulka, 1994, p. 2) suggested, "Things that are fundamentally changing for the worse. Limiting access to information and the commercialization of public space are being presented as wonderful benefits in the offing. It's a sickening con game."

The Information Superhighway metaphor itself is no longer in vogue. In 1995, the year in which the original version of this article was completed, major newspapers referred to the "Information Highway" in 4,562 stories. Four years later, in 1999, the information highway was mentioned only 842 times. During those same four years, the mentioning of electronic commerce (e-commerce) increased from 915 to 20,641 (Solomon, 2000). Once popular, the Information Superhighway metaphor was actually an inappropriate one in significant ways. As Browning (1994) aptly points out, the government built our federal highway system, but it will not be building the Information Superhighway. Similar to railways, information networks are being constructed by people who stand to profit from them. Dordick (Freedom Forum, 1993) suggests that the building of the asphalt interstate highway system also had its drawbacks, as "it served large companies, bypassed many small communities, and essentially blocked investments for public transportation for many years" (p. 25). Today, we hardly ever talk about an Information Superhighway, and the reality is that most large corporate interests are busy building commercial and/or private toll booths.

A major question for these "builders" had been whether the personal computer (a decentralized model with the Internet as a prototype) or the current television system (a centralized model) will be the principal gateway to the information highway for the masses. The AOL–TimeWarner merger represents one example of an ongoing strategy by corporate giants to integrate through content creation, packaging and marketing of content and services, and physical distribution of the packaged product. The $166 billion merger gives AOL access to Time Warner's 13 million cable customers, and Time Warner gains access to AOL's more than 20 million customers for its many media properties. Such mergers point to the future of the Internet via the ongoing convergence between the television and the personal computer.

Of course, this emerging 500-channel universe is not without it critics. Jeffrey Chester and Kathryn Montgomery (1993) envision such a universe as a "vaster wasteland" in which advertising-created programming flourishes, prohibitive rate structures make it difficult for nonprofit groups and small independent producers to gain system access, and consumers pay higher fees to obtain programming. With the onset of the 500-channel universe, they see the decline of "free" broadcast television, local news and public affairs programming, and public television as we know it today. Nancy Kranich (1994) fears that "if not controlled, industry giants will transmit 500 or more channels of highly profitable vaporware that will fall far short of serving the full spectrum of society's needs" (p. 35).

Important questions about the new media technologies, inclusive of the 500-channel universe, are not widely debated today outside of the Internet and the academic community because of corporate zeal complemented by mainstream news media behavior that more frequently resembles a corporate public relations campaign than any social watchdog function. As Schiller (cited in Ruggiero & Sahulka, 1994) suggested, "Once corporate control is given, it is alienated from the public arena and we lose rights to discuss its disposition."

## GOVERNMENT VISIONS

Vice President Al Gore was the Clinton Administration's most ardent supporter of national telecommunications reform. His vision was to bring the economic, health, and educational benefits of the information revolution to more Americans, and he publicly challenged private industry to connect every hospital, classroom, and library to the Information Highway by the year 2000. To that end, in 1993, the National Telecommunications and Information Administration (NTIA) in the U.S. Department of Commerce, under the Clinton Administration, proposed a plan for a National Information Infrastructure (NII) that would be built by private-sector investment; promote interactive, user-driven operation; and ensure universal basic service to all at affordable costs. In fact, Gore and the NTIA's version of the proposed Information Superhighway featured miles and miles of promise and potential. The Information Infrastructure Task Force Report (1993) claimed:

People could live almost anywhere they wanted, without foregoing opportunities for useful and fulfilling employment, by "telecommuting" to their offices through an electronic highway;

The best schools, teachers, and courses would be available to all students, without regard to geography, distances, resources, or disability;

Services that improve America's health care system and respond to other important social needs could be available on-line, without waiting in line, when and where you need them. (p. 3)

In February 1996, President Clinton signed a major telecommunications bill that removed legislative and judicial restrictions on telecommunications companies so that the "paving" of the highway could begin. With deregulation, telephone, broadcast and cable, and computer companies began forming manufacturing and marketing agreements. All of this seemed to spell out a continuation of national communications policy largely guided by private commercial interests in the marketplace, tempered by federal regulation for the "public interest" in areas such as technical standards, concentration of ownership, consumer pricing, and access to both users and content providers. For example, of the latter, Gore (1994) asked, "How can you sell your ideas, your information, your programs, if an intermediary who is also your competitor has the means to unfairly block your access to customers? We can't subject the free flow of content to artificial constraints at the hands of either government regulators or would-be monopolists" (p. 6).

President Clinton and Congress realized that the proposed NII plan required major regulatory reform because assymetrical regulatory models existed for the converging technologies and industries. For example, broadcasting regulation, under the Communications Act of 1934, was regulated following a public interest model. However, spectrum scarcity, the driving force behind broadcast regulation, is no longer the dominant paradigm. Once considered almost a natural resource, parts of the electromagnetic spectrum have recently been auctioned off to the highest corporate bidders. Cable was regulated principally as a local franchisee under federal guidelines, and telephone companies historically were regulated as public utility common carriers. These differing regulatory models could not simply be combined in creating new policy concerning the Information Superhighway (Geller, 1991). The NII plan recognized that the new regulatory policy needed to be flexible, adaptable, and fair in dealing with changing and emerging technologies and their applications, with business structures, and with public interest concerns that would affect distributors, content providers, and consumer users along the Information Superhighway. Important questions and problems about issues such as First Amendment rights, privacy, security, and intellectual property rights will continue to be worked out through practice, the courts, legislation, and policy decisions.

## PUBLIC INTEREST CONCERNS

While the NTIA painted a pretty picture of future possibilities, the truth is that there is a widening gap between the information haves and have-nots, often referred to as the *digital divide.* (Maybe Rodriquez wasn't joking about the absence of an Information Superhighway "off-ramp" in his neighborhood.) Even though additional millions will access cyberspace through advanced television instead of personal computers, there continues to be a legitimate concern about the "digital divide"—the gap between those who have access to and use the Internet and those who do not. Levels of education and income appear to be the most significant variables in determining Internet access and usage. At its 1999 convention, the National Communication Association (NCA) passed the following resolution on the digital divide:

> *The National Communication Association reaffirms its commitment to urge the development of free and low-cost ways of accessing the means for processing and distributing information in electronic forms. Moreover, NCA continues to urge the development of hardware and software that requires minimal training but that still allows wide use of worldwide electronic resources.*
>
> *Given these commitments, the National Communication Association resolves to take a leadership role in closing the digital divide. NCA officers and staff support legislation aimed at providing universal access to electronic means of communication. NCA members should make research on closing the digital divide a priority, and NCA should work with other organizations to ensure that communities in the U.S. and elsewhere have adequate electronic communication resources available to all.*
>
> *NCA urges its members to take an active role in increasing awareness of the digital divide through incorporating material on this problem into courses, through community consultation and education, and by advocating for appropriate policies at the state and local levels.*

The NCA is not alone in its concern. Commercial corporate interests also wish to narrow the digital divide, albeit with different motives, including expanding its consumer base and training its future work force.

Countering the corporate lobbies, public interest groups, including the Electronic Frontier Foundation, have called for universal low-cost access to public information. These groups argue for a public information carrier model that would reserve "electronic space free from corporate control and censorship" (Ouelette, 1993, p. 24). Geller (1991) believes this can be accomplished through a fiber-based integrated switched broadband telecommunications structure, with at least one line separating the conduit from the content. This means that at least one line into the home would be solely that of a common carrier with no control over content, similar to our traditional telephone system. Public interest groups see such structural regulation as key to preventing monopolistic or oligopolistic constraints that would limit diversity of expression and marginalize alternative views.

Reuben-Cooke (1993) proposes that government take a stronger public interest, access-based policy approach to regulation, considering factors such as audience receipt of ideas (e.g., the public's right to information), quantity of services (e.g., guaranteed access for content providers), cost (e.g., greater affordability through subsidies), and literacy (e.g., ability to operate hardware and use software intelligently). Although all these factors are important, it is the last factor, literacy, that often fails to be included in public interest discussions. Those who gain access to the new media environments must not only learn how to navigate but also to critically discern the quality of content in cyberspace. That is to say, whereas the future promises a diminished role for professional mass media gatekeepers and fewer controls on content, such a future also suggests the possibility of an increasing burden on individual users who will take on greater gatekeeping responsibilities). As technology progresses, audience control increases, but are individuals ready to assume control, including scanning and filtering their own information (Neuman, 1993)?

It is not difficult to envision a scenario in which some form of universal service exists, but social stratification is still clearly delineated by the ability to afford knowledge of and access to quality gatekeepers (software, people, and services that evaluate, select, sort, and package customized information). It is a scenario in which the poor and uneducated have fewer "maps" for use in new media environments and are more likely to get lost on detours or stuck at commercial roadside attractions selling entertainment and/or information in the guise of knowledge. It is all too easy to forget that information is not knowledge. Knowledge is gained by making evaluative judgments on the quality of information, which in turn is achieved through the cognitive skill of separating the significant from the irrelevant. Therefore, Reuben-Cooke (1993) and others realize that the push for low-cost, universal access must be accompanied by a push for more media literacy education.

Literacy is indeed a pertinent issue and one implicitly suggested in broader public interest concerns about our new media environments. As I see it now, the principal public interest access questions are these:

- Who will benefit most from access to the emerging telecommunications infrastructure?
- Who gets what, where, when, how, and for what purpose?
- What are the social consequences of inequitable access to information in new media environments (e.g., even greater polarization along social class lines)?
- If access is deemed a right (some Republicans are already labeling universal access as another Democrat-concocted "entitlement"), what will constitute basic service?

In addition to such basic questions about access, there are many more public interest questions, including the following, that require greater thought, discussion, and debate concerning the future of telecommunications and cyberspace:

- How can our many significant educational, health, and cultural problems be better addressed by our new technologies? (Shouldn't a major driving force behind our national telecommunications policy be the explicit goal to equate technological progress with improvements in social welfare?)
- In what new ways will users navigate through, socially interact with others, and form a sense of shared community in cyberspace?
- Once access is achieved, how will privacy be protected?
- Will virtual communities lead to a further deterioration of our older communities, especially our cities?
- What will happen to other public institutional spaces, such as tax-supported libraries, in this new age of electronic information? (For example, will the libraries go the way of the downtown stores when the suburban malls moved in, or will they serve as hubs for universal access? See Roszak, 1986, for an excellent argument for the latter.)
- Will a 500-channel universe further isolate us from one another and "individualize our approach to and our knowledge of issues of public justice and of each other," as Janette Dates asks, and will there be "more avenues for individual speech but fewer for robust, wide-open debate," as Les Brown ponders (Center for Media Literacy, 1994, p. 11)?
- As the media become more decentralized and seemingly more democratized, will old and new media serve the needs of democracy or further solidify existing power structures? There are many questions about the future of the relationship between cyberspace and politics. For example, Lawrence Grossman asks, "How do we reconcile a representative political system that is based on, and defined by, geographical boundaries—districts, counties, cities and states—with the powerful new telecommunications media that obliterate political boundaries" (Center for Media Literacy, 1994, p. 12)?
- Finally, we must ask ourselves not only what new media environments will be like, but what will we be like; that is, how will we change through communication and evolving forms of social interactions in cyberspace?

## CONCLUDING THOUGHTS

So far, I have been discussing the Information Superhighway on a national scale, but the issues are cross-cultural and international. The Information Superhighway yearns to be intercontinental and borderless, bringing us conceptually closer to

McLuhan's notion of a global village transcending time and space. But it is a village still marked by ideological and cultural conflicts, and inhabited by haves and have-nots Still, one can only hope that the emerging global information infrastructure will lead to environments that offer potential for leveling great socioeconomic inequities and for improving the quality of life for more humans.

We live during an exciting time of hype, promise and potential. Corporate ideology of the information age pervades our lives. With less powerful voices, federal and state governments and public interest groups outline their concerns, push their own agendas, and fight to keep powerful corporate entities from completely setting the parameters of the debate.

No doubt, the next decade will be a crucial time during which telecommunications policy decisions will likely influence communication and interactions in cyberspace for decades to come. What is ultimately at stake is the very nature of communications institutions, audiences/users, and the forms of relationship between them. Borrowing from Raymond Williams's (1974) interpretation of Laswell's model, we must ask ourselves anew, "Who will be able to say what to whom for what purpose and with what effect?" For no matter what your view is on or from the Information Superhighway, you are part of a significant ideological struggle about power and control.

## REFERENCES

AIM Funds. (1999). *AIM Global Telecommunications and Technology Fund Annual Report.*

Browning, J. (1994, February). Get on track: There will be no info highway. *Wired,* p. 65.

Center for Media Literacy. (1994). Visions of a brave new TV world. *Connect, 6,* 10-13.

Chester, J., & Montgomery, K.C. (1993). A public-interest perspective for the future U.S. telecommunications infrastructure. In C. Firestone (Ed.), *Television in the 21st century* (pp. 55-75). Queenstown, MD: The Aspen Institute.

Dutton, W. (1999). *Society on the line.* New York: Oxford University Press.

Freedom Forum Media Studies Center. (1993). *Media, democracy and the information highway: A conference report on the prospects for a national information service.* New York: Author.

Geller, H. (1991). *Fiber optics: An opportunity for a new policy.* Washington, DC: The Annenberg Washington Program in Communication Policy Studies of Northwestern University.

Gore, A. (1994, January 11). *Vice-president proposes national telecommunications reform.* Washington, DC: The White House Office of the Vice President.

Information Infrastructure Task Force. (1993, September 15). *The national information infrastructure: Agenda for action.* Washington, DC: U.S. Department of Commerce.

Kranich, N. (1994, November 15). Of cyberspace: Can libraries protect public access? *Library Journal*, p. 35.

Neuman, W.R. (1993). The psychology of the new media. In C. Firestone (Ed.), *Television in the 21st century* (pp. 35-54). Queenstown, MD: The Aspen Institute.

Ouelette, L. (1993, September/October). The information lockout: Is there a place for have-nots in cyberspace? *Utne Reader*, p. 24.

Reuben-Cooke, W.M. (1993). Rethinking legal and policy paradigms. In C. Firestone (Ed.), *Television in the 21st century* (pp. 55-75). Queenstown, MD: The Aspen Institute.

Roszak, T. (1986). *The cult of information: The folklore of computers and the true art of thinking.* New York: Pantheon Books.

Ruggiero, G., & Sahulka, S. (1994, March). The information superhighway: Paving over the public. *Z Magazine* [online]. Available on America Online.

Shenk, D. (1997). *Data smog: Surviving the information glut.* San Francisco: HarperEdge.

Solomon, N. (2000, January 16). *What happened to the Information Superhighway?* Creators Syndicate (online).

Williams, R. (1974). Communication as a cultural science. *Journal of Communication, 42*, 17-26.

# The Digital Divide

## Frank E.X. Dance

*For some time now, cyberspace has been characterized as an electronic frontier, democratic and open to all, but such characterizations ignore the fact that only a minority of the population of the United States, let alone the world, is actually online. In this, cyberspace's netizen's may be compared to the citizenry of the ancient Athenian democracy, a minority that excluded women, slaves, and those of foreign origins. Moreover, when access to a medium is limited to the few, they tend to gain what Harold Innis called a monopoly of knowledge, and with it they gain unfair political, economic, and social advantages. The formation of a new cyberelite, sometimes referred to as the information rich, digerati, or virtual class, has the potential to further exacerbate existing class conflicts and social stratifications. In contemporary discourse, this issue has come to be known as the digital divide, and this is the topic that Frank Dance takes up in this chapter, discussing his own concerns as a communication theorist. Of particular interest is his argument that although much attention has been focused on uneven access to information through cyberspace technologies, just as important is the all but overlooked communication gap that occurs when so many are shut out from new forms of social interaction associated with cyberspace. Outside of this section, the subject of class divisions is also addressed by Paul Lippert in Chapter 18. For alternate views on online interaction, see Gary Gumpert and Susan Drucker's comments on the disadvantages of cyberspace in Chapter 1, John M. Phelan's critique of cyberspace utopianism in Chapter 2, and the arguments concerning corporate interests in the Internet presented by James Beniger in Chapter 3, and Douglas Rushkoff in Chapter 21. For other applications of speech and rhetoric to computer-mediated communication, see Charles Larson's use of Burke's Pentad in Chapter 6, and Judith Yaross Lee's analysis of e-mail in Chapter 19.*

Since 1997 that which separates those who have access to new Internet technologies from those who do not have such access has come to be known as the *digital divide* (see Katz & Aspden, 1997).[1] Although the access digital divide currently receives the most attention, I believe that a social digital divide provides the greatest challenge for weaving new technologies into the fabric of the human life world. Efforts to close the access digital divide set the stage for playing out the drama of closing the social digital divide.

## THE ACCESS DIGITAL DIVIDE

In most instances when the topic of the digital divide is addressed the dominant focus is Internet access. On January 1, 2000, there were approximately 201 million people online. Only 2 months later, on March 1, 2000, there was an estimated 304 million people online worldwide. Big numbers, but only a fraction of the estimated 6.1 billion world population as of January 1, 2000. In early 2000, about 96% of the world's population was not online.

Given the impressive trajectory of change more up to date figures can be found online (Nua, 1995). My primary sources for Internet statistics is Nua (from the Gaelic for "new") an Ireland-based Internet survey and analysis company.[2]

In a July 1999 white paper from the U.S. Department of Commerce, it was suggested that in the time since the preceding 1997 white paper the "access digital divide" had become more rather than less evident (National Telecommunications [NTIA], 1999a). The white paper states that even though computer access has become more common, that it has been a situation in which those segments of the population who have already been using computers have grown while those segments of the population without access to computers in earlier studies have lagged behind in growth with the result that the "gap between

---

[1]Prior to 1997 the phenomenon was most often referred to as the "digital haves and have-nots."

[2]According to Nua (1995) "the art of estimating how many are online throughout the world is an inexact one at best. Surveys abound, using all sorts of measurement parameters. However, from observing many of the published surveys over the last two years, here is an educated guess as to how many are online worldwide as of September 1999. And the number is 201 million." By September 2001, this number doubled to 500 million (Nua Internet Surveys, 2001).

these groups—the digital divide—has grown over time." Some of the concluding comments, and accompanying figures, from the 1999 survey follow:

**Income.** E-mail usage increased at all income levels by fourfold or more during 1994-98. Although usage rose more than four times to 6.2% at the lowest income level (under $5,000) by 1998, the digital gap grew from 8.8 percentage points to 37.5. Unexpectedly, both the lowest income and the highest income levels experienced declines in usage from 1997 to 1998 (i.e., 7.2% to 6.2%, and 45.1% to 43.7%, respectively). At each income level, rural areas lagged behind urban and central city areas.

**Race/Origin.** All groups registered growth of 3.5 times or more. Black and Hispanic household usage remained substantially behind Whites and non-Hispanics in both 1994 and 1998. The digital gap more than quintupled during the period. The Whites' category usage of e-mail led in rural and urban areas, and also in central cities in 1998.

**Age.** E-mail usage grew at least 4.5 times at each age level during the period. Senior citizens (55+ years) trailed all other age brackets in both 1994 and 1998.The digital gap more than quadrupled, from 3.5 percentage points to 14.6.

**Education.** E-mail use and level of education are also correlated. All levels experienced at least a fourfold growth rate in usage. The digital gap between elementary school-educated and college-educated households grew from 8.7 percentage points in 1994 to 37.5 in 1998. Those households in rural areas have consistently lagged behind urban areas but surpass central cities, except at the lowest and highest age brackets.

**Household Type.** Every type of household increased e-mail use by at least a factor of 5 except for male householders with children (3 times). Usage by households composed of married couples with children led all other categories throughout the period by a substantial margin and equaled 25.9% in 1998. The latter figure decreased from that registered in 1997, 26.2%. Least usage occurred with female householders with children over the same time, registering 10.1% in 1998. The digital gap widened during the span, increasing from 3.9 percentage points in 1994 to 15.8 in 1998. Surprisingly, the gap decreased from 1997 to 1998 by 4.2%. Throughout the 1994-1998 span, rural area usage consistently trailed other areas for all household types except for the female householder with children category, where over time rural overtook both urban and central cities.

The 1999 NTIA, document substantiates the assertion that the digital divide in the United States is growing both wider, in terms of numbers, and deeper, in terms of impact and concern. It is also fairly self-evident that the digital divide often parallels the economic divide so that the digital rich keep getting richer and the digital poor, poorer.

The December 9, 1999 Digital Divide Summit held in Washington, DC and hosted by the William M. Daley, the U.S. secretary of commerce, brought together participants from corporate America, government, charitable foundations, volunteer efforts, and education to discuss possible solutions to the access digital divide (NTIA, 1999b). Representing the University of Denver and the National Communication Association, I attended the summit together with Denver City Councilman Dennis Gallagher who was one of the few representatives of local governments there. The summit had the air of a town meeting. Almost everyone attending had been involved for some time in trying to close the access digital divide for his or her particular constituency. Each participant had valuable information to share. The summit generated lots of information, lots of excitement, and lots of energy. It was evident at the summit that representatives from Internet underrepresented populations, such as African Americans, Native Americans, and Americans of Hispanic descent, among others, were committed to a rapid closure of the access digital divide for their constituencies (NTIA, 1998b).

Access is initially the most obvious of the digital divide elements and needs to be vigorously tackled. There are those who believe that the access issue will be solved by allowing free market forces to play out, whereas others believe that access should be a governmental concern calling for governmental solutions on all levels from federal to local.

With the exercise of free market enterprise and the attention of enlightened and energetic local and national governments the closure of the access digital divide in the United States will continue to be vigorously pursued. Foundation support for initiatives to close the access digital divide is also growing with the support of organizations such as the Markle Foundation, the Benton Foundation, and the AOL Foundation. In early January 2000, the Technology Opportunities Program of the U.S. Department of Commerce announced that $12.5 million in grants would be given to encourage nonprofit organizations, serving underprivileged rural and urban areas, to adopt advanced network technologies in order to improve their services (NTIA, 1998a). Obviously, efforts funded by the U.S. Department of Commerce have e-commerce ambitions. However, as discussed later, economic, business, and shopping interests may be only a small part of what it will mean for the whole world to be "online."

From my own experience in trying to excite interest and action in closing the access digital divide on the local level, I find that government tends to move very slowly. This labored movement is probably not a surprise to many readers but from my own naive perspective I found it perplexing and discouraging. I started my personal odyssey at the highest level of national government in Washington, DC, thence to the state level, then to the city and county levels and lastly to the neighborhood level. At each level I found active interest but, with some exceptions, slow progress. A few members of the U.S. House of

Representatives, such as Scott McInnis of Colorado's third district, are energetically pursuing programs such as McInnis' "Seed Project" to close the digital divide and there are some local government officials such as Councilman Gallagher in Denver who are proactive on the issue. Quite possibly closing the access digital divide will be a "trickle up" proposition rather than the result of governmental edict or law. This ascent to the grassroots may be a quest for immediacy of response, a "let's do something" attitude, even though the change is much more circumscribed in terms of geographical impact. The National Communication Association, beginning with its July 1999 summer conference on Communication and Technology, is taking an increasingly active stance and featured the role of human communication scholars apropos the digital divide issue at its November 2000 national convention in Seattle.

There are those who question the need or desirability of efforts to close the access digital divide. As a habitual technological early adopter, I was somewhat nonplussed by this attitude, but the "don't want to, don't need to" position has encouraged me to consider more closely what I had earlier taken for granted.

The question of access to new technologies has received the most attention because it is driven by what many perceive to be an economic urgency. If the situation in the United States is indicative of what the situation will soon be throughout much of the world then new technologies and their economic sequelae are destined to become a if not the major driving force of economic growth worldwide. The industries and businesses spawned by the new technologies need employees. The workplace demands are calling for individuals who have familiarity and expertise with the new technologies. There is almost no segment of the work force in the United States unaffected by the technological revolution. Jobs in computer maintenance, computer development, computer applications, computer engineering, computer science, computer sales, jobs in data entry and records maintenance, these and many others need to be filled and there simply are not enough trained workers to fill them. Agriculture, education, health sciences, research, and government are also users of the new technologies and those who would work in those arenas will be required to have appropriate familiarity and training. The need for suitable employees is going to grow not diminish. The demand will explode as more and more of the world's population gets online. Those who are unable to compete in this technological job hungry society are going to be severely disadvantaged. It is difficult to conceive of exactly what jobs will remain untouched by the computer and online revolution as we surge from an industrial society to an information society. There will be 21st-century high-tech jobs that we have not yet conceived of. There were probably very few youngsters in the late 19th and early 20th century who set their sights on becoming commercial airline pilots or going into television repair or nuclear biology.

So, from a purely self-serving, economic, wage-earning viewpoint it is essential that all members of society be assured equal access to the new technologies. This is true both for the individuals concerned as well as for the society in which those individuals live. Enlightened social self-interest should view equal access to the new technologies as an entitlement in the same manner as roads, and utilities are entitlements. To deny equal access, not to close the access digital divide, is to invite increased poverty, increased ignorance, increased computer illiteracy, increased desperation, increased hostility and increased antisocial behaviors. With the exercise of free market enterprise and the attention of local and national governments the access problem will continue to be successfully addressed. Access is moving fast and will continue to move fast as it is forced by the energy of e-commerce assisted by the growth of wireless technology and global demand.

Although "access" is initially the most apparent facet of the digital divide it is becoming, for me, the least interesting aspect. Overshadowing the access problem is the problem of adoption and usage of new technology, the social digital divide.

## THE SOCIAL DIGITAL DIVIDE

Putting everyone on the Internet, or giving every human being equal access to the Internet won't, of itself, close the overall digital divide because there are reasons other than availability and access influencing personal decisions to use the new technologies. Although Ihde (1990) suggests that almost all of us live a "technologically textured" existence, this technological life space doesn't seem to be equally attractive to all.

Throughout history, there have been divides between those who adopt and fail to adopt new technology. It took centuries for literacy to become the received position in most societies and it is still not universal. There are still those who have either no or severely restricted access to education, to literacy, to books, to adequate medical services, to refrigerators, to indoor plumbing, to radio, television, and cinema, and so on. However, there are also those who do have access to these goods and services and yet choose not to use them. Why?

There have always been those who are either slow adopters or non-adopters of new media. Some people are resistant to change for religious reasons.[3] Some have been beaten down for so long that apathy and anomie are their habitual state. There are those whose severe mental or emotional disability makes the adoption of technology too difficult for the benefits realized. There are those who are resistant to any kind of change or modernization. Some cannot see

---

[3] I came across a news story stating that Israel's leading orthodox rabbis issued a ruling banning Internet use because it introduces corruption into Jewish homes and is a threat to the survival of the Jewish people. According to the story the rabbis said that they are alarmed by the ease by which the new Technology breaks down barriers and brings the outside world into the home. I was unable to validate the URL accompanying the story. Accessed 14 January 2000. http://www.unesco.org/webworld/observatory pointing to:gopher://gopher.voa.gov/00/newswire/sun/ISRAEL_INTERNET

how the new technology would improve their life or the manner in which they do their jobs so there is no incentive to adopt new methods. Some believe that the computer and its consequences have had a negative rather than a positive impact on family, cultural, and social values and some of these folks may choose to live in a nontechnologically soiled enclave (see Montoya, 1997).[4] There are those who champion individual rights with a "Hell no, I won't go!" salute to the individual's right to illiteracy, to indolence, to nonparticipation. Finally, there are some who simply resent the hard-sell, the technological evangelist or determinist, and who display their independence and resistance by nonadoption.

## THE DIGITAL DIVIDE WILL BE CLOSED AS SOON AS PEOPLE FIND AN ALL IMPORTANT AND IRRESISTIBLE REASON TO BE ON THE WEB

Q. What do most people find important and irresistible?

A. Other people.

Tim Berners-Lee (1999), founder of the World Wide Web (WWW), observed, "In an extreme view, the world can be seen as only connections, nothing else" (p. 12). Berners-Lee's "connections," are connections between ideas but most importantly connections between people

Q. What it is that the Internet and the World Wide Web makes readily available?

A. Other people.

E-mail was the first easily available technology on the Internet and later on the Web. According to the NTIA (1999) survey, e-mail usage grew at a tremendous rate during the interval from 1994 to 1998. Usage by all races or ethnic origins grew at least 3.5 times during the span. Every income and educational level as well as labor force category exhibited growth of four times or more. All age groups have increased by at least 4.5 times while usage by household types and regions rose some fivefold.

E-mail is the first transparent technology, the technology claiming the participation of most online participants. What started out as a means of rapid communication among a relatively small community of scholars has now

---

[4]Some of the reasons given by representatives of the Hispanic middle class as to why they are apprehensive about purchasing a home computer are: (a) fear of their children accessing pornography through the Internet; (b) fear that their children will spend too much time playing computer games rather than using it for educational purposes; (c) the belief that frequent use of computers may cause antisocial behavior; (d) the high cost of online service; (e) the time it takes to learn how to use a computer, the Internet and other programs; and (f) concern that a computer will become immediately outdated after being purchased.

embraced the entire online population. If someone is online then that person is predictably using e-mail either at home Or at work.

How exactly does a spoken language theorist become entangled in the myriad questions involved in the digital divide? My entire academic life has been devoted to examining possible and probable answers to the question "What difference does it make to the human condition that human beings speak?" Spoken language is the paradigm and paragon of all human communication. Levinson (1997), I believe, recognizes this centrality of the spoken word when he felicitously alludes to what he labels the "anthropocentric" tendency of all new media, the tendency of new media to always strive for a closer approximation to human spoken language.

Spoken language has three functions that occur as an if $x$ then $y$ consequence of spoken language's presence in human beings. In addition to human communication's first function of linking humans to other humans, it has two other functions: the development of higher mental processes, and the regulation of human behavior. E-mail is the newest technological manifestation of the first function of human communication, linking human beings with other human beings (Dance, 1967). The echoes of orality found in the digital divide are one instance of the oral residue found in all media (Dance, 1999). The oral residue found in each media transformation since chirography has been treated specifically in the work of Ong (1958, 1967, 1982), and foreshadowed by Mcluhan (1962, 1964), and others.

The three functions of spoken language attest to the importance of potentiating the new technologies that carry always and in all ways the residue of spoken language. It is my belief in the importance of human linking, of mentation (or higher mental processes), and of enlightened regulation of the behavior of self and others, that demands my commitment to closing the social digital divide. In McLuhan's global village it is our duty of all and especially of all human communication scholars to seek the collaboration, networking, ratiocination, and enlightened self-government that should earmark a successful social order. E-mail has started us on the way to the possible interlinking of all human beings. Now we need to use these new tools to enhance conceptual thought and rational government. It is all so exciting! We are at the threshold not of earth shattering but of earth-integrating events. The WWW, as presaged in the writing of de Chardin (1959)[5] and the statements of Berners-Lee (1999),[6] has the potential and one hopes, the destiny, of interweaving the WWW with the web of life worldwide. Throughout the world the Internet and the WWW should heighten the profile of education, of participatory government, and of human fellowship.

---

[5]Teilhard de Chardin (1959) talks about the coming "Omega Point" or personalization of the entire world.

[6]On p. 84, while speaking of his original reasons for creating the WWW, he says: "My motivation was to make sure that the Web became what I originally intended it to be—a universal medium for sharing information."

*Education.* Almost all of the elementary and secondary schools in the United States will be wired within the next few years so the challenge is to wire the schools in the rest of the world. For example:

> Children in a remote and desperately poor Cambodian village are now some of the first in the region to go online. Three new schools in Preah Viharprovince, an isolated area that borders Thailand, were recently equipped with computers supplied by charity organizations from the United States and Japan. The computers are powered by solar energy and linked to satellite dishes providing a connection to the Internet. (Tom, 1999)

*Participatory Government.* Initiatives to set up Internet kiosks in readily available public spaces, such as transit terminals, supermarkets, libraries, are gaining momentum. The kiosks are designed to allow citizens to access tax records, to pay fines such as parking tickets, to get their licenses renewed without taking a half-day to do it, to get first-level first aid advice, to contact law enforcement agencies, and ultimately to cast their ballots both locally and nationally either from the kiosk or from the comfort of their home computer. Wow! For example:

> Thousands of people have been conducting virtual elections on the New Zealand's Electoral Commission's Web site. Communications manager Doug Eckhoff says the commission is delighted with the popularity of the site, which lets people input party list and electorate votes and translates them into the allocation of seats in the resulting parliament. (New Zealand, 1999)

*Human Fellowship.* In a way, this is what the popularity of e-mail is about but so much more is yet to be accomplished. Small initiatives help, such as private ventures that make free Web pages available to neighborhood groups for discussion of civic concerns as well as for locating traffic routes, restaurants, contacting local and state government officials, and even setting up family Web sites (Neighborhood Link, 1997). The WWW offers an opportunity to reach out to others and inside to our own better selves and to resurrect civility. For example:

> Experts say nursing home residents, even the frail ones, take to computers quickly and can revitalize their lives through e-mail and the Internet. "The Internet is a window to life," said David Lansdale, a geriatrics expert from Stanford University. "It's an elixir for these people." ("Internet glues," 1999)

Or,

> In a study of silver-surfers on the Internet the authors found that once trained, online adult learners experienced increased feelings of social support, connectivity and experienced reduced technology-related anxiety. Some learned to spend hours online each week, and some became absorbed in searching web sites, e-mailing and gathering news online. Over time, this increased connectivity and feelings of social support ought to correspond to maintaining

friendships longer, maintenance of positive self-esteem, reduced age-related stress and depression and to gains in knowledge about a wide range of topicsùmedical, travel, etc. (Cody, Dunn, Huppin, & Wendt, 1999)

Or,

Estonia, a tiny country of 1.4 million people has a burning ambition: it wants to become the world's leader in information technology. Estonians feel so strongly about this that they see access to the Internet as a basic human right. "It should be as easy as turning on the water tap or heating your home," said Enel Magi, who heads Estonia's computerization effort. "We are moving into a global world and we wanted to bring children closer to that world and give them an advantage," she said. Ms. Magi is general manager of the Tiger Leap Foundation, a non-governmental organization set up to manage Tiger Leap, as the government's information technology policy is called. (Alyank, 1999)

When the remaining 96% of the world's population gets online we will have the true opportunity for building citizens of the world and for a world citizenry. Although I am excited by the prospect, I am not so naive as to believe that it will always go smoothly. There are those who would subvert the common good to individual wealth and power. The same archetypal villains that have infested human history will be around in the immediate and more distant future. It is the chore and challenge for all of us to foster the new technologies for the common good. E-Commerce will drive the closing of the access digital divide but it is the social digital divide that most needs to be eliminated for the well being of all until the Internet and the World Wide Web is universally recognized not as a privilege but as an entitlement.

## REFERENCES

Alyanak, L. (1999). *Earthtimes News Service.* Accessed: December 1999. UNESCO Newsletter No.29. http://www.unesco.org/webworld/observatory points to: http://www.earthtimes.org/dec/businesstechnology estoniatakesdec2_99.htm

Berners-Lee, T. (1999) *Weaving the web: The original design and ultimate destiny of the world wide web by its inventor.* San Francisco: HarperSanFrancisco.

Cody, M.J., Dunn, D., Hoppin, S., & Wendt, P. (1999). Silver surfers: Training and evaluating Internet use among older adult learners. *Communication Education, 48*(4),269-286.

Dance, F.E.X. (1967). The functions of speech communication as an integrative concept in the field of communication. *Proceedings of the XVth International Congress of Communications.* Genoa, Italy.

Dance, F.E.X. (1999). *Echoes of orality in the canyons of the digital divide.* Manuscript in preparation.

Ihde, D. (1990). *Technology and the lifeworld: From garden to earth.* Bloomington: Indiana University Press.

*Internet Glues Elderly Link to Life.* (1999). Associated Press. Accessed: November 1999. http://www.lasvegassun.com/sunbin/stories/tech/1999/nov/21/112100805.html

Katz, J., & Aspden, P. (1997). *The phenomenon of who is online and who is not online: The digital divide.* New Brunswick, NJ: Rutgers University Press.

Levinson, P. (1997). *The soft edge: A natural history and future of the information revolution.* New York: Routledge.

McLuhan, M. (1962). *The Gutenberg galaxy.* Toronto: University of Toronto Press.

McLuhan, M. (1964). *Understanding media: The extensions of man.* New York: Mentor Books.

Montoya, A. (1997, November). *Why is there a gap in home computer ownership among middle class Hispanics?* Tomas Rivera Policy Institute. Accessed: January 24, 2000. http://www.cgu.edu/inst/trc_pacbell.html

National Telecommunications and Information Administration. (1998b, May 6). *Home page.* National Telecommunication and Information Administration. Accessed: January 24, 2000. http://www.digitaldivide.gov

National Telecommunications and Information Administration. (1998a, May 6). *Commerce News.* National Telecommunications and Information Administration, Department of Commerce. Accessed: January 24, 2000. http://www.ntia.doc.gov/ntiahome/press/tiiap010500.htm

National Telecommunications and Information Administration. (1999a, July 8). *Falling through the net: Defining the digital divide.* National Telecommunications and Information Administration. Accessed: July, 1999. http://www.ntia.doc.gov/ntiahome/fttn99/contents.html

National Telecommunications and Information Administration. (1999b, December 9). *Digital Divide Summit.* National Telecommunications and Information Administration, Department of Commerce. Accessed: January 24, 2000. http://www.ntia.doc.gov/ntiahome/digitaldivide/summit/index.html

Neighborhood Link. (1997). *Neighborhood Link Homepage.* Accessed: January 24, 2000. http://www.neighborhoodlink.com/public/

New Zealand Infotech Weekly. (1999). *New Zealand Infotech Weekly.* Accessed: November 1999. http://www.infotech.co.nz/current/ntvote.html

Nua Internet Surveys. (2001, October 1). *Half a billion online* (editorial). http://www.nua.ie/surbeys/analysis/weeklyeditorial/archives/index.htm.

Nua Limited. (1995a, September). *Nua Analysis,* Accessed January 24, 2000. http://www.nua.ie/surveys/analysis/graphs_charts/comparisons

Nua Limited. (1995b, September). *Nua Surveys.* Nua Limited. Accessed: January 24, 2000. http://www.nua.ie/surveys

Ong, W.J. (1958). *Ramus, method, and the decay of dialogue.* Cambridge, MA: Harvard University Press.

Ong, W.J. (1967). *The presence of the word: Some prolegomena for cultural and religious history.* Minneapolis: University of Minnesota Press.

Ong, W.J. (1982). *Orality and literacy: The technologizing of the word.* New York: Methuen.

Teilhard de Chardin, P. (1959). *The phenomenon of man.* New York: Harper & Row.

Tom, A. (1999). *Cambodia's children plug into the Information Superhighway.* Cable News Network. Accessed: January 24, 2000. http://www.cnn.com/ASIANOW/southeast/9911/18/cambodia.internet/index.html

# Risk and the Internet:
# Perception and Reality

## Eric A. Zimmer
## Christopher D. Hunter

*As an electronic frontier, the public image of cyberspace has often been one of a lawless and immoral environment, populated to a significant degree by perverts, sexual predators, and purveyors of cyberporn. Although such concerns are understandable, unsubstantiated claims and individual impressions may be problematic when they drive public policy. The value of empirical research, then, is to provide evidence for making informed political decisions. This is the rationale behind Eric Zimmer and Christopher Hunter's examination of sexual content on the Web. As they report in this chapter, the actual proportion of pornographic material on the Internet is small, comparing favorably with the typical magazine rack found in public news stands and stationery stores. The implications of their research, they suggest, is that efforts to curtail First Amendment protections of Web sites amount to unwarranted censorship. Apart from Section 2, you might compare their focus on the popular perceptions of risk associated with the Internet to Gary Gumpert and Susan Drucker's comments on the perceived dangers of city streets in Chapter 1. Also relevant to the First Amendment issue raised here is Neil Kleinman's consideration of copyright law in Chapter 4, and Camille Paglia's reflections on the online magazine Salon in Chapter 16. For an alternate take on Web content, see Stuart Moulthrop's essay on cybertext in Chapter 15.*

According to research overseen by Joseph Turow of the Annenberg Public Policy Center, fully one fourth of news articles on the Internet from October 1997 to October 1998 were alarmist in nature and two thirds of these news articles raised disturbing issues about the nature and content of the World Wide Web (Turow, 1999). Additionally, parents expressed grave concerns about the content their children may encounter on the Web. Without a doubt, much exists on the Web that is troubling to parents of school-age children and to others who do not want to be assaulted by sexually graphic content. Yet, 30 years of agenda-setting research would suggest that a link exists between these stories of the prurient and hazardous nature of Web content and the concern of parents, many of whom do not completely understand what is available on the Web, let alone how to control their children's access to it.

Agenda-setting influences also lead the public policy debate about the Internet. Concerns about the new media, driven by older media, help foster an alarmist state in which legislators define their roles in light of protecting citizens from the bogeyman of the Internet through legislative control of access to or dissemination of Internet content. Historically, however, the issue of curtailing objectionable material has not been solved by access controls; it is a long-standing social problem that will not likely be solved by legalistic or technical solutions. Politicians who might otherwise promote government taking a hands-off approach to many social issues are seen promoting legislation to monitor, cordon off, and choke off questionable sites. Although they might deplore "Big Brother" in the boardroom, they vote for the Communications Decency Act, because they desire to "protect" children from the evils of the Internet. Protectors in government and in lobbying bodies also promote the use of filtering software to keep the impressionable from the objectionable. Yet, the question arises: Why does Web content incite such fear in parents? Does it merit the press coverage it receives? Does the Web really emphasize the prurient and salacious, the vicious and the foul? Or is it, like the world around us, more a place where one must exercise caution in the dark places, but where these places are relatively limited in their number and scope?

This chapter attempts to grapple with some of these questions and to suggest public policy strategy in addressing these topics. First, we present historical background on the confluence of media scares and communication technologies, and an understanding of the nature of Internet risks and fears. Second, we present findings from a content analysis of newspaper coverage of families and the Internet, and a survey on current perceptions of the risks associated with an unfettered Web. Third, we present new findings from our content analysis of the pages found in a popular search engine's database, contrasting the perceptions and the reality of Web content. Finally, we offer some insights on reframing the policy debate in this area.

## A BRIEF HISTORY OF FEAR AND CENSORSHIP

Government and public fear about harmful Internet content, and the ensuing urge to censor such material, is nothing new. Rather, it is just the most recent manifestation of an age-old debate. Since the origin of the spoken word, communities and governments have feared the potentially corrupting influence of all new media. As Wartella and Reeves (1985) note, "With the development of each modern means of storytelling—books, newspapers, movies, radio, comics, and television—social debates regarding their effects have recurred. A prominent theme in all these debates has been a concern with media's impact on youth" (p. 119).

Perhaps the first policymaker to focus on the dangers of media content was Plato who, some 2,000 years ago, called for extensive censorship to protect the education of children, the morals of citizens, and to generally achieve a good and just society (Wolfson 1997). Indeed, in Plato's The Republic, he notes, "Then the first thing will be to establish a censorship of the writers of fiction, and . . . reject the bad." Plato goes on to argue for the censorship of playwrights, poets, and music. Warning of the influence of storytellers, Plato comments:

> Children cannot distinguish between what is allegory and what isn't, and opinions formed at that age are usually difficult to eradicate or change; it is therefore of the utmost importance that the first stories they hear shall aim at producing the right moral effect.

Based on these arguments Plato even called for the censorship of Homer.

Although Plato and the Greeks merely had to worry about spoken stories and a few written manuscripts, the invention of the printing press around 1450, confronted the Catholic Church and European rulers with a truly revolutionary medium, capable of eliminating their long held monopoly over the dissemination of ideas. The printing press and Luther disintermediated the Catholic priest and laid the seeds for mass literacy, and mass political and religious dissent (Eisenstein, 1980; Grendler, 1984). Clearly, the printed word was to be feared and, therefore, censored by the prevailing authorities.

Responding to this new technology of freedom, the Church developed one of the most comprehensive and long lasting censorship regimes in human history. In 1524, under Church guidance, Charles V of Belgium published a list of censored books. Forty years later in 1564, the Church formalized the listing of banned books by publishing the Index librorum prohibitum (*Index of Prohibited Books*). The *Index* consisted of several parts:

1. A listing of outright banned authors.
2. A listing of banned titles.
3. Rules for expurgation of books with some "error," but which were not all bad.
4. Sweeping rules for the dissemination of printed works (Grendler, 1984).

Generally speaking, the *Index* focused on doctrinal error, but it also included immoral and obscene works. This concern with the corrupting influence of content, once again seen as particularly dangerous for children, is reflected in rule number eight of the original Index:

> Books which professedly deal with, narrate or teach things lascivious or obscene are absolutely prohibited, since not only the matter of faith but also that of morals, which are usually easily corrupted through the reading of such books, must be taken into consideration, and those who possess them are to be severely punished by the bishops. Ancient books written by heathens may by reason of their elegance and quality of style be permitted, but may by no means be read to children. (*Modern History Sourcebook*, 1999)

Updated and published every 50 years until 1966, the *Index* is a strong testament to the fear and regulation of media content.

In the 19th century, the rise of mass literacy and the penny press again focused government attention on the problem of dangerous and corrupting material. In England, the infamous Thomas Bowdler took up the cause. In 1802, he helped found the Society for the Suppression of Vice, whose goal was "To prevent the profanation of the Lord's Day, prosecute blasphemous publications, bring the trade in obscene books to a halt, close disorderly houses and suppress fortune tellers" (cited in St. John-Stevas, 1962, p. 104). From 1802 to 1807, the Society successfully prosecuted between 30 and 40 obscenity cases (Tedford, 1993). In addition to his legal crusading, Bowdler authored *The Family Shakespeare*, "bowdlerized" to exclude profanity, indecency, and blasphemy (Hoyt, 1970).

The United States had a similar 19th-century morality crusader in Anthony Comstock. In 1872, Comstock founded the New York Society for the Suppression of Vice, whose state-given mandate was to suppress "obscene literature" including "vile weekly newspapers" and "licentious books" (Hoyt & Hoyt, 1970, p. 22). One year after founding the New York Society, he lobbied Congress to pass federal legislation outlawing the sending of "obscene or crime-inciting matter" through the mails. Prohibited material, under what became known as the Comstock Law, included, "every obscene, lewd, lascivious, or filthy book, pamphlet, picture, paper, letter, writing, print, or other publication of an indecent character" not to mention any material regarding contraception or abortion (Hoyt & Hoyt, 1970, p. 23). Comstock would go on to destroy countless "obscene" works as a special agent of the Post Office.

The spirit of Comstock's moral crusading continued well into the 20th century, where new groups like the National Organization for Decent Literature (founded in 1955) and The Citizens for Decent Literature (1956) gained widespread support. New types of media, including pulp-fiction magazines, comics, and films, all came under the scrutiny of such organizations. For example, speaking to the dangers of film, the *Christian Century* (1930) noted:

> Movies are so occupied with crime and sex stuff and are so saturating the minds
> of children the world over with social sewage that they have become a menace to
> the mental and moral life of the coming generation. (cited in Starker, 1989, p. 8)

## Pornography Drives Technology—Which Drives Censorship

Since the invention of the printing press, pornography has been a driving force behind the development of new media, which as a result has lead to efforts to censor all new media. Two of the most popular books produced by Gutenberg's new invention were the pornographic tales of Pietro Aretino's *Postures* (1524) and the satiric *Gargantua and Pantagruel* of François Rabelais (1530-40). *Postures* consisted of a series of engravings depicting various sexual positions; each accompanied by a ribald sonnet. Rabelais' work was more satirical, including passages such as a playful governess introducing Gargantua to sex; Gargantua's horse pissing away an army, and a woman scaring away the devil by exposing her vagina (Findland, 1993; Kendrick, 1987).

Pornography next played an essential role in the development of the paperback book. In the late 19th century, printers began publishing magazines made of cheap "pulp" paper, thus the term *pulp fiction*. One of the most popular genres of the paperback was pornography and erotica, a tradition that continues to this day, with cheap, cheesecake novels sold in the local supermarket (Johnson, 1996).

In the 19th century, pornography also accompanied the development of photography. Civil War soldiers sought more than just letters from home. Through the mails they also received large quantities of pornographic photographs. The traffic in such images was so great that Congress passed the nation's first law prohibiting the sending of obscenity through the mails. However, by the time the bill passed in 1865 the war was over, and soldiers returned home with pornography in their pockets (Johnson, 1996).

Several more modern media of communication can also attribute pornography as a contributing factor to their success. Pay-per-view cable television's first lucrative use was broadcasting X-rated films. Videotaped pornography helped drive the nascent market for videocassette players and rented videos. Pornography also helped prove the market for "900" phone services, and CD-ROMs (Johnson, 1996).

Pornography's integral role in the development of most modern media is likely attributable to two factors. First, put simply, humans enjoy sex. Second, entrepreneurs recognize this fact, and will use any medium open to them to distribute pornographic content to an eager consuming public. The Internet merely represents the culmination of this trend, providing commercial pornographers with a distribution technology capable of reaching a vast international market. How eager is the public for such material? In 1998, Americans spent $1 billion on Internet pornography and $5 billion renting pornographic videos. Globally, legal pornography is estimated to be a $56 billion industry (Morais, 1999).

Fear, Cyberporn, and the March to Censor the Web

Based on our historical fear and regulation of all forms of media content, it should be of no surprise that our newest medium, the Web, has been similarly attacked as an "evil influence," poised to "contaminate the health and character of the nation's children" (Starker, 1989, p. 5). The moral danger inherent in the Internet has been defined as the easy availability of pornography, hate speech, and violence. In the United States, and many other nations, this fear has inevitably led to calls for government regulation. We thus outline U.S. and Canadian experiences with, and responses to, the perceived dangers of Web content.

*The U.S. Experience.* On July 3, 1995, Time magazine carried the following cover article: "On a Screen Near You: Cyberporn." The article, by Time senior writer Phillip Elmer-Dewitt, cited the soon to be published research of a Carnegie Mellon undergraduate student named Marty Rimm (Wallace & Mangan, 1996). Rimm's study, eventually published in the *Georgetown Law Review*, claimed to be an exhaustive look at the amount and types of pornography available on the Internet. Rimm found that 83.5% of Usenet images were pornographic, and that more than 70% of the sexual images on the newsgroups surveyed "originate from adult-oriented computer bulletin-board systems (BBS) whose operators are trying to lure customers to their private collections of X-rated material" (Elmer-Dewitt, 1995). Furthermore, he found that many of the images analyzed were exceptionally kinky and violent.

Following the publication of the *Time* article and the actual Rimm study, many Internet analysts came forward to discredit Rimm's analysis. Taking the forefront in pointing out the study's weaknesses were Vanderbilt University professors Donna Hoffman and Tom Novak. They argued that Rimm's selection of a few sex-related newsgroups was simply not representative of the world of Usenet, or of the larger Internet. "Also, no information is provided on the degree to which these 32 newsgroups comprise the complete universe of Usenet imagery" (Hoffman & Novak, 1995). In addition to his nonrepresentative sample of newsgroups (of which there are thousands mostly relating to news, recreation, and politics), Rimm used no clear definition of pornography to classify images as pornographic.

The onslaught of articles, e-mail, and Usenet posts discrediting the Rimm study led *Time* to "admit that grievous errors had slipped past their editorial staff, as their normally thorough research succumbed to a combination of deadline pressure and exclusivity agreements that barred them from showing the unpublished study to possible critics" (Wilkins, 1997). Although for all intents and purposes the Rimm study had been discredited—shown to be a methodologically weak study conducted by an attention seeking undergraduate student—a heightened sense of the moral dangers of the Internet endured.

Despite this discrediting, the Time article and the Rimm study stirred a wild moral panic about access to pornography on the Internet. In the months that followed, several mainstream newspapers and magazines including *The New York Times, USA Today,* and *Newsweek* ran stories regarding the "threat" of Internet content. Electronic Freedom Foundation (EFF) lawyer Mike Goodwin (1998) referred to this situation as "The Great Cyberporn Panic of 1995" (p. 206). Several U.S. senators and congressmen soon weighed in with legislation to protect children from the scourge of easily accessed Internet pornography. As Margaret Seif (1997) notes, "the political football got blown up to gigantic proportions."

Senator Charles Grassley (R-Iowa) proposed the Protection of Children from Pornography Act of 1995. In support of his bill, Grassley introduced the entire *Time* article into the Congressional Record, and referred to Rimm's undergraduate research as "a remarkable study conducted by researchers at Carnegie Mellon University" (Wilkins, 1997). Grassley (1995) further noted that there is a "flood of vile pornography, and we must act to stem this growing tide." Grassley's bill did not pass, but it led to several Internet censorship bills, culminating in the Communications Decency Act (CDA) sponsored by former Senator James Exon. The bill was attached to the Telecommunications Reform Act of 1996, which was passed by Congress and signed into law by President Bill Clinton in February 1996.

Following passage of the CDA, two polls found widespread support for government regulation of the Internet. An October 1996 survey by the *Los Angeles Times* found that 56% of respondents favored "a law that would make it illegal for a computer network to carry pornographic or adult material" (Harmon, 1996). Similarly, a May 1997 ABC News poll found that 80% of respondents favored government restrictions on Internet pornography (Richtel, 1997).

Despite Congressional and public support, on June 26, 1997, the U.S. Supreme Court ruled in the case of *Reno v. ACLU* that the CDA was an unconstitutional restriction of First Amendment freedoms. Disappointed with this outcome, and boosted by polls supporting Internet regulation, 1 year later in October 1998, Congress passed the Child Online Protection Act (COPA), another attempt at limiting minors access to adult speech on the Internet (Nickell, 1998). Most recently in 1999, Congress has debated similar measures requiring Internet service providers (ISPs) to distribute Internet-filtering software ("Senate unanimously," 1999), and to require public schools and libraries to install such programs (McCain, 1999).

*The Canadian Experience.* Concurrent with battles in the United States, Canada has experienced a very similar development of public concern over the perceived dangers of the Internet. Just as in the United States, newspaper coverage of "hot button" issues, particularly child pornography and online hate speech, have led many Canadians to wonder if government regulation is needed ("Net porn," 1998). For example, a 1997 Citizen-Global poll of adult Canadians found that 66% favored government regulation of the Internet (Cobb, 1997). Similarly, a 1998 poll, by Ekos Research Associates, found that "two thirds of Canadians felt that the government should control or regulate the publication of abusive content and pornography on the Internet" ("Half of Canadians," 1998).

Likely due to such support, in July 1998 MP Chris Axworth (NDP-Saskatoon) introduced Bill C-424, the Internet Child Pornography Prevention Act, before the Canadian House of Commons. The bill called for the Canadian Radio Television and Telecommunications Commission (CRTC) to license ISPs, who would be required to block access to Internet sites where child pornography could be found (Campbell, 1998). In response to Axworth's proposal, the CRTC conducted a public review, but in May 1999 concluded "that any attempt to regulate Canadian new media might put the industry at a competitive disadvantage in the global marketplace" (CRTC, 1999).

As with the U.S. Supreme Court's rejection of the CDA, the CRTC has put a damper on legislative attempts at Internet regulation. However, in light of continued public support, and a growing debate over library and school Web filtering, Canadians will likely see further attempts to regulate online content.

## RISK

Parents with computers generally believe that it is important for their children to have access to the Web, yet many also fear what their children may encounter online. They also believe that the benefits outweigh the risks. What makes parents and legislators so concerned about their children and the Web when their children live in a world that presents more pressing dangers in everyday living?

The Web shares similar characteristics with other situations that the public finds risky. The public has a broad conception of risk that incorporates such characteristics as uncertainty, dread, catastrophic potential, controllability, equity, risk to future generations, and so forth. Some things we find risky, whereas others we may not, even though they might be equally likely to result in negative outcomes. Many people die each year from food poisoning, yet most of us give this hazard little thought. In contrast, when the news media reported the risks associated with the chemical Alar on apples, the apple industry sustained major damage to its image and a $125 million loss in income. This damage to the industry occurred even though Alar ceased to be used in 1989, only 15% of growers used it at all, and its deleterious effects were not well documented (Egan, 1991).

According to Paul Slovic; risk may be understood better when we consider two factors: how unknown the risk is, and how dreaded it is. He presents these two factors on axes and suggests that when a risk is both unknown and dreadful, people are much more likely to want it regulated (Slovic, 1987). As an example, people find the risk from radioactive waste both unknown and dreadful, and have little toleration for its presence in their lives. It is something that they cannot fathom and this lack of information about its possible effects raises the demands that radioactive waste be avoided. In contrast, the risk from something like a bicycle is neither unknown nor dreadful. Almost certainly it is the case that more people die each year in the United States from bicycle accidents (761 in 1998; National Highway Traffic Safety Administration, 1998) than from exposure to radioactive waste. People neither fear nor avoid bicycles, and they might find bicycle regulation silly.

As a society, we balance the risk inherent in different activities with the benefits they provide to us. Motor vehicle accidents result in more than 41,000 deaths per year in the United States (National Highway Traffic Safety Administration, 1998) and are one of the major sources of air pollution, yet automobiles provides us with great benefits and so people overlook the risks inherent in their use. We know the risks, but do not find the dread too high.

Internet risks, in Slovic's paradigm, are unknown risks for many people. Whether or not the risk is dreadful varies within the populace. Some may find the risk of their children discovering pornography on the Internet too dreadful to allow and may thus choose not to give their children access. Others may find it no more dreadful than watching prime-time television and thus allow the Internet in their home, subject to certain limitations.

Slovic's work also differentiates between risks that are voluntary and those that are involuntary. Research has found that "the public will accept risks from voluntary activities (such as skiing) that are roughly 1,000 times as great as it would tolerate from involuntary hazards (such as food preservatives) that provide the same level of benefits" (Slovic, 1987, p. 236). According to Slovic:

> An accident that takes many lives may produce relatively little social disturbance (beyond that experienced by the victims' families and friends) if it occurs as part of a familiar and well-understood system (such as a train wreck). However, a small accident in an unfamiliar system (or one perceived as poorly understood), such as a nuclear reactor or a recombinant DNA laboratory, may have immense social consequences if it is perceived as a harbinger of further and possibly catastrophic mishaps. (p. 236)

The Internet generally, and the Web in particular, are still unknowns to many people and will remain so until the public has a general understanding of what is available on the Internet. At that point, the fear of the available content will likely decrease and with it the concerns.

The perception of risk to vulnerable portions of the populace will not likely decrease at the same rate as the perception of risk to adults. The public, and parents particularly, will attempt to protect children, vulnerable as they are, from the perceived chaos and risk on the Internet. Media coverage has signal value for the public's perception of risk. Each media presentation of a child molester attempting to meet a young girl he has met through an Internet chat room is like a stone thrown into a calm pool of water, the effects ripple well beyond the actual entrance (Slovic, 1987). As the public hears about such an occurrence, and as the public finds the risk of the Web to be unknown, the news report imparts a greater signal than would otherwise be the case. The social impact will thus be great. The actual risk perception will likely take into account neither the fact that the child was unsupervised in this chat room, nor that the recent estimates of 107.3 million online users in the United States and Canada mean that the likelihood of a child encountering a deviant online is remarkably slim (NUA Net Surveys, 1999). This assessment does not deny the real concerns of parents and of others in charge of children, it simply offers a different perspective on the likelihood of harmful encounters on the Internet.

## Stoking the Flames: The Press and Public Opinion Toward the Internet

We notice a definite pattern in the development of Internet risks and the desire for regulation in the U.S. and Canada. First, the press treats isolated incidents of Internet pornography, sexual predators, hate speech, and so on, as if they were the norm for the Internet. To read popular media coverage of the Internet, a concerned parent might think that lurking behind every Web page link is hard-core pornography, and behind every e-mail exchange a pederast. As Ann K. Symons (1999) of the American Library Association comments, "It's not news to say that millions of kids had a safe rewarding experience on-line today." Such negative coverage generates fear in the minds of the general public and of parents in particular. This fear is reflected in the many public opinion polls cited earlier. Once public fear has been piqued, it is almost too much for legislators to avoid overly simplistic regulatory solutions.

The recent survey and content analysis conducted by Joseph Turow of the Annenberg Public Policy Center of the University of Pennsylvania supports the agenda setting-like process described earlier (McCombs & Shaw, 1972). The Annenberg study first surveyed a national sample of parents regarding their attitudes towards the Internet. They found that 76% of parents feared that their child might view sexually explicit images on the Internet. Only 40% of respondents agreed with the statement that "the Internet is a safe place for my child to spend time" (Turow, 1999, p. 14).

These survey results were compared with a content analysis of U.S. newspaper coverage of the Internet and the family. The content analysis encompassed all the articles on the Internet and the family that appeared in twelve major newspapers from October 15, 1997 to October 15, 1998. These newspapers include 6 of the 10 largest in circulation as well as another 6 between the 40th and 50th largest in circulation. For the purposes of selecting articles, all articles that used the terms *Internet, AOL, Web,* or *online* and included the words *family, families, child, children, parent, parents, youth,* or *teens.* The search resulted in 668 relevant articles. The researchers designed a questionnaire for content analysis that asked the following broad questions:

1. What issues do the papers raise about the Internet and the family?
2. What kinds of people speak about the Internet and the family in the articles, and what do they say?

Based on these questions, the researchers asked further questions on placement of stories, the positive or negative valence of stories, and whether solutions accompanied the presentation of problems.

The content analysis found that one in every four articles dealt with sex crimes against children, including sexual predation and child pornography. Although 48% of stories dealt solely with negative aspects of the net, only 33% focused on the net's benefits. Two of every three articles presented disturbing issues on the Web–family relationship. Among the negative stories, 29% dealt with material improper for children, 21% with online sexual predators, 18% with pornography, and 17% with child pornography. The positively valenced stories rarely overlapped with those presenting the social ills, leaving little to counterbalance the problems associated with the Web. Making the agenda-setting connection between survey and content analysis results, Turow (1999) notes: "the press' portrayal of the Internet is particularly significant because it directly reflects the results of our national survey" (p. 35). Although this finding is correlational, it does offer support for the connection between negative news coverage of the Internet and the reactions of parents of school-age children.

To complete the press, fear, and regulation cycle, FCC chairman William Kennard was invited to deliver a keynote speech at the conference unveiling the Annenberg results. Kennard used the opportunity to publicly support mandatory filtering policies for any public school or library receiving federal grants for Internet access (McCullagh, 1999).

The problem with this type of press, fear, regulation cycle is that the press may be overemphasizing the dangers of Internet content. If, as some anti-regulation, anti-censorship groups argue, the net contains only about 5% objectionable material, then public fear may be out of proportion to the actual risk. We thus hope to provide an objective, social-scientific measure of just how much objectionable material exists on the World Wide Web.

Media coverage creates dread risk for the public. Additionally, many parents are concerned about the risk factor of their children encountering the unknown on the Internet (Turow, 1999). The risk literature suggests that in cases of high dread risk and high unknown risk, the public will have artificially heightened risk sensitivity. Thus, in contrast to the inflammatory press coverage of Internet risks, we hypothesize that the actual percentages of objectionable content will actually be much lower.

## Methods

In order to rate the Web sites, we used the standardized Recreational Software Advisory Council's Internet rating system (RSACi), designed by Stanford

Communication professor Donald F. Roberts to rate the objectionable content of video games and to provide parents with a way to protect their children from excessive violence. Although designed for video games, with the advent of the Internet the system was adapted to allow Web site owners to self-rate their content. Currently, RSACi is the most popular system for rating content on the Internet, with more than 100,000 Web sites using it to self-rate (RSAC, 1999).

RSACi contains four content categories (language, nudity, sex, and violence) each with five levels of severity (0, 1, 2, 3, and 4). Within the language category, for example, a site may be rated 0 if it contains no objectionable language, 1 if it contains mild expletives, 2 if it has profanity, 3 with strong language, and 4 if it contains crude, vulgar language. Table 11.1 gives a summary of RSACi's rating categories.

This system was used to rate the content of 1,067 randomly chosen English language Web sites. Only the first page of all sites was rated. Links were not followed to subsidiary pages. The only exception to this rule was on pages that had no other content than an "Enter this site" link, in which case the link was followed, and the first fully developed page was rated.

We chose our simple random sample, drawn from the WebCrawler database of approximately 50 million Universal Resource Locators (URLs; Add your URL on WebCrawler, 1999), using the "Web Roulette" random link feature of WebCrawler. This feature generates a Web page containing 10 links randomly selected from WebCrawler's database (WebCrawler, 1999). We determined that a sample of 1,067 randomly chosen sites would allow plus or minus 3% accuracy at the 95% confidence level (Salant & Dillman, 1994). From September 14 through September 19, 1999 we gathered all links and placed them in a master sample file. Although this sample is an accurate random sample from the WebCrawler database, it does not represent a true random sample of all web content. Because of the Web's vast size, currently estimated at some 800 million individual pages, even the most powerful individual search engine only indexes about 16% of the Web's content (Lawrence & Giles, 1999). As such, the random sample produced by WebCrawler is only representative of the percentage of the Web indexed by the search engine.

We tested the reliability of our use of the RSACi rating system by conducting an intercoder reliability test on a 50-site subset of the larger 1,067 site sample. Overall, use of the RSACi rating system was found to be highly reliable. For the 50 sites tested, coders rated sites with perfect reliability 96.5% of the time. Intercoder reliability across all RSACi content categories and Web sites was high ($\alpha = .9313$).

Although these results point to a highly reliable coding scheme, they may be artificially high due to the large amount of nonobjectionable content in the sample. In other words, because the vast majority of sites were rated 0 for all categories by coders, there was little variation in the amount of objectionable content across the sites. This reduces the room for error among coders.

**Table 11.1**

**The Recreational Software Advisory Council Internet Rating System**

| Level | Violence | Nudity | Sex | Language |
|---|---|---|---|---|
| 0 | none of the below, or sports related | none of the below | none of the below, or innocent kissing; romance | none of the below |
| 1 | injury to human beings | revealing attire | passionate kissing | mild expletives |
| 2 | destruction of realistic objects | partial nudity | clothed sexual touching | moderate expletives or profanity |
| 3 | aggressive violence or death to humans | frontal nudity | nonexplicit sexual acts | strong language or hate speech |
| 4 | rape or wanton, gratuitous violence | provocative frontal nudity | explicit sexual acts or sex crimes | crude, vulgar language or extreme hate speech |

## CONTENT ANALYSIS OF WEB SITES

Our content analysis of 1,067 Web sites produced the results displayed in Tables 11.2 through 11.5.

**Table 11.2**

### Levels of RSACi Language Categories

|       |                                           | Frequency | Percent | Valid Percent | Cumulative Percent |
|-------|-------------------------------------------|-----------|---------|---------------|--------------------|
| Valid | None                                      | 1,009     | 94.6    | 94.6          | 94.6               |
|       | Mild expletives                           | 18        | 1.7     | 1.7           | 96.3               |
|       | Mod. expletives/profanity                 | 1         | .1      | .1            | 96.3               |
|       | Strong lang./hate speech                  | 9         | .8      | .8            | 97.2               |
|       | Crude, vulgar lang./extreme hate speech   | 30        | 2.8     | 2.8           | 100.0              |
|       | Total                                     | 1,067     | 100.0   | 100.0         |                    |
| Total |                                           | 1,067     | 100.0   |               |                    |

**Table 11.3**

### Levels of RSACi Nudity Categories

|       |                    | Frequency | Percent | Valid Percent | Cumulative Percent |
|-------|--------------------|-----------|---------|---------------|--------------------|
| Valid | None               | 1,020     | 95.6    | 95.6          | 95.6               |
|       | Revealing attire   | 11        | 1.0     | 1.0           | 96.6               |
|       | Partial            | 7         | .7      | .7            | 97.3               |
|       | Frontal            | 5         | .5      | .5            | 97.8               |
|       | Provocative frontal | 24       | 2.2     | 2.2           | 100.0              |
|       | Total              | 1,067     | 100.0   | 100.0         |                    |
| Total |                    | 1,067     | 100.0   |               |                    |

## Table 11.4

### Levels of RSACi Sex Categories

| | | Frequency | Percent | Valid Percent | Cumulative Percent |
|---|---|---|---|---|---|
| Valid | None, or innocent kiss | 1,038 | 97.3 | 97.3 | 97.3 |
| | Clothed sexual touching | 3 | .3 | .3 | 97.6 |
| | Nonexplicit sex acts | 2 | .2 | .2 | 97.8 |
| | Explicit sex/sex crimes | 24 | 2.2 | 2.2 | 100.0 |
| | Total | 1,067 | 100.0 | 100.0 | |
| Total | | 1,067 | 100.0 | | |

## Table 11.5

### Levels of RSACi Violence Categories

| | | Frequency | Percent | Valid Percent | Cumulative Percent |
|---|---|---|---|---|---|
| Valid | None, or sports related | 1,058 | 99.2 | 99.2 | 99.2 |
| | Injury to humans | 2 | .2 | .2 | 99.3 |
| | Aggressive violence/death to humans | 6 | .6 | .6 | 99.9 |
| | Rape or wanton gratuitous violence | 1 | .1 | .1 | 100.0 |
| | Total | 1,067 | 100.0 | 100.0 | |
| Total | | 1,067 | 100.0 | | |

Overall, the rate of objectionable content was very low; 92.8% of all Web sites in the population have no content that rated even 1 on the scale. We find that 95.1% had no scores above 1. Compared to the level of violence on television, where 61% of U.S. television shows have violent content, these percentages are very low (Federman, 1999).

## DISCUSSION

The results from our content analysis suggest that the Internet contains a very small percentage of offensive material. These data call into question the press's coverage of the Internet as a dangerous place, the public's fear of the Internet, and government's attempts to impose Internet content controls. Just as a large city will have some dangerous areas among a majority of safer ones, the Internet and the Web consist of mostly constructive, not to say innocuous, sites that offer sports scores, library supplies, dictionaries of e-mail "emoticons," and shingles for various professionals. The sample we obtained for this study did have its share of provocative sites. From graphic heterosexual sex to bestiality, from fecal eroticism to "barely legal" pictures of teenagers, the 2.8% of sites with graphic sexual content offered much that the prurient mind might desire and gave credence to the argument that pornography has and continues to drive communication technology. Although online pornography is clearly very big business, the small percentage of objectionable content in this sample suggests that the people use the Web for far more than titillation. Yet it is not news that the vast majority of children are not getting into trouble on the Internet (Symons, 1999).

What does one say to the statement that children do not go randomly to sites, but follow links, click on banner ads, and punch in searches for any variety of interests? They can easily get into any variety of problematic areas on the Internet, from chat rooms to porno sites. Concerned parents and legislators may note that even a small percentage of objectionable Internet content should not preclude regulation. After all, although pornography, hate speech, and so on, are only a small percentage of the total Internet, children can actively seek this content out. Unlike the real world where dirty magazines are stored behind the counter or placed behind blinder racks to prevent child access, there are few such barriers in cyberspace. Proponents of regulation argue that government enforced access controls are necessary to ensure that children do not wander into the "free-fire zones and red light districts of cyberspace" (Gore, 1999).

Although this argument has some validity in a society in which children often grow up far too quickly, its implementation comes with a high cost. Due to the Internet's vast size and distributed nature, it is difficult to keep track of objectionable content subject to government access restrictions. Software filters, or proxy servers that maintain lists of blocked sites, usually impose these restrictions. Artificial intelligence web spiders that classify content according to key words found in the text of a Web page follow links and track the pages that fall inside or outside of the list boundaries. Unfortunately, these spiders have proved to be extremely context insensitive, blocking sites dealing with breast cancer and safe sex merely due to the presence of off-limits words. Such false positives create a situation where far more than the 3% of truly objectionable sites are blocked. Indeed, one study has concluded that filter software incorrectly blocks 21% of nonobjectionable Internet content (Hunter, 1999). Such findings raise troubling societal questions.

Authorities throughout history have attempted, and often succeeded, in controlling access to information and various media. Yet, in most Western societies advocates of free speech have increasingly foiled these efforts. The value placed on unfettered access to information has resulted in fewer and fewer controls on speech content. The Web is a medium in its infancy. Like previous communication technologies, it has been used to disseminate pornography and violence of the most graphic kind. We postulate that, as with past technologies, time will show that the Web will be used in far more pedestrian and useful ways than we can possible predict. Although pornography has been the cash cow of the Net to date, it will pale in comparison to the business to business uses that have already arisen, and will continue to arise in the future. Any use of legislation to regulate speech on the Internet will likely come into place too slowly to address the perceived issues and will be unable to address the international scope of Web content. Certainly, in the future the technology of filtering will increase in its subtlety, but so to will the expert little fingers that desire to circumvent such filters.

In the meantime, parents rightly concern themselves about their children's access to the Web. What might one say to these concerned caregivers? The majority of parents, more than 80%, in online households set limits on their children's use of the Internet and keep an eye on what the children do online. For such parents of children between the ages of 8 and 12, two thirds do not allow their children to go online without a parent present (Turow, 1999). Currently, 32% of parents with online connections use filtering software. These parents have a solution of sorts already. These data suggest that parents, for the most part, are quite capable of minding their own children on the Internet. This finding is mirrored in the newspaper coverage of families and the Internet, where journalists placed the burden of addressing Web problems on the shoulders of parents. Certainly the less parents cede jurisdiction to government authorities, the better they will maintain control over their children in this and other potentially risky behaviors.

This study has addressed the history of concerns that arise when new communication technologies are introduced to the public. We have considered how print journalism inflames the fears of society about pornography, violence, and foul language on the Internet and how the agenda-setting aspects of such press coverage correlate with the concerns of both parents and policymakers. Such concerns need to be tempered by the realization that the vast majority of

Web sites are benign and by the fact that parents, generally speaking, have the situation well in hand through their own supervisory powers and through their use of personal filtering software.

The debate will continue as to whether or not governments should move to block a significant percentage of nonobjectionable and valuable content at the source in order to get at the much smaller percent of objectionable content. For now at least, the United States and Canada have concluded that this tradeoff is unacceptable. However, in light of continued negative press coverage of the Internet, public pressure may well lead to such an outcome.

## REFERENCES

Campbell, K.K. (1998, July 16). Porn prevention. *The Toronto Star*, p. J8.

Canadian Radio Television and Telecommunications Commission. (1999, May 17). *CRTC won't regulate the internet* (news release). Author.

Cobb, C. (1997, December 22). Majority wants curbs on Internet. *The Ottawa Citizen.*

Egan, T. (1991, July 9). Apple growers bruised and bitter after Alar scare. *The New York Times,* Section A, p. 1, column 2.

Eisenstein, E. (1980). *The printing press as an agent of change: Communications and cultural transformations in early-modern Europe.* Cambridge: Cambridge University Press.

Elmer-Dewitt, P. (1995, July 3). On a screen near you: Cyberporn. *Time Magazine.*

Federman, J. (Ed.). (1999). *National television violence study* (vol. 3). Santa Barbara, CA. Available at www.ccsp.ucsb.edu

Findland, P. (1993). Humanism, politics and pornography in Renaissance Italy. In L. Hunt (Ed.), *The invention of pornography: Obscenity and the origins of modernity, 1500-1800.* New York: Zone Books.

Goodwin, M. (1998). *Cyber rights.* New York: Random House.

Gore, A. (1999, May 5). *Remarks on the Internet. White House Office of the Press Secretary.* Available at http://www.whitehouse.gov/WH/New/html/19990505-4219.html.

Grassley, C. (1995, June 26). *Senate testimony.* Congressional Record. S9017-S9023.

Grendler, P. E. (1984). The advent of printing. In *Censorship: 500 years of conflict.* New York: New York Public Library.

Half of Canadians Experienced Negative Effects of Computers. (1998, February 24). *The Globe and Mail.* Available at http://www.nua.net/surveys/?f=VS&art_id=888342560&rel=true.

Harmon, A. (1996, October 7). The cutting edge: Technology poll special. *Los Angeles Times,* p. D4.

Hoffman, D., & Novak, T. (1995). *Rimm commentary.* Project 2000. Available at http://www2000.ogsm.vanderbilt.edu .

Hoyt, O.G., & Hoyt, E.P. (1970). *Censorship in America.* New York: Seabury.

Hunter, C.D. (1999). *Filtering the future?* Unpublished master's thesis, Annenberg School for Communication, University of Pennsylvania, Philadelphia, PA.

Johnson, P. (1996). Pornography drives technology: Why not censor the Internet. *Federal Communications Law Journal, 49,* 217.

Kendrick, W. (1987). *The secret museum: Pornography in modern culture.* New York: Viking.

Lawrence, S., & Giles, C.L. (1999, July). Accessibility of information on the web. *Nature.*

McCain, J. (1999). *Childrens' Internet Protection Act.* Senate Bill 97. Available at http://www.thomas.loc.gov/.

McCombs, M.E., & Shaw, D.L. (1972). The agenda-setting function of mass media. *Public Opinion Quarterly, 36,* 176-187.

McCullagh, D. (1999, May 5). Click here for safe surfing. *Wired News.* Available at http://www.wired.com/news/news/politics/story/19505.html.

Modern History Sourcebook. (1999). *Rules on prohibited books.* Available at http://www.fordham.edu/halsall/mod/trent-booksrules.html.

Morais, R.C. (1999, June 14). Porn goes public. *Forbes.*

National Highway Traffic Safety Administration. (1998). *Traffic safety fact sheet. 1999.* Available at http://www.nhtsa.dot.gov/people/ncsa/factshet.html.

Net porn hysteria overhyped, prof says. (1998, 21 March). *St. Catharines Standard Press,* p. A2.

Nickell, J. (1998, October 22). Groups challenge antiporn law. *Wired News.* Available at http://www.wired.com/news/news/politics/story/15762.html.

*NUA Net Surveys.* (1999). Available at http://www.nua.net/surveys/how_many_online/index.html.

Plato. (1977). *The Republic* (S. Buchanan. Ed.). New York: Penguin.

Recreational Software Advisory Council. (1999). *About RSACi.* Available at http://www.rsac.org/.

*Reno v. ACLU.* (1997). 117 S.Ct. 2329.

Richtel, M. (1997, May 16). Poll: Protect kids from porn. *Hotwired.* Available at http://www.hotwired.com/netizen/97/19/special4a.html.

Salant, P., & Dillman, D.A. (1994). *How to conduct your own survey.* New York: Wiley.

Seif, M. (1997). Symposium comments. Cited in *B.U. Journal of Science and Technology Law, 3.*

Senate unanimously passes filtering bill. (1999, May 13). *Bloomberg News.* Available at http://www.news.com/News/Item/0,4,36540,00.html.

Slovic, P. (1987). Perception of risk. *Science, 236*(17), 280-285.

Starker, S. (1989). *Evil influences.* New Brunswick, NJ: Transaction Publishers.

St. John-Stevas, N. (1962). The church and censorship. In J. Chandos (Ed.), *To deprave and corrupt.* New York: Associated Press.

Symons, A.K. (1999, May 4). *Keynote address presented at the Annenberg national conference on the Internet and the family.* Available at http://www.ala.org/pio/speeches/annenberg.html/.

Teford, T.L. (1993). *Freedom of speech in the United States* (2nd ed.). New York: McGraw Hill.

Turow, J. (1999). *The internet and family: The view from parents; The view from the press.* Philadelphia, PA: Annenberg Public Policy Center.

Wallace, J., & Mangan, M. (1996). *Sex, laws, and cyberspace.* New York: Henry Holt.

Wartella, E., & Reeves, B. (1985). Historical trends in research on children and the media: 1900-1960. *Journal of Communication, 35*(2), 118-133.

WebCrawler. (1999). *Add your URL on WebCrawler, NP. 1999.* Available at http://www.webcrawler.com/info/add_url/.

WebCrawler. (1999). About WebCrawler. http://www.webcrawler.com/.

Wilkins, J. (1997, September 17). Protecting our children from Internet smut: Moral duty or moral panic? *The Humanist, 57*(5), 4.

Wolfson, N. (1997). *Hate speech, sex speech, free speech.* Westport, CT: Praeger.

# 12

# Constructing the Virtual Organization: Using a Multimedia Simulation for Communication Education

## Terri Toles Patkin

*There has been a great deal of speculation and fantasizing over virtual reality technologies, but what are the practical applications of virtual worlds? In this chapter, Terri Toles Patkin focuses on the technical and psychological challenges of constructing a simulation to aid in teaching organizational communication. Emphasizing a human factors (e.g., cognitive, instrumental, normative) approach to the design of human-computer interfaces, she explores the many features of multimedia and virtual reality that may contribute to the process of education, and profiles current work relating to the development of a "virtual organization" as a learning tool/environment. In Sections 1, 3, and 4, additional discussion on virtual reality appears in Herbert Zettl's aesthetic study in Chapter 5, Charles U. Larson's rhetorical analysis in Chapter 6, and Sue Barnes's ecological analysis in Chapter 13; other research on education can be found in Stephanie Gibson's examination of the pedagogy of hypertext in Chapter 17, and research also relevant to organizational communication includes Philip Thompsen's theoretical study of flaming in Chapter 20.*

Virtual Reality (VR) has been in the headlines often recently, usually in juxtaposition with some exotic entertainment with a futuristic twist. Media personalities appear decked out in the requisite high-tech bodysuit as they try their hand at a new game, compare the results to Star Trek's holodeck, and snicker nervously about the possibility of teledildonics replacing the real thing. But is virtual reality simply the newest whiz-bang toy, or might it be used for serious applications in education? Certainly, with its ability to provide realism in an immersive computer simulation, virtual reality has the potential to alter the meaning of "experiential learning" significantly. Computer applications can provide substitutes for reality across a range of human activities and properly constructed and utilized simulation can provide valuable practice in merging mind and body for interaction in real life (Richards, 1998; Turkle, 1996). This chapter reviews the current literature on virtual reality's human factors, particularly in relation to education, and proposes the construction of one prototype desktop education-oriented virtual reality, the Virtual Organization.

## WHY A VIRTUAL ORGANIZATION?

The advantages to students participating in a Virtual Organization go well beyond simple participation in a classroom exercise. Properly developed, the Virtual Organization will allow communication students to hone communication skills at their own pace and to focus on weaknesses. If needed, basic drill-and-practice exercises in grammar and punctuation could be incorporated for some students, whereas others could be challenged with more advanced techniques.

More significant than such short-term gains, however, would be the opportunity for students to wear a number of virtual hats. Communication students who get the chance to intern in organizations today generally report dissatisfaction with the tasks they are assigned. Dreams of creative fulfillment tend to be misplaced among the filing, telephone duty, and fact checking that typically constitute the intern's job description. Often the experience of a corporate environment and the chance to "network" provide more valuable experiences for the student than the substance of the assigned tasks.

The Virtual Organization would complement such internship experiences by providing students with a substantive example of organizational communication. As students progress through the simulation, they will be able to build on their knowledge and test their ability to perform new and interesting tasks. Although the real intern might prepare a mailing list, the virtual intern could also design the entire advertising campaign and test its effectiveness.

Different types of organizations, with differing cultures and unique communication needs, could also be developed. Students could try working in a small family business or a Fortune 500 headquarters during a single semester. They could then select the type of organization they would prefer to concentrate their efforts on in the future. The Virtual Organization simulation would supplement, not replace, current classroom and internship experiences.

## VIRTUAL TECHNOLOGY AND REALITY

Virtual reality is a computer interface that enables people to participate directly in real-time three-dimensional environments created from computer-generated simulated environments, digitized images of people and objects, or imported video. Most inclusive are full-immersion systems that provide first-person interaction within the computer-generated world via head-mounted stereoscopic displays, gloves, bodysuits, and audio systems, in which computers generate images on goggles with liquid crystal displays, offering the user the sensation of being in a different place. Less-immersive environments include "through-the-window" approaches, in which the user sees a 3D world through the computer screen and steers via a spaceball or flying-mouse, and video-projected worlds that provide a second-person experience where the viewer stands outside the imaginary world but communicates with characters or entities inside it.

The origins of virtual reality include computer graphics, computer-aided design and drafting (CADD), auditory interfaces, military research (especially flight simulators), video games, mediated entertainments (such as the 1950s Sensorama depicting a motorcycle ride through New York City), video art exhibits (such as Videoplace, Video Living Rooms, etc.), literature and film (especially science fiction and cyberpunk, particularly Gibson's *Neuromancer,* 1984), and entrepreneurial firms that produce hardware such as the dataglove for use with virtual reality. Applications can be found in CADD, computer games, the military, museums, theme parks, training and education, medicine, and manufacturing, to name just a few. Other application possibilities include remote performance of dangerous industrial tasks (e.g., nuclear disaster cleanup) or repairing spaceships or satellites from earth. Architects design buildings, tennis games are simulated, and surgeons practice delicate techniques (Krueger, 1991; Rheingold, 1991; Woolley, 1992).

Many of the current developments in virtual reality focus on entertainment, such as the Battletech Multiplayer Simulators that allow users to suit up in camouflage gear and practice driving a virtual tank, or amusement park games and rides that offer particularly realistic sensations. Of course, military applications have played a crucial role in the development of VR technology, and the military has sponsored the largest networked virtual simulation to date. The Department of Defense's SIMNET project has linked as many as 250 tank and helicopter simulators at multiple U.S. and European sites, allowing soldiers to practice on a virtual battlefield.

Virtual teleconferencing, manipulation of graphically rendered objects, telepresence surgery, architectural design, and vehicle movement are only a few examples of current civilian projects using VR techniques. Most work in this area is theoretical at present; only a few completed projects are on the market or even available as demonstrations despite rapid advances in imaging technology in recent years. The most common projects include architectural walkthroughs that allow students to test design modifications, flight simulators, biological visualizations, and telepresence surgery.

Most of the VR projects described are simply too expensive, both financially and computationally, for widespread public use. However, low-end virtual reality is possible today. Price-competitive game machines targeted at the home market are driven primarily by the entertainment aspects associated with virtual reality rather than the simulated reality function. Because games and animated cartoons do not strive to duplicate the real world, they can create an internally consistent artificial world that provides an enjoyable and cost-effective experience. Important parameters for VR game displays include local pixel quality (smooth), global display appearance (fast response, readable text), global economic specifications (perception of telepresence even in a relatively narrow field of view, color, resolution), and unit manufacturing cost (low) (Becker, 1991).

At present, there seem to be more social prognostications regarding the effects of virtual reality than there are working VR environments. Technical barriers to development of virtual environments include tactile feedback, a slow frame rate, flat appearance of three-dimensional scenery, user resistance to the goggles and gloves required for sustained high-end applications, a lack of network support for multiple players, and the high cost of fully immersive environments. The literature seems split between highly technical data and social forecasts, but some work has been done on specific human factors relating to virtual reality.

**Human Factors**

*Human factors* refers to aspects of human performance, behavior, and desire that must be considered when designing any machine or information system, including issues relating to sensation, perception, participation, and experience. Some of what we know from experimental psychology about the basics of sensation may be applied to virtual reality, especially questions regarding perceptions of depth, shape, motion, texture, flavor, and localization. Making the experience of being in the virtual world as transparent as possible to the user is a primary goal of VR developers.

Some examples of human factors that must be considered in designing communication and human-computer interfaces include cognitive, instrumental, normative, expressive, and somatic factors. Cognitive factors include perception and psychophysics, attention, motivation, decision making and judgment, procedural memory, and semantic memory factors. Instrumental factors include individual, social, and organizational communication goals and the relationship to other communication instruments. Normative factors include cultural variation in communication expectation, performance or norms, contextual and environmental factors, and ethical considerations. Expressive factors include code usage and message variability, and somatic factors include anthropometry and biomechanics (Biocca, 1993).

## Visual Factors

Current human factors research in virtual reality concentrates on visual and psychomotor testing, including vision testing (people are functionally nearsighted in the virtual world), color blindness, subject recognition, turning ability, search-and-locate tests, and manipulation tests. The battery of tests takes about two hours. Many of the tests are being done specifically for military applications and have predictable difficulties with generalizability beyond those scenarios (Morie, 1992). One test, for instance, involves recognizing a soldier as "ours" or "other" based on his uniform and weaponry.

It takes some practice to get used to navigating in a virtual environment. Game players report that they need to play the game three or four times in order to feel comfortable with basic maneuvers, even after a brief video training session and assistance from the game attendant. Similarly, many VR users find it difficult to differentiate a virtual painting from simulated reality and tend to bump into the "wall" on which it is displayed (Latta, 1992).

## Auditory Cues

One of the most overlooked aspects of the VR experience has been the rhythmic nature of visual, auditory, and kinesthetic experience: Poetic meter, musical beat, and behavioral cadence all have been shown to affect humans at primal levels, as the Muzak Corporation has so profitably shown. The most popular commercial video games are not necessarily those with the flashiest graphics or the most interesting storyline; they are the ones that start off at about 70 beats per minute and steadily increase in speed. Incorporating audio cues is an important feature contributing to the participant's perception of "realness" in a virtual environment and costs are relatively low (Jones, 1993; Orr, 1992).

## Social Factors

Early research into virtual reality has suggested that the emotional state experience of being in the virtual world is almost equivalent with that of being in the "real world," as measured by semantic differential scores of an architectural space. Certainly, experimental and field research in computer-mediated interaction indicates that despite the lack of nonverbal cues, low social presence, low media richness, and lack of social context cues, social bonds form and communities emerge (Walther, 1992).

In over 2,500 demos completed at the University of Washington's Human Interface Technology Laboratory, researchers have found that a large proportion of people do not even think to turn around with the VR helmet on because they simply are not used to the hardware. Users wearing headsets found it almost impossible to point to a physical object, whereas locating objects within the virtual world was easy. It may be that we can carry only one cognitive map in our head at a time (Weghorst, 1992). Novice users in particular require the support of another person familiar with the technology (McLeod, 1992).

### Philosophical Issues

Cyberphilosophers warn about the importance of integrating the real body with the virtual body. The emotional attachment that a player holds for his or her computer construct can be intense, as evidenced by the strong bonding made by players in text-based virtual realities (MUDS; Multi-User Dungeons). Players in these virtual communities evince a close affective bond with their online personae and can experience very real distress when their "cyberalter ego" suffers a setback.

The human cost of VR use can include some significant psychological and physiological symptoms, including brain-body lag, self-identity split, and a split between primary body and cyberbody (Heim, 1993), particularly for heavy users of the technology. Health issues may include headaches from spending too much time in a virtual environment, disease transmission from the equipment, pain, fatigue, disorientation, motion sickness, and trauma (Latta, 1992). Some have raised concerns about the potential for addictive or abusive behavior via VR technology, but the question of ethics remains largely unexplored.

Rather than the traditional view of the computer as rival (a chess partner or artificial intelligence adversary), virtual reality's conception of the computer is paradigmatically different: The computer functions as a contact lens—transparent but still affecting what and how the user sees. Cyberspace weaves together language, technology, architecture, and mathematics to create a place where mind and machine merge (Benedikt, 1991). Unlike previous computer interfaces, virtual reality includes the viewer inside the message; the medium is not only the message, it is also the viewer.

## EDUCATION AND VIRTUAL REALITY

The use of virtual reality in educational settings is based on the assumption that active learning provides a superior experience to passive learning, a notion that can be traced back at least as far as Dewey. Most students who participate in responsive learning environments in which they become engaged in full body-mind kinesthetic learning not only retain more information but also manifest a fuller understanding of the information presented.

One of the key assumptions of VR work is that the brain can process information better when it is presented through sight, sound, and touch instead of just text and numbers. Putting a virtual environment at the disposal of teachers could allow students not only to observe, for example, daily life in ancient Greece, but also allow them to participate in interactive discussions of philosophy with Socrates or science with Aristotle. Alternate paths could be explored; students might restage the Civil War or experiment with a variety of physical or historical concepts.

Computer-based instructional simulations allow learners to practice the skills needed for real-life situations without the risks of injury or equipment damage that actual practice might involve. Flight simulators, space station operations, nuclear reactor repair, and police work have all successfully provided scenarios for virtual practice grounds. One distinct advantage of the virtual environment lies in its ability to present a simplified reality to the beginner, with complicating factors stripped out of the scenario until the student is ready to handle more complexity. First the pilot learns to land the plane, then he or she can try it in a crosswind.

Virtual learning environments promise to be more active than traditional classrooms, less formal, perhaps more fun, and provide a greater range of experiences. The attributes of virtual reality that make it potentially useful for education include flexibility in the creation of virtual worlds, ability to support a feeling of presence, the ability of the user to control and interact with objects and characters within the virtual world, and physical feedback from the virtual world. Whether original source materials (videos or documents) or simulated environments (computer generations) are used, users may participate in problem solving, concept development, and creative expression. Three primary applications exist: visualization (seeing connections and relationships that would otherwise be difficult to comprehend, such as architectural structure), simulation (synthetic replication of some real-life experience, such as flying a plane), and constructing participatory virtual environments (such as a rainforest or the Lascaux caves; Ferrington & Loge, 1992; Middleton, 1992; Randall, 1992).

Although most projects have to date simulated physical actions (behavior of water, wind, molecules, etc.), there is no reason that virtual reality might not be used for more abstract skills as well, although graphical representation is more challenging. Virtual reality might, for example, be applied to the training of people in cross-cultural communication; for instance, an American business traveler could practice appropriate negotiation skills with a virtual Japanese client. Portions of the scenario could be practiced as many times as necessary for comprehension or success, and continual feedback can focus the student's efforts on weak areas (Meyer & Dunn-Roberts, 1992).

Early work has shown that students can effectively learn new tasks such as spatial navigational skills in virtual reality, and students report that it is possible to interact with the illusory world as if it were real (Regian, Shebilske, & Monk, 1992). Such simulations effectively train students to apply specific knowledge to new situations. When students play a role (such as tank commander in a military simulation), their newly acquired knowledge can be effectively translated into a field setting (Shlecter, Bessemer, & Kolosh, 1992).

## CONSTRUCTING THE VIRTUAL ORGANIZATION

The Virtual Organization represents an electronic case study approach in which the communication student is given the opportunity to solve a variety of problems in a simulated organizational setting. The immersive graphical interface allows for interactive exercises in organizational communication to take place. Simulations can be created using any of the desktop VR toolkits, such as Virtual Reality Studio, Virtus VR, or VREAM, all object-oriented VR development systems that allow the user to design, build, enter, and interact with virtual worlds using a windowed, mouse-driven graphical user interface on a desktop PC. Higher end VR hardware such as head-mounted displays, three-dimensional tracking systems, and gloves may also be incorporated. The prototype described here simply utilizes a through-the-window approach with a standard PC.

The structure of the simulation somewhat resembles a game. A game requires that users be given a goal, most often through providing an increase in a "score" following the performance of a series of actions. In an entertainment setting, this could include finding a treasure, solving a puzzle, or winning a battle against an object or another player. In the organizational setting, points can be earned for such activities as correctly proofing a press release, following guidelines for scheduling a press conference, planning a crisis response, or resolving a conflict.

The student begins the game as a part-time intern assigned the most routine tasks, such as editing an already prepared press release. When a certain number of tasks have been completed, the student is offered a summer job, in which more complicated problems are presented, such as writing a press release from already assembled facts. Successful completion of this level earns the player a full-time job offer in the Virtual Organization at the level of Communication Assistant. Here the tasks become more complex again and require a greater level of independent thought until the student progresses through a number of ranks and finally is promoted to Vice President for Corporate Communication. The tasks become progressively less reactive (in-basket exercises, decision making, negotiation tactics), and students must ultimately plan a long-term communication strategy for the organization.

A good game must have both breadth and depth. Breadth is the extent to which the simulation is able to deal with things the players want to do. If there is water, the players may want to swim; if there are trees, players may want to climb them. Depth expresses a sense of the level of detail provided. Games with good depth generally model the real world to some extent. For example, a glass object will break when dropped on a hard surface, but not if it is dropped on a soft surface. Although this can become computationally expensive, its judicious use enriches the player's experience of the "reality" of the illusion. In the Virtual Organization, the illusion is enhanced by the graphical interface that permits visualization of an office space, ranging from a cubicle for the Assistant to a spacious corner office for the Vice President, as well as cartoon-like representations of coworkers, clients, and supervisors.

Text can also contribute to the sense of reality. Interactions can be simulated through careful compilations of text that guide the player through the scenario at hand. For example, dialogue in a software code inspection simulation is dynamically constructed using the history of the current game, simulated situation, and character definitions given by the player as guidelines (Christel, 1992).

Interactivity provides perhaps the most sophisticated sense of reality for the user. Interactivity is built through software links, in which certain conditions (pushing a button on a radio) will cause certain responses (music is played). Links may be triggered by actions of the viewer (touching or moving an object, entering a room) or actions of objects within the world (a thrown object collides with a wall and bounces accordingly). The simulation will utilize text windows as one linked response. For example, students who take initiative beyond the minimum requirements of the simulation may enable a link to a window in which a glowing letter appears in their virtual personnel file. Links can also be performed with external calls to a program, batch file, or DOS command. Students who touch the virtual in-basket could be transported to a word processing program, CD-ROM, spreadsheet, or database, and then returned to the virtual office once they have completed the assigned task.

Later versions of the simulation would additionally incorporate complete multimedia capabilities, including full-motion video, audio, and hypertext links. Students may be able to interview characters online through careful editing of stock phrases uttered in response to some keyword (Summitt, 1993, offers a parallel structure for creating a virtual newsroom). Eventually, the scenario could even be distributed on CD-ROM, which would increase the flexibility and portability of the simulation (Smith, 1992). In later versions, the student's response will influence the scenario itself. A poorly prepared press release could lead to negative news coverage, which might in turn influence sales, thus necessitating a series of follow-up actions by the student.

The ultimate interactivity, of course, comes from human interaction. The Virtual Organization simulator could incorporate multiple players, perhaps an entire class, with full electronic mail and interactive chat capabilities added to the scenario. Interactivity is the critical element in computer media, and the interactivity of multiple users within virtual reality potentially creates the most interesting experience. In a study of a text-based "virtual classroom" setting, no significant differences in mastery of course material occurred between the virtual and traditional classrooms, but the majority of students reported that the virtual classroom improved the quality of the learning experience, particularly when "group learning" was experienced (Hiltz, 1993).

Interestingly, the Virtual Organization concept has already been introduced by some not-at-all-virtual organizations through the introduction of computer-mediated communication at all levels of the workforce (Lee & Varey, 1998). For example, the Social Virtual Reality project at Xerox PARC is extending

MUD technology into nonrecreational settings, particularly in the scientific community. A social virtual reality is a software system that allows several people to interact in pseudo-spatial settings that are text based. Real-time audio and video as well as window-based graphical user interfaces complement the text base to make the computer-mediated experience competitive with face-to-face communication in the workplace (Curtis & Nichols, 1993). The Virtual Organization simulation could one day be a student's first experience with an organizational media environment that will later be encountered on the job.

## REFERENCES

Becker, A. (1991, July). *Virtual reality for home game machines.* Paper presented at the Virtual Reality Symposium, Tokyo.
Benedikt, M. (Ed.). (1991). *Cyberspace: First steps.* Cambridge: MIT Press.
Biocca, F. (1993). Communication research in the design of communication interfaces and systems. *Journal of Communication, 43*(4), 59-68.
Christel, M. (1992). Virtual reality today on a PC. *Instruction Delivery Systems, 6*(4), 6-9.
Curtis, P., & Nichols, D.A. (1993). *MUDs grow up: Social virtual reality in the real world.* Palo Alto, CA: Xerox PARC.
Ferrington, G., & Loge, K. (1992). Virtual reality: A new learning environment. *The Computing Teacher, 19*(7), 16-19.
Gibson, W. (1984). *Neuromancer.* New York: Ace Books.
Heim, M. (1993). *The metaphysics of virtual reality.* New York: Oxford University Press.
Hiltz, S.R. (1993). Correlates of learning in a virtual classroom. *International Journal of Man-Machine Studies, 39,* 71-98.
Jones, S. (1993). A sense of space: Virtual reality, authenticity and the aural. *Critical Studies in Mass Communication, 10*(3), 238-252.
Krueger, M. (1991). *Artificial reality II.* Reading MA: Addison Wesley.
Latta, J.N. (1992). The quest for virtual reality applications. In *Proceedings, DPMA Virtual Reality Conference.* Washington, DC.
Lee, H., & Varey, R. (1998). Analysing cultural impacts of computer-mediated communication in organisations. In *Proceedings, Cultural Attitudes Towards Communication and Technology* (pp. 321-326). Sydney, Australia.
McLeod, D. (1992). Art and virtual environments. In *Proceedings, DPMA Virtual Reality Conference.* Washington, DC.
Meyer, C., & Dunn-Roberts, R. (1992). Virtual reality: A strategy for training in cross-cultural communication. *Educational Media International, 29*(3), 175-180.
Middleton, T. (1992). Applications of virtual reality to learning. *Interactive Learning International, 8*(4), 253-257.

Morie, J.F. (1992). Multi-disciplinary history of VR and IST in VR research. In *Proceedings, DPMA Virtual Reality Conference*. Washington, DC.

Orr, J.N. (1992). Anthropocybersynchronicity: Rhythm and intimacy in VR. In *Proceedings, DPMA Virtual Reality Conference*. Washington, DC.

Randall, J.P. (1992). The emerging potential of virtual reality in postsecondary education. *New Directions for Teaching and Learning, 51*, 77-81.

Regian, J.W., Shebilske, W.L., & Monk, J.M. (1992). Virtual reality: An instructional medium for visual-spatial tasks. *Journal of Communication, 42*(2), 136-149.

Rheingold, H. (1991). *Virtual reality*. New York: Summit Books.

Richards, C. (1998). Computer-mediated communication and the connection between virtual utopias and actual realities. In *Proceedings, Cultural Attitudes Towards Communication and Technology* (pp. 173-184). Sydney, Australia.

Smith, D. (1992). VR and multimedia: An evolutionary approach. In *Proceedings, DPMA Virtual Reality Conference*. Washington, DC.

Shlecter, T.M., Bessemer, D.W., & Kolosh, K.P. (1992). Computer-based simulation systems and role-playing: An effective combination for fostering conditional knowledge. *Journal of Computer-Based Instruction, 19*(4), 110-114.

Summitt, P.M. (1993). *News, information and knowledge in cyberspace*. Unpublished manuscript.

Turkle, S. (1996). *Life on the screen: Identity in the age of the Internet*. London: Weidenfeld & Nicolson.

Walther, J.B. (1992). Interpersonal effects in computer-mediated interaction. *Communication Research, 19*(1), 52-90.

Weghorst, S. (1992). Human factors in virtual reality design. In *Proceedings, DPMA Virtual Reality Conference*. Washington, DC.

Woolley, B. (1992). *Virtual worlds*. Cambridge: Blackwell.

# 13

# Online Education
# Unbound

## Paul Levinson

*The school has traditionally been the center of education, but what happens when we trade in the physical classroom for its cyberspace equivalent? How does the activity of teaching change when face-to-face communication is removed from the educational equation? What is gained and what is lost when students and instructors are separated in space, linked only by technology? As a pioneer in online schooling and the founder of a nonprofit distance education provider, Paul Levinson addresses these and other questions in this chapter. His position is that the computer has, on balance, been a boon for learning, freeing education from the arbitrary constraints of buildings and bodies. In other sections of this book, additional discussion of cybereducation can be found in Stephanie Gibson's analysis of the pedagogy of hypertext in Chapter 17; see also Paul Lippert's discussion of abstract and concrete modes of communication in Chapter 18, and Judith Yaross Lee's analysis of text-based interpersonal communication in Chapter 19. Levinson's optimism about cyberschooling can be contrasted to the critiques of cyberspace presented by Gary Gumpert and Susan Drucker in Chapter 1 and John Phelan in Chapter 2.*

Like most activities as old as humanity, the underlying structures of education seem so obvious as to be taken for granted. Formal learning requires a teacher, a student, a subject to teach, and a place to teach it—whether in the personal tutor and small academies of the ancient world or the clusters of buildings teeming with classrooms in our present day. The advent and evolution of writing, culminating in mass-produced books, changed the equation a little, bringing into play the possibility that some kinds wisdom could first be engaged and acquired outside of the classroom. But even in education mediated by books, the nub of the process—the essence of the education—takes place in the physical classroom, the place to which students bring back the lessons they have acquired in books, for confirmation, clarification, and elaboration. (See Marrou, 1956, for the impact of writing on education in the ancient world, and Levinson, 1997, for the printing press and public education.)

When environments are as deeply ingrained in our culture as the classroom, their limitations are difficult to see. Thus, most of us accept without much objection the fact that once the physical classroom is vacated, the active dialogue of the class is put on hold until the next class meeting. If obstacles of time and/or geography prevent us from attending a specific class, or taking a particular course, or, for that matter, attending a university that is too far away, we tend to accept that also as something that just flows from the very nature of education—in much the same way as we accept (though may not like) that a book we want to read may be out of the library, or that we need to stay silent when someone else is talking in a class because two people cannot talk and be understood at the same time.

But imagine a classroom equally available to anyone, anywhere in the world—or, for that matter, off of the world—with a personal computer and connection to a phone system. Think of a classroom whose discussions, proceeding asynchronously, went on continuously, 24 hours a day, with no absolute limitation on how many people could participate at any one time. And picture yourself with access to a library comprised of papers that could be read by thousands of people, all at once, and yet these texts would still be there for you whenever you wished.

Such conditions are not only not imaginary, they are not even near future. They are, in fact, the basic structures of online education—a radically new mode of learning that has been quietly underway for nearly two decades.


## A THUMBNAIL HISTORY OF ONLINE EDUCATION

The advantages of a computer as a communications tool—as distinct from a programming instrument, data manager, or word processor—were first developed in various government and corporate sites (such as Xerox's "PARC" in California) in the 1960s and 1970s. In those days, people used "dumb" terminals that could do nothing other than connect to a central mainframe computer, on which people could word process, send and receive messages, and therein engage in all manner of discussion, trivial and profound.

By the early 1980s, the introduction of relatively inexpensive personal computers and modems had given this process a dramatic boost: People could now log on any time they pleased, from their homes or places of business, provided only that they had access to a telephone, which of course almost everyone did. Commercial online networks like CompuServe and the Source (later purchased by CompuServe) began flourishing. The Western Behavioral Sciences Institute in 1982 began offering a 2-year program of noncredit "executive strategy" seminars offered completely online to busy CEOs and government officials, at a cost of $25,000. Two years later, the New York Institute of Technology began offering a few courses for undergraduate credit online at a more reasonable tuition. And in the fall of 1985, Connected Education (the organization I founded with my wife, Tina Vozick) began offering a series of online graduate-level courses for credit granted by the New School for Social Research in New York City. By 1988, this program had developed into a full-fledged Master of Arts curriculum, with a specialization in Technology and Society—offered entirely online. More than 2,000 students from 40 states in the United States and 15 countries around the world including China, Japan, Singapore, Senegal, The United Arab Emirates, Colombia, and most countries in Europe took courses in that program—all without having to leave their families or means of employment.

Although transmission speeds have increased more than a hundredfold since the mid-1980s—from 300 to 56,000 bps on traditional modems, and much faster on other equipment—the features of online education have remained pretty much the same since its inception. In that sense, online education, especially its current general dependence on text rather than images, icons, and graphic interfaces, serves as a middle- or even low-tech oasis in an otherwise galloping, high-tech computer world. This allows people to participate with equipment costing hundreds rather than thousands of dollars, and is also consonant with the traditional image of the scholar in an environment somewhat removed from the hustle and bustle of the beaten commercial track.

Of course, advanced personal computer equipment is always "downwardly compatible" with text modes, meaning that those who have more expensive systems can take full advantage of online education, and indeed retrieve its written lessons via icon command, and read and write them via fancy fonts and windows, or via speech synthesizer in some cases, and interspersed with all manner of images and sounds if appropriate. In some specialized courses—say, a course on the poetics of relativity, where an equation or two might be useful—such specialized graphics might even be recommended. But even in these courses, the heart of online education is the text.

## ON THE INSIDE OF AN ONLINE COURSE

The actual process of online education works much like e-mail, except rather than one person communicating to another or a group of people, many people communicate to many, with the Web site or external computer system playing the crucial role of keeping track of who in the group has read who else's messages. Here's how it works.

I taught an online master's-level course called "Artificial Intelligence and Real Life" from 1985 to 1995. The course carried three graduate-level credits (awarded by the New School for Social Research), and took place over a 2-month period of time online. This time frame contrasts sharply with that of an equivalent "in-person" course, which at the New School and most other "place-based" universities would usually extend 3.5 months—almost twice as long as the online course. Why is this? The answer lies in the intensity of learning that takes place in a course continuously in session online—a course in which students can constantly log on with their thoughts, comments, and questions, and read not only what the faculty member has to say, but, in some ways even more usefully, what all the other students have to say as well.

Prior to the start of the online course, I prepared an "opener" (the equivalent of a first day's lecture in an in-person class), and a course outline. The opener not only sketches out what the course will be about, but invites students to jump in immediately with questions about the course and brief descriptions of who they are. In an online course, participation in the form of entering messages into the course is essential. Unlike the in-person class, in which the teacher can have a sense of how well the class is following the curriculum just by looking at the expressions on the faces of students, the online class requires actual writing by students if they are to have an online identity and role in the course. Thus, a highly significant subsidiary benefit of taking any online course is that it sharpens the student's writing ability.

In "Artificial Intelligence and Real Life," the posted outline indicated that the course would proceed very differently in each of its two months. The first month would entail students reading and discussing, with my input and guidance, basic texts in the field, including nonfiction works such as Bolter's (1984) "Turing's Man" and relevant fiction such as Isaac Asimov's robot series (e.g., 1983). This part of the course would be most like an in-person course, although the dynamics of the in-person classroom and out-of-class readings would be fused together and transformed into a much more fluid, steadily progressing dialogue online. The second part of the course would take advantage of the online environment in a more unique way: Students would play roles in a mock trial, in which a human captain in space is accused of murdering an android.

In a classic *Twilight Zone* episode starring Jack Warden and Jean Marsh ("The Lonely," written by Rod Serling and first broadcast November 13, 1959), an innocent man (Warden) is found guilty of a heinous crime he did not commit, and is sentenced to solitary life imprisonment on a barren asteroid. A captain takes pity on him, believes in his innocence, and brings a beautiful android (Marsh) along on one of his stops to serve as company for the prisoner. The prisoner at first rejects her, then falls in love in with her. The captain returns the next year with good news: The prisoner's innocence has been established, and he can come home. But there is no room on the ship for the android, and the captain eventually has to blow her head off, leaving her wires rudely dangling, to make his point. Here the *Twilight Zone* episode, and Rod Serling's original story, end.

But I always thought that there was an additional story that needed to be told here. It is several years later, back on Earth, and the freed prisoner brings the captain up on charges of murder. This is where our online trial begins. I play the freed prisoner, and the students play all other roles—the captain, defense and prosecuting attorneys, expert witnesses of various sorts, and the jury. The goal of this role-playing is to encourage students to confront more directly than usual such profound philosophic questions as what is it that makes us human, can sentience be programmed, and the like. In an online class of 8 to 10 students, this works well.

In the 10 years I conducted this trial online, it worked well with as few as 5 and as many as 15 students. And these numbers are the flexible lower and upper limits for any successful online course taught by one teacher—fewer students leave an online discussion without sufficient critical mass, greater numbers can overwhelm any instructor's capacity to respond constructively to each of the students.

Let's look more carefully at how an online course progresses on an hourly basis.

As indicated earlier, on the first day of an online course, I post my opener and outline. I live in New York, but that hardly matters—I have on occasion started and conducted courses from places in England and numerous cities around the United States. But let's say on this occasion I "upload" my opener and outline to the central course topic at 10 a.m., EST, from New York City. As soon as those messages have been entered, all registered students are admitted to the course topic. At 11:05 a.m. EST—actually 4:05 p.m. London time—John logs on from London, and "downloads" my message. Downloading means he has a copy of it now in his personal computer; he could also have printed it out at that time, or he may wish to print it later. He logged on using a local Internet provider he already had in England, but he could have just as easily used his CompuServe account to reach the Web site on which our course is to be conducted. Next, Laurie, an early riser in San Francisco, logs on to our course site at 11:20 a.m. EST, 8:20 Pacific time via an America Online account node that's a local call for her, and similarly obtains my opener and outline. But she has a few minutes, and is in a contemplative mood, so after logging off she writes (on whatever word processing program she has handy) a few paragraphs about who she is and why she is taking the course. And she also asks a question: "What exactly is the difference between an android and a robot?" She reconnects to our online course, and uploads her text to our course topic at 8:55 a.m. her time, 11:55 a.m. New York time. Message 1 in the course is my opener; Message 2 is my outline; Message 3 is Laurie's note. Now Joichi logs on from Tokyo and reads these first three messages. He decides to enter a few lines about himself while still online, and also to answer Laurie's question. He types, "My understanding is that an android is a robot that looks like a human—either has flesh and blood, or seems to." That's Message 4. Two hours later, John logs back on from London, and enters about six paragraphs of text explaining who he is— he's a student completing his doctorate in evolutionary biology at Cambridge with a term off right now—and why he's taking this course.

I log back on now at 4:00 p.m., New York time, and am delighted to find this multi-national dialogue already under way. Five more students located in various cities in the United States and Canada have yet to log on, but I can see already that the course is off to a good start. Three students have already logged on. Furthermore, one has posed a good question, and another has answered it. Students teaching each other is a prime dividend of online education. At the end of the month, when each student submits a midterm essay to me online, I will make them available to all other students in the course who have submitted essays. Students thus get the benefit not only of my comments on their essays, but the comments of their colleagues. By the time our online trial begins in the second month, a potent online learning community will have coalesced in our course, with students who have never met each in person developing strong intellectual and often personal attachments. And these will be strengthened further in the give and take of our online trial, as students get caught up and energized in the role-playing, and the philosophic issues that pervade it.

But for now, I post notes that welcome Laurie, Joichi, and John; express real pleasure at Laurie's question; compliment Joichi for an excellent answer; and go on to provide a little more context and background of my own, including some detail on the origins of the term *robot* . . . We're off and running.

## ADVANTAGES OF ONLINE EDUCATION

Edmund Carpenter (1973), a colleague of Marshall McLuhan, observed that "Electricity makes angels of us all—not angels in the Sunday school sense of being good or having wings, but spirit freed from flesh, capable of instant transportation anywhere." The online student—and teacher—certainly partake of intellect freed from the restraints of flesh, in a milieu in which obstacles of distance, time, and many other sorts are either completely eliminated or significantly reduced.

We can make a list of these obstacles, and how online education overcomes them.

### Obstacles of Geography

This is the most obvious impediment removed by online education. With information travelling to and from the Web site or e-mail list in seconds and minutes, even with slower modems, the online student who lives across the street from the action is no closer to the online course than the student who lives across the world. Indeed, with speed of light being the only ultimate underlying limitation on speed of online communication, students could easily take online courses from a space station or even a Mars environment with faculty back on Earth, and vice versa.

## Obstacles of Time

One of the basic constraints of in-person education is not only that classes must meet at given places, but at given times. But at any particular time, either faculty or students might be ill, or plagued by subtler problems that make that time not the best for learning to take place. The problem rarely if ever arises in an online course, in which people are by and large able to log on at times of their own choosing. (The limit here would be that even an online course has a beginning and end, and a time for assignments to be completed and evaluated.) The result of such choice over when one participates in the online course means that all parties—faculty and students—tend to participate at their best, when they are likely to derive the most benefit from the experience. Furthermore, important thoughts that may occur to students and faculty after a vigorous in-person class session may be lost to that class; in contrast, in an online course, participants can log on the next morning, or even in the middle of the night if that's when the thought occurs, and enter it into the online discussion that is literally ongoing throughout the extent of the course.

## Obstacles of Retention

As every student knows, taking notes in an in-person class is an inefficient method of storing information—the act of taking the note usually renders you incapable of hearing what else is being said at that moment. In contrast, everything that goes on in an online course is automatically and continuously available. This intellectual safety net for ideas makes for a richer, more informed, educational experience.

## Obstacles of Economics

This is closely related to the geographic and temporal limitations of in-person education. For many people, the need to work for a living puts them in a place too far away to take a course; or perhaps renders them too fatigued to take a course during the evening when they are off work. Online education overcomes both such problems—and greatly increases the number of people who can take part in what Comenius called the Great Dialogue. And this is why, to return to a point raised earlier, online education must be careful not to introduce economic restrictions of another kind, in the form requiring expensive equipment to participate. Such expenses work against the natural democratizing tendencies of online education.

## Obstacles of Teacher Domination

Students learning from other students is a basic dynamic of online education. This does not mean that online faculty abdicate their responsibility to teach; but it does mean that, rather then attempting to inject or spoonfeed information into passive student minds, the ideal online teacher is rather someone who attempts to elicit active student learning, in the tradition of such educational theorists as Montessori, Dewey, and Piaget (see Perkinson, 1982, for more about the active learner).

## Obstacles of Physical Disability

Despite recent strides made in facilitating access of physically disabled students and faculty to in-person classrooms, such access is by no means easy or comprehensive. Access ramps at urban universities provide no help in getting wheelchairs through traffic-clogged streets that lead to the university. Furthermore, impairments of hearing and seeing can make the in-person classroom a difficult place in which to learn, regardless of how easily one might be able to get there. The online class eliminates most of these impediments. One of Connected Education's first students, in the mid-1980s, was someone who had been deaf since birth. I met him in one of my in-person undergraduate courses at Fairleigh Dickinson University, where he struggled to keep up with the proceedings by tape recording my lectures and discussions with the students, and having them transcribed for later reading. His capacity to contribute to the class via this second-hand participation was of course severely limited. But within days after he registered for his first online course, he was playing a leading role in online discussions: in an educational environment in which intellect was already freed from the flesh, his intellect was able to roam and create with the same verve as anyone else's online. In another case, one of our most dynamic online teachers, Tzipporah BenAvraham, conducted her "Technology and the Disabled" course from her wheelchair. She is legally blind. But voice synthesizers conveyed all the words on the screen to her. Just as lack of hearing was irrelevant to my online student, so lack of vision was irrelevant to Dr. BenAvraham when she taught online. Or rather: lack of external eyesight was irrelevant, just as lack of the outer voice was to my student. What counts online is the inner voice and the inner vision.

In view of the above advantages, one may wonder why online education has not taken the academic world by storm. Although many schools offer courses with some online component, or a course or two offered entirely online, only a few schools—such as the University of Phoenix (San Francisco) since 1987— have ever offered anything approaching a full-scale online program, or a degree that could be earned completely online. (See McGinn, 2000, for a description of several current courses and programs; Columbia, Stanford, and Duke University are among the traditional schools offering some online courses; researchers at

"InterEd" estimate that 75% of universities in the United States would be offering at least some online course-work in the next few years.) The reasons for the dearth of complete online programs are twofold. The first has to do with some of the intrinsic limitations of online education. The second has to do with our continuing, strong attachment to traditional "in-person" modes of education.

## DRAWBACKS TO ONLINE EDUCATION: INTRINSIC AND IMAGINED

### No Panacea

The first and foremost limitation of online education that must be acknowledged is that it is not a panacea: If a person, for reasons having nothing to do with geographic location, time constraints, and the like, does not want to take part in a university course and its requirements in reading, writing, and thinking, then no amount of flexibility in time and place of access can result in this person's having a successful online experience.

### Comfort With Writing Required

Success in online education—for faculty as well as students—also presupposes a facility, even a pleasure, in the written mode, which remains the essential currency of online communication even on a Web that increasingly incorporates sounds and images. Of course, participation in an online course can elicit and sharpen one's written skills—several of Connected Education's most successful students were dyslexic. But an underlying confidence in text as a mode of expression was apparently a prerequisite even in those cases.

### Not for Brain Surgeons-in-Training

The importance of text in online education points to another intrinsic limitation: Not all subjects can be taught with equal effect online. Certainly, the liberal arts and humanities, the theoretical aspects of the sciences, and professions like the law are well suited for the online curriculum. But other areas—ranging from horticulture to ceramic science to surgery—seem inextricably in need of hands-on tutoring. New virtual reality imaging techniques available on the most sophisticated online systems can convey a sense of full physical presence, but the personal touch seems an irreducible prerequisite especially in medical schools, where the grades after graduation can be life and death.

### Lure of the Campus

Intrinsic limitations to online education are thus substantial. But they are buttressed by considerations that can be described more aptly as states of mind than reality. Humans have strong attachments to technologies of their childhood and early adulthood—the world in which they came of age. The fountain pen had devotees years after the advent of the far more functional ballpoint. The better "flow" of the fountain pen was perhaps in part responsible, but comfort with what we know was likely a far more powerful inducement (see Levinson, 1997, 1999, for more; the fountain pen still enjoys a following as a nostalgic fashion statement). Most of us have a deep-seated expectation that education entails a teacher in a classroom—our species has been going to school that way for hundreds, even thousands, of years. Whatever the benefits of education in cyberspace, however logically we may see these, they are nonetheless mediated by the tug of tradition in real space. This tug is in our genes—it runs far deeper than the appeal of the fountain pen. And it works, for better or worse, as a balance for all transactions in cyberspace.

## The Stigma of TV

Online education is beset by another tradition, one that pits new media against literacy. Beginning with motion pictures at the start of the last century, and continuing with television in the middle, presentations on screens have been condemned by academic and cultural critics as destructive of literacy, traditional education, and their values (McKeever, 1910, is an early example; see Levinson, 1999, for discussion of this and more throughout the 20th century). People who see computers and the Web as yet another species of screen (see, e.g., Postman, 1994) are inclined to take the same view of online education—an oxymoron, at best, in which the online part undermines any educational value. But the primacy of text online means that Web screens function much more like books than televisions. And when we add to this textual power the capacity of online participants to question the written words, to shape them in dialogue, we obtain a medium having almost nothing in common with television and its one-way communication of pictures and sounds. Socrates' yearning for an "intelligent writing"—one which responded to questions put to it, as in a dialogue, rather than preserving a "solemn silence"—is fulfilled online.

## HUMAN OPTIONS

We of course know best our in-person environments—our family lives, the classrooms we attend as children, the people most of us work with on a daily basis. From such a vantage point, the prospect of an online community—of people getting to know each other online, learning from each other, even caring about each other—may seem far-fetched. The computer, after all, for much of its still brief tenure in our popular culture, has usually been assigned the role of a cold, impersonal, programming instrument.

But the reality of online communities and online education is different. Students in online courses become good friends, visit each other in diverse cities years after their online courses are over. Online education, although not satisfying every educational need, is as human an option as the classroom. It just responds to different kinds of human needs.

There are obviously some human activities that cannot work well or at all in cyberspace—walking hand-in-hand on a windswept beach, dining in a fine restaurant with wine and candlelight.

But education, the realm of human activity that deals with the life of the mind par excellence, is in most respects not one of them.

## REFERENCES

Asimov, I. (1983). *The robots of dawn.* New York: Doubleday.

Bolter, J. D. (1984). *Turing's man.* Chapel Hill: University of North Carolina Press.

Carpenter, E. (1973). *Oh, what a blow that phantom gave me!* New York: Bantam.

Levinson, P. (1997). *The soft edge: A natural history and future of the information revolution.* New York & London: Routledge.

Levinson, P. (1999). *Digital McLuhan: A guide to the information millennium.* New York & London: Routledge.

Marrou, H. L. (1956). *A history of education in antiquity* (G. Lamb, Trans.). New York: Mentor.

McGinn, D. (2000, April, 24). College online. *Newsweek,* pp. 54-58.

McKeever, W. A. (1910, August). Motion pictures: A primary school for criminals. *Good Housekeeping,* pp. 184-186.

Perkinson, H. (1982). Education and learning from our mistakes. In P. Levinson (Ed.), *In pursuit of truth: Essays on the philosophy of Karl Popper* (pp. 126-153). Atlantic Highlands, NJ: Humanities Press.

Postman, N. (1994, February). *The John Culkin Memorial Lecture.* Lecture delivered at The New School for Social Research, New York City.

# SECTION 3

# FORM: VIRTUAL REALITY AND HYPERMEDIA AS NEW KINDS OF SPACE AND NAVIGATION

Cyberspace may be intended to perform the same functions as physical space, but it does so by introducing new forms that are intrinsically different from real space and from other forms of mediated space (e.g., books, film). Through virtual reality and hypermedia, new perceptions and conceptualizations of space, location, dimension, direction, travel, and navigation are created. Of course, we cannot actually step into the computer and slide along the neural pathways of the CPU as movie characters sometimes do. In fact, the point of cyberspace communication is that it all can take place from the comfort of a chair. The illusion of immersion in a virtual landscape is based on the interface between user and computer: the graphic user interface (GUI) such as Windows or the Macintosh desktop; the keyboard, mouse, or joystick; the hypermediated Web page and links; or virtual reality and telepresence interfaces. Out of this interface with the digital world, familiar environments and objects gain new forms, and the boundaries between forms dissolve. Navigation takes on new meaning as well, as travel in cyberspace can be accomplished with a single keystroke; we can "move" from northeastern United States to southwestern Australia without having to get out of our chairs and without any sense of motion, so seamless is most electronic navigation; on the other hand, it is quite easy to become "lost" in dataspace.

Sue Barnes begins the section by examining several forms of cyberspace, including virtual reality, telepresence, and ubiquitous computing in real spaces. Surveying such phenomena as cyberpunk, cyborgs, artificial intelligence, and artificial life, she explores the ecological pressures of this new environment and the forms of life and consciousness adapted to it. In doing so, she argues that bodiless existence in cyberspace is characterized by a number of paradoxes. Stuart Moulthrop concentrates on typographic form, as it makes the transition from paper to screen, in the next chapter, which takes its name from Writing on the Edge (an electronic journal also produced in traditional print). Moulthrop argues for taking the plunge into complete immersion in electronic texts; if Moulthrop had his way you would be reading this on your screen, not holding a traditional printed book in your hands. In this piece he examines some reasons why print remains a dominant medium and electronic text still struggles to get inside the gate of the academic castle.

Camille Paglia provides a more positive take on online publishing in this section's third chapter. As a regular contributor to the online magazine Salon, as well as an author of traditional typographically produced books and articles, she is in a good position to compare the two forms of publication. Thus, she discusses the different formal demands inherent in writing for the Web as opposed to print media, as well as the changes brought on by working with a medium whose content does not require physical distribution. In arguing for the advantages of electronic text, Paglia also points to the ways in which this new medium breaks up the old knowledge monopolies of print-based publishers, and has a democratizing effect on journalism.

Continuing, in the fourth chapter of this section, with an examination of hypertext and hypermedia forms, Stephanie Gibson gives a broad overview of the pedagogical issues surrounding hypertext in the classroom (and as a classroom). Examining both positive and negative possibilities, and providing a comparison with printed text books, Gibson considers the impact of this new, more open form of textuality on teacher-student relationships. She also discusses its paradigmatic implications for both curriculum and canon. Finally, in this section's fifth chapter, Paul Lippert steps inside traditional cinema to examine the new routes carved out by cyberspace technologies. In a thoughtful piece that discusses class implications of concrete and abstract symbolic forms, Lippert proposes that cyberspace is itself digital, and representations of it are unnecessarily analogic. Ultimately, he is critical of postmodern and cyberpunk attempts to reify virtual space.

Communications technologies have traditionally altered our relationships with space and navigation. The telephone, for instance, allowed our physical selves to be in one spot while our voice and ears traveled metaphorically to another. The places we went were real, and there was an exchange of actual sensory experience. Because of the telephone, the manner in which humans interact has been irrevocably altered. What impact will cyberspace technologies have on human understanding and interaction? Some surprising food for thought follows.

✧✧✧✧ *14*

# Cyberspace:
# Creating Paradoxes for
# the Ecology of Self

## Sue Barnes

*A recurring theme in this anthology is the impact of the cyberspace environment on conceptions of the self. In this chapter, Sue Barnes employs an ecological approach, taking the reader on a tour of artificial environments and the life forms that are or may be adapted to them. In doing so, she explains the trend-setting desire of cyberculture aficionados to create and maintain consciousness solely in cyberspace, and the resulting philosophical and social paradoxes. Covering topics as diverse as science fiction, cyberpunk style, artificial intelligence and artificial life, virtual reality, telepresence, and ubiquitous computing (in which computers are installed into physical environments, creating media spaces), she is concerned with all forms of digital incursion into everyday life and their impact on the delicate balance between self and environment. Aside from this section of the book, other perspectives on cyberspace and the self can be found in Jay David Bolter's essay in Chapter 7, and Lance Strate's discussion of cybertime in Chapter 23; see also Terri Toles Patkin's piece on the virtual organization in Chapter 12, and Paul Levinson's discussion of the educational implications of computers in Chapter 13. An alternative to the environmental perspective appears in Gary Gumpert and Susan Drucker's piece on social space in Chapter 1.*

By erasing the boundaries between what is real and artificial, cyberspace creates a series of paradoxical situations that undermine the natural balance of self. Paradoxes occur in cyberspace because it blurs the distinctions between living people and artificial environments. In traditional physical environments, a concept of self is developed through face-to-face encounters with other people and objects. In contrast, cyberspace interaction takes place symbolically in a media-generated space. Depending on the computer system, the individual interacts in a digital environment of written language, images, video, sounds, three-dimensional computer-generated objects, virtual people, and artificial life. Therefore, the perceptual experience of one's physical environment is replaced by the sensations of being in a symbolic or artificial one. Moreover, the physical self is replaced by a digital representation of self. This digital self can be distributed throughout a network of cyberworlds to interact with other digital selves.

The concept of creating a digital self to exist in electronic media is a theme in the work of science fiction writers (Gibson, 1984, 1986, 1988; Harry, 1996; Stephenson, 1992; Sterling, 1988), cyberpunk authors (Kroker, 1993; Sirus, 1992), and scientific researchers (Minsky, 1986; Rucker, 1982). Their writings reflect a shift in attitude about the relationship between living humans and digital technology. In contrast to early science fiction writings that viewed human nature as being more important than machines, these works remove the human from its privileged position and advocate human-machine equality. Human nature no longer controls the machine. In some cases, the machines and cyberspace are viewed as superior to natural existence. Human-machine equality is a cultural paradigm shift in thinking about human relationships to technology. This shift has profound implications for the natural ecology of self and the development of self in digital environments.

Currently, a new generation of computer technology is emerging that enables people to separate themselves from physical space and reality in order to enter the artificial worlds of cyberspace. These technologies include personal computers, computer networks, virtual reality, media spaces, teleconferencing, and ubiquitous computing. To enter cyberspace, people create a digital persona. The self that exists as a unified mind and body in a physical space becomes a separate and distributed digital self. This new digital self encounters paradoxical situations in cyberspace that could threaten the ecological self that inhabits a natural world.

## DEFINITIONS OF CYBERSPACE

*Cyberspace* is a term that is used synonymously with other phrases such as cyberia, virtual space, virtual worlds, dataspace, the digital domain, the electronic realm, the information sphere, virtual reality, computer networking, and the Internet. The word was originally introduced by William Gibson (1984) in his science fiction novel Neuromancer to describe a futuristic computer network. However, Gibson (1991) states that he assembled the word *cyberspace* as an "act of pop poetics" to describe today's postmodern culture. Although Gibson's stories take place in the future, they are based on his observations about our present relationship to technology. For example, Gibson's inspiration for the term cyberspace came from watching kids playing video arcade games. In an interview, he described these games as "a feedback loop with photons coming off the screens into the kids' eyes, neurons moving through their bodies, and electrons moving through the video game. These kids clearly *believed* in the space games projected" (cited in McCaffery, 1992, p. 272). Gibson observed that video game kids and computer users seem "to develop a belief that there's some kind of *actual space* behind the screen, someplace you can't see but you know is there" (p. 272; emphasis in original). It is a "nonspace," a hyperdimensional realm that we enter through technology. Therefore, in his books, *cyberspace* became a term to denote the nonspaces created by futuristic electronic media.

However, Gibson's term takes on additional meanings when it is applied to current media such as personal computers (PCs) and computer networks. For example, "now that PCs are linked through networks that cover the globe and beyond, many people spend real time out there in 'cyberspace'—the territory of digital information. This apparently boundless universe of data breaks all the rules of physical reality" (Rushkoff, 1994, p. 2). From home, people can explore information in cyberspace stored at any geographic location. When the term *cyberspace* is applied to computer networks, it moves out of the realm of science fiction and into everyday life.

Gibson's original use of the word *space* in cyberspace relates to electronic spaces created by computer-based media. Today, it has been adapted by an emerging *cyberculture* as a general term for digital media space. Cyberculture represents the merging of the present and the future and the total encroachment of technology into human lives. *Cyber-* has become the prefix of the 1990s—cyberspace, cyberpunk, cybernaut, cyberart, cybergames, cybersex. It is derived from the word *cybernetics*, a term coined by Norbert Weiner (1954). Weiner applied it to an entire discipline of communication theory that studies the transmission of messages in animals, machines and society. Weiner (1954) states he derived cybernetics "from the Greek word Kubernetes, or 'steersman,'" (p. 7). In Gibson's (1984, 1986, 1988) science fiction novels, the term *cyberspace* encompasses the idea of people steering through a matrix of digital information.

## CYBERPUNK COUNTERCULTURE

Since the publication of Gibson's books, an entire cybercounterculture has evolved. Science fiction writers Wilhelmina Baird (1993), Ben Bova (1989), Alan Dean Foster (1990), Neal Stephenson (1992), and Bruce Sterling (1988) have all written books using the concept of cyberspace. Magazines such as *Mondo 2000* and *Wired* feature articles describing cyberspace and its counterculture.

Additionally, the term *cyberpunk* has appeared to refer to its inhabitants. Cyberpunks are people who explore the digital landscapes of electronic space. It is a word that has "escaped from being a literary genre into cultural reality. People started calling themselves cyberpunks, or the media started calling people cyberpunks" (Sirius, 1992, p. 64).

For example, *Cyberpunk* is the title of Katie Hafner and John Markoff's (1991) book about the "outlaws and hackers on the computer frontier." They use the term to describe people who are involved in illegal computer activities, such as breaking into networks. In contrast, Bruce Sterling (1992) describes *cyberpunks* as "perhaps the first SF [science fiction] generation to grow up not only with the literary tradition of science fiction, but in a truly science-fictional world. For them, the techniques of classical 'hard SF—extrapolation, technological literacy—are not just literary tools, but an aid to daily life'" (p. 344). Computers that were once the tools of science fiction characters are now in the hands of the cyberpunk generation.

Cyberpunks have developed ideologies based on the work of Arthur Kroker (1993) and Jean Baudrillard (1983). These authors write about human relationships to technology. It is a relationship that blurs the boundaries between human and machine. Cyberpunks want the human nervous system to merge with the computer matrix by making reality and hallucinations collapse into each other in an electronic universe. Mind invasion is their technological theme. It includes: "brain-computer interfaces, artificial intelligence, neurochemistry—techniques radically redefining the nature of humanity, the nature of self" (Sterling, 1992, p. 346). Additionally, the cyberpunk perspective encompasses the idea of body invasion—implanted circuitry, cosmetic surgery, prosthetic limbs, and genetic alteration. These visions of mental invasion and biological alterations correspond to Gibson's imaginative writing.

Gibson's characters immerse themselves in information by entering "a new universe, a parallel universe created and sustained by the world's computers and communication lines" (Benedikt, 1991, p. 1); this universe generates "a three-dimensional field of action and interaction: with recorded and live data, with machines, sensors, and with other people" (p. 129). Cyberpunk fictional characters are fitted with surgical implants and "jack-in" to cyberspace directly through their brains. Software programs "create computerized virtual bodies to exist inside the computer matrix, the boundary between human and computer is erased and the nature of the human psyche is redefined in accordance with the computer paradigm" (Springer, 1993, p. 721).

Neal Stephenson (1992) describes this process in *Snow Crash*. His characters create a computer-generated "avatar" that dwells in a parallel world called the "Metaverse": "Your avatar can look any way you want it to, up to the limitations of your equipment. If you're ugly, you can made your avatar beautiful. . . . You can look like a gorilla or a dragon or a giant talking penis in the Metaverse" (p. 36). Your physical appearance is only limited by the hardware you possess. Human bodies become obsolete as the mind circulates through the software. In cyberjargon this is referred to as "getting rid of the meat." In the philosophy of cyberpunk, "the ultimate revenge of the information system comes when the system absorbs the very identity of the human personality, absorbing the opacity of the body, grinding the meat into information" (Heim, 1991, p. 66). The mind becomes immersed in the medium while the body is left behind in physical space.

## THE PHILOSOPHICAL PARADOX

In an interview with Woolley (1992), Gibson states that the word cyberspace meant to suggest "the point at which media [flow] together and surround us. It's the ultimate extension of the exclusion of daily life. With cyberspace as I describe it you can literally wrap yourself in media and not have to see what's really going on around you" (p. 122). But Gibson is an usher rather than a participant in cyberspace. In reality, his books draw nihilistic conclusions about mankind's current relationship to technology. Although traditional science fiction "frequently problematizes the oppositions between the natural and the artificial, the human and the machine, it generally sustains them in such a way that the human remains surely ensconced in its privileged place at the center of things. Cyberpunk, however, is about the breakdown of these oppositions" (Hollinger, 1992, pp. 204-205). Human nature is no longer superior to the machine. Cyberpunk "invokes a rhetoric of technology to express the natural world in a metaphor that blurs the distinctions between the organic and the artificial" (p. 205).

Cyberpunk is a philosophy whereby hyperreal or virtual icons of human simulations infiltrate reality. The physical environment is replaced with a symbolic media-generated landscape. Prosthetic devices "plug the human sensorium into interactive communion with the computer, so that the user transcends—and, all too often in this context, elides—not only his (or her) being in an imperfect human body, but also the imperfect world that we all 'really' materially create and physically inhabit" (Sobchack, 1993, p. 575). Cyberpunks contend that escape from the physical world into an artificial one is notable because the "earth is this incredibly boring place" (Turin, 1993, p. 48). By connecting ourselves to artificial worlds in cyberspace we not only leave our physical bodies, but also the physical world in which we live.

Immersion into this world of data distances the individual from physical culture. As a result, "lifestyle has fled its basis in the domain of personal ethics, becoming an empty floating sign-object—a cynical commodity—in the mediascape" (Kroker, 1993, p. 6). Cyberpunk becomes "a virtual theory of those organs without bodies that come to dominate the electronic landscape of digital culture" (p. 6). It is a virtual reality that escapes the vicissitudes of the physical body by replacing the natural with the artificial: "Virtual reality, the ideology of which could be triumphantly described by Marvin Minsky of MIT's Multi-Media

Research Lab as the production of cyber-bodies with the soft matter of the brains scooped out, and skulls hard-wired to an indefinite flow of telemetry" (p. 7). Cyberpunk seeks to replace flesh and blood with silicon and chips. Human and machine merge together, and the machine takes control as the natural body is gradually eliminated.

For academics, cyberpunk ideology raises serious questions about human relationships to technology. Forgetting the body may be a Cartesian trick to place the mind in a different category than the body, but it has profound implications. Cyberpunk authors view the human body as "meat" and as being obsolete as soon as consciousness can be uploaded into a computer network. But the human body is a complex technical hardware device that must function properly to perform complex software operations, such as thinking. Its "software, human language, is dependent on the condition of the hardware [body]" (Lyotard, 1991, p. 13). Stone (1991) states: "Cyberspace developers foresee a time when they will be able to forget about the body. But it is important to remember that virtual community originates in, and must return to, the physical. No refigured virtual body, no matter how beautiful, will slow the death of a cyberpunk with AIDS. Even in the age of the technosocial subject, life is through bodies" (p. 113). Human consciousness is rooted in the physical body and without the body, consciousness does not exist.

From an academic perspective, cyberpunk ideology demonstrates the frailty of Cartesian philosophy that separates the body from the mind or the concrete from the abstract: "The mind is a property of the body, and lives and dies with it. Everywhere we turn we see signs of this recognition, and cyberspace, in its literal placement of the body in spaces invented entirely by the mind, is located directly upon this blurring boundary, this fault" (Novak, 1991, p. 227). Thus, by grinding the meat to eliminate the physical body, cyberpunks would simultaneously be destroying the human hardware that is necessary for consciousness and thinking to exist. From a philosophical perspective, destroying the body paradoxically destroys consciousness or the thinking mind. Once the mind is destroyed, the self ceases to exist.

## CYBERCULTURE AND SCIENCE

Getting rid of the meat to explore cyberworlds is an imaginative theme for science fiction books; however, it becomes an ominous vision when it crosses from the realm of fiction into the research of legitimate science. Sterling (1992) states: "Technical culture has gotten out of hand. The advances of sciences are so deeply radical, so disturbing, upsetting, and revolutionary, that they can no longer be contained" (p. 345). For example, John von Neumann introduced "The General and Logical Theory of Automata" in the late 1940s: "An automaton is a machine that processes information, proceeding logically, inexorably performing its next action after applying data received from outside itself in light of instructions programmed within itself" (Levy, 1992, p. 15). Simply stated, von Neumann argues that machines could be internally programmed to react to outside stimulus. This led to the idea of self-replicating machines and factories. Scientists during the 1950s considered the possibility of sending robots to the moon to design and build a self-growing lunar facility. The robots would be preprogrammed on earth to find the raw materials, manufacture the parts, and construct the factory. Once sent to the moon, the robots would self-replicate and build.

Von Neumann's theory was based on the mechanistic perspective that views life literally as an automation process. Scientists reasoned that if life is an automata, then machines could be designed to self-replicate and think. During the late 1960s and early 1970s, the discipline of artificial intelligence (AI) had high hopes of digitally duplicating the human thinking process: "Nearly all authorities agree that artificial intelligence seeks to produce on a computer, a pattern of output that would be considered intelligent if displayed by human beings" (Gardner, 1985, p. 11). AI researchers postulated that computers could behave like thinking minds. But their original approach to creating "thinking machines" was top-down. Structures were not encouraged to emerge, but imposed. Programs for AI were solution oriented: "They posed a question to the computer and tried to make the computer answer it in the way a human being would" (Levy, 1992, p. 158). Hubert L. Dreyfus (1979) in *What Computers Can't Do* explains why the original AI researchers failed. In the book, he argues that computers "can't think like people because there's no way to represent all the background knowledge of ordinary human life—the stuff we associate with common sense—in some form a computer can understand" (cited in Rose, 1984, p. 84).

With the failure of an imposed top-down approach to AI, these researchers started to explore other ways of creating artificial life. For example, Marvin Minsky (1986) in *The Society of Mind* argued that "nature's approach toward intelligence and behavior was decentralized" (cited in Levy, 1992, p. 285). Moreover, he states that computers can be designed to duplicate natural processes. From Minsky's (1986) perspective, the mind is a process or activity of the brain. Therefore, he argues that biological human brain cells could be replaced with computer chips. This replacement creates a substitute machine that "would reproduce the same processes as those within your brain" (p. 289). Minsky goes on to state: "There isn't any reason to doubt that the substitute machine would think and feel the same kinds of thoughts and feelings that you do—since it embodies all the same processes and memories" (p. 289). He then asks, "*Would that new machine be the same as you?*" Minsky believes microscopic differences would exist because "it would be impractical to duplicate, with absolute fidelity, all the interactions in the brain" (p. 289). These microscopic differences, he argues, do not matter because we are always changing as we age. Because people are never the same from one moment to the next, you cannot claim that your brain machine is not you. In essence, the artificial you is the same as the physical you. Therefore, from Minksy's view, there is no difference between the real you and your digital clone.

Minsky's concept of the possibility of digital duplication is supported by mathematician/cyberpunk writer Rudy Rucker. Rucker uses mathematical theory to claim that machine consciousness can exist. Rucker (1982) states: "If one gets an artificial leg, kidney, or heart, one is still the same person. I maintain that it is possible to envision a time when one could even get a new artificial brain" (p. 197). But, Rucker's perspective goes beyond the mechanistic view that argues "neither men nor robots are anything but machines" (p. 197). He states that "everything, whether man or machine, participates in the Absolute" (p. 197). Therefore, machines can have souls because they exist the same way that human beings exist. Rucker directly challenges the idea that human beings are superior to machines. According to his view, humans and machines are equal—both can exist with souls.

The work of von Neumann, Minsky, Rucker, and Kurzweill reflect a paradigm shift in scientific thinking. The boundaries between real and artificial life are eliminated. The human being is no longer placed in its privileged position at the center of things, but is now on the same level as machines.

The work of these scientists has influenced the relatively newer discipline of artificial life (a-life). In contrast to AI research that focuses on the thinking mind, a-life looks at self-reproducing artificial organisms: "The premise being that the basis of life is information, steeped in a dynamical system complex enough to reproduce and to bear offspring more complex than the parent" (Levy, 1992, p. 22). A-life "studies ways of building systems that act as if they are alive. This broad area of study encompasses chemical attempts to synthesize self-replicating molecules, the linguistic analysis of self-perpetuating belief systems, robotics, and the design of computer programs capable of evolving into new forms" (Rucker, 1992, p. 30). Intrigued with the concept, Steven Levy (1992) in *Artificial Life* describes the work of a-life researchers to create and study lifelike organisms and computer systems that are built by humans. According to Levy, a-life research has two different points of view. The purpose of "weak" a-life research "is to illuminate and understand more clearly the life that exists on earth and possibly elsewhere" (p. 5), and this "weak" research tends to be conducted by biologists, astronomers, and physicists. Bolder practitioners engage in "strong" a-life research: "They look toward the long-term development of actual living organisms whose essence is information. These creatures may be embodied in corporeal form—a-life robots—or they may live within a computer" (Levy, 1992, p. 6). In general, a-life researchers replace organic molecules and chemical compounds as the essence of life with information.

## THE "ARTIFICIAL VERSUS HUMAN" PARADOX

Currently, strong a-life researchers work with digital information instead of living compounds and organs (referred to as *wetware*). Despite the fact they work with digital software instead of living wetware, this research is still clouded by the legacy of Mary Shelly's *Frankenstein* (1963). In Shelley's story the monster destroys his creator. Upon meeting his creator the monster states: "Do your duty towards me, and I will do mine towards you and the rest of mankind. If you will comply with my conditions, I will leave them and you at peace; but if you refuse, I will glut the maw of death, until it be satiated with the blood of your remaining friends" (p. 95). This powerful image of a manmade creation gone awry raises moral questions about a-life research. For example, what will happen if these new life forms are unleashed on the world? Will they go out of control, and could they harm human life? Based on examples of existing software patterns, the answer is most likely yes.

In *Digital Woes*, Lauren Ruth Wiener (1993) argues that software is unreliable. In her book, she describes 13 tales of how software can go wrong. Some of the stories are comic, but others are tragic. For example, she describes how the AT&T telephone system went down on January 15, 1990 as the result of a common software error. Wiener states: "It isn't that the people who design, build, and program computers are any less careful, competent, or conscientious than the rest of us. But they're only human, and digital technology is unforgiving of human limitations" (pp. 3-4). The details that must be tracked in a software program are so enormous that the "job of testing a software program could take decades . . . centuries . . . sometimes even millennia" (p. 4). She argues that depending on software to run human-related systems is risky. Future system failures could result in injury or fatalities to plants, animals, owners, operators, users, future generations, and the life-sustaining qualities of the earth.

Another example of software failure that is more closely related to a-life is computer viruses: "The dangers of viruses are a vivid paradigm of the perils inherent in any realized form of a-life" (Levy, 1992, p. 333). Releasing uncontrolled viruses into the information ecosystem "can certainly reap unhappy results for those who depend on the stability of that system" (p. 333). For example, Robert Tapan Morris unleashed a computer virus that all but shut down the Internet. According to Hafner and Markoff (1991), Morris got one of the numbers wrong in his program. As a result, his virus went out of control and a major human communication system was affected. Currently, software unreliability creates a paradoxical situation in cyberspace. The more we depend on artificial software systems, the larger the risk to human systems of all kinds.

## CYBORGS AND POPULAR CULTURE

In popular culture, the merging of people and artificial systems is the *cyborg*. Cyborgs are fictionalized in films, videos, books, computer games, and popular magazines (Jamison, 1994). "A cyborg is a cybernetic organism, a hybrid of machine and organism, a creature of social reality as well as a creature of fiction" (Haraway, 1991, p. 149). An examination of the fictional cyborg reveals social attitudes about the relationship of people to machines. For example, films such as *Robocop* and *Terminator* "embrace technology at the same time as they armor the human against the technological threat. There is, underlying these works, an uneasy but consistent sense of human obsolescence, and at stake is the very definition of the human" (Bukatman, 1993, p. 20). A cultural attitude in cyborg fiction begins to emerge that challenges our concept of what it means to be a human being rather than a machine (also see Hayles, 1999).

The cyborg symbiosis of machine and human questions the very essence of human personality. For example, novelists Amy Thomson (1993) and Marge Piercy (1991) write about the process in which cyborgs develop a sense of self. In *Virtual Girl*, Thomson describes how a female cyborg named Maggie struggles to digitally develop her memory and sense of identity. Similarly, Piercy in *He, She and It* discusses the socialization process of a male cyborg and how he attempts to develop a personality and life separate from his creator. In both cases, the cyborg strives to be accepted as human. Through software manipulations and adjustments, the cyborg engages in interpersonal human relationships. By viewing human personality through the eyes of the cyborg, these authors begin to examine the idea of what it means to be human, machine, and a hybrid of both.

The cyborg is representative of a new type of human persona. It is a human personality that "is replaced by pure information whose configurations 'signify' disembodied human sensoria, personality constructs, and artificial intelligences" (Tomas, 1991, p. 35). Today, the cyborg is representative of two new cultural myths. First, digital cyborg personalities could be equal to human personalities. Second, the human personality could be duplicated in a digital format.

## THE "HUMAN UNIQUENESS" PARADOX

Cyborg digital identities create a paradox. The cultural acceptance of digital personalities opens up the possibility of personality duplication and memory alteration. If memories are stored in a digital format, they can be enhanced, augmented, erased, or changed according to electronic models. The ability to alter memories has profound implications: "Since memories form the foundation of human identity, loss of memory is equivalent to loss of self. . . . Thus it suggests that advanced technologies can potentially be used to destroy human uniqueness" (Springer, 1993, p. 723). For example, Baudrillard (1983) states that the automation of the robot is "a perfect double for man, right up to the suppleness of his movements, the function of his organs and intelligence" (p. 93). The mechanical robot body can double for the human body, or eventually replace it. If this occurs, the original human presence would be replaced by a cyborg personality because digital personality could be copied. A contradiction occurs when human identity is duplicated by computer technology. In the process of copying ourselves we destroy the very nature of what makes us individuals.

Social theorists argue the mind and body together are an integral part of our unique presence: "Our bodily existence stands at the forefront of personal identity and individuality" (Heim, 1991, p. 74). Replacing the physical body with a cyborg simultaneously eliminates oneself. Thus, the cyborg paradox occurs when digital duplication of body and mind destroys the essence of what it means to be a unique human being. Although the cyborg remains an imaginary creature, the cultural attitudes represented in its myth challenge our existing concepts of what it means to be a unique living person.

## TRADITIONAL THEORIES OF SELF

Social theorists Mead (1959) and Berger and Luckmann (1966) argue the mind and body together are necessary to develop a sense of self. Writing from a monist perspective, they believe the mind is "inseparably associated with and dependent upon the physical organism known as body" (Hintz, 1960, p. 105). A person's "experience of himself [herself] always hovers in a balance between being and having a body" (Berger & Luckmann, 1966, p. 51). Without experiencing the physical body a person cannot develop a sense of self. For example, the work of Mead (1959, 1962) depicts how an individual self evolves through body interaction with objects and other people.

According to Mead (1959, 1962), in the first stage of self-development, the actions of physical objects become internalized within oneself. For example, taking hold of a hard object stimulates oneself to exert an inner mental effort. The individual begins to make a relationship between holding an object and the effort of pressure in the action of holding. When the individual takes the attitude of the object (holding), the object becomes a part of an individual's inner experience.

In the next stage, a transference takes place when the individual "in grasping and pushing things is identifying its own effort with the contact experience of the thing" (Mead, 1959, pp. 121-122). In other words, after making the relationship between the object and pressure, the individual must then realize that he or she is exerting the effort to hold the object. At this point, the individual now becomes aware of him- or herself as an object that exists with other objects in an environment. As surrounding colors, shapes, and objects come in contact with the body, they begin to occupy a defined place within an individual's world. The pressure of the body and grasping of the hands localizes objects from an inside attitude, and the individual becomes aware of him- or herself as an object through body interaction with other objects. Simultaneously, while the individual is becoming aware of him- or herself, he or she is also becoming aware of "other" individuals in addition to objects.

Mead (1959) stated: "The others and the self arise in the social act together" (p. 169). An individual self is established by organizing the attitudes of other individuals toward the self and toward one another through participation in social interaction. For example, a social act is playing the game of baseball. Each team member knows his or her role in the game as well as the roles of every other player. Because each player understands the role of the "other" players, each player can socially interact according to the game's rules. Every individual player takes on the roles of others and addresses themselves in their multiple roles as well as in their singular role. Simply stated, a person could not play the role of the batter, if he or she did not understand the roles of the pitcher and catcher. Thus, by understanding the role of others, we can develop our own individual roles and consequently a sense of self. Mead (1962) invents the term the *generalized other* to describe "the organized community or social group which gives to the individual his unity of self" (p. 154). The generalized other is the "attitude of the whole community" or, as described previously, the baseball team.

Summarizing Mead's view, the formation of self involves encounters with objects in the physical world and social interaction with other people: "The formation of the self, then, must also be understood in relation to both the on going organismic development and the social process in which the natural and the human environment are mediated through the significant others" (Berger & Luckmann, 1966, p. 50). An underlying concept is the idea that the self is formed through body interaction in a natural space. Monist theories of self argue that the physical body is an integral part of self-development. Touching, feeling, and having access to all five senses is essential to interacting with objects and people. According to this perspective, a separation of mind and body in cyberspace will inhibit self-growth. Therefore, integrating the physical body with the digital representation of self in cyberspace would be essential for developing self-identity.

## THE INTEGRATION OF THE PHYSICAL
## BODY WITH THE DIGITAL SELF

Currently, a new generation of computer technologies are developing to integrate the physical body with a digital self. These technologies fall into two types of computer development. The first is virtual reality and the second ubiquitous computing. *Virtual reality* (VR) is essentially "the use of computers to create a simulated reality" (Zachmann, 1992, p. 107). It is immersing ourselves into a computer-generated world "to tighten the bond between humans and computers, and allows us to more directly enter those digital worlds that, until now, we could only passively observe through the window of the computer screen" (Porter, 1992, p. 43). The physical self wears goggles, gloves, and/or body suits to interact in computer generated space. In contrast, *ubiquitous computing* is a "computing environment in which each person is continually interacting with hundreds of nearby wireless interconnected computers" (Weiser, 1993, p. 7). Computers are invisibly woven "into the fabric of everyday life until they are indistinguishable from it" (p. 94). Virtual reality is immersing the self in cyberspace; in contrast, ubiquitous computing is transparently placing hundreds of computers within our real-world environments. However, by integrating computers with real space, the lines between reality and cyberspace are blurred. On the one hand, virtual reality and ubiquitous computing may appear to be different approaches. But on the other, they both have the same goal of integrating the physical body into virtual space. In the future, the information we receive in the virtual world may rival the information we receive in actual real-world face-to-face encounters.

William Gibson is "credited with inspiring the idea of virtual reality with his concept of cyberspace" (Woolley, 1992, p. 36). The goal of VR development is to integrate the physical senses into a computer-constructed environment and create experiences that are "life-like" interactions. This is accomplished through the use of peripheral devices that are connected to the body such as glasses, head-mounted displays, three-dimensional interactive sound, data gloves, tactile feedback controllers, and body suits. The body is integrated into cyberspace through peripheral attachments and clothing. Ideally, the entire body would become the *interface* or point of contact for computer interaction. Virtual reality "is the technology used to provide a more intimate 'interface' between humans and computer imagery. It is about simulating the full ensemble of sense data that make up 'real' experience" (p. 5).

Virtual reality made its grand entrance at a panel session called "Virtual Environments and Interactivity: Windows to the Future" during the 1989 SIGGRAPH Conference on computer graphics. Audience members (myself included) listened to Jaron Lanier (1989), a pioneering developer of virtual reality, explain the concept:

> It's a simulation of a reality that can surround a person that's created with computerized clothing. It's rather like the physical world in that it's an externally perceived reality that you perceive through your sense organs and the physical world. You perceive sensation on the outside of your eyes and your ears and your skin, and what you do in a virtual world is you put on clothing that generates stimulation right on top of those sense organs. (p. 7)

VR research attempts to create technologies that engage all of the senses in the process of interacting with computers. For example, VR interfaces enable people to explore virtual worlds and hold objects. Taking hold of a virtual object simulates the feeling of pressure. Or in Mead's vocabulary, holding the virtual object stimulates oneself to exert an inner mental effort—pressure. In these systems, the "virtual object" feels like the "real object." The system simulates the feeling of holding a real object through the use of tactile feedback controllers. But this is an example of only one type of VR interface now under development. Current VR research

> can be split into four broad categories: desktop systems (navigating through 3-D on a monitor), partial immersion (navigating through 3-D on a monitor with enhancements such as gloves and 3-D goggles), full-immersion systems (head gear, gloves, and bodysuits), and environmental systems (externally generated 3-D, but with little or no body paraphernalia). (Reveaux, 1993, p. 34)

Examples of these four categories include, respectively, the following: 3-D computer games including Microsoft's Flight Simulator, interacting with a computer monitor wearing 3-D glasses, VR arcade games in which players wear a head-mounted display helmet and data gloves, and projecting three-dimensional computer-generated images on walls of physical space. In addition to these four general categories, innovative developers are also adding puppetry and a-life to virtual environments.

"Over the past few years, several real-time animated digital puppets have been created for entertainment and promotional purposes" (Graves, 1993, p. 38). A well-known project is a system developed for Nintendo. It is a 3-D head of Mario, of the *Super Mario Brothers* computer game. "The Mario puppet is controlled by an actor who wears a face armature that has sensors to track the actor's head, face, and lip movements" (p. 38). The actor's movements control the computer-animated head of Mario. Another example of a digital puppet is "Neuro-Baby," a project under development at the Fujitsu laboratories in Japan. Neuro-Baby is a digital puppet that "seems to have a mind of its own, learning from its interactions with human beings through the use of *neural-network* software" (Reveaux, 1993, p. 38). A neural network is "a form of computation inspired by the structure and function of the brain" (Illingworth, 1990, p. 303). Neural network research involves researchers from a variety of disciplines:

> The work has attracted scientists from a number of disciplines: neuroscientists who are interested in making models of the neural circuitry found in specific areas of the brains of various animals; physicists who see analogies between the dynamical behavior of brain-like systems and the kind of nonlinear dynamical systems familiar in physics; computer engineers who are interested in fabricating brain-like computers; workers in artificial intelligence (AI) who are interested in building machines with the intelligence of biological organisms; engineers interested in solving practical problems; psychologists who are interested in the mathematics of such neural network systems; philosophers who are interested in how such systems change our view of the nature of mind and its relationship to brain; and many others [including entertainment and game companies]. (Rumelhart, Widrow, & Lehr, 1994, p. 87)

VR developers claim that applying neural network and a-life research to virtual reality "provides the interest, action, and real-time changes in behavior that occur in a living world. A-life makes the virtual world as intriguing as the real world" (Kelly, 1994, p. 21). In an entertainment context, "a-life lets the inhabitants of a world adapt to their environment, learn, and evolve in response to new players and new circumstances" (p. 21). In addition to entertainment, developers of these environments are working on a-life applications for business to predict financial trends and in education to "construct virtual worlds that explain themselves as they evolve" (p. 21). Rucker (1992) states: "Present day applications of Alife [sic] programs include computer graphics that draw themselves, methods of finding solutions to intractably difficult problems, and, of course, robotics. In the future we can expect to see large numbers of Alife [sic] organisms wandering around in cyberspace—this will keep virtual reality from being sterile and boring" (p. 32).

## THE "ARTIFICIAL VERSUS REAL BEHAVIOR" PARADOX

Although VR developers and cyberpunk enthusiasts welcome the idea of immersing ourselves in cyberspace, there are warnings about possible consequences. L. Casey Larijani (1994) states that there is "concern about the exaggerated susceptibility and vulnerability exhibited by subjects within immersive environments" (p. 8). When the medium disappears in virtual reality, events we perceive in virtual situations "become incorporated into our own, ever-evolving 'realities'" (p. 8). According to Larijani, some researchers fear that virtual reality will open doors to excessive and abusive behavior in virtual environments. Exaggerated behavior will then become integrated with normal behavior in the real world. This idea represents a potential cyberspace paradox in progress. Simultaneously, while researchers are building virtual worlds to better understand scientific and medical knowledge, the individuals who immerse themselves in virtual environments may be altering their individual knowledge of real-world experience.

Today, examples of behavior alteration in the real world based on cyberspace relationships are beginning to be discussed. For example, the introductory issue of *Wired* magazine ran an article about a woman whose real life changed as a result of her "online" or digital persona. In real life the woman was described as "a rather mousy person—the shy type who favored gray clothing of a conservative cut—and was the paragon of shy and retiring womanhood" (Van Der Leun, 1993, p. 74). In contrast, her digital persona was called "The Naked Lady," in which she was a sexy, lewd, bawdy, man-eating female. As months of cyberspace interactions with men progressed, a transformation occurred in the woman's real life. "She got a trendy haircut. Her clothing tastes went from Peck and Peck to tight skirts slit up the thigh. . . . Her speech became bawdier, her jokes naughtier" (p. 74). In short, she became her digital persona.

Reports of real-world behavioral changes as the result of VR and cyberspace interactions raise new concerns about the possible affects of digital technologies on human behavior. These concerns "include the ethical or political issues of specific VR technologies, consideration of VR as related to the arts, theories of scientific management systems and questions of cognitive learning and behavior" (Larijani, 1994, p. 10). Additionally, VR can induce intersensory conflict such as eye displacement that alters hand–eye coordination (Biocca & Rolland, 1995). What will happen when the "generalized others" we relate to are VR simulations, digital personas, and artificial life forms? Will a baseball game played in cyberspace invoke the same responses as a game played on a baseball field? As VR technology improves these are topics that will require serious discussion.

## THE PHYSICAL BODY IN MEDIATED SPACE

In contrast to the VR interface approach that integrates the body into cyberspace, ubiquitous computing wants to turn physical space into a computer interface. Where VR wants to fool the user into leaving the everyday physical world behind, ubiquitous computing wants to integrate computers into physical space. Because human activity occurs in the real world, ubiquitous computing makes computers disappear into the background of physical environments. For example, computerized objects such as wall-sized interactive screens and clip-board-sized computer terminals will be placed in physical spaces.

Ubiquitous computing is based on earlier research on media spaces. Media spaces are "computer-controllable networks of audio and video equipment used to support synchronous collaboration" (Gaver, 1992, p. 17). Media spaces create the appearance of a physical visual environment with the use of computers, projection screens, and video cameras: "The concept of media spaces is not new, Captain Kirk of the television program Star Trek communicated with other captains of other space ships via a huge projection screen. Captain Kirk could see and hear the person and the person's surroundings, and the other person with whom he was communicating could see and hear him as well" (Barnes & Greller, 1994, p. 10). Presently, media spaces enable the two-way transmission of auditory and visual information across geographic space.

Although media spaces span geographic space, they attempt to send and receive the visual and auditory messages people would experience in face-to-face communication. By setting up large screens with video cameras in physical spaces such as meeting rooms, hallways, and recreational areas, media spaces attempt to provide interpersonal interaction that is close to face-to-face encounters. People interact with each other in the following ways: through chance encounters in hallways and recreational areas, video phone conversations, group discussion, formal presentations, and social activities. Of all the cyberspace technologies, media spaces are the closest to actual reality because they create synchronous or real-time acoustic and visual environments that are based on physical ones. Moreover, they support normal human behavior patterns in real-world activities. But instead of being face to face in the same room, people's "telepresence" is transmitted through video, audio, computer, and telephone technologies: "*Telepresence is defined as the experience of presence in an environment by means of a communication medium.* In other words, presence refers to the natural perception of an environment, and *telepresence* refers to the *mediated* perception of an environment" (Steuer, 1992, p. 76; emphasis in original).

The concept of telepresence developed in teleconferencing and telerobotics applications. *Teleconferencing* is setting up a meeting in a special location that can transmit the images and sounds from other locations. For example, a conference room is set up where people sit on one side of a table and look at a group of people sitting on the other side. In reality, the table is next to a projection screen. The first group is in one location and the second group geographically somewhere else. The screen helps to simulate the illusion that both groups are meeting in a single space. Information such as gestures, facial expression, eye movement, and other nonverbal signals that are lost in standard telephone conversations are transmitted through telepresence. Thus, teleconferencing solves the problem of trying to be in two places at the same time. Additionally, the concept of telepresence can be applied to the telephone: "For example, while you're talking on the telephone to someone, it is as though your ears were in some remote place. You can hear what's going on miles away and then create sound (through the telephone) without actually being there" (Aukstakalnis & Blatner, 1992, p. 247). The difference between the telephone and teleconferencing is the addition of visual information to verbal electronic exchanges. However, adding the visual information to these exchanges is altering the meaning of face-to-face communications. With teleconferencing systems, face-to-face communication is no longer two people in the same room. The meaning is expanded to include the ability to see a person's face in a media space.

Telepresence research originally began at NASA as a way of controlling robots: "Since it is better to send machines than humans into hazardous environments like space, the NASA research team aimed to provide a wrap-around technology that would give the machine operator the feeling of 'being' in the place of the machine being operated" (Woolley, 1992, p. 126). For example, robots would be sent outside to repair space ships, while the human operator remained safely inside the space craft. Scott Fisher (1989), a NASA researcher working on telepresence, describes his project:

> What our particular lab, NASA Ames in California, is trying to do is . . . to make you really have the sense of being present in that remote environment and be able to interact with it as much as possible. Really the bottom line here is to go

from personal computer to personal simulator in a sense. To be able to simulate whatever it is you'd like to move around inside of. (p. 14)

To simulate the illusion of actually being in another location, the NASA researchers placed cameras in a robot that were "connected to a head-mounted display so that the wearer could see what he or she would see if actually there. Similarly, a glove or exoskeleton (that is, a series of hinges and struts clamped to the body, like an articulated splint) could be used to reproduce the wearer's movements in the robot's arm and hand or to provide tactile feedback" (Woolley, 1992, p. 126). Communication between the robot and operator has a complete range of sensory feedback and response. The operator is now telepresent through robot information links.

## THE ORWELLIAN PARADOX

Telepresence through ubiquitous computing, media spaces, and teleconferencing has Orwellian implications. Although people are mentally and physically immersed in cyberspace, their actions and locations can be monitored and digitally recorded because these technologies require the user to be physically interacting with computer systems. For example, in ubiquitous computing environments individuals wear an "active badge": "With an active badge system, every computer you sit down at is your computer, with your custom interface and access to your files, because your active badge sends it information via infrared signals" (Rheingold, 1994, p. 94). The paradox of this system are the Orwellian possibilities. Individuals can freely connect to cyberspace through any computer system, but, at the same time, the locations of researchers wearing the active badges can be monitored at all times by a central system. Individual freedom of motion is counteracted by the surveillance of physical location (see Lyon & Zureik, 1996). Similarly, media spaces and teleconferencing activities can be recorded digitally or on videotape while individuals are communicating in these environments.

As media transform into digital formats, the ability to interactively gather personal information will increase because convergence will make it easier to exchange data between them. A distinguishing difference between digital media and traditional mass media is the channel of communication. Mass media is a one-way channel; in contrast, digital media is two way. Two-way communication enables companies to monitor and respond to human messages and media interaction. For this reason, marketers are especially interested in discovering software methods for directly identifying and interacting with consumers. For example, cookies, small data files that are stored on an individual's computer by a Web browser, collect personal information about the user and his or her use of the Web. Although programmers (Erwin, 1996) argue that cookies are harmless, computer magazines report that cookies have been used to retrieve user's e-mail addresses, real names, and Web activities (Galkin, 1997; Staten, 1996). This personal information can be fed into other types of database systems and computer users are often unaware of how this information is going to be utilized. As a result, the use of technology to collect personal information raises a number of privacy concerns in both personal and professional contexts.

## THE SELF IN CYBERSPACE

In cyberspace communication, such as e-mail and chat, people to travel across time and space without a physical body. But in contrast to ubiquitous, media, and teleconferencing spaces, computer networking systems do not include personal visual information. Heim (1993), in *The Metaphysics of Virtual Reality*, states that "being a *body* constitutes the principle behind our separateness from one another and behind our personal presence" (p. 100; emphasis in original). Eliminating visual information about the physical body in cyberspace communication has positive and negative implications. On the one hand, eliminating the body makes us more equal because we no longer have access to the visual information of sex, age, or race. But on the other hand, the quality of human relationships narrows, because unlike face-to-face communication, we do not have a full range of visual and verbal sensory information: "No other form of social relating can reproduce the plentitude of symptoms of subjectivity present in the face-to-face situation" (Berger & Luckmann, 1966, p. 29).

As a result of cyberspace communication, "the boundaries between the subject, if not the body, and the 'rest of the world' are undergoing a radical refiguration, brought about in part through the mediation of technology" (Stone, 1991, p. 101). People can now communicate and develop relationships without ever meeting each other in a face-to-face situation (Rheingold, 1993), because technology enables people to communicate with each other in electronic space instead of real space. People exchanging messages in electronic space are creating new "symbolic" (Gergen, 1991) or "virtual" communities (Rheingold, 1993): "Symbolic communities are linked primarily by the capacity of their members for symbolic exchange—of words, images, information—mostly through electronic means" (Gergen, 1991, p. 214). The formation of symbolic or virtual communities raises the issue of how people will develop a self-identity when they communicate through electronic media instead of face-to-face interaction. In Mead's terms, what happens when the generalized other becomes the "electronic other?"

The relationship between media and developing a sense of self is the topic of a number of books (Gergen, 1991; Meyrowitz, 1985; Poster, 1990). These authors argue that "electronic media have changed the significance of space, time and the physical barriers as communication variables" (Meyrowitz, 1985, p. 13). We can now speak to someone in New York while sunning in

California: "The technological achievements of the past century have produced a radical shift in our exposure to each other" (Gergen, 1991, p. xi). Advances in radio, telephone, transportation, television transmission, computers, and cyberspace are exposing us "to an enormous barrage of social stimulation. Small and enduring communities, with a limited cast of significant others, are being replaced by a vast and ever-expanding array of relationships" (p. xi). As a result of these technologies, our amount of social participation is expanding.

We are now exposed to views, values, and visions that we would not normally come in contact with through face-to-face encounters. Electronic media "have rearranged many social forums so that most people now find themselves in contact with others in new ways. And unlike merged situations in face-to-face interaction, the combined situations of electronic media are relatively lasting and inescapable, they therefore have a much greater effect on social behavior" (Meyrowitz, 1985, p. 5). Because the formation of self depends on social behavior, media effects on social behavior will consequently affect the development of self. For example, Gergen (1991) and Poster (1990) argue that electronic media is fragmenting self-conceptions. In electronic media "the self is decentered, dispersed, and multiplied in continuous instability" (Poster, 1990, p. 6). Gergen (1991) describes this condition as the "saturated self": "The evening at home, once quiet, relaxed, and settling, is now—by dint of telephone, automobile, television, and the like—a parade of faces, information, and intrusion. One can scarcely settle into a calming rut, because who one is and the cast of 'significant others' are in continuous motion" (p. 67). Moreover, Gergen argues, "the fragmentation of self-conceptions corresponds to a multiplicity of incoherent and disconnected relationships" (p. 7). Relationships that form in cyberspace fall under this description. Computer network users interact with each other through disconnected and many times incoherent e-mail messages. Additionally, a myriad of electronic relationships can invite "us to play such a variety of roles that the very concept of an 'authentic self' with knowable characteristics recedes from view" (p. 7). Through electronic discourse, people can experiment and play with digital personas, such as The Naked Lady.

The lack of personal visual information in network exchanges allows people to test new personalities and even create totally fictitious ones. For example, in "The Strange Case of the Electronic Lover," Lindsy Van Gelder (1991) describes how a prominent male New York psychiatrist was "engaged in a bizarre, all-consuming experiment to see what it felt like to be female, and to experience the intimacy of female friendship" (p. 365). As a result of his experiment, many of the women he developed electronic relationships with felt that they had been "mind raped" by the fraud. In cyberspace the unity of personality associated with physical presences dissolves because individuals create digital characters of self that engage in correspondence with other digital personas. Thus, the ecology of self once grounded in physical reality becomes separated and distributed in a network of digital relationships. According the Gergen (1991), "the fully saturated [or digital] self becomes no self at all" (p. 7).

To summarize, Poster (1990) states when computer communication replaces face-to-face communication the subject is affected in the following ways: (a) new possibilities for playing with identities is possible, (b) gender cues are removed, (c) existing hierarchies in relationships are destablized, and (d) the subject is dispersed and dislocated in space and time. He further states: "The subject is changed in computer communications, dispersed in a postmodern semantic field of time-space, inner/outer, mind/matter" (p. 115). The subject is no longer represented as a physical human being. In cyberspace the physical self is represented by bits and bytes of information that disperses through the electronic nervous system of the network. Although, the physical body disappears in contemporary cyberspace interaction, the body can be used as a metaphor to understand a communication paradox in progress.

## THE COMMUNICATION PARADOX

Cyberspace can be directly related to McLuhan's (1964) use of the body as a metaphor to describe communication systems:

> Today, after more than a century of electric technology, we have extended our central nervous systems itself in a global embrace, abolishing both space and time as far as our planet is concerned. Rapidly, we approach the final phase of the extension of man—technological simulation of consciousness, when the creative process of knowing will be collectively and corporately extended to the whole of human society, much as we have already extended our senses and our nerves by the various media. (p. 19)

McLuhan's vision of extending our physical bodies through electric media has been realized in cyberspace. It extends our senses and annihilates physical space as it enables us to encounter the collective views of human society. We can now create, duplicate, and distribute a digital persona throughout the World-Wide Web of computer systems. However, although we are bridging the barriers of time and space through global communications media, we are simultaneously destroying the unity of self. As our communications technologies extend our senses into a united global embrace, the ecology of self dissolves. This is the final paradox of cyberspace.

## REFERENCES

Aukstakalnis, S., & Blatner, D. (1992). *Silicon mirage: The art and science of virtual reality.* Berkeley: Peachpit Press.

Baird, W. (1993). *Crashcourse.* New York: Ace Books.

Barnes, S., & Greller, L. (1994). Computer-mediated communication in the organization. *Communication Education, 43,* 1-10.

Baudrillard, J. (1983). *Simulations.* New York: Semiotext(e).

Benedikt, M. (1991). *Cyberspace: First steps.* Cambridge, MA: MIT Press.

Berger, P. L., & Luckmann, T. (1966). *The social construction of reality.* New York: Anchor Books.

Biocca, F.A., & Rolland, J.P. (1995). *Virtual eyes can rearrange your body: Adaption to visual displacement in see-through head-mounted displays.* Available at http://mindlab.msu.edu/mind/presence/presence.html

Bova, B. (1989). *Cyberbooks.* London: Mandarin Paperback.

Bukatman, S. (1993). *Terminal identity.* Durham, NC: Duke University Press.

Dreyfus, H.L. (1979). *What computers can't do.* New York: Harper & Row.

Erwin, M. (1996, June). Baking browser cookies. *Boardwatch Magazine, 10*(6). Available at http://www.boardwatch.com/mag/96/jun/bwmll.htm

Fisher, S. (1989, December). Virtual environments and interactivity: Windows to the future. *Computer Graphics: SIGGRAPH '89 Panel Proceedings, July 31-August 4, Boston, Massachusetts, 23*(5), 7-18.

Foster, A.D. (1990). *Cyber way.* New York: Ace Books.

Galkin, W.S. (1997, January). Your clickstream is showing: Privacy of online consumer information. *Computer Law Observer, 22.* Available at http://www.lawcircle.copm/issue22.html

Gardner, H. (1985). *The mind's new science.* New York: Basic Books.

Gaver, W.W. (1992). The affordance of media spaces for collaboration. In *ACM 1992 Conference on Computer-Supported Cooperative Work, Sharing Perspectives, October 31 to November 4, 1992, Toronto, Canada* (pp. 17-24). New York: Association for Computing Machinery.

Gergen, K.J. (1991). *The saturated self: Dilemmas of identity in contemporary life.* New York: Basic Books.

Gibson, W. (1984). *Neuromancer.* New York: Ace Books.

Gibson, W. (1986). *Count Zero.* New York: Ace Books.

Gibson, W. (1988). *Mona Lisa Overdrive.* New York: Bantam Books.

Gibson, W. (1991). Academy leader. In M. Benedikt (Ed.), *Cyberspace: First steps* (pp. 27-29). Cambridge, MA: MIT Press.

Graves, G.L. (1993, January). Invasion of the digital puppets. *New Media,* pp. 38-39.

Hafner, K., & Markoff, J. (1991). *Cyberpunk: Outlaws and hackers on the computer frontier.* New York: Simon & Schuster.

Haraway, D.J. (1991). *Simians, cyborgs, and women: The reinvention of nature.* New York: Routledge, Chapman & Hall.

Harry, E.L. (1996). *Society of mind.* New York: HarperCollins.

Hayles, N.K. (1999). *How we became posthuman.* Chicago: The University of Chicago Press.

Heim, M. (1991). The erotic ontology of cyberspace. In M. Benedikt (Ed.), *Cyberspace: First steps* (pp. 59-80). Cambridge: MIT Press.

Heim, M. (1993). *The metaphysics of virtual reality.* New York: Oxford University Press.

Hintz, H.W. (1960). Whitehead's concept of organism and the mind-body problem. In S. Hook (Ed.), *Dimensions of mind* (pp. 100-109). New York: New York University Press.

Hollinger, V. (1992). Cybernetic deconstructions: Cyberpunk and postmodernism. In L. McCaffery (Ed.), *Storming the reality studio: A casebook of cyberpunk and postmodern fiction* (pp. 203-218). Durham, NC: Duke University Press.

Kurzweil, R. (1999). *The age of spiritual machines.* New York: Viking.

Illingworth, V. (1990). *Dictionary of computing* (3rd ed.). Oxford: Oxford University Press.

Jamison, P.K. (1994, February 28). Contradictory spaces: Pleasure and the seduction of the cyborg discourse. *The Archnet Electronic Journal on Virtual Culture* [On-line serial]. Available: LISTSERV@KENTVM.KENT.EDU. Archived as JAMISON V2N1.

Kelly, R.V., Jr. (1994). Move over, Dr. Frankenstein. *Virtual Reality Special Report, Premiere Issue,* pp. 19-25.

Kroker, A. (1993). *Spasm: Virtual reality, android music and electric flesh.* New York: St. Martin's Press.

Lanier, J. (1989, December). Virtual environments and interactivity: Windows to the future. *Computer Graphics: SIGGRAPH '89 Panel Proceedings, July 31-August 4, Boston, Massachusetts, 23*(5), 7-18.

Larijani, L.C. (1994). Homo Faber or Homo Sapiens? *Virtual Reality Special Report, Premier Issue,* pp. 7-10.

Levy, S. (1991, November). Cyberspaced. *MacWorld,* pp. 61-66.

Levy, S. (1992). *Artificial Life: A report from the frontier where computers meet biology.* New York: Random House.

Lyon, D., & Zureik, E. (1996). *Computers, surveillance, & privacy.* Minneapolis: University of Minneapolis.

Lyotard, J. (1991). *The inhuman.* Stanford: Stanford University Press.

McCaffery, L. (1992). *Storming the reality studio: A casebook of cyberpunk and postmodern fiction.* Durham, NC: Duke University Press.

McLuhan, M. (1964). *Understanding media: The extensions of man.* New York: Signet Books.

Mead, G. H. (1959). *The philosophy of the present.* LaSalle, IL: Open Court.

Mead, G. H. (1962). *Mind, self, & society.* Chicago, University of Chicago Press.

Meyrowitz, J. (1985). *No sense of place.* New York: Oxford University Press.

Minsky, M. (1986). *The society of mind.* New York: Simon & Schuster.

Novak, M. (1991). Liquid architectures in cyberspace. In M. Benedikt (Ed.), *Cyberspace: First steps* (pp. 225-254). Cambridge, MA: MIT Press.

Piercy, M. (1991). *He, she and it.* New York: Knopf.

Porter, S. (1992, March). Virtual reality. *Computer Graphics World,* pp. 42-43.

Poster, M. (1990). *The mode of information.* Chicago: University of Chicago Press.

Reveaux, T. (1993, January). Virtual reality gets real. *New Media*, pp. 32-41.

Rheingold, H. (1993). *The virtual community: Homesteading on the electronic frontier*. Reading, MA: Addison-Wesley.

Rheingold, H. (1994, February). PARC is back! *Wired*, pp. 91-95.

Rose, F. (1984). *Into the heart of the mind: An American quest for artificial intelligence*. New York: Harper & Row.

Rushkoff, D. (1994). *Cyberia: Life in the trenches of hyperspace*. San Francisco: HarperCollins.

Rucker, R. (1982). *Infinity and the mind*. New York: Bantam Books.

Rucker, R. (1992). Artificial life. In R. Rucker, R.U. Sirius, & Q. Mu (Eds.), *Mondo 2000: A user's guide to the new edge*. New York: HarperCollins Publishers.

Rumelhart, D.E., Widrow, B., & Lehr, M.A. (1994, March). The basic ideas in neural networks. *Communications of the ACM*, pp. 87-92.

Shelley, M. (1963). *Frankenstein*. New York: Signet Classic.

Sirus, R.U. (1992). Cyberpunk. In R. Rucker, R.U.Sirius, & Q. Mu (Eds.), *Mondo 2000: A user's guide to the new edge*. New York: HarperCollins.

Sobchack, V. (1993). New age mutant ninja hackers: Reading Mondo 2000. *The South Atlantic Quarterly Review, 92*(4), 569-584.

Springer, C. (1993). Sex, memories, and angry women. *The South Atlantic Quarterly Review, 92*(4), 713-733.

Staten, J. (1996, March 13). Netscape tricks raise security concerns. *MacWeek*. Available at http://www.zdnet.com/macweek/mw_1001/gw_net_tricks.html

Stephenson, N. (1992). *Snow crash*. New York: Bantam Books.

Sterling, B. (1988). *Islands in the net*. New York: Ace Books.

Sterling, B. (1992). Preface from Mirrorshades. In L. McCaffery (Ed.), *Storming the reality studio: A casebook of cyberpunk and postmodern fiction* (pp. 343-348). Durham, NC: Duke University Press.

Steuer, J. (1992). Defining virtual reality: Dimensions determining telepresence. *Journal of Communication, 42*(4), 73-93.

Stone, A.R. (1991). Will the real body please stand up?: Boundary stories about virtual cultures. In M. Benedikt (Ed.), *Cyberspace: First steps* (pp. 81-118). Cambridge, MA: MIT Press.

Thomson, A. (1993). *Virtual girl*. New York: Ace Books.

Tomas, D. (1991). Old rituals for new space: Rites de passage and William Gibson's cultural model of cyberspace. In M. Benedikt (Ed.), *Cyberspace: First steps* (pp. 31-47). Cambridge, MA: MIT Press.

Turin, D. (1993). Welcome to the machine: Clever Hans and his expert systems future. *Mondo 2000, 11*, 47-51.

Van Der Leun, G. (1993). This is a naked lady. *Wired, Premier Issue*, pp. 74, 109.

Van Gelder, L. (1991). The strange case of the electronic lover. In C. Dunlop & R. Kling (Eds.), *Computerization and controversy* (pp. 354-375). Boston: Academic Press.

Weiner, N. (1954). *The human use of human beings: Cybernetics and society.* Garden City, NY: Doubleday Books.

Weiser, M. (1991, September). The computer for the 21st century. *Scientific American,* pp. 95-104.

Weiser, M. (1993, July). Some computer science issues in ubiquitous computing. *Communications of the ACM,* pp. 75-84.

Wiener, L.R. (1993). *Digital woes: Why we should not depend on software.* Reading, MA: Addison-Wesley.

Woolley, B. (1992). *Virtual worlds.* Oxford: Blackwell.

Zachmann, W.F. (1992, March 31). Simulation: The ultimate virtual reality. *PC Magazine,* p. 107.

✧✧✧✧ *15*

# Getting Over
# the Edge

## Stuart Moulthrop

*For some time now, scholars and critics have tried to answer questions such as "Is print dead?" or "Is the book dead?" Computer technologies are the latest in a long line of electronic and/or audiovisual media that have threatened to render typographic form obsolete. The introduction of electronic writing further complicates these questions, as it both extends and undermines print media. Stuart Moulthrop clarifies the issues involved in current discussions and debates over the "new edge" technologies and worldviews, as well as exposing some of the inherent contradictions in print-based discourse in an electronic environment. He also examines the progression that led to the development of hypertext and considers the staying power of traditional print. In Sections 1, 2, and 4, other views of electronic textuality can be found in Neil Kleinman's historical study of intellectual property in Chapter 4 and Jay David Bolter's arguments concerning print-based discourse and virtual reality in Chapter 7; also relevant to the future of the book are Terri Toles Patkin's discussion of virtual education in Chapter 11 and Paul Levinson's piece on distance learning in Chapter 12, Judith Yaross Lee's survey of text-based computer-mediated communication in Chapter 19, and Lance Strate's exploration of cybertime in Chapter 23. For an alternate take on cyberculture, see Douglas Rushkoff's essay on information warfare in Chapter 21.*

> The only responsible intellectual is one who is wired.
> —Taylor & Saarinen (1993, p. 13)

Millennium season has arrived. Every month now the rhetoric of technology salesmen, never much known for subtlety, resets the record for hyperbole. The airwaves are filled with trailers for the future. AT&T promises surfside faxes, power breakfasts in your skivvies, your medical history on a credit card. Maybe you do not desire this stuff just yet, but don't worry . . . *you will.* Meanwhile, on MCI's side of the highway, Anna Pacquin lisps that *everything is information*—digitized, lightspeed quick, annihilating distinctions of time and space. In the new regime *there will be no more "there!"* Or, as we might cynically observe, *there goes the neighborhood.* So begins "our violent descent into the electronic cage of virtual reality," says Arthur Kroker (1994), with trademark hysteria; down we go into the "floating world of liquid media where the body is daily downloaded into the floating world of the net, where data is the real, and where high technology can fulfill its destiny of an out-of-body experience" (p. 36). There goes the body, too, drowned in recombinant buzz. Shuffled off into "bodiless exultation" (Gibson, 1984), we hang out in cyberspace awaiting further prophecies. *Where do you want to go today?* asks Microsoft, but it is less a question of going than of knowing—knowing where we are. We have come to that liminal zone called "The New Edge" (Rucker, Sirius, & Mu, 1992). The gulf between the now and the new yawns impatiently.

This is an ambiguous, ambivalent state. Our millennium calls for heavy irony. Vivian Sobchack (1992), commenting on the cyberhip magazine *Mondo 2000*, says "In my sober and responsible moments I bemoan our culture's loss of gravity and fear the very real social dangers of disembodied ditziness, but holding this Christmas present to myself, all I want is a head shot" (p. 583). It is particularly easy to feel this way if one is of a certain age. Cyberculture may be the last holiday orgy of the yuppies, replete with silicon sugar plums for all. There is something seductively regressive about the New Edge, with its smart drugs, mind machines, data networks, body-piercing narcissism, and dreams of virtual sex without secretions. Personal computing these days seems little more than an exclusive toy shop, especially considering the present craze for CD-ROM and "multimedia." More often than not this buzzword refers to prerecorded sequences of sound and video, a *techne* that seems distinctly familiar. As Greg Ulmer (1990) says, "Everything now, in its own way, wants to be television" (p. 11). Except for television, of course, which wants to be something new, improved, and "interactive," but whose vision of the future turns out to be Oliver Stone's *Wild Palms*, or Beavis and Butthead in cyberspace.

In large part the New Edge may be just another *trompe l'oeil* shadow; although it may not be entirely without significance, even so. In the era of simulation, as Baudrillard (1983) pointed out, the production of illusions becomes a crucial enterprise. Consider the thesis of "digital convergence," the last "vision rollout" put on by John Sculley before he left Apple Computer for wilder company. Taken at its glossiest, this concept means the wholesale integration of personal data services; much the same thing that is intoned over that stolen Peter Gabriel riff in all those AT&T spots. If the industrialists get their way, then nearly all our information will be mediated by a very small number of boxes and perhaps a single skein of cable.

Consequences of this change could be great. No more personal computers, no more television sets, no more fax machines, just a single appliance strung into "the dataline," as Pat Cadigan (1990) calls it. Nor would consumer electronics be the sole area of impact. Imagine a world without bookstores, in which one has only to connect to a publisher's electronic catalog to download, in whole or part, anything that one can plausibly afford. The implications for retailing are astonishing, as Barry Diller and others in the media marketing business have recognized (Carlin, 1993). Sculley's convergence seems likely to be realized any day now; it has considerable momentum both economically and politically. His vision maps closely onto Vice President Gore's National Information Infrastructure (NII) initiative, in which a "partnership" of communications companies, information providers, computer makers, and government will build the fabled digital superhighway. Because this strategy seems equally acceptable to the resurgent right (or at least the Speaker of the House), it seems sure to go forward.

Discussion of the NII usually centers on its implications for business. Under "time-based competition," in which product development cycles can be measured in weeks, some method of fast, copious, and efficient data exchange becomes essential (Peters, 1992; Zuboff, 1988). Complex, densely interrelated tasks must be adequately documented and represented for managers. Large engineering enterprises like the aerospace industry require flexible software tools for complex and dynamically changing work groups (Malcolm, Poltrock, & Schuler, 1991). But the implications of this development go well beyond industrial competition. Autobahns and interstate highways support commerce (and military mobilization), but they also change profoundly the way we organize ourselves as a culture. Just ask anyone who grew up in the suburbs and later returned to the urban core. As Fred Pfeil (1990) points out, the coming of the concrete highways contributed crucially to the atomized, post-Oedipal condition of the "PMC," Pfeil's shorthand for both Professional-Managerial Class and Postmodern Culture. The new fiber-optic data routes might bring similarly sweeping changes to cultural life. But what will these effects be? Can they be understood in terms not saturated by science fiction visions or pitchman hyperbole?

When Arthur Kroker (1994) writes about bodies "downloaded into the floating world of the net" (p. 7), he is of course fantasizing. Whether the "destiny" of "high technology" lies in "an out-of-body experience," even our highest technologies of the moment come nowhere close to that objective. The body, like the material world in general, turns out to be more complex and sophisticated the more closely we examine it. Digital convergence is one thing; digital conversion quite another. Uploading or downloading people into information networks is the stuff of Star Trek's 24th century (i.e., of television), not of the present era. What we transfer into the network, now or in the foreseeable future, is not our literal mind or body but some representation: some text. As Donna Haraway (1991) says: "Writing is pre-eminently the technology of cyborgs, etched surfaces of the late twentieth century" (p. 176). Questions about cyberculture thus lead away from "edges" (new or otherwise) and back toward surfaces—or to scenes of writing.

At the moment our cyborg texts remain heavily invested in preelectronic technologies. We are living in what Jay David Bolter (1991) calls "the late age of print" (p. 2), a moment in history when the old, industrial paradigm of alphabetic literacy collides with the younger agenda of electronic communication. Outlines of a new order have begun to emerge, yet the old regime remains stubbornly present. Alhough promoters of multimedia may try to turn everything into television, for a while the main front of development in electronic media remains verbal and textual; there is good reason to think that the word will not wither away anytime soon (Moulthrop, 1993). *Cyberspace* as we know it in the 1990s is largely a system of texts and intertexts. Consider the current most popular lane on the information highway, the distributed writing system called the World-Wide Web. This vast congeries of information is really nothing like an electronic book or even a virtual library. The flow of information on the Web is much more dynamic and much less invested in stable objects than such metaphors suggest. Yet its component elements are still referred to (and to some extent designed) as "pages." Authors representing themselves on the Web organize their work around the comforting notion of a "home page" (December & Randall, 1994).

If we recognize today's electronic environments as what Bolter (1991) calls "writing spaces" (pp. 10-12) then we may begin to understand the emerging cultural front of cyberspace. Is the library the home we never left? Or is it the object of our frustrated returning, the home to which we cannot come again? The cyberpunks and New Edgers dream about cyberspace in the comfort of predigital media. They operate in the book and magazine markets, old foundations of the print age. They are often, strange as it may seem, staunch defenders of high literacy and even the canon (e.g., Stephenson, 1993). Too often their projections assume that crucial aspects of print culture—analysis, reductive formalism, Aristotelian *agon*, and discrete authorship—will be carried wholesale across the new frontier.

They are probably dead wrong about this. In the environment of electronic communications, write the "media philsophers" Mark Taylor and Esa Saarinen (1993), "all philosophy must be interactive. Monologue becomes dialogue or, more precisely, polylogue" ("Ending the Academy," p. 1). Cyberspace may be a textual domain, but it is not the Gutenberg Galaxy, same as it ever was. Textuality in the new writing space is not constrained by the rigid ordering principles native to preelectronic media. This means that we must fundamentally rethink our position as subjects of electronic textuality. We must come to grips with yet a third kind of "convergence," a phenomenon George Landow (1992) calls "the convergence of contemporary critical theory and technology" (p. 4). This intersection may have more significance, in the short run at least, than either the vision of integrated data services or the dream of human-machine fusion.

The subject of Landow's interest, like that of Bolter, is a relatively modest item on the high-technology agenda, a form of electronic writing called *hypertext*. (For background on this concept, see Bolter, 1991; Halasz, 1987; Landow, 1992; Nelson, 1990; Slatin, 1990.) The term was coined in the mid-1960s by the computing visionary Theodor Nelson (1990) to describe "non-sequential writing"

(p. 3/19), a scheme for using interactive computing systems to deliver documents in variable form, as opposed to the strict sequence imposed by book binding. Hypertexts cannot be translated into print. They retain a dynamic or "interactive" component that no nonelectronic reduction can adequately represent. In hypertext, a body of writing is formally divided into arbitrary units or *lexias* as Landow calls them, borrowing from Roland Barthes. The reader's path from one lexia to another is determined partly by active engagement: The reader selects a word in the present lexia, chooses an option from a menu, issues a command, or otherwise indicates some wish for further development. The program responds with another piece of writing that may or may not match the reader's desires, but that articulates in some way to the previous passage. In the most ambitious, "constructive" versions of this writing system (Joyce, 1994), the reader may not only follow predefined pathways, but may alter the connections and add new lexias to the system, creating complex textual hybrids.

Hypertext is a characteristic product of the late age of print, which is to say, it is deeply ambiguous. Although still dependent on alphabetic literacy, algorithmic programming, linearity, hierarchy, and other trappings of Gutenberg culture, hypertext implicitly challenges the episteme from which it sprang. Although any hypertextual document remains a limited and definable object, this object is much more like Roland Barthes's notion of "text"—a dynamic network of ideas, indefinite in its boundaries and mutable over time—than like a teleologically closed literary "work" (Landow, 1992, p. 23). The precise nature and boundaries of a hypertext are hard to define. The experience of reading for any two people who traverse its verbal space may be radically different: "polylogue," not monologue. When multiple writers are involved, authorial voice and intention come in for serious questioning. In the World-Wide Web, for instance, a single document may contain scores of references to other texts stored at various far-flung points around the Internet. A single reading may involve writings (and writers) from Baltimore to Bombay; and because many documents on the Web are regularly revised and updated, both the authorial corps and the textual corpus are subject to change.

These aspects of hypertextual writing lead Landow to his particular vision of "convergence." As he sees it, the current interest in hypertext represents the happy union of two cultural forces that have worked for 20 years in adjacent ivory towers. On one side of this new synthesis are information scientists, men like Douglas Engelbart and Andries Van Dam, who created the first practical hypertext systems. On the other flank stand poststructuralist theorists like Barthes, Michel Foucault, Jacques Derrida, and Julia Kristeva, whose critiques of print culture, or logocentrism, appear to parallel the hypertextual enterprise. As Landow (1992) sees it, the technology of the printed book:

> engenders certain notions of authorial property, authorial uniqueness, and a physically isolated text that hypertext makes untenable. The evidence of hypertext, in other words, historicizes many of our most commonplace

assumptions, thereby forcing them to descend from the ethereality of abstraction and appear as corollaries to a particular technology rooted in specific times and places. (p. 33)

Landow does not claim that hypertext represents an "applied grammatology," to borrow Ulmer's phrase, only that there is a compelling and useful analogy between poststructuralist theories of the text and the development of electronic writing. "What is perhaps most interesting about hypertext," Landow (1992) explains, "is not that it may fulfill certain claims of structuralist and poststructuralist criticism but that it provides a rich means of testing them" (p. 11). What Landow means by "testing" here, or what anyone else might mean by it, remains very much at issue. Hypertext enables its users to invent new forms for arranging and passing on information. These forms do not map onto the claims of poststructuralist critics in any simple, literal way. But if Landow is right, hypertext should allow us to *articulate* poststructuralist concepts within the emergent practices of digital culture. *Articulation* here might mean a process of connection in which one creates contingent unities among moving differences (for the roots of this concept, see Grossberg, 1992). This enterprise seems entirely in line with Haraway's cyborg politics. If such a process is possible, then hypertext might lend some substance to all that loose talk about digital highways, electronic frontiers, and a "floating world of liquid media." But this remains to be seen.

At the moment we face a more primary and practical cultural problem: the disturbing presence of the past. Contrary to the testimony of the 1960s, print is not dead, nor is it merely sleeping. The cultural complex of print (a metonymy taking in publishing houses, academic institutions, reviewers, advertisers, and, these days, multimedia conglomerates) is actually *undead*, which is to say that it lingers on, monstrously transformed, haunting us in the dead of night. According to Taylor and Saarinen, who have laid the strongest claim yet to Marshall McLuhan's mad media prophecies, technologies such as hypertext portend a cultural paradigm shift. This would be a change from monologue to polylogue, from edifice to improvization, from *Bildung to bricolage.* "Expert language," they say, "is a prison for knowledge and understanding. A prison for intellectually significant relationships. It is time to move beyond the institutional practices of triviledge, toward networks and surfaces, toward the play of superficiality, toward interstanding" (Taylor & Saarinen, 1993, "Communicative Practices," p. 8). Neologism is an essential part of the game here. *Triviledge* indicates the privilege of institutional learning, or the trivilality of knowledge; *interstanding* names the way of knowing appropriate to hypertext, the exploration of what Joyce calls "interstices" and "contours," or what Gilles Deleuze and Félix Guattari (1987) call "lines of flight" (p. 3). "When depth gives way to surface," Taylor and Saarinen write, "under-standing becomes inter-standing. To comprehend is no longer to grasp what lies *beneath* but to glimpse what lies *between*" (Taylor & Saarinen, 1993, "Interstanding," p. 1). In moving from the page to the interstice, from understanding to interstanding, we ostensibly reverse figure and ground, transforming the condition of textuality.

But how much is genuinely new here? As Pete Townshend might have said: *Meet the new Logos; same as the old Logos.* The problem is that scholars, critics, developers, and designers cling desperately to the same old ways of doing what we do. "Triviledge" represents our ultimate home on the page. Those optical networks and etched surfaces that might redeem us seem strangely hard to engage. Take Taylor and Saarinen's book as a depressingly perfect case in point. Like McLuhan and Fiore's *The Medium is the Massage* (1967), whose design it emulates, *Imagologies* puts up a deeply irreverent front. "The triviledge that legitimizes the academic critic renders him impotent," Taylor and Saarinen proclaim. "Merely a Peeping Tom who gazes from afar but refuses to enter the fray, he becomes nothing more than a limp dick" (Taylor & Saarinen, 1993, "Ending the Academy," p. 7). But how much difference can these words make, even when they are made-up or bawdy words? How much difference can a book make—for even though it is as irreverent and iconoclastic in design as it is in content, *Imagologies* is still very much a book. Taylor and Saarinen (1993) do consider this objection, but their answer fails to satisfy:

> If an electronic text can be published in printed form, is it really electronic? The alternative would be to give up print and publish an electronic text. But the technology necessary for accessing electronic texts is still rather limited. Furthermore, most of the people we want to reach remain committed to print. There is no sense preaching to the converted. Our dilemma is that we are living at the moment of transition from print to electronic culture. It is too late for printed books and too early for electronic texts. Along this boundary we must write our work. ("Telewriting," p. 5)

Much of this argument makes sense—although the sense that it makes deeply undermines the primary claim. There is indeed no point in "preaching to the converted." If we understand hypertext we know that there is no point in preaching at all, just as there is no sense in worrying about the limpness of the next man's transcendental signifier, or your own. If technologies like hypertext really do open possibilities for cultural renewal, then, as Taylor and Saarinen (1993) say, they ought to help us climb out of the muck of triviledge and simple-minded agonistics. This might mean that we can indeed give up print and do something other than write books—that it is not too soon for electronic texts. The new networks ought to provide Landow's testing ground for poststructuralist critique, a space in which we can experiment with alternatives to the Logos as we know it. Have you ever reconceived yourself entirely outside the grounds of Western metaphysics? *You will. . .*

Or maybe you won't. As any scientist knows, most experiments fail. Even after we have given up on print, the majority of "really electronic" text will be hopelessly contaminated with the old ways of knowing. What we must carry forward is a strong sense of foundational irony. The past is always present; we are Gutenberg creatures no matter how hard we play at revolution—there is no such thing as "nonsequential writing." We make our way by recursion, by folding a new order back on and into its predecessor. The relations among media, as McLuhan discovered and as Neil Postman (1992) has clarified, belong to a complex, mutually modifying ecology. Drastic, monumental changes are rare in most ecologies—and disastrous when they do occur. In the place of such upheavals, in our day-to-day survival, we find articulations, contingent complications of the old order that may, in their nontotalizing, fractal context, create some space for "interstanding." Or so we may hope.

So is there really a new world coming? If books are still being written about cyberspace (including this book), then it must be too soon to tell. There is only one thing about which we can be reasonably sure: We must stop writing our work along the boundaries. We must step off the edge and onto the shifting surfaces. This writing is finished, or unfinished. Its electronic address is: *http://raven.ubalt.edu/staff/moulthrop/essays/edge.html*

## REFERENCES

Baudrillard, J. (1983). *Simulations* (P. Foss, P. Patton, & P. Beitchmann, Trans.). New York: Semiotext(e).

Bolter, J. (1991). *Writing space: The computer, hypertext, and the history of writing.* Hillsdale NJ: Erlbaum.

Cadigan, P. (1990). *Synners.* New York: Bantam.

Carlin, P. (1993, February 28). The jackpot in television's future. *New York Times Magazine,* pp. 36-41.

December, J., & Randall, N. (1994). *The World Wide Web unleashed.* New York: SAMS.

Deleuze, G., & Guattari, F. (1987). *A thousand plateaus: Capitalism and schizophrenia* (B. Massumi, Trans.). Minneapolis: University of Minnesota Press.

Gibson, W. (1984). *Neuromancer.* New York: Ace Books.

Grossberg, L. (1992). *We gotta get out of this place: Popular conservatism and postmodern culture.* New York: Routledge.

Halasz, F. (1987). Reflections on NoteCards: Seven issues for the next generation of hypermedia systems. *Communications of the ACM, 31*(7), 836-852.

Haraway, D. (1991). *Simians, cyborgs, and women: The reinvention of nature.* New York: Routledge.

Joyce, M. (1994). *Of two minds: Hypertext pedagogy and poetics.* Ann Arbor: University of Michigan Press.

Kroker, A. (1994). *Spasm: Virtual reality, android music, electric flesh.* New York: St. Martin's Press.

Landow, G. (1992). *Hypertext: The convergence of contemporary literary theory and technology.* Baltimore: Johns Hopkins University Press.

Malcolm, K., Poltrock, S., & Schuler, D. (1991). Industrial strength hypermedia: Requirements for a large engineering enterprise. In P.D. Stotts & R.K. Furuta (Eds.), *Hypertext '91 Proceedings* (pp. 13-24). San Antonio: Association for Computing Machinery.

McLuhan, H.M., & Fiore, Q. (1967). *The medium is the massage.* New York: McGraw-Hill.

Moulthrop, S. (1993). You say you want a revolution? Hypertext and the laws of media. In E. Amiran & J. Unsworth (Eds.), *Essays in postmodern culture* (pp. 69-97). New York: Oxford University Press.

Nelson, T. (1990). *Literary machines.* Sausalito, CA: Mindful Press.

Peters, T. (1992). *Liberation management: Necessary disorganization for the nanosecond nineties.* New York: Knopf.

Pfeil, F. (1990). *Another tale to tell: Politics and narrative in postmodern culture.* New York: Verso.

Postman, N. (1992). *Technopoly.* New York: Vintage.

Rucker, R., Sirius, R.U., & Mu, Q. (1992). *Mondo 2000: A user's guide to the new edge.* New York: St. Martin's Press.

Sobchack, V. (1992). Reading Mondo 2000. *South Atlantic Quarterly, 92*(4), 581-597.

Slatin, J. (1990). Hypertext: Order and coherence in a new medium. *College English, 52,* 870-883.

Stephenson, N. (1993, September 13). Smiley's people. *New Republic,* p. 52.

Taylor, M., & Saarinen, E. (1993). *Imagologies: Media philosophy.* New York: Routledge. [This book is paginated in individual sections. Citations are given by section name and page number.]

Ulmer, G. (1990). *Teletheory: Grammatology in the age of video.* New York: Routledge.

Zuboff, S. (1988). *In the age of the smart machine: The future of work and power.* New York: Basic Books.

# Dispatches From
# the New Frontier:
# Writing for the Internet

## Camille Paglia

*Writing is often thought to be an abstract activity, but it in fact involves writing materials, instruments, and environments that influence the process of composition. Chiseling words into stone naturally leads to a more economic style of writing than putting pen to paper. Bound books suggest cross-referencing possibilities difficult to implement when working with scrolls. Print media place greater emphasis on layout and homogeneity of form than manuscripts. Electronic text is less fixed, more easily altered than words written in stone, or on paper. Writing for the Web, too, has its distinctive qualities, as Camille Paglia explains in this chapter. As a contributor to the online magazine Salon, as well as a successful writer in the traditional world of print, Paglia is in a good position to contrast the two forms of composition. Additionally, she argues for the anti-elitist, democratizing potential of online publication. In other sections of this book, Paglia's perspective on writing can be compared to Jay David Bolter's comparison of hypertext and virtual reality in Chapter 7, Judith Yaross Lee's examination of e-mail in Chapter 19, and Lance Strate's views on text and temporality in Chapter 22; see also Neil Kleinman's analysis of copyright law in light of cyberspace technologies in Chapter 4. Paglia's general perspective on online activity can be compared to Levinson's essay on distance education in Chapter 13, and the critiques of cyberbusiness put forth by James Beniger in Chapter 3, and Douglas Rushkoff in Chapter 21.*

## BIRTH OF A MEDIUM

Although I had co-hosted public online chats for new Web sites like AOL, my work for the Internet began in earnest in November 1995 with the inaugural issue of *Salon*, the first general-interest Webzine. As this chapter goes to press, *Salon*'s financial condition is shaky and its ultimate survival in doubt. It has always had to rely principally on advertising revenue, while its chief rival, *Slate*, is safely bankrolled by billionaire Bill Gates, founder of Microsoft, Inc.

For my first *Salon* piece, editor-in-chief David Talbot asked me to comment on conservative social critic William Bennett's recent attack on "trash TV" as a debasement of moral standards and a bad influence on the young. I charged Bennett in turn with elitism and argued that he seriously misunderstood popular culture: Our rowdy daytime talk shows in fact reflect the actual tastes and raw comic energy of the mass audience, whose loyalties translate into sky-high ratings.

*Salon* was created during a newspaper strike by Talbot, then arts and features editor of the *San Francisco Examiner*, with a team of like-minded editors and reporters from the *Examiner* and KQED-TV. My professional association with him had begun 4 years earlier when he interviewed me for the *Examiner's* weekly magazine, *Image*, an entire issue of which he devoted to excerpts from my academic exposé, "Junk Bonds and Corporate Raiders," which had just appeared in the the Spring 1991 issue of *Arion*, a classics journal at Boston University.

As a 1960s progressive who had co-written a study of the sexual revolution, Talbot sympathized with my thesis that liberal '60s principles had become distorted by political correctness in the 1980s, when campus speech codes were threatening free expression. As the son of a Hollywood actor (Lyle Talbot, the "king of B movies"), Talbot also appreciated my respect for popular culture, which my 1990 book, *Sexual Personae*, meshed with the fine-arts tradition and hailed as a pagan phenomenon connected to classical antiquity.

In 1990, I had begun writing op-ed pieces on hot-button current affairs for newspapers (an unusual forum at that time for humanities professors). Hence Talbot asked me to contribute to the *Examiner.* From late 1992 on, I wrote for him on Amy Fisher, the "Long Island Lolita"; comedienne Sandra Bernhard as the heir of Lenny Bruce; and Bill and Hillary Clinton, where I analyzed the pivotal role played by TV in the rise of an obscure Arkansas governor to the White House.

When Talbot left the *Examiner* to start *Salon*, I went with him. He envisioned international editions of *Salon* as well as an arts-and-ideas *Salon* TV show that was eventually contracted to Bravo. A *Salon* radio project was also later announced. For what seemed to be managerial as well as funding and personnel problems (the in-house staff, for example, may have been expanded too rapidly), none of these projects materialized. Reprints of *Salon* articles, however, do appear via an international syndication service.

My first fleeting encounter with the Internet occurred in 1991 at the Massachusetts Institute of Technology after a lecture I gave called "Crisis in the American Universities". A visitor from the Boston area approached me at the podium and asked, "Are you aware that you're all over the *Well?*" "What is the *Well?*" I asked, completely baffled. He promised to send me some information.

A week later, a packet arrived at my office in Philadelphia. I brandished the thick print-out at my colleagues: "What IS this?" I sputtered. "Look—a person in Boston is arguing about my ideas with someone in Tennessee, and they're both arguing with someone else in San Francisco!" None of us in the humanities department could decipher the method or rationale of this peculiar document, nor did we guess that it was our first bulletin from a dawning communications revolution.

The co-creator of the *Well* was Stewart Brand, founder of the *Whole Earth Review*. Much later, when he interviewed me for the premiere 1993 issue of *Wired* (whose "patron saint" is Marshall McLuhan), I realized that he was another 1960s veteran actively reassessing U.S. cultural history. The *Well* had been launched in 1985 by Brand and Larry Brilliant as the first general cyber forum, turning the Internet away from its early orientation as a bulletin-board service for scientific and military exchanges. Like *Salon*, the *Well* was based in northern California and staffed by independent, tech-savvy thinkers outside both the academic and the east coast media establishments. They shared my fatigue with the strident polarization of conservatism versus liberalism and were looking for something new, which did in fact materialize in the libertarianism and pro-sex feminism of the 1990s.

Brand recognized how deeply I had been influenced by McLuhan (1964), who had been swept away in the 1970s by French and German theory. By the 1980s, popular culture was being routinely condemned from two sides: by conservatives on the grounds of immorality and vulgarity and by leftists on the grounds of sexism, racism, and economic exploitation, with capitalism stereotyped as a brutal tool of Western imperialism. Very little in the new academic approaches to media—abstract semiotics, the Frankfurt School, British Marxist cultural studies, or Franco-American postmodernism—made sense to me as a McLuhanite. Furthermore, there seemed to be a willful blindness to the role modern capitalism had played in enhancing individualism, raising the standard of living, and liberating women. And it was capitalism, via the technological marvel of the personal computer, that would make the Internet so powerful a vehicle of free thought and free speech around the world.

It was in fact via the Internet that the heirs of McLuhan, scattered across North America like defeated soldiers of a civil war, identified each other in the 1990s and regrouped. My commitment to the Internet is partly inspired by gratitude: It was the *Well*, I later saw, that had helped spread the word about my controversial and long-delayed first book, a 700-page tome that its publisher (Yale University Press) did not expect would find a wide audience (Paglia, 1990). In an era of political correctness, which had taken root on campus and in the major media, the Internet was operating like an invisible, subterranean resistance movement.

## PROCESS AND PRACTICE

Since the mid-1990s, the Internet has caused a tremendous cultural shift whose most profound impact has been on young people. It will take another 30 years before the Internet's effects are clearly understood. The computer has literally reshaped the brain of those who grew up with it, just as television and rock music reshaped the brains of my baby-boom generation and made our thinking so different in form and content from that of writers and critics born just before World War II.

College students, even in the Ivy League, may spend from 2 to 5 hours a night on the Internet. Most middle-aged professionals, including teachers, have yet to appreciate the scope or depth of what is happening. As late as 1997, for example, a prominent reporter at the *Boston Globe* tried to discourage my writing for *Salon* ("No one reads things on the Internet"); he exhorted me to focus on contributing to the major media instead. But one of my primary motivations in writing for *Salon* was to speak directly to young people who have no loyalty to newspapers: Today's college students were born in the 1980s, when newspapers, a major melting-pot medium for a century since the start of the immigration era, had already lost ground to television.

Campus literature departments were caught flat-footed by the sudden rise of the Internet. Throughout the 1990s, elite universities inflicted a cruel cognitive dissonance on their humanities students, who were forced to read antiquated French and German theory (based on premises and methodology predating World War II), while cyberculture was exploding all around them. This was a principal factor in the decline in prestige and power of humanities departments in that period, when the number of literature majors steadily fell. The young knew perfectly well that the language of the future was now the computer and the Web.

Some theorists tried to shore up their system by redefining the Internet as a postmodern medium, but the idea was misconceived. The fragmentation or discontinuity they thought they saw was really the proliferation, multiplicity, and rapid pulses of electronic media that McLuhan correctly interpreted in physiological and neurological terms. Surfing the Web (significantly, a nature-sports metaphor) means catching its wave motion and feeling its tides and eddies. The Web has weather, particularly when news events unleash storms of popular sentiment. Although the body is quiet and dormant at the computer, the Web works by sensory overload, through which the surfer navigates along a zigzag track like a sailboat tacking at sea.

One reason I find writing for the Internet so fulfilling is that the Web's natural rhythms and strong, personal voices (contradicting the effete poststructuralist doctrine of the "death of the subject") seem to be in the direct line of the body-oriented, incantatory, anti-academic American poetry of the 1950s and 1960s that influenced me heavily in college. Beat and Black Mountain poems were performance pieces meant to be recited. The fountainhead of this American style was Walt Whitman, whom Allen Ginsberg in particular invoked as an influence.

Whitman's "Leaves of Grass," as I see it, oddly prefigures Internet style: The poem's impressionistic sections and cascading verse-paragraphs resemble the way *Salon* articles are split into pages linked by provocative hypertext grabbers. My columns for *Salon* have consciously assimilated Whitman's salutations to the reader; his pluralist dwelling on social class; and his mix of street slang with oracular pronouncements. Whitman shows how to juxtapose the homely minutiae of everyday life with both contemporary politics and grand perspectives on nature.

But the key to Internet writing for me is visual, not verbal. Ever since computer operating systems progressed from half-mathematical ASCII to today's lively, colorful, high-resolution graphics HTML format, the Internet has become a mercurial hybrid of word, image, and sound. Television was the key, leading to the personal computer screen and thus the Internet. Nowhere in the world has TV been so dominant a cultural presence as in the United States. Close to three generations of Americans have learned from childhood not just how to look at TV but how to live with it in virtually every room of the house (and now car).

More pertinently, only in the United States do commercials intrude at predictable intervals into newscasts, talk shows, sports, and drama. Elsewhere in the world, commercials are grouped at the start or end of programs, which thus may begin at odd times rather than on the hour or half-hour. Visitors to the United States sometimes become confused or lose focus when commercials burst into a story line every few minutes.

I submit that the stop–start rhythm of a half-century of commercial TV viewing was Americans' basic training for Internet communication, active or passive (i.e., writing or reading). "And now for a word from our sponsor," we used to hear; today it's "Hold that thought," as the host sternly stops even the most high-ranking guest mid-flight to cut away for a series of eye-assaulting commercials. The jump or truncation is an American specialty; it is precisely our suffusion in mass media that has allowed us to keep identity, thought, and mood intact as we vault over the alleged discontinuities of modern life that have proved so disabling to literati from T.S. Eliot and Samuel Beckett to the postmodernist theorists who drove aesthetics off the academic map for 25 years.

The puzzling failure of humanities professors to contribute in any substantial way thus far to the leading Webzines stems, I conjecture, from their long ambivalence about TV. Although prominent academics have made occasional appearances in *Salon* and *Slate,* they strangely fade away, retreating to the online special-interest groups where they resume the same professional conversation they have at conferences. Their lack of interest in addressing a general audience is remarkable in this period when the "public intellectual" (a questionable and overused term) is so much prized.

Some academics may feel that Internet writing, like the TV image, is evanescent, but the opposite is true. Ever since it switched from live to tape, TV is the great medium of the re-run, where nothing is ever lost; so with the Web, where not only do the search engines net up every obscure, years-old crackpot rant like debris from the sea floor but where on the best-organized Web sites all past articles are miraculously available by push-button access in their archives. The Web is an ever-expanding, if still ill-sorted and error-filled encyclopedia of Alexandrian dimensions.

Another reason for academics' reluctance to join the Webzines may be the blinking marginalia of advertising logos that now adorn every *Salon* page. Perhaps academics feel that their text is swamped or compromised by so much visual distraction, like the banks of flashing bulbs at a casino or penny arcade. But I feel quite at home in this milieu, which replicates the jump-cuts and blizzard of special effects on commercial TV. Web pages crowned or rimmed by ads sometimes resemble medieval illuminated manuscripts, with their fantastic, embellished lettering, and also Art Nouveau books and prints, with their undulating borders of running tendrils.

My premises about advertising, in any case, are quite different from those of most academics. Like Andy Warhol, I always regarded ads, logos, and product packaging as an art form and probably for the same reason: As a child, I visually processed them as analogues to the lavish, polychrome iconography of the Italian Catholic church. (Warhol's eastern European church was Byzantine and therefore even more ornate.) I remain fascinated by advertising slogans as folk poetry, which over time taught me how to speak in quotable "sound bites."

In writing for *Salon*, I regularly use many more voices and shifts of tone than I do in writing, for example, for *The Wall Street Journal*: My op-ed pieces for the latter are usually sober in tone and organized in a conventional, linear way, with a timely lead followed by factual evidence and a conclusion. In *Salon*, on the other hand, I've absorbed the hectoring personae of old-time radio and TV: the host, the stand-up comic, and the pitchman, a descendant of the carnival barker. Even when most of the column addresses serious issues, I often borrow its transitions from the evening talk-show form perfected by Johnny Carson on *The Tonight Show*, where a topical opening monologue yields to a series of guests and where the host may turn up in costume as cranky Aunt Blabby or that caped clairvoyant, Carnac the Magnificent.

The column began as a strict Q & A, a sequel to the parody "agony aunt" column, "Ask Camille," that I wrote for *Spy* magazine in 1993. As *Salon* reader questions, as well as my replies, got longer, however, the format broadened, so that the "host" voice opens, closes, and directs throughout. Another TV genre helping me organize material is the variety show, a form (descended from vaudeville) that was in its heyday in my adolescence but is now defunct due to sheer expense. At their height, *The Ed Sullivan Show* and *The Carol Burnett Show* struck a balance between mainstream offerings and controversial, cutting-edge acts. In writing my column, I try to draw in as many segments of the Web-reading public as possible—no easy task, since political junkies and pop fans, for example, now haunt their own ghettoized sites.

During the 2000 presidential campaign, I began weaving into the text longer passages than usual from reader letters on incendiary issues like gun control, so that the column began to resemble (as Talbot was the first to observe) a call-in AM radio show. In the media work I have been invited to do over the past decade, the most dynamic has unquestionably been AM shows in the "drive-time" slots, when commuters are trapped in their cars and craving diversion and relief. The quarrelsome blare of AM radio, born in the obnoxious disc-jockey days of early Top 40 rock, is a truly modern voice, the embodiment of McLuhan's (1964) classification of radio as a "hot" medium. AM's abrasive high energy contrasts with the repressed mellifluousness of National Public Radio, geared to the velvety FM band. My *Salon* column consciously taps into AM's proletarian brashness rather than NPR's upper middle-class gentility.

In writing for the Web, I've also found that text must be visually designed: Its ideal basic architecture consists of sharply delineated, single-spaced paragraphs. Although newspaper and magazine readers can flip through and scan the whole of an article before focussing in on it, the online reader typically sees no more than a half page at a time and would have to tediously scroll downward and jump by hypertext to successive pages to survey the whole. Because the eye of the online reader tires and needs refreshment, I build blank space into the article through regular paragraphing. I conceive of the text as floating blocks, much like the hovering rectangles in Mark Rothko's misty paintings. The paragraphs must be monumental and yet in motion.

The point-and-click method of advancing text produces a freeze-frame effect onscreen. These jumpy rhythms (finger-triggered by the mouse exactly as by the TV remote control) are positively new to reading experience and are so inconstant and improvisatory that they resemble syncopated jazz or jitterbug (once called "jump" music). At final-draft stage, I strip my paragraphs of excess words so that the sentences seem abrupt, which powers the text forward.

I also choose vocabulary that *looks* interesting on the page, which usually means juxtaposing blunt Anglo-Saxon nouns and high-action verbs with polysyllabic Greco-Roman abstractions. I use far more exclamation points, slang terms, alliterations, rhetorical questions, and expostulations than I would for a mainstream newspaper or magazine. Finally, I favor raucous sound effects, inspired by the reedy "honking" of alto-sax players. The text should be palpable and not just a remote stream of cyphers on a glassy wall.

Because of the blitzkrieg quality of Web bulletins—some of which notoriously turn out to be false—I strongly feel that Internet writing descends from the telegraph, that once high-tech innovation so vital to America's economic and political development as the frontier moved west. The wire services, which started up in the 1840s, reduced and condensed information to the atomized bits of Morse Code, a radical remaking of language that looked forward to modernism at its most minimalist. During the Civil War, telegraphed dispatches from the front transformed newspaper writing, not only creating the "inverted pyramid" protocol of news stories, where breaking news comes first, but drastically simplifying American English syntax and vocabulary.

There was as huge a gap in style between the punchy, telegraph-transformed, late 19th-century newspapers and their more literary, periphrastic 18th-century precursors as exists today between mainstream or Web journalism and the still dismayingly turgid essays in academic journals like *PMLA* (quarterly of the Modern Language Association). While cast in more lucid prose, the leading articles on literature and culture even in the current *New Republic* or *New York Review of Books* are often amazingly verbose, taking pages to make simple points: It's as if the thought processes of the authors and editors remain untouched by the media revolution of the past century. Internet text at its best is *streamlined*—a cardinal artistic principle of modernism extending beyond the Bauhaus to an American source, the late 19th-century Chicago school of architecture.

Online articles that sustain reader attention beyond the first page are those, in my view, that take the telegraph as their ancestor. Simplification and acceleration are the principles. The Internet's residual telegraphic element has brought the frontier or battlefront into every wired home, so that any surfer can play dispatcher, flooded by urgent messages from all over the map. For this reason, I find *The Drudge Report*, almost universally disdained by upscale journalists, to be a unique and invaluable Internet resource. As a rough-hewn insurgent and outsider without institutional support, Matt Drudge, who styles himself after stentorian columnist Walter Winchell, provides constantly updated, siren-flashing news alerts and links to the world press, a format now widely imitated by other Web sites. Drudge's range of subjects has a tabloid flamboyance—from Washington and Hollywood scandals to earthquakes, airplane crashes, grisly crimes, and sentimental animal stories.

The Internet's flair for the "news flash" is something I try to capture in my columns—the on-street excitement that used to be generated by "extras" run off by urban dailies in the pre-TV era when big news broke between the morning and evening editions. The Internet democratizes the news, allowing the average citizen to get information straight off the wires before TV producers and print journalists can shape and doctor it. This unfiltered flow of information direct from stringers on location comes like a bolt of electricity into the private home.

In *Salon*, I also report on and weigh rumors, which I would never do for mainstream publications. Rumors have a life of their own and often are the first sign of a shift in popular thought, particularly in campaign years; a rumor is myth in the making. (The standard was set in the fifth century B C. by Herodotus, who collected and analyzed rumors for his "Histories.") An Internet column allows one to monitor and comment on contemporary life as it's actually happening. Because it is linked by hypertext to past columns and other sites, the text has an organic connection to the entire Web, an amplitude of reference analogous to the ponderous footnote material of print books that never appears, for reasons of space, in newspapers. Organic also is the Webzines' ability to correct factual errors or typos in already posted articles—a luxury unavailable to print journalists, who are stuck forever with embarrassing mistakes (as when copy editors fresh from college maddeningly introduce grammar errors at deadline).

In topic sequence, my column has begun to resemble *Time* magazine, which I grew up with and virtually cut my teeth on in its classic era of superb reportage and acid-etched prose. Although *Time* has distressingly declined over the past 15 years, it generally retains its old format, with high-impact national and international political news at the front, followed by science, sports, movies, books (much reduced), and celebrity gossip.

*Time's* revolutionary innovation was to package the week's news when the United States had just become a power on the international stage in the decade after World War I. And the magazine addressed a brand-new national audience, recently created by movies and radio. The Webzines have gone one step further by expanding their readership internationally. E-mail responses to my column have come not just from Canada and England but from Iceland, Hungary, Russia, Chile, South Africa, Australia, and Japan. Because of this global reach, I carefully adjust my column so that American personalities, events, and places are discreetly identified for overseas readers.

A primary aim of mine has been to keep the column resolutely independent and nonpartisan; hence I try to critique all invested positions. (For example, though a registered Democrat who voted for Bill Clinton twice, I have been scathing about the failures of the Clinton Administration.) As a consequence, the column has had an unusually broad following. While negative mail is of course a constant for anyone who writes for a public forum, I am always surprised at the ideological and sociological range of supportive letters, which come from evangelical Christian home-schooling moms, conservative retired military officers, harried public school teachers, anxious grad students, cross-dressing bisexuals, movie-trivia fanatics, opera connoisseurs, and struggling young rock musicians. To bring all these people together—many of whom lack the time or money for multiple magazine and newspaper subscriptions—is a testament to the power of the Web as a potentially universal medium.

## MOBILIZATION UNDER FIRE: A CASE STUDY

Because Internet publication is unconstrained by traditional printing-press deadlines, the Webzines can dispense with a fixed production schedule, an opportunity that *Salon* was the first to take advantage of. Its rivals used to operate in slow motion, randomly dribbling out new articles in late morning or the afternoon without regard for timeliness or drama. That *Salon's* chief editors originally worked for a daily (rather than a biweekly, like *Slate's* editor) has certainly given *Salon* a more militant intensity.

Each edition of *Salon* is finalized in San Francisco by the end of the prior business day, Pacific time, though breaking news stories can be inserted at any hour. The issue goes online around midnight, east coast time. Hence, *Salon* is seen and read in the United Kingdom and Europe 5 hours before the work day begins in the United States. Many times, I went to sleep in Philadelphia before my column went online and awoke to find faxes and e-mail queries from the London press, who had been reading *Salon* at the start of their workday (between 3 and 4 a.m. EST). Of the domestic newspapers, only *The New York Times* (or, less so, *The Washington Post*) has that kind of reach to European capitals.

The fluid press deadline newly created by the Web was never clearer than in the tragic episode of the death of Diana in a car crash in the early hours of August 31, 1997. This was a landmark in the early history of Web journalism, where *Salon*, because of its quick reaction, broke Web records in sheer volume of reader "hits."

That chronology should be documented as the first important example of a Webzine outmaneuvering the print press. And in the process, *Salon* scooped and humiliated its rival, *Slate*, which had closed its east coast offices for the last week of August before Labor Day (the staff presumably decamping to the Hamptons). In personal terms, this was by far the most traumatic of all my media experiences because I had been a longtime analyst of the Diana saga for both North American and British media.

The accident occurred just after midnight on a Saturday night in Paris. By chance, I was listening to the radio at home when the first news flash came just after 7:00 p.m., Philadelphia time. The initial report said Diana was merely injured. Television responded immediately (as it had so memorably done for the assassination of John F. Kennedy in 1963), but already scheduled network programming went on, interrupted by intermittent bulletins. More than 2 hours passed before all the networks and cable channels switched to continuous coverage. The top news stars were slow to appear on air because they had to return to the studio from their vacation retreats (the Hamptons again).

Just after 10 p.m. EST, the correspondents relayed the official announcement from a Paris hospital that the Princess of Wales had been declared dead. Hence, U.S. residents heard the terrible news before they went to bed, whereas most of the British public, fast asleep in the middle of the night, still had no idea an accident had even occurred. The British woke up on Sunday morning to a stunning fait accompli, while many Americans had had 3 tense hours after news of the crash to prepare for the worst.

The accident occurred too late on Saturday night to make the Sunday newspapers in either the United Kingdom or the United States. On weekdays, the press deadline for major U.S. dailies is between 5 and 6 p.m., and it is much earlier on Saturdays. Hence, it was not until Monday morning that newspapers could report on Diana's shocking death, which had occurred more than a full day earlier.

Into this press vacuum, when for more than 30 hours there was nothing substantive for shocked people to read about the event, leapt *Salon*. The editors in San Francisco sprang into action ("like firehouse dogs," Talbot later said) as soon as Diana's death was announced on Saturday night. They immediately solicited reaction and commentary from within *Salon*'s staff and outside it: the articles went online by stages from midday Sunday on and received a mammoth amount of traffic from all over the world. On following days, more pieces of reportage and background were added, and the epic Diana package remained flagged on *Salon*'s main screen for weeks.

The perils attendant on Web publishing are illustrated by an unexpected reaction to my first remarks about the accident in *Salon*, where I lamented that Diana had been foolish to trust her safety and security to the Egyptian playboy Dodi Fayed (a point later substantiated by the inquest report). After the translated article was reprinted several days later in *Le Monde*, two rather menacing air-mail letters from Paris arrived at my university office accusing me of fomenting anti-Muslim prejudice and propaganda. Despite the risk of incurring a fatwa, however, writing for *Salon* has been a golden opportunity to contribute to the World Wide Web at a pivotal point in its cultural development. Though I retired my column in the fall of 2001 to focus on book projects, I intend to return to online journalism when time allows.

Whatever *Salon*'s fate, it has already been enormously influential in creating the paradigm for online magazine publishing. Its graphic and tech design has been consistently cutting-edge. And its feature writers and columnists developed, through trial and error, the distinctive tone and style of online commentary, now imitated by Web sites across the political spectrum. In literary history, I submit, *Salon* can be compared to two bold and witty London periodicals, Richard Steele's *The Tatler* (1709-11) and Steele and Addison's *The Spectator* (1711-12; 1714). Despite their short lives, *The Tatler* and *The Spectator* prefigured and helped beget the rhetorical forms and strategies of modern journalism.

## REFERENCES

McLuhan, M. (1964). *Understanding media: The extensions of man*. New York: McGraw-Hill.

Paglia, C. (1990). *Sexual personae. Art and decadence from Nefertiti to Emily Dickinson*. New Haven, CT: Yale University Press.

✧✧✧✧ 17

# Pedagogy and Hypertext

## Stephanie B. Gibson

*From text to classroom to curriculum and canon, the fluid and disembodied character of cyberspace dissolves forms and disrupts established procedures and relationships. In this chapter, Stephanie B. Gibson examines some of the pedagogical possibilities that may be called forth by a shift from the use of traditional printed text to that of hypertext. Providing an overview of hypertext and hypermedia forms, and an exploration of typography's relationship to education, she casts hypertext characteristics in contrast to the paradigmatic structures summoned by traditional printed text and offers some thoughts on the presence of educational hypertext in the academy. Aside from Section 3, other discussions of textuality can be found in Neil Kleinman's study of intellectual property and electronic publishing in Chapter 4, Jay David Bolter's comparison of text and virtual reality in Chapter 7, and Judith Yaross Lee's research on text-based, computer-mediated communication in Chapter 19; related examinations of cyberspace education appear in Terri Toles Patkin's profile of the virtual organization in Chapter 11 and in Paul Levinson's reflections on online learning in Chapter 12.*

The University of Maryland, Baltimore County (UMBC) was built in 1967 without a computer science building because it was thought that that obscure discipline would not attract students. In 2002, from grade school to graduate school, students are using hypertext as an integral part of their studies. Those people who were attracted to the study of computers (contrary to the thinking of many more schools than just

UMBC) went on to design computer programs that now invisibly pervade our everyday lives. ATMs, Game Boys, palm pilots, cell phones, Nintendos, cars that think, appliances that make phone calls, and the Internet itself, to name just a few manifestations, are integral parts of American life. A great shift has taken place from traditional, printed text to cyberspatial, electronic text. The movement has been from the tangible and physical to the ephemeral and digital, from text as object to text as environment. It seems only fitting that one of the areas most greatly affected by these developments has been education.

Almost all our contemporary ideas about pedagogy have been anchored firmly in a paradigm informed by the printed word. These assumptions about the world have driven interactions in the classroom to such an extent that the room physically resembles print: We see rows and columns, we hear silence, and up above the cursive alphabet—although most of us have long ago abandoned handwriting for anything other than the most personal of composition—lingers in our memories. Until this moment there has been little challenge to that way of understanding theories about learning and teaching. We now find ourselves at a crack in the window that allows us to examine the present in the blazing light of what is (perhaps, always perhaps) to come.

The impact of this new cyberspatial manner of apprehending text can be seen in a number of different domains. This chapter addresses how ideas about pedagogy have been, and may be, reconfigured by the introduction of hypertext into the educational system at all levels—from kindergarten through postdoctoral work.

## WHAT IS IT?

Any program that allows readers to navigate nonlinearly through a body of text, sometimes a single text, but frequently a database of related materials with hundreds of nodes of text linked together forming a network of relevant material, may be considered a *hypertext*. Hypertext is text that exists only in cyberspace. It is impossible to put hypertext into traditional page-bound print; doing so would so radically alter its nature that it would simply no longer be hypertext.

Hypertext is called by many names, the most common being *hypertext, multimedia,* and *hypermedia*. It may also be considered to be many different things: a stand-alone text version on disk or CD-ROM that a student may read on his or her personal computer, or text (or even a database) accessed online through any one of a number of available library or network systems, or a program used in the classroom to create a text—in other words, the possibilities are quite broad. Although the World Wide Web has become an integral part of the work in many classrooms, this distributed online world is beyond the scope of this particular text. Although the Web creates many new relationships in the world of education, the comments in this chapter solely focus on other types of hypertexts. Designers of hypertext and hypermedia packages are concerned with the differences between their products and traditional texts assigned for classroom use (Crane, 1990; Crane & Mylonas, 1988; Newman, 1991). A number of scholars have addressed the question of how hypertext and hypermedia differ from traditional printed text in their epistemological, ideological, political, and cultural biases (Bolter, 1991; Delaney & Landow, 1991; Kaplan, 1991; Landow, 1992; McDaid, 1991; Moulthrop, 1991b; Slatin, 1991). Some investigate how the hypertext environment differs from that of the traditional computer environment (Herrstrom & Massey, 1989; Rubens, 1989; Smith, 1991). Hypertext is not simply more text, or text arranged differently. It is qualitatively different from traditional text and engages us in qualitatively different activities. A horseless carriage is not simply a vehicle that moves without benefit of animal power, it alters our position in the universe. Hypertext, too, calls into being a completely new set of attitudes about who we are and our relationship to our written world, as pointed out by Jay David Bolter and Sue Barnes, among others, in Chapters 6 and 14, respectively, of this volume. Hypertext is not simply a larger book. A few of the physical differences may be illuminating: It contains more, covering the ground that could be covered by hundreds of books in a single hypermedia package. Readers do not have to get up and go to another book; when another text is needed a single keystroke summons it to the screen. It may contain different modalities: printed text, photos, animation, video, diagrams, or sound. It can keep track of the path you have followed through the text. Perhaps, most significantly, it can make connections between a piece of text and more than one other piece of text in a nonlinear fashion that is impossible in traditional print. Sometimes the medium is "write-to" as well as read, meaning any reader can add commentary and links, which then become part of the text.

Because it is so different from traditional printed text, hypertext's appearance in the classroom calls into question many accepted ideas about how text is used. Much like traditional printed text, a significant characteristic in hypertext is control of the text; but the locus of control in hypertext can be very different from that of traditional print. Some important questions grow out of the different nature of this new text. What does hypertext allow readers and writers to do that traditional text does not? What does hypertext allow teachers and students to do that traditional text does not? And what assumptions about the classroom (and curriculum and canon) are called into question as a result of these different interactions?

Several scholars have discussed the movement from traditional print to hypertext as an inevitable shift. O.B. Hardison (1989) maintains that hypertext is part of what he sees as a natural progression—literary, social, and technological—wherein American culture is slowly disconnecting from its history and floating into what he calls paradigmatic isolation—the cutting off of culture from any heretofore familiar paradigms of interaction. George Landow (1992), on the other hand, sees the "convergence of contemporary critical theory and technology"—the coming together of postmodern critique and hypertextual practice—subtitling his book thusly. McDaid (1991) maintains that nothing less than the transformation of consciousness is at stake in a relationship with hypertext. Jay Bolter (1991) says that hypertext will alter the manner in which realities are constructed. And Richard Lanham (1993) insists that the new electronic writing of hypertext will bring us full circle to classical rhetorical forms. Whatever their specific conclusions, these scholars and critics all indicate that hypertext radically alters traditional hierarchical structures both within writing systems and between author and reader. It is in this alteration in the relationship between author and reader that the fundamental differences between traditional print and hypertext lie, and these differences seem likely to cause a shift in pedagogy.

## TRADITIONAL TEXTBOOKS IN THE CLASSROOM

The relationship of textbooks to their respective disciplines has been the object of examination for some time. In 1979, Frances FitzGerald showed a relationship between textbooks and contemporary social values. Earlier, Paolo Friere (1970) made a powerful argument that classroom agendas are integrally tied to political agendas. In the years since these and other works, this issue has been addressed by scholars in many disciplines (e.g., English, 1986; Gagnon, 1987; Kaplan, 1991; Knoblauch & Brannon, 1984). A 1991 study by Gibson found that although communications textbooks mention issues addressed in professional communications scholarship, the translation process they undergo renders them in an entirely different light. Textbooks are seen, at their most powerful, as a driving force behind curriculum decisions and, at their least powerful, as simple auxiliary tools to classroom interaction. The various truths probably lie somewhere between those two possibilities.

The thought in which scholars engage, in many ways, constitutes a field. Textbooks traditionally represent this thought in a much different format than that of its original presentation. Obviously, the two bodies of text—professional scholarship and textbooks—are asking their audiences to engage in two different activities. Scholars, presumably well versed in the theory and methods of the field, read journals to engage in debate about the current direction of the discipline. Conversely, students read textbooks to gain entry (which may be interpreted in several ways) to the discipline. Briefly, some characteristics that set traditional classroom textbooks apart from other types of text can be seen in the following.

Journals and academic language notwithstanding, textbooks are not inviting reading. They present their text in a manner peculiar to textbooks. Physically they resemble no other type of written text. They are often printed on heavy paper to withstand excessive handling, wide margins are provided for comments by readers, questions are frequently posed at the close of a chapter to test the reader's comprehension of what he or she has read, side bars attempt to illustrate particularly difficult material. These characteristics send readers the message that the text arrives at the interaction with the student with an attitude of authority (Gibson, 1991; Moran, 1971).

Traditional classrooms are a reflection of this noninteractive environment. The design and layout of this classroom is static, like print on a page. No matter how a reader moves, or moves through the pages of a book, the print remains anchored firmly to its place on the page. In a mirror relationship chairs often remain attached to desks (do those things have a name?). Sometimes both are bolted solidly to the floor. Much traditional classroom activity also reflects the unidirectionality of traditional print. The lecture, the blackboard, the overhead projector—these are the staples of a print-driven classroom, all of them traditionally controlled by the teacher. The printed textbook carries with it these same assumptions about the relationship between teachers and students—that one is in charge, the other a mere vessel.

How teachers use textbooks in the classroom is not at issue here; clearly, there are many ways to contextualize textbooks in the classroom. What is fascinating is that the majority of texts in print say that they encourage one thing—critical thinking—while presenting their content in a manner that attempts to both block and trivialize that activity by being markedly uncritical of their own assumptions. When methods other than that which informs the book are acknowledged, it is only in passing, and the prevailing attitude is to explain that such other methods exist, but to dismiss both the concepts and other methodology as neither valid nor valuable. This sort of internal disqualification is accomplished in several ways. First, and most significant, the method and paradigm that drive the book itself are rarely acknowledged. Texts often see relationships in the world they describe as unidirectional, which is the same attitude they take in relating to their audience. Textbooks rarely engage in self-reflection, in which they explain that paradigmatic strictures involve basic assumptions about what is important and that this drives decisions about what appears in the text and how. Even when textbooks discuss the notion that assumptions about reality may be embedded in theory and method, they rarely indicate any recognition of the assumptions embedded in the theory that guides the composition of their own text. The unspoken assumptions of a discipline, as Kuhn (1970) pointed out, are difficult enough to see, let alone question. When underlying assumptions are articulated and examined by the author, it then becomes easier to show how agendas exist in other theoretical methods. When books not only do not do this, but present material as unquestionable truth, contradictory messages are being given. The text wants its readers to become better critical thinkers, but it removes one of the most important tools they can be given for doing this. It does not allow them to examine the text. In examining two message levels of the text—content and pedagogic—clear problems exist. To the uninitiated novice, much of what is contained in traditional textbooks appears to be knowledge carved in stone.

Textbooks are, as Olson (1988) states, "compilations of the given" (p. 30). Presentation of scholarly discourse in journals is different because the very nature of the journal is that it is in flux. The appearance of responses to articles and responses to those responses indicates the existence of an ongoing dialogue—quite different from what happens in textbooks. The literature of scholarship begs a different engagement from its audience. It assumes readers have an extensive background in the field, that they are mature enough thinkers to follow a sometimes complex line of reasoning, and—most important—it asks that readers engage in debate about the thinking and the direction of the discipline. It is clear from the authority with which textbooks approach their audience that they do not wish to be questioned about their methodology. I do not intend to address here the question of whether it is possible, or even desirable, to close the gap between professional scholarship and what students read. It is significant that a major difference exists between the texts of scholars and the activities requested by those texts, and the texts used in the classroom by students and the activities requested by those text. The relationships of the texts to their audiences are different; the overt and covert, content and pedagogical messages are different. And as a result, related educational arrangements are affected.

## HYPERTEXT IN THE CLASSROOM

The hypertext form is utilized in quite a wide variety of ways. For instance, *afternoon* by Michael Joyce (1987), *Victory Garden* by Stuart Moulthrop (1992), and *Uncle Buddy's Phantom Funhouse* by John McDaid (1992), are three examples of classic hypertext fiction. The first two are solely text based: The reader reads a node of text and, depending on his or her selection of navigation methods, moves to any one of several possible text blocks to continue reading. The third example incorporates a multimedia experience that takes advantage of object-oriented programming in presenting the reader with "objects," graphics, sound, and some movement. The reader moves through this text in the same way as he or she navigates through the first two—either by using an arrow set up by the writer or by selecting a bit of text he or she wishes to pursue and clicking on it. Many other educational hypertext packages are available; most incorporate multimedia such as written text, sound, graphics (including illustration and photographs), and frequently video. Many of these packages are extremely large databases of material, compared to what we are accustomed to having access to in one spot, and they allow many different pathways of navigation. For instance, one of the first constructed was the *Perseus Project*. This hypertext package strives to make available (to its credit—it is still, several years into the project, being worked on) much of ancient Greece. There are archeological photographs and diagrams, photos of period artwork, plays in the original Greek with translations, contemporary commentary, maps, and several glossaries, all linked together to allow myriad approaches to the material. All this is available at a single keystroke. *Ulysses* is another example of an early hypertext project, described in some detail by Jay Bolter in Chapter 6, which combines video of actors reading Tennyson's *Ulysses*, scholars discussing the piece, the poem itself, and other material. Readers can select portions of the database they wish to study. Yet another type of hypertext is that frequently used in writing classrooms. A writing program, like Storyspace, is used by composition teachers to give students open access to each other's work. In Storyspace, writers may compose nodes of text, link them to any number of other text nodes, and leave the project open for others to add their text nodes and links. Unlike some hypertext fictions and composition programs, these classroom multimedia packages do allow users to also become authors and linkers. All these programs, although fundamentally different in tremendously significant ways, are considered hypertext.

All the qualities of hypertext encourage vastly different habits of thought than does traditional print. Hypertext has been called a democratizing medium because it allows everyone access to both production and decoding. This may be said of it both internally and within its larger environment. Internally, for example, hypertext is able to show clearly interconnectedness between ideas by linking them together. Although this is not completely impossible in print, it is structurally difficult to include massive amounts of material in a single text. It also goes against all accepted authoring practice; the idea behind composing text is, for the most part, to exclude anything that might be only tangentially related and to include only that which is directly pertinent. In particularly large traditional textbooks, it is difficult to show connections among all the disparate material compiled within. In authoring a hypertext it is possible to allow the text to branch in several directions at once, representing many relevant paths of thought. As a result, ideas can be contextualized historically as well as theoretically in ways impossible in traditional print. For example, The *Perseus Project* contains what would amount to several printed books, audio, and video, all linked together through many different pathways allowing readers to traverse the material searching for many different types of relationships. To do this with traditional printed text would require several trips to the library, several armfuls of books, and an ability to imagine connections and translations that might seem overwhelming to beginning students.

Because students are permitted to see primary sources, many more interpretative choices are open to them. In much the same way that the Bible in its first vernacular translations allowed the masses direct access to the "words of God," allowing—even encouraging—students to explore a variety of primary materials provides them with original background heretofore only available to scholars. When everyone can read the original, all kinds of choices become possible. What is more, readers are viewing primary material, commentary, and criticism—not solely material that has been digested and represented in a simplified fashion for their ease. This is particularly significant because although primary material is not always easy for readers to wrestle with, it gives a picture of the discipline that commentary two or three times removed cannot provide.

The epistemological and pedagogical ramifications of these qualitative differences between the two types of text are many. Because no margins literally exist, there is neither actual nor figurative marginalization. No text node has any more or less significance than any other node of text because they all appear in the same manner on the screen. Of course, both positive and negative points can be made about this. Some say that not all pieces of information are equal in value or importance. When whatever is summoned to the screen becomes primary, this equalizes Aristotle and the college freshman. Some applaud this new equality; others decry the elimination of gatekeepers saying hypertexts without them lack legitimacy. (It must be noted that not all hypertexts allow readers to also function as writers and link makers; in fact, most hypertexts do not.)

In many hypertexts there is no hierarchy of ideas as is evidenced in a table of contents or outline. Instead of the linear sequencing of items characteristic of most printed texts, nonlinear, web-like organization drives hypertext. After the opening screen announcement of what the package is, there is no one direction one must take through the text; many equally interesting paths are available. In other words, no particular node must be read before moving on to any other node. This, of course, challenges the notions that one concept is more important than another or that certain knowledge must precede other knowledge. This sort of organizing principle spreads ideas or pieces of text out in a manner that shows their relationships not in order of importance, calling into question not only hierarchies of ideas, but the notion of prerequisites.

The dynamic nature of hypertext is another significant difference. Books are static; their layout remains the same no matter how the reader chooses to experience the text. But hypertext moves about on the screen, always presenting the reader with a different primary node. And although CD-ROMs are completed pieces, other hypertext structures, those on the Internet in particular, are dynamic in an even larger sense. Books embody, as Ong (1982) and Bolter (1991) both state, a sense of closure, the idea that what the reader holds in his or her hands is the completed subject, an area that has been both literally and figuratively covered. The kinetic environment of hypertext always allows new material to be added, new relationships to be delineated.

A host of differences are evidenced between traditional print and hypertext in the writing classroom. Scholarship in the field of composition theory has directed attention to how write-to hypertext alters the nature of the interactions among all classroom participants—students, teachers, and all combinations thereof. Space prohibits a thorough consideration about the nature of the composition classroom with hypertext, but a brief glance reveals that composition researchers are also examining radical changes not only in the nature of the interactions and the quality of the work produced, but in the nature of the work produced. Collaborative work produced using write-to hypertext programs such as Storyspace uses entirely different writing and thinking skills than do traditional composition techniques. These techniques approximate dynamic learning structures, such as those described by Knoblauch and Brannon (1984), Treisman (1985), and Douglas (1994a, 1994b), much more closely than does the isolated writing used in most composition classrooms.

## SOME IMPLICATIONS FOR CLASSROOM, CURRICULUM, AND CANON

General classroom policy and activities have the possibility of being heavily impacted by these differences in the move from traditional text to hypertext. First, control is shifted away from the teacher to the user of the text. The pedagogical implications in the classroom are that the teacher must relinquish some measure of control, and, as a result of this, the relationship between student and teacher is altered. When using a hypertext package as an adjunct to a course, the student will have access to material not traditionally available in both volume and structure. Although it is certainly possible for students to skip ahead in textbooks, they do not do so often, usually because they have no way of knowing what in the subsequent text is linked conceptually to what they are presently reading. Traditional printed text signals to students: This is what will be covered in class, and usually in this very same order. Not so with hypertext. In using a hypertext, the reader has access to a significantly larger database of material than when using a traditional printed text. Not only is more material available, but this is frequently material used in preparation of the course, in other words, primary text material and scholarly critique. This is material that is almost never made available to students as a matter of course. But in a hypertext database it is highly accessible to them.

Traditional classroom relationships are altered because the teacher no longer has control over who will read what texts, when, or in how much depth. This is not to say that these primary texts have heretofore been unavailable to students if they search for them. But that is the key phrase—searching, on a somewhat grand scale, was necessary. Not many typical students exhibit this type of interest in their course material. When a body of literature is right at their fingertips, however, the question of exploration is different. When students have access to primary material and connecting ideas are made easier to follow, they can often see conceptual maps that teachers frequently keep private. Some of the information they may be reading may even be contrary to the conceptual agenda of the course. Students may now pursue, on their own, links among ideas that may or may not be planned as a part of the course material. If they are part of the course, students may be ahead of the class progression and ask questions that anticipate these links. If they are not planned as part of the class material, students may force the issue, making the instructors examine ideas they had originally planned not to cover. Unless teachers are prepared to dictate each time they are confronted with an unexpected question, student access to hypertext material will force teachers to deal with material they may not have planned for, in a time not their own.

This altered relationship mirrors the internally democratizing elements of hypertext. There is no marginalization within the text of ideas or in the classroom of readers who wish to pursue different paths. When students have control of what they can read, they also have control of what connections they will make. This is not without even considering the enormous database available to them online on the Internet.

These are some of the ideas about teaching that are embedded in the technology of hypertext. This is how relationships in the classroom may be altered, as may be the structure of how people interact with each other and their material, what the teacher can and cannot do, what he or she may expect of the students, and what they may expect of the teacher.

Some have even suggested that hypertext will bring with it a paradigm shift as radical as that ascribed to the shift from manuscript to print (Bolter, 1991; Kaplan, 1991; Landow, 1992; McDaid, 1991). Charles Ess (1991) indicates that students gain a better idea of connectedness and the ability to grasp highly complex material when working with hypertext as opposed to traditional printed textbooks. Both Landow (1992) and Moulthrop (1991a) address the notion that a new rhetoric must necessarily grow out of our use of hypertext both as a composition tool and as a reading instrument. Landow discusses the rhetoric of arrivals and departures because this is what readers do as they read hypertext—leave one screen and arrive at another. This traveling among texts, this linking of ideas together in space, leaves readers with a more developed idea about how a particular piece of text is related to another piece of text. When writing in hypertext, Ess's students came away with clearer notions of how ideas were related to one another.

Hypertext's ability to democratize the classroom by showing interconnectedness, not marginalizing less popularly held points of view, and having no embedded hierarchy, all argue for a more open classroom in which students feel free to ask, and also answer, questions. The kinetic characteristics of hypertext seem to lend themselves to showing students that the world is constantly evolving and that knowledge is not carved in the proverbial stone. Hypertext lends itself to collaborative learning: techniques in which the students are engaged on a fundamental level with the text, with each other, and with the teacher. In learning in which students are allowed to discover connections and realities for themselves we have seen a more complete grasp of material and a greater interest in continuing to learn. Moreover, the dynamic attributes of hypertext provide the possibility of allowing all users to do what only scholars have traditionally done—engage in debate.

Implications for curriculum and canon can be seen in this examination of the microcosm of the classroom. Issues of control are central. If classroom control must shift, the administrative grip on curriculum will also be challenged. In the alteration of access, the politics of choice will be dramatically shifted to the forefront. When access is expanded, as it is when hypertext is used, choice lies much more dramatically with the reader. Control of the canon may be dispersed when access is available to everyone connected with the academy.

A principal change may occur in the material being used to teach courses. Many courses use textbooks instead of primary material. Even in literature courses a leaning exists toward using anthologies frequently containing only parts of works. I have argued elsewhere (Gibson, 1993) that what we offer students in (particularly introductory) textbooks actually constitutes the canon. What makes it through the obstacle course of academic gatekeepers and into the classroom texts constitutes the discipline. All else is scholarly debate. As observed earlier, academic journals request different activities of their readers than do textbooks, among those activities are the milling over of what may be permitted to enter the canon. The body of material that is the core of what we talk about when we refer to a discipline; the core of what we want novices to know about a discipline; material that has passed the test of relevance, understandability, and importance; and finally material that is believed to be true is what is found in textbooks. This is canon. Hypertext, with included supporting material, links to lesser known texts, commentary, and criticism, even other disciplines, reconfigures what is available to students and reconfigures the canon. In addition to reconfiguring the canon in any single discipline, hypertext allows for the mating of several areas of study. In fact, the medium of hypertext has a Postmanesque (1992) way of insisting that more than a single discipline be included in the database.


## THE SHIFT


It seems inevitable that classrooms will shift from using traditional print textbooks to hypertext, perhaps not to meet all of their needs, but certainly for many purposes. At a workshop I attended back in 1994, at which the *Ulysses* package was discussed, teachers were immediately drawn to it. At that seminar several high school and college English teachers asked excitedly where they could procure the package for their institutions. An oft-heard comment during that summer workshop, and since, is that hypertext is a way to hold student interest. It is dynamic, contains several approaches to the material, and appears to give readers/users a choice about how the material will be experienced and studied. (It also contains minimal printed stimulus, most of that particular package using video as its primary platform.) Will this change initiate a paradigmatic shift? A brief examination of some of the epistemological biases of print and electronic text will provide a clearer answer here.

Just as textbooks construct their own authority and in so doing obscure the foundations of the belief systems that inform them, hypertext can easily do the same. Although many possibilities of openness exist with hypertext, as cited earlier, the fact remains that many hypertexts lead and limit the reader in much the same way as does traditional print. Although with print it is obvious that the artifact is saying "examine me in this particular order, and when you come to the end—stop," with hypertext such a relationship can be constructed without the reader knowing he or she is being so directed. A book has a beginning, middle, and end, and the physical nature of the object informs the user of the appropriate method of engagement. Hypertext is artifactless, except on the metalevel, and so it exists without self-apparent user directions. Directions are embedded at a much deeper level.

As a result of these possibilities, not all hypertext is as free as has been described. It is certainly possible to construct a hypertext so that it leads the reader in as structured a way as does traditional print. They can be more structured, in fact, because in traditional print the reader is free to skip from any one page to any other page. In a computer environment, it is possible to program the user's every move. This goes against the principal of what most hypertext authors maintain as the medium's intention, many of them stating that the nature of the medium is to fight against this type of constraint. Nevertheless, it is possible to lead a reader in hypertext in a manner inconceivable in print, and I have seen several hypertexts that do just this. In hypertext the reader has no concept of what he or she is not seeing because the artifact shows neither size nor content. When the reader does not know the possibilities of the text, it is possible to program gates within the text that do not allow progress through the program until certain other nodes have been read and/or questions (some have quizzes programmed into them) have been answered. This type of hypertext is every bit as directed (and deadly boring) as the traditional printed text with questions at the end of each chapter quizzing a somnambulistic reader on the contents therein. Neither does every hypertext exist in a write-to mode; in fact, few hypertexts allow the reader to contribute. In spite of all that is written about the marvels of allowing readers to add text, create new links, and alter existing paths, few hypertexts allow the reader to do any of this. Even in composition programs, in which these types of contributions are invaluable, not all programs in use allow them. When the text leads the reader on a predetermined path and does not allow contributions, alterations, or wanderings, there is certainly a sense of hierarchy—the text is in charge, and the text will tell the reader what is important. In some highly structured hypertext environments, readers may still have the illusion of constructing the text, but when a choice is path A or path B and the end of the path is always the same stroll through the text, this choice is a deception, making this type of hypertext suspect. Is it worse to have no choice or to have the illusion of choice?

Without the mutability characteristic of the hypertext most people discuss, there is certainly an epistemological attitude of a body of knowledge being "covered" completely—no questions need be asked nor are they, quite literally, permitted.

When hypertext is constructed in this way, the responsibility shift spoken of here does not occur. The teacher need relinquish no control, he or she has just as much as always. The teacher controls the text, how much students may read, and where they may wander. He or she controls what contributions they may make to class and what questions they may ask.

Clearly the possibilities for conundrums peculiar to hypertext are myriad. The same qualities that open possibilities for hypertext also provide the opportunity for problems. In a database so enormous that it includes several thousand nodes of primary and secondary text, where does authority lie? And what of the concept of authorship—will it be entirely done away with? Will, as my students maintain, we become a nation of expert linkers able to draw connections, but without original thought. And what of the concept of closure that Bolter (1991) and Ong (1982) say traditional print affords us? The closure of traditional print leaves readers with the impression of a certain amount of expertise and authority. Both write-to and closed but enormous databases may relieve individual authors (and linkers) of the responsibilities of expertise. Many scholars see the gatekeeping function of print and its politics as an important method of safeguarding the academy. Hypertext presents the possibility of genuine revolution—epistemologically and pedagogically with all the attendant implications for classroom, curriculum, canon, and cultural paradigm.

It seems unlikely, however, that such a revolution will occur. Most scholars today do not view open hypertexts as authoritative acceptable sources. There is still great disagreement as to the acceptability as research material of unmoderated lists and World-Wide Web sites. The need, created by books, for a sense of authority, authorship, and authenticity will not fade softly away. Electronic texts will be required to have closure, control of their subject matter, and responsible expert editorial boards in order for them to be acceptable classroom adjuncts. With all this it seems unlikely that there will be any significant challenge to the practice of presenting text as if it had no agenda. Hypertexts must still make assumptions about what is worthy of inclusion, and it remains to be seen if the possibilities of size will allow the inclusion of possibly competing worldviews.

Based on what we know about the functioning of textbooks in the classroom, it seems obvious that it is not the desire of the current educational system that our initiates engage in the same activities as do seasoned scholars. It is not in the interests, politically, socially, or intellectually of any established discipline for newcomers to the field to engage directly in debate. Aside from the oft-cited practical reasons for the necessity of coming into possession of the canon prior to admission into the dialogue, the notion of legitimate challenge has historically been ill received (Fleck, 1939/1979; Kuhn, 1970). Based on the traditional relationships among texts, disciplines, scholars, and novices, relationships driven not simply by a quest for knowledge but by a host of intrigues, it seems probable that future analysis of hypertext in the classroom will continue to indicate the same sort of self-reflective myopia present in traditional printed textbooks.

## CONCLUSIONS ARE NOT YET POSSIBLE

At this point most open and write-to hypertexts are being used and positively discussed only in writing classrooms (Douglas, 1994a, 1994b; Forman, 1991;

Joyce, 1988). Given the current state of the educational system in this country it seems unlikely that hypertexts with truly "democratizing" qualities will be accepted into mainstream use outside of composition workshops. There may be *some* hope. Seymour Papert (1980) traveled to France in the late 1970s to introduce his computer program Logo into grade-school classrooms. Although a tremendously significant purpose of elementary education—teaching youngsters appropriate social behavior—was omitted from his resultingly optimistic discussion of that experiment, the experiment still yielded primarily positive results.

In spite of the possible "mis"uses of hypertext cited previously, the technology does encode a new worldview, different from that of traditional print. I have discussed the primary differences between the two. Pedagogically, hypertext both allows and encourages more genuine participation by students. It permits access to primary material. It also seems to open up the classroom in ways that would encourage collaborative learning. Whether teachers will be willing to give up some control of their classrooms is a question similar to that brought about by the introduction of the printing press. The academy hated seeing authority shifted, but it was as inevitable as sunrise. Not knowing what may happen in a particular class is uncomfortable and requires a flexibility and a range of material many instructors may be unwilling to embrace. As hypertext breaks down the barriers between disciplines by contextualizing bodies of knowledge historically and conceptually, it will demand a more well-rounded classroom that admits not only opposing points of view, but points of view from seemingly disparate fields. Faculty will be forced to adapt; we are already seeing the results of this in newly formed interdisciplinary departments and schools all around the country.

Hypertext will also have an impact on an epistemological scale larger than classroom pedagogy. It calls into question several different relationships of academic authority. Not only will instructors in individual classrooms have their authority challenged, but the larger ideas of curriculum and canon will be forced to account for themselves in ways heretofore unimagined. As attitudes that inform the construction of hypertext make their way into curriculum planning, and beyond, traditional elements such as prerequisites, required reading, and single-discipline classrooms may find themselves in jeopardy. The wider contextualization allowed by hypertext will most certainly force changes in the manner in which disciplines are conceived and expertise is attributed. When the text is mutable, all notions about authority and authorship are called into question.

The habits of thought encouraged by the dynamic and visual environment of hypertext and other cyberspace applications are already apparent in our culture in the guise of, for example, MTV and computer games. Rhetorical traditions in all venues will be severely challenged by this. It has become convention now, for example, that what is possible visually, whether or not it is logical, is expected. Whether these visuals make traditional and logical sense in the world of the real no longer demands the imperative consideration it used to.

We are already seeing the impact of hypertext both in the classroom and in the culture. Most children and students are more computer literate than we are; and certainly they are less intimidated by the possibilities of computers than we were at their age. Although this chapter has not even touched on the World Wide Web, we must wonder whether it will be a democratizing medium as so many think, or will it simply produce a nation of people with short attention spans and good eye-hand coordination, as others contend? I am in favor of anything that asks us to examine our traditional agenda. Particularly when that agenda has been, for the most part, a hidden one. Whether the emergence of hypertext will result in a pedagogical shift remains to be seen, perhaps not by us. But I suspect we will all be examining these questions for some time to come.

## REFERENCES

Bolter, J.D. (1991). *Writing space.* Hillsdale, NJ: Erlbaum.

Crane, G. (1990). Challenging the individual: The tradition of hypermedia databases. *Academic Computing, 1,* 22-38.

Crane, G., & Mylonas, E. (1988, November). The Perseus Project: An interactive curriculum on classical Greek civilization. *Educational Technology,* pp. 25-32.

Delaney, P., & Landow, G.P. (1991). Hypertext, hypermedia and literary studies: The state of the art. In P. Delaney & G.P. Landow (Eds.), *Hypermedia and literary studies* (pp. 3-50). Cambridge, MA: MIT Press.

Douglas, J.Y. (1994a). Making the audience real: Using hypertext in the writing classroom. *Educators' Tech Exchange, 1*(3), 17-23.

Douglas, J.Y. (1994b). Technology, pedagogy, or context: A tale of two classrooms. *Computers & Composition, 11,* 275-282.

English, R. (1986). Can social studies textbooks have scholarly integrity? *Social Education, 50,* 46-48.

Ess, C. (1991). The pedagogy of computing: Hypermedia in the classroom. In P.D. Stotts & R.K. Furata (Eds.), *Hypertext '91 Proceedings* (pp. 277-289). New York: Association for Computing Machinery.

FitzGerald, F. (1979). *America revised.* Boston: Little, Brown.

Fleck, L. (1979). *Genesis and development of a scientific fact* (F. Bradley & T.J. Trenn, Trans.). Chicago: University of Chicago Press. (Original work published 1935)

Forman, J. (1991). Computing and collaborative writing. In G.E. Hawisher & C.L. Selfe (Eds.), *Evolving perspectives on computers and composition studies* (pp. 65-83). Urbana, IL: National Council of Teachers of English.

Friere, P. (1970). *Pedagogy of the oppressed* (M.B. Ramos, Trans.). New York: Continuum.

Gagnon, P. (1987, Summer). Democracy's untold story. *American Educator,* pp. 19-25, 46.

Gibson, S.B. (1991). Professional scholarship and introductory communications textbooks (Doctoral dissertation, New York University, 1991). *Dissertation Abstracts International, 52*, 1931A-1932A.

Gibson, S.B. (1993, November). *Textbooks as canon.* Paper presented at the Speech Communications Association Convention, Miami, FL.

Hardison, O.B. (1989). *Disappearing through the skylight.* New York: Penguin.

Herrstrom, D.S., & Massey, D.G. (1989). Hypertext in context. In E. Barrett (Ed.), *The society of text* (pp. 45-58). Cambridge, MA: MIT Press.

Joyce, M. (1987). *afternoon, a story* [Computer software]. Watertown, MA: Eastgate Systems.

Joyce, M. (1988). Siren shapes: Exploratory and constructive hypertexts. *Academic Computing. 4*, 11-14, 37-42.

Kaplan, N. (1991). Ideology, technology, and the future of writing instruction. In G.E. Hawisher & C.L. Selfe (Eds.), *Evolving perspectives on computers and composition studies* (pp. 11-42). Urbana, IL: National Council of Teachers of English.

Knoblauch, C.H., & Brannon, L. (1984). *Rhetorical traditions and the teaching of writing.* Upper Montclair, NJ: Boynton/Cook.

Kuhn, T.S. (1970). *The structure of scientific revolutions* (2nd ed.). Chicago: University of Chicago Press.

Landow, G.P. (1992). *Hypertext: The convergence of contemporary critical theory and technology.* Baltimore: John Hopkins University Press.

Lanham, R.A. (1993). *The electronic word: Democracy, technology and the arts.* Chicago: University of Chicago Press.

McDaid, J. (1991). Breaking frames: Hyper-mass media. In E. Berk & J. Devlin (Eds.), *The hypertext/hypermedia handbook* (pp. 445-458). New York: McGraw-Hill.

McDaid, J. (1992). *Uncle buddy's phantom funhouse* [Computer software]. Watertown, MA: Eastgate Systems.

Moran, T.P. (1971). Education and persuasion: A propaganda analysis of English language textbooks used in New York City academic high schools (Doctoral dissertation, New York University, 1971). *Dissertations Abstracts International, 32/10-A*, 5747.

Moulthrop, S. (1991a). Beyond the electronic book: A critique of hypertext rhetoric. In P.D. Stotts & R.K. Furata (Eds.), *Hypertext '91 Proceedings* (pp. 277-289). New York: Association for Computing Machinery.

Moulthrop, S. (1991b). The politics of hypertext. In G.E. Hawisher & C.L. Selfe (Eds.), *Evolving perspectives on computer and composition studies* (pp. 253-274). Urbana, IL: National Council of Teachers of English.

Moulthrop, S. (1992). *Victory garden* [Computer software]. Watertown, MA: Eastgate Systems.

Neuman, D. (1991). Evaluating evolution: Naturalisitc inquiry and the Perseus Project. *Computers and the Humanities, 25*, 239-246.

Olson, D.R. (1988). Mind and media: The epistemic functions of literacy. *Journal of Communication, 38*(3), 27-36.

Ong, W.J. (1982). *Orality and literacy: The technologizing of the word.* New York: Methuen.

Papert, S. (1980). *Mindstorms.* New York: Basic Books.

Postman, N. (1992). *Technopoly: The surrender of culture to technology.* New York: Knopf.

Rubens, P. (1989). Online information, hypermedia, and the idea of literacy. In E. Barrett (Ed.), *The society of text* (pp. 3-21). Cambridge, MA: MIT Press.

Slatin, J. (1991). Reading hypertext: Order and coherence in a new medium. In P. Delaney & G.P. Landow (Eds.), *Hypermedia and literary studies* (pp. 153-170). Cambridge, MA: MIT Press.

Smith, C.G. (1991). Reconceiving hypertext. In G.E. Hawisher & C.L. Selfe (Eds.), *Evolving perspectives on computer and composition studies* (pp. 224-252). Urbana, IL: National Council of Teachers of English.

Treisman, P.M. (1985). A study of the mathematics performance of black students at the University of California, Berkeley (Cooperative learning, remedial, honors programs, affirmative action) (Doctoral dissertation, University of California, Berkeley, 1985). *Dissertation Abstracts International, 47,* 1641A.

# 18

# Cinematic
# Representations
# of Cyberspace

## Paul Lippert

*Cyberspace, although computer-generated, has seen many representations in cinema, itself a media space. Paul Lippert uses films such as TRON as a jumping-off point to discuss the significance of computer media's peculiar mix of the analogic and the digital. Noting how the concrete and the abstract have historically functioned as metaphors for each other, he connects symbolic form with social class, the elite leaning toward literacy and the masses toward speech and imagery. Ultimately, he is critical of postmodernists who celebrate cyberspace as a metaphor for computing and cyberpunk as a lifestyle. In the other sections of this book, alternate critical discussion of virtual space can be found in Herbert Zettl's analysis of the metaphysics of virtual reality in Chapter 5 and Jay David Bolter's comparison of VR and text in Chapter 7; for a different take on social class, see Frank Dance's discussion of the digital divide in Chapter 10. Other related critiques of a more general nature include John M. Phelan's essay in Chapter 2, and Ron Jacobson's discussion of policy in Chapter 9, and Douglas Rushkoff's comments on information warfare in Chapter 21; also see Lance Strate's arguments concerning cyberspace versus cybertime in Chapter 22 as a variation on Lippert's distinction between concrete and abstract forms.*

Two neon-lit figures with dim yet unmistakably human faces engage in a life-and-death Frisbee match, supported by a gridwork of similar neon lines that hang in a black void. Cartoon-like, yet strangely iridescent motorcycles race on an illuminated plane, leaving linear barriers of light behind them. With these images, Walt Disney Productions introduced the general public in 1982 to what is now known as cyberspace. The film they appear in, TRON, has since become a major case study for postmodernists interested in the cultural impact of computer technology. Basically a children's film, with good-guys-beat-bad-guys plot and seemingly prepubescent characters, it is considered to be a cultural landmark for its depiction of such "space."

Yet in considering these brightly colored and excitingly kinetic images, it is possible to be distracted from the fact that what is being depicted (i.e., the computer's functions) is in actuality not a space at all but, in practical terms, its opposite. In a certain sense, one can even say that space was the *problem* that the computer was invented to *solve*. Bureaucracies, needing to process ever-increasing amounts of information, were faced with a growing impediment of space; the space of ever-lengthening forms and documents, ever-widening file folders, ever-multiplying file cabinets, ever-more crowded offices, ever-growing distances between offices, people, and sources of information. The computer helped to remove this impediment by storing and processing information in what is to a great extent a nonspatial medium. When we use the term *cyberspace*, we are using the concept of space as a metaphor for something that in some ways can be made to function like a concrete space, but that is actually much more abstract. Such cinematic representations of the computer's functions as can be found in *TRON*, or any one of a number of other recent science fiction movies, utilize the actual space of the screen for such metaphoric purposes. In this case, it is not the linguistic *concept* of space alone, but the *directly visible* spaces on the screen's surface that are used as metaphors for abstractions about the computer.

But how can such graphic spatial metaphors be used to capture the complex, invisible nature of the computer's influence on our lives? Why would they be chosen over more literal, language-based methods of explanation? Most important, what are the social implications of this choice? This chapter contextualizes these questions through an examination of the media environment in which they arise in order to suggest possible answers to them.

The use of spatial metaphors for abstractions is nothing new. As Walter Ong (1967) has pointed out, the cultural transition from orality to literacy is marked by a shift from a temporal to a spatial phenomenology of the word. In the early days of print culture, knowledge began to be cast into object-like form and subjected to a logic of spatial arrangement on the depthless, denatured surface of the printed page. When applied to physical entities, like planets, whose characteristics are manifest by means of their positions in actual space, like orbits, this logic led to productive developments in the natural sciences. When applied to more abstract entities, it tended to reify them, to conceptualize them as if they actually had the characteristics of objects situated in space. A prime example of this is the very notion of *system*. Originally this term was applied specifically to the schematic representation of planets in their orbits. So influential was the concept, as advanced in such works as Copernicus's *De Revolutionibus* in 1543, that suddenly all sorts of phenomena began to be represented in such diagrams as systems. Even human psychology took on a geometric form (Ong, 1951).

It is a paradoxical feature of writing, and especially of print, that they facilitate the contemplation of the abstract by rendering it in the concrete form of object-like, visible words situated on the space of the page (Havelock, 1963, 1976). Because both language and the alphabet are digital symbol systems, the form of the signifier is purely arbitrary and conventional. At least ideally, it is nothing more than a technical convenience; it need not affect the semantic status of the signified. In fact, it functions best when its physical form is transparent (Havelock, 1976). Inevitably, an analogic habit of mind tends to come into play, especially when new questions are being addressed. As the increasingly abstract nature of new knowledge makes it ever more difficult to grasp, not only the signifiers but the signified concepts themselves are concretized (reified), translated, consciously or not, into spatial form. Poststructuralist writing well exemplifies this habit, from the work of Michel Foucault, in which all sorts of phenomena are reduced to "things" in "places," to a recent author (Bukatman, 1993), who asserts about his book on cyberspace: "*Terminal Identity* constructs a trajectory that propels the subject into the machine" (p.17). Not only is the cultural impact of computer use here depicted through the image of a human subject actually inhabiting a machine (as in the science fiction movies), the very text that describes this state of affairs itself figures as a sort of mechanical device that somehow puts it there.

As the print environment is gradually supplanted by electronic technologies, it is ironic not only that these spatial metaphors continue to proliferate, but they are even being applied to a technology that in large part was developed specifically for its nonspatial character. And yet, cyberspace is not usually described in terms of the dull, lifeless space of the printed page. Instead, it is a colorful, exciting, dynamic, even dramatic space that is depicted in most writing on the subject as well as in the movies. The cybernetic Frisbee players of *TRON* have their equivalents in serious writing on the subject that describes human subjects leaving their "obsolete" bodies to enter the "dramatic arena" of cyberspace (Bukatman, 1993, p. 201). How can we account for this?

Two important features of this writing are related to the fact that its subject is a technology. First, the metaphor, to a large degree, precedes the phenomenon. Unlike natural phenomena, technologies are conceived before they actually exist. Second, the phenomenon can be altered so as to correspond to the metaphor, as well as vice versa. Technology can be adapted to popular tastes. Therefore, writers are addressing themselves to something that is not only in the process of becoming, but whose path of development is subject to alteration. It is even possible that self-fulfilling prophesies are being made. But if they are not based on the experience of a completed, existent phenomenon itself, where do these prophesies come from?

Part of the answer, I believe, can be found by placing the computer in the context of the history of the development of communication media. From the very beginnings of human communication to the advent of the print era (one might even say, to the development of the telegraph), media have rather consistently evolved in the direction of increasing digitalization of form. After this point, as the age of electronic media began, this process seemed to reverse direction, as media became increasingly analogic and began to evolve toward the representation of direct experience (Levinson, 1979). The computer, obviously, represents a branch from this line of evolution that reverses the direction of change yet again toward digitalization. So we now can see two fairly distinct lines of media evolution heading in opposite symbolic directions. If the digital abstractions of print tended to give way to analogic spatial metaphorizing, just what might be expected from the even more digital computer? Although it had no intrinsic equivalent to the space of the printed page, it soon adopted the video monitor from its analogic cousin—the television—whose content traditionally and even still today derives largely from film.

Considered apart from its analogic content, television actually has an affinity with the computer. In their near-instantaneous operation, in their rendering space in effect irrelevant, in their connecting of displaced, decontextualized information, both represent a break from the linear continuity and spatial context of the printed page. And with the addition of the video monitor to the computer's standard apparatus, both are capable of the same kind of visual display of content. Both are capable, that is, of a visual display suitable to the symbolic content of film.

Although basically an analogic medium, film has a spatial bias similar to that of print. Signifiers are given visual form and are subjected to a logic of spatial arrangement. And yet, its analogic form causes its space to generate meaning differently. For unlike the physical form of digital symbols, that of analogic symbols is not merely a technical convenience. It is directly expressive of meaning. Unlike the use of spatial metaphors in the print environment, which tends to concretize what is abstract, their use in that of film tends to make abstract what is concrete. If a character, for example, is standing in the foreground of a shot, and thus takes up a greater amount of screen space than others within the same frame, although a mere concrete spatial arrangement is denoted, at the same time a more abstract connotation is being expressed about that character's relation to the others. Popular film's essential mode of operation, then, is to represent a concrete narrative through images whose spatial characteristics serve as metaphors for the story's abstract connotations.

This process of using imagery for abstraction did not begin with film. In oral cultures, whose languages are relatively devoid of abstract terms, the dominant form that knowledge takes is concrete, image-evoking narrative. Although abstract meanings are implicit in the storyline, they are not directly expressed in words. Instead, they are symbolized by images called to mind by verbal description. For this reason, Eric Havelock (1963) calls preliterate Greek culture one of "image thinkers." The image, though, as in radio drama, has to be constructed in the mind mainly on the basis of these verbal descriptions. Film is different in that it articulates the image in explicit form on the space of the screen. The mind, in a sense, has its visualizing done for it. But once the mind has possession of the image, the act of using it to represent the abstract is the same with both speech and film media.

These two types of spatial metaphorizing—one, characteristic of print, which concretizes the abstract; the other, characteristic of film and oral narrative, which abstracts the concrete—arise in response to opposite epistemic problems. The former reacts to an overload of abstraction, characteristic of literacy. The latter reacts to a lack of it, characteristic of orality. The computer, interestingly, can be associated with both, although in very different applications. In its mathematical and scientific uses, as when abstract equations are given graphic form, it is functioning like print. In its more recent entertainment uses, as when images of fictional characters and their narrative actions are spatially manipulated to express the more abstract interactions of games, it is functioning like film.

Historically, these two types of spatial metaphors and their related epistemic problems have been associated not just with different media, but with different social classes. Since the invention of writing, orality and literacy (that is, oral and literate modes of thought, embodied for the most part in oral and literate people) have coexisted in what Ong (1967) calls media interface culture. Rhetoric is an art developed by literate elites in order to persuade mostly oral audiences. In many respects, it represents an interaction between the two sensibilities. Such interaction is an important characteristic of the Age of Rhetoric, which came to an end with the advent of typographic culture.

In many respects, the cultural transition from print to electronic media seems to be bringing with it a return to this rhetorical orientation in society (Lanham, 1993). Our present culture, in spite of whatever print era ambitions of universal literacy and cultural equality that may linger, can be understood in terms of media interface. As print and literacy, generally, increasingly become the dominant media of only the elite, and while the masses turn to the speech and imagery of the electronic media's "secondary orality," society is divided epistemically. This societal split corresponds to the split in the path of media evolution described earlier: The elite embrace ever more digital forms, whereas the masses go analogic. In terms of content, as the elite explore ever higher levels of abstraction, popular culture revels in the graphic and the concrete.

Equipped with the video monitor, the computer has been adapted for mass marketing by means of software that creates an analogic user interface. As with traditional rhetoric, literate resources are being used to appeal to an essentially oral sensibility. Giving this highly digital medium an analogic persona facilitates its representation in the mythology of popular film as well. This "selling" of the computer, both as consumer product and as cultural icon, represents an interface not only between the two branches of media evolution, but between two social classes. Whereas one class concretizes the abstract, translating the computer's meaning into the imagistic terms of cinematic space, the other class abstracts the concrete, trying to understand the computer in these terms. Both processes, I believe, are evident in cinematic representations of cyberspace; yet each operates through distinctly different cinematic elements.

The mass audience's tendency to abstract from concrete images has its surest foothold in the narratives of these films. The narrative of *TRON*, for example, exhibits features that are the same as those of the mythologies of oral cultures (Ong, 1982). It centers around the actions of a hero or protagonist with whom the audience establishes a mimetic identification. The plot is agonistically toned, consisting of the struggles between clearly defined forces of good and evil. The new and unknown is presented in the form of magic or even religion, as a machine mysteriously transforms live human beings into digitized data and a "Master Control Program" approaches the status of a deity. Its extremely flat characters seem to have no interiors; for the most part, their presence is expressed kinetically. Technology is represented animistically, with computer programs taking on human form. All these characteristics serve to concretize the narrative, rendering it in a form in which its spatial representations can be used metaphorically to express the abstract.

The tendency of the elite, corporate and intellectual, to concretize the abstract finds its expression in these films' mise-en-scene (the visual elements placed within the frame at any particular time during the course of the narrative). Here we find spatial metaphors not only for concepts about the computer, but for theories of postmodern culture in general. *TRON*'s depiction of absolute Cartesian space divided by abstract linear coordinates, of irradiated light neither reflected nor blocked by anything solid, of decentered presences and actions, of depthless yet semantically inflated surfaces in its mise-en-scene has been interpreted in much postmodernist writing as representing ideas that address both of these highly abstract topics (Bukatman, 1993; Sobchack, 1988). As found in this and several other recent science fiction films, these spatial elements have risen to the status of authoritative pronouncements not just on the supposed wonders of the computer, but on nothing less than the "cultural logic of late capitalism." It is remarkable about these cinematic representations and their critical interpretations that they exhibit such a close similarity between the social viewpoints of the creators of popular cultural commodities and "Marxist" literary critics. That mass culture merchants and supposed counterculturists would engage in such mutual flattery and collaboration is deeply disturbing to this writer. It is a broad phenomenon in our culture today, best epitomized by the recent "hip" commercial William Burroughs did for Nike and discussed in detail elsewhere (Hayward, 1993; Roszak, 1994; Savan, 1994). More significant here is the question of how this common elite viewpoint is received by the mass audience.

Kinetically led into this space through the concrete narrative, the audience is subjected to a visual environment that is rather drastically at odds with common-sense notions of what is natural, or even real. In those films, like *TRON*, whose narratives employ a reassuringly conventional action-adventure plot structure—in which we know in advance that the good guys will beat the bad guys and all problems will be solved by the end of the story—it seems that the mise-en-scene would make little more impression than that of an extended chase scene through an amusement park. In more recent cyberspace-related films, such as *The Fortress, Future Shock, Ghost in the Machine, Homewrecker, Mind Warp,* and *Lawnmower Man,* the "trip" into this new realm tends toward the generic conventions of the horror film: not an encouraging sign. For whatever our "liberated" postmodernists may say about horror visually articulating "anxieties about the body" (Whose body? Whose anxieties?), the nonmonstrous characters in these films seem to want to keep their bodies in one solid piece, untechnologically modified and alive (in the traditional sense of the term). I assume that the audience goes along in reacting negatively to the mise-en-scene.

Yet most revealing of the postmodernist/audience media interface as expressed through the interaction of narrative and mise-en-scene are those works that tend toward the conventions of the detective novel and the film noir. The novel *Neuromancer* (Gibson, 1984), although not a film, plays a prominent role in discussions about representations of cyberspace. What is remarkable about this book's reception is the tendency of the technophilic not even to notice its unremitting pessimism, to, in the author's words, "read me and just take bits, all the cute technology, and miss about fifteen levels of irony" (cited in McClellan, 1989, p. 70). Utopian prophesying tends to be based on descriptions of the story's setting (the print equivalent of mise-en-scene) without taking much account of what effects that setting is having on the characters, their actions, or the plot generally. For those who have an interest in the characters and what happens to them, the conventions of the narrative set up a number of expectations that, depressingly, are never fulfilled: expectations of desire, love, coherence, and purpose. Trapped within a mad technological environment, the characters' human impulses wither.

A similar yet not quite so hopeless example is the film *Blade Runner,* which, although not explicitly centered around conceptions of cyberspace, is considered by many to be a prime example of the expression of the postmodern (and cyberpunk) through its mise-en-scene. What is especially ironic about this film is that the director, who is known primarily for his talents in scene design, was forced by the producers to strengthen the narrative elements of the film before they would release it. This primarily involved the addition of a voice-over narration that stressed the protagonist's struggle to find coherence in his bizarre surroundings as well as to answer questions about his own humanity. A small cult has formed around the later-released "director's cut" of the film, as postmodernists pick over the symbolism of scenic details. Yet it seems to me that the producers knew the mass audience's reaction to this environment and insisted that it be incorporated into the narrative.[1]

---

[1]For more about reactions to postmodern elements of recent science fiction films, especially the reemergence of film noir elements as signs of opposition, see Lippert (1993).

What this all amounts to, I think, is a situation in which postmodernists and typical audience members see very different things in these films. Although the former embrace concretely glowing schematizations as symbols of conceptually glaring cultural prognostications, the latter struggle to maintain an existential footing on the narrative path. Dazzling one another in their kaleidoscopic dance of antifoundationalist imagery, the postmodernists fail to see the significance, indeed, even proclaim the "obsolescence," of narrative as it is known to the average person. But for the audience, it is the narrative that grounds the experience of images in the human lifeworld, which is where this experience ultimately originates. It is in this lifeworld that humanity has found what Susanne Langer (1939) calls "charged" symbols of life orientation since time immemorial. But as science and technology increasingly have distanced us semantically and experientially from this lifeworld, our ideas and their images have become similarly remote.

As ever-more brave new abstractions materialize on the cinema screen, the audience encounters them on their narrative journey. The narrative paths chosen so far seem to approach these "spaces" and "things" from such a perspective that they seem artificial and unreal to most people. Perhaps it is that they do not understand, that in their concrete modes of thought they cling to nostalgic notions of what is natural. But perhaps it is that they understand only too well, that in such spaces they recognize the alienated existences that they have already begun to live in the "space" of their daily lives.

## REFERENCES

Bukatman, S. (1993). *Terminal identity: The virtual subject in postmodern science fiction.* Durham, NC: Duke University Press.

Gibson, W. (1984). *Neuromancer.* New York: Ace Books.

Havelock, E.A. (1963). *Preface to Plato.* Cambridge, MA: Harvard University Press.

Havelock, E.A. (1976). *Origins of western literacy.* Toronto: Ontario Institute for Studies in Education.

Hayward, P. (1993). Situating cyberspace: The popularisation of virtual reality. In P. Hayward & T. Wollen (Eds.), *Future visions: New technologies of the screen* (pp. 180-204). London: British Film Institute.

Langer, S.K. (1939). *Philosophy in a new key.* Cambridge, MA: Harvard University Press.

Lanham, R.A. (1993). *The electronic word: Democracy, technology, and the arts.* Chicago: University of Chicago Press.

Levinson, P. (1979). *Human replay: A theory of the evolution of media.* Unpublished doctoral dissertation, New York University, New York City.

Lippert, P.J. (1993). Beyond postmodernism in science fiction film. In M.T. Newman (Ed.), A *rhetorical analysis of popular American film* (pp. 117-134). Dubuque, IA: Kendall/Hunt.

McClellan, J. (1989, December). From here to reality. *The Face,* p. 70.

Ong, W.J. (1951). Psyche and the geometers: Aspects of associationist critical theory. *Modern Philology, 49,* 16-27.

Ong, W.J. (1967). *The presence of the word.* New Haven, CT: Yale University Press.

Ong, W.J. (1982). *Orality and literacy: The technologizing of the word.* New York: Methuen.

Roszak, T. (1994). *The cult of information* (2nd ed.). Berkeley: University of California Press.

Savan, L. (1994, September 6). Over-the-counter-culture: Corporations harvest hip. *Village Voice,* pp. 50-53.

Sobchack, V. (1988). *Screening space: The American science fiction film.* New York: Unger.

# SECTION *4*

# MEANING:
# CYBERCOMMUNICATION
# AND CYBERCULTURE

Communication abhors a vacuum. Electronic communication calls into being electronic space. Computer-mediated communication (CMC) calls into being computer-mediated space. That these new spaces are much more than alternatives to physical space is a point that is central to this volume. As products of communication, they constitute new forms of social space; this is the case for all forms of electronic communication, but doubly so for interactive media such as the telephone and the computer. Although in some ways cyberspace mimics and substitutes for actual locations and forms of transportation, performing social functions and imitating the form of physical reality, in other ways we are introduced to an entirely new set of phenomena. And as part of the process of adapting to such new and different environmental factors, we change the ways in which we communicate, both in format and in content. Communication adjusted to meet the demands and biases of cyberspace is cybercommunication, and as communication and culture are intimately linked (to some they are consubstantial), culture itself is also altered. Thus, the focus of this section is on the ways in which cyberspace is influencing both communication and culture.

Human communication is characterized by the use of symbol systems; we compose our messages by drawing on established codes. This is the subject of the first chapter in this section, Judith Yaross Lee's study of the codes of electronic mail. Surveying the various forms of text-based, computer-mediated interpersonal communication, Lee argues that the symbol systems of cyberspace combine literate, oral, and iconic modes, juxtaposing novel symbols and familiar forms in new and unprecedented ways. Thus, Lee believes that it is through the combinations in particular that a unique and distinctive form of rhetoric has emerged in cyberspace. One of the most discussed phenomena associated with this form of cybercommunication is flaming; it is also one of the most misunderstood, as Philip Thompsen demonstrates in this section's second chapter. His analysis provides extended theoretical discussion of online hostility, offering a model that frames flaming as both a message encoded by a source and a meaning decoded by a receiver and therefore influenced by a variety of factors on both sides of the transaction.

As a site of new forms of communication, cyberspace gives rise to new cultural formations and entirely new forms of culture. CMC is commonly used as an abbreviation for computer-mediated communication, but could just as well stand for computer-mediated culture, also known as cyberculture. But culture also implies continuity, and Douglas Rushkoff, in the third chapter in this section, argues that the culture industries have colonized cyberspace. He describes the process as a form of information warfare. Placing cyberspace in the historical context of cultural imperialism, Rushkoff argues that cyberculture has been coopted by commercial interests, rendering true cybercommunication impossible. In the final chapter, Lance Strate explores the neglected topic of cybertime both as supplement and alternative to the notion of cyberspace. As much a part of any communication context as the sense of place, time according to Strate is central to the formation of culture, community, identity, and, ultimately, meaning. Strate explores the characteristics of cybertime resulting from computer technology's time-keeping functions, from computer media's ability to present symbolically a sense of "virtual time" and from the individual's experience of time when interacting with and through computers.

Throughout this section, the core issue is the problem of generating meaning in a electronic environment. As new codes and new forms of signification are developed against the ground of the cyberscape, new meanings and new ways to make meaning are born. Moreover, meaning cannot be confined to cyberspace itself. Cyberculture has its origins in the "new culture" of computer professionals and hobbyists, which itself is changing as more and more members of the general public find themselves going online. At the same time, the impact of cyberspace and cybercommunication extend beyond the electronic domain. American culture and Western culture in general are influenced by and converging with cyberculture, itself becoming increasingly synonymous with global culture.

# 19

# Charting the Codes
# of Cyberspace: A Rhetoric
# of Electronic Mail*

## Judith Yaross Lee

*At present, communication in cyberspace generally takes place by entering data through an alphanumeric keyboard. As such, cybercommunication by electronic mail, conferencing, discussion group, or live "chat" is an extension of such older forms as writing, printing, and typing. Thus, the media code of electronic mail and related genres borrows heavily from the conventions of typography and letter and memo writing, as Lee makes clear in this chapter. She argues, however, that e-mail diverges significantly from preelectronic writing and printing, and even from such channels as the electronic book and hypertext, by retrieving elements of oral media such as telephone conversations, oral performance, and face-to-face communication; e-mail produces a sense of immediacy and informality missing in more traditional relationships between writer and reader. Lee therefore argues that*

---

*My thanks to the many people who have generously helped me research and compose this chapter: Rita Rahoi of the School of Interpersonal Communication at Ohio University, for her skillful assistance in the library and her patient downloading of some 500 e-messages; Joe Amato of the Humanities Department at Illinois Institute of Technology, for his gracious sponsorship of this project to the members of the *Technoculture* list; Sue DeWine, Director of the School of Interpersonal Communication at Ohio University, for sharing her e-mail correspondence; and Lance Strate, of the Communications Department at Fordham University, for his sensitive commentary on an earlier draft of this essay.

*e-mail is a hybrid medium, "a junction where orality and literacy, in their extreme or purest forms, meet." Consequently, e-mail also brings into play nonverbal iconic elements such as the emoticon or smiley face :-) as well as other innovations in the use of typographic characters for visual and affective communication. Thus, Lee demonstrates that communication through this new cyberspatial code constitutes a new and highly significant form of rhetoric. Outside of Section 4, a different type of rhetorical analysis can be found in Charles U. Larson's Burkean exploration of virtual reality in Chapter 6; see also Frank Dance's argument that cybercommunication constitutes a form of speech. Other examinations of textuality include Neil Kleinman's historical study of intellectual property in Chapter 4, Jay David Bolter's comparison of text and VR in Chapter 7, Stuart Moulthrop's discussions of the future of the book in Chapter 15, Camille Paglia's essay on online publishing in Chapter 16, and Stephanie Gibson's overview of hypertext and education in Chapter 17.*

Communicating in any medium calls for choosing from the sign systems we call codes, which constitute form and content, matter and manner. Some codes are imposed by the medium, some sanctioned by social authorities, others entirely novel, still others adapted from ancillary purposes. Not every choice succeeds, but even failure invokes social and textual meanings, and the result is always rhetoric. Any new medium can illustrate how rhetors adapt existing codes to new situations, but electronic mail (e-mail) offers a unique look into the emerging codes of cyberspace. Often referred to as *computer-mediated communication* (CMC) because it involves the online composition and retrieval of electronically transmitted text, e-mail actually embraces several distinct genres: personal correspondence (dyadic communication), public announcements (varying from small group notices to mass messages, akin to flyers and junk mail), discussion lists (sometimes called *bulletin boards*, or simply *lists*, which involve messages between dyads and among small groups of members), and e-conferences (which attempt to replicate small or large group discussion). Through its particular union of the textual and the oral, e-mail constitutes cyberspace: it is a social site where messages, rather than people, meet. This chapter presents a rhetoric of electronic mail[1]—describing, classifying, and explicating the codes used in e-mail messages—in order to map the new territory we call *cyberspace*.

In the 40 years since Marshall McLuhan (1964) claimed in *Understanding Media* that "the medium is the message,"[2] examinations of orality and literacy have confirmed that language changes when communication media shift. Such examinations have, however, focused more on characterizing the effects of print than on interpreting the impact of electronic interaction. The

---

[1] I am following the examples of Kenneth Burke in *A Rhetoric of Motives* (1950) and Wayne Booth in *The Rhetoric of Fiction* (1961) *and A Rhetoric of Irony* (1974) in using *rhetoric* to denote a communication phenomenon, the analysis of that phenomenon, and the text presenting the analysis.

[2] The phrase serves as the title of the first chapter of *Understanding Media*.

classic history of economics and politics in the Renaissance and Reformation by Elizabeth Eisenstein (1979), *The Printing Press as an Agent of Change*, probably the most authoritative account of how media affect culture, antedates the computer revolution. The provocative discussions of rhetoric and secondary orality in Walter Ong's *Orality and Literacy* (1982) and Eric Havelock's *The Muse Learns to Write* (1986), among other scholarship from the early 1980s (Pattison, 1982; Tannen, 1982; Scribner & Cole, 1981), likewise appeared before the personal computer left its mark on the writing of individuals. The theorists who have undertaken to explain the impact of the computer on written language, on the other hand, largely ignore electronic mail and, perhaps because of our culture's bias toward print, emphasize instead the product-oriented aspects of electronic communication. Michael Heim (1987), for example, takes up word processing in *Electric Language;* Jay David Bolter's *Writing Space* (1991) and George P. Landow's *Hypertext* (1992) look at hypertext narratives. Richard A. Lanham (1993) does consider the rhetorical dimension of many varieties of *The Electronic Word*, as he calls it in a text tantalizingly issued in both conventional codex and Macintosh diskette, yet his cultural argument, like James J. O'Donnell's in *Avatars of the Word* (1998), remains high above the daily reality of e-mail—as does Mark Poster's analysis in *The Mode of Information* (1990), although his chapter "Derrida and Electronic Writing" describes some e-mail phenomena. Discussions explicitly about e-mail, by contrast, for the most part ignore philosophical, cultural, and rhetorical implications (an exception is Thompsen & Ahn, 1992, whose title makes the point: "To Be or Not to Be: An Exploration of E-Prime Copula Deletion and Flaming in Electronic Mail"). Instead, discussions of e-mail tend to focus rather narrowly on how organizations can set up and manage effective networks (see, e.g., Caswell, 1988; Radicati, 1992; Vallee, 1984).

The hybrid nature of e-mail has important consequences for the form and content of its messages, whose textual conventions are evolving and stabilizing with use. With its immediate electronic transmission of typographic text, e-mail stands midway between the telephone call and the letter. As the materiality and formality of the typed letter yield to the immediacy and intimacy of the telephone call, e-mail messages not only contain less contextualizing or background information than the business letter, but also flaunt informal vocabulary, phonetic spellings, and colloquial sentence structures. Appropriately enough, considering that cyberspace is quite literally neither here nor there, correspondents in this virtual community use codes reflecting both orality and literacy. In addition to its own insiders' jargon, e-mail has given rise to new paralinguistic signs (including nonverbal symbols such as the happy face and typographical glyphs such as the column of greater than signs [>] used to indicate words quoted from a previous message) that exploit the technology of the computer keyboard and screen. This chapter examines writers' rhetorical choices in two dominant genres of e-mail messages: individual correspondence and the Internet bulletin board (or *list*), in which people metaphorically "post" messages for anyone interested to see. Discussion in the

*Technoculture* and *Voices* lists featured here ranges from the personal to the professional—academic considerations of technology and culture in the former, a women's hypertext collective in the latter. The e-textual counterparts of naturally occurring talk exemplify e-mail in its social contexts, whereas the list members' sophistication as writers and e-mail users gives them particular insight into e-mail phenomena. Contrasting messages from both e-mail genres with their conventional textual and oral counterparts shows how cyberspace is changing the written word.

Social psychologists have observed that the absence of "a distinctive etiquette" forces users of new communication technologies to learn new ways of behaving toward information and each other (Kiesler, Siegel, & McGuire, 1984). E-mail conventions, as constructed democratically online, constitute just such an etiquette, in both the descriptive sense of "common practice" and the prescriptive sense of "appropriate practice." Prescriptive rhetoric has tended to dominate discussion, however, largely because Anglo-American writing has institutionalized the elitist concept of "reputable custom." As the Scottish theorist George Campbell (1776/1963) defined it in his influential *Philosophy of Rhetoric*, "reputable custom" arises from the premise that "the generality of people speak and write very badly" (p. 141). Campbell's work incorporated some of the 18th-century's most advanced ideas about psychology and philosophy, but his notion of reputable use reflects the social politics of the late Middle Ages, when the medieval *ars dictaminis* (art of letter writing) offered instruction in the rhetorical practices of the elite.[3] From a political standpoint, the *ars dictaminis*, like Campbell's notion of reputable use, extended the elite class's power of credible written communication down to the lower classes.

E-mail rhetoric, on the other hand, reflects the democratizing power of computers. Despite the universal recognition of e-mail's ability to flatten hierarchies, many people fail to see how that same power elevates common use over reputable use. In the 20 years since Peggy Porter (1984) asked plaintively, "Where is the Emily Post or Miss Manners to help us enter this alien culture which we have newly encountered?" discussions of e-mail etiquette have tried to comply by offering lists of do's and don'ts.[4] Their efforts are as futile as those of

---

[3]Until fairly recently, etiquette books explicitly aimed to teach members of lower classes the behavioral rules of the aristocracy. In that sense, they also followed the pattern of the *ars dictaminis*. Such instruction presumes, of course, that people outside those elite groups need skills to function within them. Even today, candidates for upper management seek guidance in acquiring suitable manners, and parents chide their children for behavior that seems "vulgar"—common. More obviously, contemporary models abound for correct business letters, wedding invitations, and the like.

[4]More recently, Philip Elmer-Dewitt (1994) of *Time* asked, "If e-mail represents the renaissance of prose, why is so much of it so awful?" (p. 66). See also Goode and Johnson (1991), who recommend that users proofread messages for spelling errors before pressing the send button, and tailor content and tone to the culture of the intended audience, among a dozen other "guidelines . . . in the spirit of encouraging electronic mail and networking" (p. 64). Experienced users seem to recognize the futility of such recommendations. Dern (1994), for example, includes a section on "Netiquette" in his chapter on Internet citizenship, but he focuses on social rather than linguistic rules.

English teachers who insist that *everyone* needs a singular pronoun, not *their*. The top-down rhetorical practices of literate culture do not apply to oral culture, in which everyone does *their* own thing.

E-mail's immediacy and democratic power have their nearest parallels in oral communication, but e-mail is not an oral medium; rather, e-mail converts correspondence into a virtual conversation. In this new genre of mock-oral prose, much as in such older examples as Mark Twain's *Adventures of Huckleberry Finn* (1884/1985), literate and oral codes mingle and swap juices.[5]

## RHETORICAL IMPLICATIONS OF E-MAIL FORM

Even familiar functions take new forms as codes adapt to cyberspace. E-mail messages, for example, alter the basic format of the typewritten memorandum, which standardizes correspondence with its rigid to-from-date-subject template. As McLuhan (1964) has argued, such standardization is one of the hallmarks of alphabetic literacy, and it has carried over into e-mail, which transmits typographical messages electronically. Most e-mail systems require a sender to fill in a memo template with its prescribed "To," "From," and "Subject" lines. Because it reveals both sender and receiver at the very beginning, e-mail has no need for the conventional "Dear John" or "Sincerely, Sue" of paper correspondence. The absence of a salutation and closing alters the familiar dynamic of correspondence, revealing in the process important differences between electronic and paper language.

From the reader's standpoint, the receipt tracing (e.g., "Received 25-Jan-1994 02:24pm") at the bottom of the screen or printout signals the end of the message. As the last element in the message, the tracing confirms the end of communication in much the same way as the blank space at the end of a letter or memo. Formalist theory suggests that the blank space at the bottom of a page confirms (with the redundancy typical of complete communication) elements in the text, such as the closing phrase and the writer's name, that declare the message complete. That is, as the textual equivalent of the phone call's "thanks for calling" or "good talking with you," the closing phrase provides a transition between the body of the message and the final textual element, the signature or name indicating that

---

[5] I am indebted to Shelly Fisher Fishkin (1993) for the connection between *Huckleberry Finn's* mixed codes (African-American and Euro-American, in her case) and Huck's preference for a "barrel of odds and ends . . . [where] things get mixed up, and the juice kind of swaps around, and the things go better" (p. 2). Although mock-oral prose is best known in Mark Twain's writing, it was already a familiar technique to Americans by the 1830s in the Down East writings of Seba Smith's Jack Downing (see, e.g., Blair & Hill, 1978).

the correspondent is, quite literally, signing off. The power of writing to reorder time and space asserts itself in the convention by which writers reveal themselves by name only at the end.[6] Thus the blank space that follows the text reassures the reader that the writer has said goodbye (unless there is a P.S., or postscript, which by definition means "after the writing"). These conventions need to be invented for the computer writing space. Because a blank screen would bring anxiety, not reassurance, basic e-mail systems signal "end of text" with additional text, the receipt tracing. E-mail software for the wide consumer market deflects anxiety with graphics rather than text; a metaphorical paper letter appears on the screen, framing the message, including any blank space not filled by text, with a graphic border around the edge of the screen to simulate a piece of paper. The program also attaches a signature file (but not a signature) when the message is sent.

In contrast to the software solution, the typical e-mail writing space invites correspondents to revise how they signal the end of their messages. Although some writers import the conventional "Sincerely yours, Joe," from paper mail, the usage has not caught on. In fact, John Seabrook (1994), writing in the *New Yorker* of his early e-mail exchanges with Bill Gates of Microsoft, reports that he began to view his own use of "Dear Bill" and "Yours, John" as an "etiquette breach" (p. 48) after observing how Gates began and ended his messages abruptly, without either salutation or closing phrase. Reliance on the familiar boundary markers of the paper letter underlines not only our tendency to understand new technologies in terms of older ones—as early rhetorics imposed the values of oral performance on writing—but also our insecurity with the lesser redundancy of electronic communication, compared with print. Electric language is, as Mark Poster (1990) has observed, immaterial.[7] Conventions based on material media like ink and paper do not quite fit.

The immateriality of the written trace contrasts sharply with the multiplication of copies of stored versions—whether in backup disks or tapes or in printouts—as anyone in a so-called paperless office can attest. Richard Lanham (1993) has recognized the basic paradox involved: "The electronic word embodies a denial of nature" (p. 18) so that we now can have our cake, eat it, *and* give it away to someone else! Despite e-mail's similarity to talk, which remains the most ephemeral communication medium in general use, at least one e-mailer suspects that "the memory for digital signs will be _longer_ [sic] than that of written signs. Perhaps even as long as the life of signs on clay tablets!" He has reason to think so: A total stranger once presented him with a printout "nicely preserved under a plastic cover" of a posting he had made some three years

---

[6]The convention also suggests that personalized stationery represents an effort to assert the political over the technical.

[7]The term *electric language* is from Michael Heim (1987). On the power of the computer to "dematerialize the written trace," see Poster (1990, p. 111). The immateriality of all language is, of course, an ongoing topic among contemporary theorists—especially followers of Derrida—who begin by exploding the structuralist union of sign and signified as a metaphorical convenience and extend the argument to include all attempts to inscribe thought.

earlier (*TNC*, 1993, March 29, 2:29 p.m.). Nonetheless, some danger exists of what one scholar called "fetishizing . . . the digital sign," which in its immateriality grants digital language particular powers or limitations of signification, a viewpoint that ignores "the failure of the sign (any sign) to capture the saturation of meaning or narrative/descriptive closure it appears to promise" (*TNC*, 1993, April 3, 9:14 a.m.). At the very least, the paradox that makes e-mail texts at once both durable and fragile comes across in the greater redundancy of some components than others.

The reliance on print-based boundary conventions may be more common among novice users and writers who export regular computer text via e-mail than among correspondents composing online. But frequent e-mailers adopt one of three distinct conventions. Many sign off with only a word or phrase: "Thanks!" is common; Gates ended one letter "Enough for now" (Seabrook, 1994, p. 54). Others use informal renderings of their names. Prevailing usage favors first name only or initials (sometimes in lower case and usually without periods or spaces between the letters), but communication between strangers sometimes leads to use of first and surnames (almost never including middle names or initials). Familiarity is the general rule. Among friends, that can lead to intimate in-talk, as when an American professor on leave in Israel signed himself "Dovidl," the diminutive of his Yiddish—not Hebrew—name, which would be used mainly by family members. Given the redundancy of any of these solutions to the problem of closure, however, many writers opt for a third practice: They simply stop writing. Adopting this approach requires strong faith in e-mail technology and the durability of the electronic word.

Requiring the user to fill in the e-mail template before beginning a message means that every e-mail message designates an addressee from the very start. E-mail thus confirms Mikhail Bakhtin's claim that every utterance "is oriented toward an addressee" (Voloshinov, 1973, p. 85). It also identifies the sender. Most e-mail software automatically generates a "from" line revealing at the very least the sender's user ID, if not the complete electronic address (e.g., "PP609" or "LEEJ"). The address communicates other information as well. Internet messages reveal through their address syntax the name of the sender's computing unit, the institution or organization, occasionally the brand of computer system (*vax*, for instance, referring to the DEC mainframe), and the network domain (e.g., *bitnet, edu, gov, uk, com*).

Every element of the address thus has the potential (not always exploited) to carry social meaning as well as technical information. Although user IDs may simply contain someone's name or assigned code, they may also express personal interests or politics (e.g., "feminist"). Subdomains sometimes contain puns or acronyms, as when Ohio University changed its name from *UCLS* (University Computing and Learning Services) to *CATS* (Computer and Technology Services). Of greater social interest, however, is the network or top-level domain, which identifies networks as American or international, and indicates which of the former belong to educational, government, or commercial systems. The Internet grew out of links among research and governmental computing systems, so addresses on these networks have higher status than those of such Johnny-come-latelies as America Online (whose domain is *aol*). Another indicator of status is one's proximity to the "Net"—that is, the number of subdomains in one's address. The shorter one's address, the higher one's status (Lohr, 1994), perhaps because a longer address provides more information about a sender, thereby defining the person more by function and membership than by personal traits. Viewed through a metaphorical mailbox or list of new messages received, these addresses function much like envelopes, allowing the receiver to attach priorities to messages even before reading them. The template thus links e-mail to its literate origins in the memorandum.

As a negative consequence of the template's information, e-mail has acquired what Andrea Ovans (1992) has called "the pitfalls of the memo culture" (p. 128), whereby people pretend not to have received a message, answer only those messages that suit them, or toss into the wastebasket (if only metaphorically) messages they dislike. But other consequences of the template are more positive. Having the sender's name at the beginning of a message, and sometimes at the end as well, gives e-mail a more casual, personal character than a printed letter. Although the ease of e-mail fosters the distribution of junk messages and unnecessary "I agree" replies, it can also discourage formal, institutional pronouncements. Sending an anonymous or institutional message may require a user to exert special effort, such as logging on under a new account or shifting to another predefined memo layout. From a visual standpoint, shifting layouts seems the electronic equivalent of changing from one kind of stationery to another, but from a rhetorical perspective it represents exchanging one's individual persona for institutional facelessness. In fact, a recent case study suggests that such official messages tend to appear on paper rather than e-mail (Deatsch, 1994). The less formal purpose of e-mail thus combines with its personal face to compress the distance between writer and reader. In that sense, by discouraging anonymity, e-mail captures for writing some of the personal presence of face-to-face communication.

## The Textual Self

Not that anonymous messages or false representations are impossible. Some e-mail software permits users to define several "personalities," or profiles. People are always free, in whatever medium they use, to adopt a new persona for a new interaction. I remember as a teenager playing a game in which my friends and I gave false names and telephone numbers to boys we met at the beach, and college students routinely come home for winter vacation with new nicknames or modes of interaction. Internet folklore recounts many examples of falsified genders, ages, and other personal factors. A recurring theme focuses on the opportunity to hide behind one's e-mail text—for good or ill.

The ill effects of the invisible persona have received the most attention. Deborah Tannen (1994), editorializing in a sidebar to a *Newsweek* feature on e-mail, specifically blames "the anonymity of networks" for emboldening some men to "deluge women with questions about their appearance and invitations to sex" (p. 53)—to harass them in ways that society no longer permits. Although sexual harassment merits serious concern in any context, Tannen's explanation amounts to blaming the messenger for bad news. Because list users commonly enforce social conformity by the practice of *flaming,* overwhelming a violator's mailbox with angry replies sent via the e-mail answer function (a practice that would be impossible if e-mail were truly anonymous), facelessness and network morality are more likely contributing factors than first cause.

That honor probably goes to gender imbalance. An academic study by Eric Jorgensen (c. 1994) of MIT estimates that Internet discussion lists are about 87% male.[8] Why would the male-dominated groups of cyberspace be more willing than the male-dominated clubs and workplaces of a few years ago to make women welcome? Or to discourage their members from making sexually provocative comments to women? Jorgensen's decision to censor his own message in anticipation of being flamed illustrates how flaming promotes social conformity, but because complaints constituted only 0.00657, rather than the 0.50 he expected, it is unclear whether the strategy was successful or unnecessary.[9] Women have already begun insisting that online intimidation stop (Price, 1993), and experience suggests that network users' tolerance for online harassment will diminish as the political power that women have achieved in other arenas extends to cyberspace. After all, only recently have sexual jokes come to constitute harassment, as opposed to camaraderie, and many Americans today—30 years after the feminist movement was launched—resist even that change.

In contrast to the antisocial few, many other men and women find opportunities for play in the chance to fabricate a textual self. A cartoon in the *New Yorker* a few years ago showed two canine computer buffs gloating that "on the Internet no one knows you're a dog." Similarly, a group of women reportedly collaborated on a series of love letters, a deception they saw as "Cyrano on the internet, with the innocent male cast as Roxanne" (*TNC*, 1993, March 29, 2:29 p.m.). The mere conception of such a ruse indicates that paper texts have no patent on insincerity or fiction. And what's in a name, anyway? Everyone on the *Technoculture* list knows that "Tomato" is Joe Amato, so the pseudonym is no disguise. But it does differentiate this persona from those developed in his other writing and in his personal relationships.

---

[8]Jorgensen's survey of Internet USENET demographics resulted in a sample of 4,566: 86.5% men ($N = 3,948$) and 13.5% women ($N = 615$).

[9]Network administrators also have a vested interest in avoiding inflamatory messages because the resultant flames can cause the computer system to crash. The manager of the system that forwarded two lawyers' advertisement to the Internet was pretty irate himself. "They crashed our computer about 15 times . . . because of the volume of incoming complaints," he fumed. "I lost an entire week dealing with [it]" (Lewis, 1994, p. C1).

## THE RHETORIC OF VIRTUAL CONVERSATION

Women's anger at online harassment reflects e-mail's simulation of social presence. Virtual presence is, of course, what gives cyberspace its sense of place, but it also explains some of the more unusual phenomena of computer communication, including flaming. Conventional correspondence does not lend itself particularly well to heated discussion because of the extended time lag between turns. The whole affair tends to fizzle out after a few angry exchanges have been composed, committed to paper, and sent off—partly because moods and objects of attention shift over time, partly because the effort needed to maintain the fight becomes disproportionate to benefits received from doing so. Telephones offer combatants much more gratification by allowing voice-to-voice confrontation, but one party can gain the upper hand by hanging up. If, as this comparison suggests, verbal fights are a phenomenon enhanced by physical presence, then their appearance on e-mail confirms that cyberspace functions as a physical location where people behave as they do in conventional spaces.

Such an interpretation explains why, as one *Technoculture* member put it, "people feel obligated to 'leave' the list (whether in a tizzy or a huff or just a sad, sad shufflin' away) instead of bringing up another topic to see what happens" (*TNC*, 1993, March 12, 12:19 p.m.). It also explains the case of a woman "who was forced off a list by physical threats from one of the other subscribers" (C. Guyer, personal communication, December 9, 1993) because the threat of violence shows how e-mail communication collapses the distinction between virtual and real communities. The very terms *lurking* and *lurker* for a nonparticipating observer of online discussions suggest the in-group's hostility to nonparticipants—characterized by Internet slang as voyeurs peeking in from the outside—and the idea that lists are clubs for "members only" intensifies the sense of space defined by the participants. One must either participate or leave; lurkers are trespassers. In such a community, in which the metaphorical has become functional, the gendered communication patterns familiar to real-space groups continue to operate. A member of a women's hypertext collective contrasted "the kind of offense/defense maneuvering and displays which happen on other lists like TNC" with the "exceedingly polite" communication of the women's group running the *Voices* list (C. Guyer, personal communication, December 9, 1993). In contrast to the multiple flames within six months of *Technoculture* postings, *Voices* had none. Other women's lists appear equally tranquil (Kantrowitz, 1994).

The memo template's subject line points to a second manifestation of e-mail's lesser redundancy: Writers do not need a full sentence to contextualize their remarks ("I am writing in regard to your letter of November 4, 1993") and may sometimes avoid any reference to their motives for writing. Seabrook (1994) described the subject line as "a little like . . . a publicity release for what you have to say" (p. 52), but the announced subject may in fact have nothing to do with the message. Rather than look up or retype a cumbersome Internet address, senders may choose to reactivate it by invoking the reply mode to an old message. (I have carried on six months of conversation with one friend on varied subjects under the subject line "Re: Testing," which was my answer to her original message to verify my address.) Typically, however, the subject line provides most of the context the writer deems necessary. It may even be the whole message. A writer who titled a message "Lunch Monday noon at Uptown Chinese?" would have little, if anything, to add in the body of the message, whereas a writer who entered "Lunch" in the subject space of the template might need a message as long as "Are you free for lunch on Monday? How about noon at Uptown Chinese?" By contrast with e-mail's opportunities for brevity, telephone calls (as Harvey Sacks, 1992, points out) commonly contain a reason for the call early in the message.

E-mail replies also tend to lack contextual information. Indeed, a reply may consist of only a single word, such as "Thanks!" or "Great!" or a phrase, such as "oh, john. really!" (*TNC*, 1993, March 25, 2:47 p.m.). E-messages may lack substance in ways that paper texts cannot partly because the subject line makes additional explanation redundant, but largely because the reply function compresses actual time between conversational turns. Virtually speaking, no time has elapsed between utterance and reply if I answer a message as soon as I read it. So it makes perfect sense for someone to respond to a message titled "Idea" by writing "Good input! I'm still thinking...." (Sue DeWine, personal communication, May 11, 1994, original ellipses). An e-mail message requires less contextualizing content than a letter or paper memo because the context is already present, as in oral conversation. The same does not apply, however, to the response that reaches *its* destination divorced in time and space from the stimulus message. Only the subject line ("Re: Idea") links a reply to the prior message, requiring the reader to complete the context through memory. The reply itself, of course, becomes an immediate context for the next response, in true dialogic fashion.

Two alternatives have emerged for handling messages when elapsed time disrupts the reading-reply cycle. One is a convention for quoting relevant portions of the stimulus message. Instead of using quotation marks, the familiar literate symbol, to frame or enclose retyped text, e-mail writers typically *import* the text from the previous message into the reply; the software signals the importation with a row of mathematical greater-than signs (>) running down the left margin. This convention brings the past into the present, creating the illusion of zero-elapsed time in replying to it. As the reliance on typographical symbols suggests, this convention adapts the customs of letter writing ("In regard to your letter of May 3, when you requested . . . ") and thereby reflects e-mail's debt to the codes of literacy. The second alternative applies to private e-mail and discussion lists as well as to oral conversation in groups. So much time may have passed between the original message and the opportunity to reply that a context for reply is lost. The result is silence. This circumstance, familiar to students whose teachers finally call on them long after their response had any relevance, represents another similarity between e-mail and oral conversation: Context is created *between* turns rather than *by* turns. In "snail mail," by contrast, the expected time lag between turns diminishes the irrelevance of a delayed answer, even as it increases the need to contextualize that answer.

The virtual conversation created by such turn-taking leads to another affinity between e-mail and oral communication: Breaking off is hard to do. Although an e-mail sequence may end after the requested information has been provided, a few superfluous turns often follow the completion of business: "Glad I could help" might be followed by "Thanks again," which itself might lead to "Looking forward to seeing you at the meeting in October," and (in an extreme case) a final "I'll be there!" Such chatter serves no function related to content; rather, each message confirms receipt of the previous nicety. This phenomenon, however, can exist only when it costs little in time and effort. Interminable goodbyes belong to the jokelore about discussions with friends and neighbors on the front steps (Garrison Keillor once illustrated the problem in song) because the phenomenon belongs to the world of oral, social conversations. The effort and money required for a business letter—or, in some cases, a long distance telephone call—mean that few verbal responses will be generated solely to confirm the receipt of prior messages.

The memo form affects the language of e-mail messages as well as their structure. Perhaps because the memo form has a conventional association with informal, internal communication—between people who already know each other or who share institutional links—the vocabulary and grammar of e-mail lack the formality of many other genres of professional communication. Joshua Meyrowitz (1985) claims that "the more slowly messages are encoded, sent, and received, the more formal their typical content" (p. 110), but a case study of one manager's written communication indicates that encoding and transmission time may themselves be functions of social purpose (Deatsch, 1994). The messages in that study revealed a distinct pattern between medium and purpose: letterhead for official personnel matters, memo format for formal requests and announcements (thereby creating a paper trail for future reference), e-mail for informal requests, announcements, and individual persuasion.

Institutional factors enhance e-mail's informality by establishing a sense of direct communication between equals. High-ranking executives such as Bill Gates of Microsoft answer their own e-mail, whereas secretaries act as gatekeepers over their telephone calls and paper mail. In the process, e-mail exerts democratizing pressure as it bypasses the hierarchies of power and status that telephones preserve. The template itself, with its institutional blandness, eliminates other hierarchical power issues, especially those associated with elegant or prestigious stationery, providing a greater sense than paper allows of communication between equals. Additional factors may also help flatten hierarchies, but the linguistic evidence is clear: The aristocratic formality of writing is diminished—some would say eliminated—in e-mail. In its place, *vox populi, vox Dei.*

## E-MAIL TEXT AS VISUAL TALK

### Slanguage and Mock-Oral Writing

The insiders' jargon that creeps into e-mail content helps drive the informality while also benefiting from it. E-mail's origin as a hackers' medium has a role in the phenomenon, but now even people who cannot tell a spool drive from a punch card speak knowingly about "lurkers on the Net" (people who read but do not contribute to discussion lists) and "snail mail" (regular postal service). Some terms use initials as acronyms or shorthand: btw (by the way), MUD (Multi-User Dungeon), MOO (Multi-User, Object-Oriented), MUSE (Multi-User Simulation Environment), GOK (God only knows), OIC (Oh, I see!). Like other forms of specialized language, jargon helps create and define e-mail communities, and new members embrace the lingo as signs of belonging. (America OnLine provides a glossary for new users.) E-mail replaces the redundancy of formal communication (for instance, a name repeated on the letterhead, in the signature, and typed below) with informal brevity.

Colloquial vocabulary and syntax thereby rule the day. Sentences need not be either complete or grammatical. "Trying to get ahold of you, but the addresses aint working" is a typical example (*TNC*, 1993, March 11, 10:04 a.m.). Punctuation tends to be haphazard ("lets find the common ground by which we may construct bridges between mechanical, electronic and social engineering. My my. I"m [sic] all for that" (*TNC*, 1993, March 12, 8:07 a.m.). Abbreviations abound: One writer curses, apparently in mock anger, "yer a great b-word," whereas another describes a friend as "enthusiastic about the conf at MIT" (*TNC*, 1993, March 11, 6:17 p.m.; S. J. Weininger, personal communication, October 17, 1992). As these examples suggest, deviations from formal grammar usually signify efforts to visualize talk. It would make no *phonetic* difference, for example, if Joe Amato's request to me (personal communication, February 3, 1993)—"I wonder if you could do me a favor (more work, she sez)"—had the correct spelling *says*, but the friendly, casual quality of the text would be lost. The ongoing discussion on computer-mediated conferences and electronic bulletin boards, in particular, fosters such mock-oral writing, which has a long tradition in American popular culture as the textual representation of the colloquial speaker. A skilled writer can imply vocal modulation with considerable precision. One contributor to the *Technoculture* list represented four changes of pitch and tone—musing, aspirated, dropped, raised—in as many sentences: "Lemme see, here. Hoo-kay. (I know I'm gonna regret this, but....) Anyways" (*TNC*, 1993, March 12, 12:19 p.m.; original ellipses). E-mail merges the literate emphasis on sight with the breezy informality of talk, with its many variations of sound.

## Emoticons

More important than e-mail's linguistic variations, however, are the visual symbols called *emoticons*. Illustrations constituted by punctuation marks and other symbols (primarily nonalphanumeric) from the keyboard, emoticons adapt both oral and literate codes. In some ways, emoticons are miniature, screen-based versions of the banners and graphic printouts (e.g., Bugs Bunny composed of *X*'s and *O*'s) that hackers developed more than 40 years ago. Their reliance on characters from the computer keyboard reflects their literate origins. On the other hand, emoticons have more in common with hieroglyphics than with the alphabetic, phonetic writing on which Western literacy is based, and emoticons' visual representation of the speaker or listener's frame of mind brings nonverbal aspects of oral communication to written text. As a hybrid code, the emoticon is a perfect fit for a hybrid medium.

Emoticons have acquired various textual and social uses. Because they are read sideways, an element of play enters the text even before the reader decodes the symbols. Some emoticons exist mainly as jokes, passed along from one person to the next as examples of wit. This category tends toward elegant or complex examples, such as those featured by Tom McNichol (1994) in his introduction to the Internet for readers of *USA Weekend*, a national newspaper supplement:

Charlie Chaplin    C):-(EQ)
Ronald Reagan    7:-)

As these examples illustrate, joking emoticons have very little use in constructing messages. They offer denotation nearly devoid of connotation.

When emoticons do contribute to the meaning of a message, however, they modulate the verbal text rather than substitute for words or phrases. In her study of switching between oral and written language, Denise Murray (1988) saw emoticons (she called them "icons") as transitional signs and predicted that their use would decline as other conventions developed—particularly asterisks (to indicate verbal stress), multiple vowels (for changes in intonation), and multiple question marks and exclamation points (for emphasis). But she mistakenly grouped orthographic conventions for visualizing sound with signifiers of attitude. E-mail writers use pairs of asterisks to indicate that the bracketed word, usually an adjective or adverb but occasionally a verb form, should receive verbal stress. Similarly, multiple question marks or exclamation points signal the reader to intensify the degree of rising intonation in a question or the loudness of an assertion. Both features appear quite clearly in this insistent statement, "Of course none of you are *obliged* to get involved with this!!" (*Voices*, 1994, February 12, 3:49 p.m.), and they indicate that the convention amounts to little more than an adaptation of conventional punctuation to the computer keyboard. Similarly, the list member who wrote "Like I said a loooooooong time ago, I like to tell stories" (*TNC*, 1993, March 14, 1:10 p.m.) relied on conventional rules of English phonics, not specialized codes of cyberspace.

Using emoticons, on the other hand, does require understanding a specialized code. Who among the uninitiated would recognize 8-0 as a sign of astonishment, or know when to use (8-o for "Oh, no! It's Mr. Bill!"? These examples, although extreme, nonetheless illustrate that emoticons are inherently different from alphabetic signs—a difference that explains, in part, why we view them from a different angle. Rather than represent sounds, they represent attitudes. That is, emoticons are literate symbols with no grounding in oral language. Hence, we read them sideways, in a different axis from verbal text.

## The Body in the Text

Ranging from the simple sideways smiley face :-) to elaborate caricatures of public figures, the connotative emoticon serves a simple function: to express an attitude toward the statement that precedes it. The reader must determine from the context, however, whether the emoticon signifies the writer's own attitude or a representation of the attitude that he or she wishes to invoke in the reader. When telecommunications expert Tom Reid (local communication, February 16, 1994, 6:19 p.m.) concluded a systemwide announcement about the establishment of new modem lines and protocols with the statement "You don't have to know what all this jargon means! ;)" the winking face represented his own face, offering good will to the bewildered and confiding technical knowledge to the hackers. In a somewhat different use of a smiley—"If you wish to change something already there you can ask the author of the note to do it! Or argue about it ! :-)" (*Voices*, 1994, February 8, 5:52 p.m.)—a member of a writing collaborative indicated that controversy and conflict were normal, even enjoyable, aspects of the group process. The smiley face can also, however, attempt to suggest or impose an attitude on the reader. The list member who wrote "George, what do you say? I admit I haven't finished your book :-)" (*TNC*, 1993, March 12, 10:04 a.m.) clearly intended the smiley to represent the desired approval from George, urging him to abandon any irritation he might feel about the preceding discussion. As these uses suggest, the emoticon contributes to written communication a sign system usually limited to oral communication: facial expression.

## E-Mail as Performance Space

This inscription of the body into the text, particularly when combined with text as visual speech, explains the tendency of discussion list participants toward the dramatic and oratorical. Alluding to the dialogue conventions of popular dramas enhances the mock-oral dimension of the electronic text. One aggrieved list member portrayed himself as a character in a western, using phonetic spellings to represent the stereotypical cowboy's accent. "Wahl, I kin see we don't want no FED'RAL AGENTS on this list," he charged in the body of his message (*TNC*,

1993, March 12, 2:34 p.m.), and its explicit orality and western inspiration encompass the title as well. The subject line, "WANTED (not)," invokes the posters of criminals in the sheriff's office as it begs the reader to imagine a spoken voice chanting "not!" in the manner of current slang. The dramatic impulse extends from cultural icons to more elaborate metaphors, such as the one constructed by this writer *cum* prospector or tour guide, who represents his writing space as a site with three dimensions:

> Hi . . . uh, wait just a sec, there's some snow drifted across my information superhighway <<STAMP!>> <<STAMP!>> there, got it off my boots, don't want to track it into your nice dry Macintoshes.
>
> Where was I? Right—I want to suggest that . . . (*TNC*, 1993, March 14, 11:24 a.m.)

The playful qualities of these messages remind us, as Meyrowitz (1985) has taught, that electronic media blur work and play, humor and seriousness, along with generational, social, and physical boundaries. In addition, these examples reveal that e-mail—with its blurring of present and past, here and there—inspires writers to try controlling the sound and duration of their messages, just as they would if they were physically present.

Readers join writers in seeing the discussion list as drama. (Readers become writers, of course, when contributing to the discussion.) From their vantage point as spectators, however, dramatic performance concerns not sound and time, but space. Kali Tal, for instance, envisions the list as a dance floor. Defending another list member's post, she argued that discussions need not be orderly and coordinated, but ought to allow each member to choose a suitable mode for participation:

> And it aint that I think the dood is always right . . . or even always on the right track. It's a style thing, a voice thing, a rhythm thing. He doan wanna arm wrestle. He wants to *dance*. Me too. It's a big floor. There's room for us all. (TNC, 1993, March 14, 11:12 p.m.)

Istvan Cizerny-Ronay makes a similar, if less metaphorical, observation. In comparing screen with stage, he recognizes that beyond the oratorical element lies a physical component that he identifies as "presence," using quotation marks to distinguish physical from virtual presence.

> The screen is like a stage. . . . the one thing that holds me fascinated is the performance. . . . the ease of exchange makes opinions and even hard information pre-texts for imaginative "presence." . . . I don't separate the "issues" from the voices. I guess I take the ideas more seriously, the more involved I get with the voice. Not every voice will do. (*TNC*, 1993, March 13, 5:49 p.m.)

Although Cizerny-Ronay *compares* screen with stage, he *identifies* discussion with performance, text with voice, voice with body. He and Tal envision virtual dramas in which they take part, dramas several steps closer to "reality" than the theoretical, metaphorical dramas envisioned by Erving Goffman (1959). In the process, Cizerny-Ronay illustrates the power of the e-mail text to embody the writer while also creating a site for the writer's performance. E-mail thus demonstrates in practice Bakhtin's claim in Part III of *Marxism and the Philosophy of Language* that "a word is a territory shared by both addresser and addressee" (Voloshinov, 1973, p. 86).

## AT THE JUNCTION OF ORALITY AND LITERACY

More important for the purposes of this chapter, the embodiment of the writer in the text clarifies the nature of e-mail's hybridness. Rather than represent a middle ground moderating the characteristics of oral and written language, e-mail constitutes a junction in which orality and literacy, in their extreme or purest forms, meet. One reason is obvious: e-mail adapts the technology of the keyboard, a by-product of print, to the requirements of talk. For instance, the convention of upper and lower case letters, a visual and spatial distinction devised for print, becomes a means for indicating loudness. Similarly, the emoticon converts the finite alphanumeric keyboard into a source of nearly infinite signs. Unlike manuscript characters (which can be varied infinitely) or moveable types (which can be turned sideways or upside down), the standard keyboard restricts the placement of its 107 characters[10] to specific horizontal and vertical positions. Creative combinations of characters in the emoticon's sideways axis allow writers to transcend the keyboard's limitations, controlling and varying the glyphs through which they express meaning as speakers have always controlled and varied their sounds. Reading e-mail is thus akin to reading a musical score: To the initiated, both sound and emotion reside in the text.[11] An experienced e-mail reader can hear the unhappiness in the following report from a member of the *Technoculture* list (*TNC*, 1993, April 9, 9:39 a.m.):

> my first VW [virtual world] experience a few years ago . . . was a virtual kitchen containing virtual appliances. The very first thing that I did was to go over to the stove and put my disembodied hand on one of the burners—I wanted to hear it sizzle. A MAJOR disappointment :- (

Like virtual reality simulators, e-mail seeks to unify textual and physical experience. By requiring us to bend at the neck and look sideways at the message, emoticons transform reading from a mental to a physical process. Both readers' and writers' bodies can be inscribed in the e-mail text.

---

[10]Ten numeric characters and their shift-key alternates, 26 alphabetic characters in upper and lower case, 11 punctuation and mathematical marks with shift-key alternates, and an additional 10 keys, slash, asterisk, and period on the number pad.

[11]For a fascinating discussion of the historical process wherein musical texts became "the music," see Dehnert (1990).

The virtual physicality of reader, writer, and message—despite all our sensory evidence to the contrary—explains some of the difficulties of fitting e-mail into existing rhetorical, social, and legal structures. One writer saw the rhetorical problem in terms that illustrate as well as describe it:

> the notions of textuality I am trying to enact, to emplot myself within, won't fit the technology: this is a space, someone might say, for a ludic post-modernism, the freeplay of digitized signifiers, one in which my insistence on a deliberated, hold-things-together impulses and rhetoric (or poetics, for that matter) is an anachronism that could, should I persist, cost me my sanity. (Or somebody might also say, "Lighten up, jerk!"). (*TNC*, 1993, March 15, 7:14 a.m.)

The conflict expressed here points to parallels between the introduction of e-mail and the introduction of print. According to the classic interpretation by Elizabeth Eisenstein (1979), print decentralized control of information and thus paved the way for Protestant and secular disruptions of political control by the scribal information culture of the Roman Catholic Church. E-mail, similarly, presses against the boundaries of grammar and rhetoric defined by print culture. Moreover, it presses against the boundaries of work and play. In a culture that has seen the work week increase and leisure decline, this paradox of electronic communication points to one of contemporary life's great ironies: Labor-saving devices make more work.

A second paradox centers on e-mail's underlying metaphor, by which we toss messages into a "wastebasket," "open" our "mail," and receive notices of undeliverable messages from a "postmaster." Of course, we really identify bits of magnetic tape for erasure, convert stored signals to glyphs on our screen, and receive error messages from computers that cannot find a match between the addressee's user ID and the one on the message. The metaphorical process, however, elides the distinction between immaterial and material. Speech and the electronic trace on the screen become indistinguishable from writing on paper or magnetic tape. Is e-mail therefore public like speech or television? Or is it private like manuscript writing?[12]

This distinction goes beyond questions of rhetoric or technology to matters of law. When an alumnus of the University of Michigan sought access to senior administrators' e-mail under the state's freedom-of-information law, on the premise that e-mail is analogous to written documents, the university declined on two grounds: first, that e-mail is more akin to telephone calls, which

---

[12]An interesting problem arose in the process of my writing this chapter because some members of *Technoculture* considered their postings private correspondence covered by copyright (which gives control of a letter to the writer, according to the most recent legislation), whereas others saw their work as public presentations. Because all the postings are archived and thus available, like any published text, to whoever chooses to look them up, I saw them as subject to the fair use provisions of publications. Although I have cited by name only those contributors who gave me permission to do so, I have cited by date and title other postings whose writers did not specifically grant permission.

go unrecorded and therefore fall outside the boundaries of the law; second, that the federal Electronic Communications Privacy Act shields the university from screening e-mail to determine whether it concerns public business covered by the state law (DeLoughry, 1994).

As the courts struggle to define how such print-based legal concepts as tampering with the mail and intellectual property apply to electronic communication, the more nebulous questions of social use remain equally challenging for the lay public. May one send a message of condolence by e-mail? A wedding invitation? Must one reply immediately to an e-mail message? The absence of a response within a few days may offend the writer, who may feel like a visitor stranded on the front doorstep knowing that the person inside is ignoring the bell. In that sense, although e-mail systems offer some of the advantages of writing over speech—the chance to deliver an entire thought without interruption, the chance to plan out one's remarks for maximum effect— the receiver holds all the cards in an e-mail conversation, as in other modes of communication. A reader can refuse to open a letter, avoid replying, let the phone ring without answering (or hang it up afterwards), and so on, thereby reminding us that in cyberspace, as in other media, a message is a gambit, an invitation that one may accept or decline. E-mail receivers have further control over the physical form of the message, which they can print on whatever paper and in whatever fonts they choose. In this case, as in others, e-mail intensifies the essential characteristics of both writing and speech.

Although e-mail's rhetorical features express distinctions from conventional writing, telephony, and speech, the conventions of e-mail are as dematerialized and fluid as cyberspace itself, for this hybrid is almost certainly transitional. When interactive digital video merges with e-mail, as computer researchers now predict (Markoff, 1994), the resultant video mail will displace literate textual codes with nonverbal ones. Although this new communication medium will almost certainly rely on familiar facial and body "language," users will find themselves in unfamiliar waters as they attempt, anew, to chart its codes. Nonetheless, the example of e-mail makes clear that communication itself creates cyberspace. Perhaps more important, e-mail demonstrates that natural languages are flexible enough and users creative enough to adapt to new media. As writing and print stabilized and diffused aristocratic dialects and usage, so e-mail is generating new vocabularies and modeling a new rhetoric.

In this sense, e-mail fulfills the goal of alphabetic literacy. As the alphabet renders sound in visual space, so e-mail converts writing to speech. By allowing readers and writers to meet in cyberspace, e-mail repairs the disjunction between authors and their discourse that philosophers from Plato to Derrida have found problematic. Plato's lament in the *Phaedrus* that writing renders a speaker silent becomes Derrida's (1967/1976) complaint in *Of Grammatology:* Writers must die for writing to speak. Although he agrees with Derrida on almost nothing else, Walter Ong (1982) noted, similarly, in *Orality and Literacy,* that writing by definition is "discourse [that] has been detached from its author" (p. 78). Not so for the e-mail writer. The electronic text embodies the author—the virtual speaker who meets the reader, who becomes embodied by a similar process in response. Thus, although e-mail derives from both writing and speech, it does not homogenize traits from each into a synthetic mixture or blend. Rather, like a child, it has some traits from one parent and some from the other, and the combination has a life of its own.

## REFERENCES

Blair, W., & Hill, H. (1978). *America's humor: From Poor Richard to Doonesbury.* New York: Oxford University Press.

Bolter, J.D. (1991). *Writing space: The computer, hypertext, and the history of writing.* Hillsdale, NJ: Erlbaum.

Booth, W.C. (1961). *The rhetoric of fiction.* Chicago: University of Chicago Press.

Booth, W.C. (1974). *A rhetoric of irony.* Chicago: University of Chicago Press.

Burke, K. (1950). A *rhetoric of motives.* New York: Prentice-Hall.

Campbell, G. (1963). *Philosophy of rhetoric* (L.F. Bitzer, Ed.). Carbondale: Southern Illinois University Press. (Original work published 1776)

Caswell, S.A. (1988). *E-mail* (Converging Technology Series). Boston: Artech House.

Deatsch, J.A. (1994). *Investigating the stereotypes: One woman manager's written language.* Unpublished manuscript.

Dehnert, E. (1990). The consciousness of music wrought by musical notation. In J.W. Slade & J.Y. Lee (Eds.), *Beyond the two cultures: Essays on science, technology, and literature* (pp. 99-116). Ames: Iowa State University Press.

DeLoughry, T.J. (1994, January 26). U. of Mich. refuses to release e-mail of administrators. *Chronicle of Higher Education,* p. A28.

Dern, D.P. (1994). *The Internet guide for new users.* New York: McGraw-Hill.

Derrida, J. (1976). *Of grammatology* (G.C. Spivak, Trans.). Baltimore: Johns Hopkins University Press. (Original work published 1967)

Eisenstein, E.R. (1979). *The printing press as an agent of change: Communication and cultural transformation in early-modern Europe.* New York: Cambridge University Press.

Elmer-Dewitt, P. (1994, July 4). Bards of the Internet. *Time, 144*(1), 66-67.

Fishkin, S.F. (1993). *Was Huck black? Mark Twain and African-American voices.* New York: Oxford University Press.

Goffman, E. (1959). *The presentation of self in everyday life.* New York: Anchor.

Goode, J., & Johnson, M. (1991, November). Putting out the flames: The etiquette and law of e-mail. *Online, 15*(6), 61-65.

Havelock, E.A. (1986). *The muse learns to write: Reflections on orality and literacy from antiquity to the present.* New Haven, CT: Yale University Press.

Heim, M. (1987). *Electric language: A philosophical study of word processing.* New Haven, CT: Yale University Press.

Jorgensen, E. (n.d.). *Background: The survey and why I did it.* Unpublished manuscript.

Kantrowitz, B. (1994, May 16). Men, women & computers. *Newsweek,* p. 55.

Kiesler, S., Siegel, J., & McGuire, T.W. (1984, October). Social psychological aspects of computer-mediated communication. *American Psychologist, 39*(10), 1123-1134.

Landow, G.P. (1992). *Hypertext: The convergence of contemporary critical theory and technology.* Baltimore: Johns Hopkins University Press.

Lanham, R.A. (1993). *The electronic word: Democracy, technology, and the arts.* Chicago: University of Chicago Press.

Lewis, P.H. (1994, April 19). An ad (gasp!) in cyberspace. *The New York Times,* pp. C1-C2.

Lohr, S. (1994, June 6). Can e-mail cachet = jpmorgan@park.ave? *The New York Times,* pp. A1, C4.

Markoff, J. (1994, March 13). The rise and swift fall of cyber literacy. *The New York Times,* pp. 1, 5.

McLuhan, M. (1964). *Understanding media: The extensions of man.* New York: McGraw-Hill.

McNichol, T. (1994, January 21-23). Fellow travelers on the info highway. *USA Weekend,* pp. 4, 6.

Meyrowitz, J. (1985). *No sense of place: The impact of electronic media on social behavior.* New York: Oxford University Press.

Murray, D.E. (1988). The context of oral and written language: A framework for mode and medium switching. *Language in Society, 17,* 351-373.

O'Donnell, J.J. (1998). *Avatars of the word: From papyrus to cyberspace.* Cambridge, MA: Harvard Univesity Press.

Ong, W.J. (1982). *Orality and literacy: The technologizing of the word.* London: Methuen.

Ovans, A. (1992). Can e-mail deliver the message? *Datamation, 38*(11), 128.

Pattison, R.P. (1982). *On literacy: The politics of the word from Homer to the age of rock.* New York: Oxford University Press.

Porter, P. (1984). 'Dear PP05': Interpersonal communication and the computer: Entering a brave new world. *Library Hi Tech, 2*(1), 22-27.

Poster, M. (1990). *The mode of information: Poststructuralism and social context.* Chicago: University of Chicago Press.

Price, W.T. (1993, August 6). Harassment goes on-line. *USA Today,* pp. 1B-2B.

Radicati, S. (1992). *Electronic mail: An introduction to the X.400 message handling standards.* New York: McGraw-Hill.

Reid, T. (1994, February 16, 6:19 p.m.). *Higher speed modem pool for off-campus use.* Ohio University All-in-1.

Sacks, H. (1992). May 8: Reason for a call: Tellability. In G. Jefferson (Ed.), *Lectures on conversation* (pp. 773-783). Oxford: Blackwell.

Scribner, S., & Cole, M. (1981). *The psychology of literacy.* Cambridge, MA: Harvard University Press.

Seabrook, J. (1994). E-mail from Bill. *New Yorker, 69*(45), 48-61.

Tannen, D. (1994, May 16). Gender gap in cyberspace. *Newsweek,* pp. 52-53.

Tannen, D. (Ed.). (1982). *Spoken and written language: Exploring orality and literacy.* Norwood, NJ: Ablex.

Thompsen, P.A., & Ahn, D.K. (1992). To be or not to be: An exploration of e-prime, copula deletion and flaming in electronic mail. *Etc., 49,* 146-164.

*TNC.* [*Technoculture* Internet discussion list]. LISTSERV@GITVM1. GATECH.EDU. (INDEX TNC).

*TNC.* (1993, March 11, 10:04 a.m.). Re: Calling David Sewell.

*TNC.* (1993, March 11, 6:17 p.m.). Re: More advice (was: re: voice and authority).

*TNC.* (1993, March 12, 8:07 a.m.). Re: Unwanted?

*TNC.* (1993, March 12, 10:04 a.m.). Re: Bob Black's rant.

*TNC.* (1993, March 12, 12:19 p.m.). Re: Bob Black's rant.

*TNC.* (1993, March 12, 2:34 p.m.). WANTED (not).

*TNC.* (1993, March 13, 5:49 p.m.). Re: Authority.

*TNC.* (1993, March 14, 11:12 p.m.). Amato's staying power.

*TNC.* (1993, March 14, 11:24 a.m.). Authority & community.

*TNC.* (1993, March 14, 1:10 p.m.). Re: Back again, hopping mad.

*TNC.* (1993, March 14, 11:12 p.m.). Amato's staying power.

*TNC.* (1993, March 15, 7:14 a.m.). Re: Amato's staying power.

*TNC.* (1993, March 25, 2:47 p.m.). Re: Brief tangent/fractal expansion.

*TNC.* (1993, March 29, 2:29 p.m.). Re: The evanescence of public e-text.

*TNC.* (1993, April 3, 9:14 a.m.). Re: Texte a texte a fetishism.

*TNC.* (1993, April 9, 9:39 a.m.). Re: Helmets and tears.

Twain, M. (1985). Adventures of Huckleberry Finn. In W. Blair & V. Fischer (Eds.), *The Mark Twain library.* Berkeley: University of California Press. (Original work published 1884)

Vallee, J. (1984). *Computer message systems.* New York: Data Communications.

Voloshinov, V.N. [Bakhtin, M.]. (1973). Verbal interaction (L. Mattejka & I.R. Titunik, Trans.). In *Marxism and the philosophy of language* (pp. 83-98). New York: Seminar Press.

*Voices.* [Internet discussion list]. VOICES-L@ECL.WUSTL.EDU.

*Voices.* (1994, February 8, 5:52 p.m.). Extra links.

*Voices.* (1994, February 12. 3:49 p.m.). Project and paper for C&W conference.

# 20

# What's Fueling the Flames in Cyberspace? A Social Influence Model

## Philip A. Thompsen

*As in any other communication environment, social interaction in cyberspace also includes behavior that may be judged antisocial, such as the widely discussed phenomenon of flaming in computer-mediated communication and cyberculture. Although flaming, as an expression of hostility through the codes of cyberspace, may seem to be a simple and straightforward form of communication, in this chapter Thompsen demonstrates that there is considerable disagreement as to the definition and nature of this phenomenon. Rather than viewing flaming simply as a certain type of message or behavior, Thompsen suggests that flaming involves a relationship established through computer media, and therefore that the interpretation of another's message or behavior as flaming is equally a part of the concept of flaming; in other words, flaming can be understood as an act of decoding as much as an act of encoding. He argues that a broader approach that takes into account the negotiation of meaning, as it is influenced by a variety of factors, offers a better understanding of this phenomenon than explanations that focus on the limited communication modes available through e-mail. Apart from this section of the book, other perspectives on the social character of cyberspatial communication include Gary Gumpert and Susan J. Drucker's essay on social space in Chapter 1, John M. Phelan's critique of cyberculture in Chapter 2, Terri Toles Patkin's profile of the virtual organization in Chapter 12, and Sue Barnes's ecological approach to cyberspace in Chapter 14.*

Consider the following scenario: You have recently subscribed to what you thought was a rather serious e-mail discussion list for scholars in your field. You are reading the messages, trying to follow the discussion, looking for ideas. Seemingly out of the blue, two of the participants get angry, call each other names, use profanity, and hurl out ad-hominem arguments. Then things turn really nasty. You check the return addresses on these messages and discover, much to your surprise, these are not sophomoric punks who have little respect for civility. These are people you know, respect, even admire. What is going on here? Why are otherwise decent folks beating each other up with digital bits of vivid vitriol?

Welcome to the flame wars. If you are wondering what is behind these spontaneous combustions in cyberspace, you are not alone. The phenomenon of flaming has caught the attention of many who engage in computer-mediated communication (CMC), from casual "net-surfers" to serious scholars. The literature on flaming ranges from exaggerated tales of terror to carefully controlled experimental investigations. Yet despite a decade of speculation on the causes and consequences of flaming, there is still little agreement on what is fueling the flames in cyberspace. Many believe the technological constraints of computer media encourage people to lose themselves and let their emotions fly. Others think the population of cybernauts simply has an unusually high concentration of hotheads. And still others feel flaming is merely a reflection of human nature, not much different from other forms of conflict.

Who is right? Perhaps they all are, for what causes flaming depends on how flaming is defined and how narrow the causal boundaries are drawn. The diversity of explanations for flaming reflects more than a rigorous debate over the effects of CMC—it reveals a theoretical fuzziness that hinders the advancement of substantive knowledge claims. To bring flaming into sharper focus, this chapter draws on the "social influence model of technology use" (Fulk, Schmitz, & Steinfield, 1990, p. 121) to provide a structure for the integration of research findings. Although previous studies are cited in support of the model's propositions, the model as a whole remains untested. It is offered, therefore, not as an authoritative representation of the "way things are," but rather as a source for developing testable questions about flaming from within a comprehensive theoretical framework.

Before the model is presented, the chapter first looks at how flaming has been defined, both as an abstract theoretical construct and as a measurable research operationalization. Next is a critique of the major theoretical perspectives guiding inquiry into flaming. In response to this critique, a social influence model of flaming is advanced. The model's propositions are formally stated, and each of the factors identified in the model are described. The chapter concludes by considering the implications and limitations of this model.

## DEFINING FLAMING

The term *flaming* apparently evolved from the "hacker" computer subculture. One of the earliest definitions found in the literature is offered in *The Hacker's Dictionary* (Steele et al., 1983): "to speak rabidly or incessantly on an uninteresting topic or with a patently ridiculous attitude" (p. 158). Although this definition suggests flaming is merely an annoying peculiarity that should not be taken seriously, the term appears to have been broadened over time to include a variety of generally negative antisocial behaviors, including the expression of hostility, the use of profanity, and the venting of strong emotions.

Here is a sampling of some of the definitions of flaming found in the popular and scholarly press:

- speaking incessantly, hurling insults, [and] using profanity (Baron, 1984)
- the practice of expressing oneself more strongly on the computer than one would in other communication settings (Kiesler, Siegel, & McGuire, 1984)
- rudeness, profanity, exultation, and other emotional outbursts by people when they carry on discussions via computer (Eckholm, 1984)
- emotional outbursts of rudeness, profanity, or even exultation among users of computer conferencing systems (Spitzer, 1986)
- heated, emotional, sometimes anonymous, venting by a participant (Selfe & Meyer, 1991)
- rabid, abusive, or otherwise overexuberant outbursts sent via computer (Stewart, 1991)
- impoliteness, swearing, charged outbursts, and often a high use of superlatives (Hawisher, 1992)
- the hostile expression of strong emotions and feelings (Lea, O'Shea, Fung, & Spears, 1992)
- the heated exchange of messages expressing hostility or defensiveness toward others on a computer network (Thompsen & Ahn, 1992)
- insults, swearing, and hostile, intense language (Walther, 1992)
- the spontaneous creation of homophobic, racist, and misogynist language during electronic communication (Dorwick, 1993)
- vitriolic online exchanges (Dery, 1993)
- the tendency to react more critically or with greater hostility over this medium, leading to an escalation of conflict (Rice & Steinfield, 1994).

These definitions for flaming may not at first seem incongruent. But a closer examination reveals some subtle differences. Some emphasize the emotional quality of a message, whereas others focus on the expression of hostility. Some place the locus of flaming in the sending of a message, some in the reception of a message, and some in the exchange of messages. This diversity of definitions begs a number of questions. Is flaming a behavior, a message characteristic, a subjective reaction, or a linguistic genre? Does flaming arise from a relaxing of inhibitions or an intensifying of interpersonal friction? Is flaming reflective of strong tempers, incessant banality, or immature histrionics?

To be fair, theoretical constructs are inherently abstract (Judd, Smith, & Kidder, 1991), and perhaps this diversity of conceptual definitions should be of less concern than the extent to which researchers agree on operational definitions of flaming. In other words, what do researchers measure when they claim to measure flaming? Here the situation is clearly problematic. In their reviews of past research, both Anderson and Walther (1992) and Lea et al. (1992) have noted that flaming has not been consistently operationalized in past research. Widely divergent operational definitions have been employed by researchers in the effort to measure flaming.

For example, many studies have defined flaming in terms of uninhibited behavior, but have operationalized "uninhibited" in very different ways. Some studies counted insults and name calling (Siegel, Dubrovsky, Kiesler, & McGuire, 1986; Weisband, 1992), whereas others measured flirting and the expression of personal feelings toward others (Kiesler, Zubrow, Moses, & Geller, 1985). Sproull and Kiesler (1986) used self-report measures of "increased willingness to communicate bad news or negative information" and the "flouting of social conventions" (p. 1508). Lea and Spears (1991) counted uses of paralanguage and swearing. Still others have employed the categories of Interaction Process Analysis (Bales, 1950) to assess negative socioemotional content (Hiltz, Johnson, & Turoff, 1986; Rice & Love, 1987; Thompsen & Foulger, 1993).

Certainly multiple operationalizations of a construct can be useful in establishing convergent and discriminant validity (Campbell & Fiske, 1959). The diversity of operational definitions may reflect a healthy debate in the research community over the essence of flaming. Yet the work to date has provided little evidence for establishing the conceptual validity of flaming as a research variable. It may not be overstating the case that flaming has been appropriated in some studies as a provocative term to use in the service of advancing various perspectives on media effects. Flaming has been a "hot" topic for CMC research, but as the following critique suggests, we may have been burned in the rush to contain the blaze.


## A CRITIQUE OF PREVIOUS EXPLANATIONS OF FLAMING


A number of nomological nets have been cast to catch the elusive essence of flaming. Deindividuation theory (Festinger, Pepitone, & Newcomb, 1952; Zimbardo, 1969), which suggests that anonymity and reduced self-awareness leads to uninhibited behavior, is one of the most frequently cited explanations for flaming (Kiesler et al., 1984; Lea & Spears, 1991; Spears, Lea, & Lee, 1990;

Sproull & Kiesler, 1991). From this perspective, computer users experience an erosion of self-control by being submerged in a massive matrix of anonymous voices. Citizens of cyberspace develop a kind of mob mentality, in which social norms and constraints are presumably less influential than in "normal" settings. People lose their sense of social identity—they become "deindividualized"— exposing a dry hotbed of uncivilized humanity in which flames are easily ignited.

Social presence theory (Short, Williams, & Christie, 1976) is another popular explanation for flaming. This perspective holds that the inability of CMC systems to transmit much of the social information present in face-to-face interaction leads to more impersonal communication (Hiltz et al., 1986; Rice, 1984; Steinfield, 1986). When people talk face to face, they have a keen sense of the "social presence" of each other; eye contact, facial expression, tone of voice, and other cues contribute much to the quality of the interaction. When people talk online, however, this sense of social presence is greatly reduced by the limitations of the computer as a communication medium. As a result, computer conversations are more impersonal, more blunt, and more likely to produce the kind of friction that leads to flaming.

A third explanation for flaming is offered by the information richness theory (Daft & Lengel, 1986). This perspective holds that CMC systems are relatively inferior for communicating "rich," multifaceted information. Ranking communication media according to their ability to transmit information richness places face-to-face meetings and telephone calls toward the top of the list and e-mail and computer conferencing toward the bottom. Information-rich media foster the reinforcement of a message through extraverbal channels, so less effort is needed to communicate clearly. But information-poor media constrain messages to a limited range of expression—such as the ASCII character set used in many CMC systems—and consequently more information is needed to compensate for this narrow "bandwidth." Because electronic mail messages are typically short and contributions to a computer conference rarely exceed a few lines, ambiguity abounds, intentions are easily misinterpreted—and the slightest spark can touch off a flame war.

Although some empirical evidence has been offered in support of these theories, research findings are largely inconsistent. (For a review of the extant research on flaming, see Lea et al., 1992.) As one critique put it, "in the rush to describe and catalogue effects, theories may have developed and become reified prematurely" (Walther & Burgoon, 1992, p. 52). As a whole, this body of theoretical work has been widely criticized (Baldwin & Holmes, 1992; Culnan & Markus, 1987; Fulk et al., 1990; Walther, 1992; Williams, Rice, & Rogers, 1988). The critique offered here focuses on four points of concern.

First, the influence of time is typically ignored. Most explanations of flaming have adopted some variant of what Culnan and Markus (1987) called the "cues filtered out" perspective. Flaming is said to arise because some of the social and communicative cues used to regulate interaction and inhibit hostile behavior in face-to-face communication—such as indicators of status, facial expression, and tone of voice—are "filtered out" by the computer medium. But there is evidence that, given the time often denied them in experimental comparisons, CMC users develop strategies to overcome the lack of communicative cues (Blackman & Clevenger, 1990; Holmes & Berquist, 1990; Walther & Burgoon, 1992). The influence of time may be crucial in understanding flaming in electronic mail discussion lists and other forms of asynchronous CMC, in which interactions take place over relatively long periods of time. Similarly, the immediacy of response in synchronous forms of CMC, such as the real-time computer conferencing popularized in the "chat rooms" of commercial online services, suggests that the influence of time may be an overlooked factor in understanding how the lack of communicative cues contributes to flaming.

Second, explanations of flaming have typically displayed a bias toward face-to-face communication. As Culnan and Markus (1987) point out, the "cues filtered out" perspective assumes that face-to-face communication is the standard by which CMC should be compared, and "ignores the possibility . . . that the electronic media have capabilities not found in face-to-face communication" (p. 431). In his study of computer conferencing at IBM, Foulger (1990) found evidence that computer media "allow people to communicate in new ways, and perhaps more effectively than has been possible in the past" (p. 89). A perspective that begins with the assumption that face to face offers "the most" and CMC can only provide something "less" may miss valuable insights.

Third, previous explanations of flaming suffer from what Roth (1987) has dubbed "meaning realism." Flaming is said to be found in the objective attributes of a message. From these perspectives, a flame is a flame is a flame; all reasonable observers will be able to tell a flame apart from a message that is not a flame (a flicker perhaps). Few of the extant explanations for flaming consider the interpretation of a communication interaction, yet it may be more theoretically satisfying to acknowledge that flaming emerges when a reader attributes this quality to messages. Flaming does not exist in a vacuum; it requires the "fuel" of interpersonal interaction and the interpretation of that interaction by social actors. From this perspective, flaming is an emerging quality attributed to a sequence of messages by human actors involved in an interpretive process of meaning creation (Anderson & Meyer, 1988; Leeds-Hurwitz, 1992). Put simply, a flame is not a flame until someone calls it a flame.

Finally, explanations of flaming have typically looked for causes in the distinctive characteristics of technology, rather than in the social settings in which technology is used (Baldwin & Holmes, 1992; Fulk et al., 1990). Computer communication media are seen as having relatively fixed, invariant attributes that influence all users in similar ways. Flaming is assumed to be an effect of technology, whereas possible social influences are minimized or ignored. But examination of social influences can be most illuminating (Compton, White, & DeWine, 1991). Lea and Spears (1991) argue that "earlier research underestimated the role of social contextual factors and normative processes in CMC," and that "compared with face-to-face interaction, the social and normative context may be of even greater importance in computer-mediated communication" (p. 299). It is conceivable that flaming may be related less to supposed constraints of technology than to social norms that value uninhibited behaviors (Lea et al., 1992).

In sum, previous explanations of flaming have largely failed to incorporate the element of time, exhibited a myopic bias toward face-to-face interaction, suffered from meaning realism, and typically ignored the role of social influence. Although flaming has been researched from a variety of perspectives, the claims that have been made about flaming arguably rest on shaky foundations. What CMC research needs, to use the words of Steinfield and Fulk (1990), is a stronger "theoretical infrastructure—a tree to which individual findings can be grafted to generate the synthesis and integration needed to support knowledge claims" (p. 13). The following model is an attempt to move toward that goal.

## A SOCIAL INFLUENCE MODEL OF FLAMING

A theoretical perspective on technology that offers promise for providing a more solid foundation for grounding claims about flaming is Fulk et al.'s (1990) "social influence model on technology use." This model evolved from an earlier version, a "social information processing model" (Fulk, Steinfield, Schmitz, & Power, 1987), which in turn drew on the work of Salancik and Pfeffer (1978). Although none of these works originally addressed flaming, they provide a basis for developing a model of flaming that can address many of the weaknesses of previous explanations while yielding new and potentially useful insights.

The social influence perspective holds that the choices people make regarding technology use are neither entirely rational nor entirely subjective, but rather are "subjectively rational." Explanations of media use need to move beyond rational models based on the supposedly invariant influence of technological constraints on behavior and consider the widely variable influence of social environments on the subjective interpretation of behavior. Fulk et al. (1990) argue that:

> The limitation of traditional media use theories is their over-reliance on rational processes to explain the entire range of media-choice situations. A realistic understanding of behavior requires knowledge not simply of objective features of the environment, but also the social milieu that alters and adjusts perceptions of that environment. (p. 127)

A social influence perspective on flaming thus considers both the behavior of flaming and the social negotiation of what that behavior means. To use the terms of Fulk et al. (1990), flaming is both a media use and a media evaluation—a CMC behavior and an interpretation of that behavior. Technological characteristics of the computer medium—such as the lack of nonverbal cues—may indeed contribute to the behavior of flaming, but from the social influence perspective, this is only a partial explanation. A more complete explanation of flaming would account for the sense-making norms that influence people to interpret some CMC behavior as flames. The social influence perspective focuses the effort to explain flaming on articulating the factors that contribute to these two sides of flaming—the behavior of flaming and the interpretation of those behaviors as flaming.

So what are these factors? Fulk et al. (1990) identify a number of factors in their model which, when extended to flaming, provide a framework for integrating previous research. This framework is built on two propositions:

Proposition 1: The behavior of flaming is a function of (a) social influence, (b) media experience and skills, (c) media evaluations, (d) task evaluations, and (e) situational factors.

Proposition 2: The interpretation of flaming is a function of (a) social influence, (b) media experience and skills, (c) media features, and (d) prior use of other media.

These propositions are presented schematically in Figure 20.1. Note that two factors influence both the behavior and the interpretation of flaming: (a) social influence and (b) media experience and skills. These two major influences on flaming are considered next, followed by a discussion of those remaining factors that the model associates with either the behavior or interpretation of flaming.

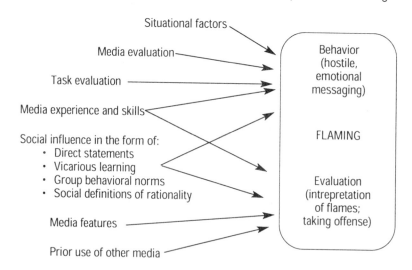

Figure 20.1. A social influence model of flaming

## SOCIAL INFLUENCE

Unlike those explanations for flaming that have focused on technological limitations, social influence occupies a central role in this model, affecting both the behavior and the interpretation of flaming. According to Fulk et al. (1990), social influence may be exerted in at least four ways: (a) direct statements by others, (b) vicarious learning from others, (c) group norms, and (d) social definitions of rationality. Although social influence is not necessarily limited to these four manifestations, these categories provide a useful framework for understanding the impact of social influence on flaming.

### Direct Statements

There is some evidence that flaming may be moderated (or intensified) by direct statements by others outside of the CMC context (Thompsen, 1994). In settings in which CMC is supplemented by face-to-face communication, direct statements relating to an incident of flaming can help douse the fire or fan the blaze. Furthermore, direct statements may contribute to the interpretation of flaming behavior. A hostile e-mail message from someone who is perceived by his or her peers as antagonistic outside of the CMC context is likely to be interpreted (and crafted) differently than a flame from a "cyberspace cowboy"—someone who may be mild-mannered in person, but dons a flamboyant CMC persona when online (perhaps as compensation for failures in interpersonal relationships; see Turkle, 1984).

### Vicarious Learning

People undoubtedly learn much about flaming by watching others flame. When users witness a "flame war," they vicariously learn the techniques and consequences of flaming specific to that incident. One need not participate in a flame to learn about flaming; indeed, many people stay on the sidelines in CMC discussions, preferring to remain quiet spectators, known as *lurkers* in network jargon (Brown, 1984; Romiszowski & deHaas, 1989). Although this area of social influence has yet to be fully explored with respect to flaming, the model suggests a reasonable hypothesis that vicarious learning has a significant influence on both the behavior and the interpretation of flaming.

### Group Behavioral Norms

Although some proponents of deindividuation theory hold that computer media reduces the influence of group behavioral norms, there is some evidence that the opposite is true. Lea and Spears (1991) found group norms to be a significant predictor of flaming, particularly those norms related to the appropriateness of uninhibited behavior. Groups in which uninhibited, aggressive argumentation is the norm are likely to experience quite different flaming behaviors than groups in which the norm is passive acceptance of leadership. In some groups, flaming may be a reflection of shared group norms rather than a violation of common rules of civil discourse.

### Social Definitions of Rationality

What is perceived as rational behavior in one CMC forum (e.g., the USENET newsgroup alt.flaming) could be perceived as quite irrational in another (e.g., the newsgroup misc.kids). Lea et al. (1992) suggest that flaming may be reflective of a "computer hacker subculture" that embraces social definitions of rationality that "run counter to the expectations and standards of industrial or educational organizations from which perspective they might be considered deviant or uninhibited" (p. 23). The definitions of rationality at work in a social environment may be the key difference between those groups that condemn flaming as blatantly vicious hostility and groups that celebrate flaming as an artistic expression of cyberspace machismo.

To review, the model asserts that social influence is one of the major factors contributing to flaming, whether flaming is viewed as an objective behavior or as a subjective interpretation. Social influence, as revealed through direct statements, vicarious learning, group behavioral norms, and social definitions of rationality, represents a potentially significant influence on flaming, one that has yet to receive much attention from the research community. The incorporation of social influence into a comprehensive model of flaming may help illuminate this research opportunity by offering a more culturally sensitive and less technologically dependent explanation.


## MEDIA EXPERIENCE AND SKILLS

Although social influence plays a significant role in this model, flaming is also held to be a function of the experience and skills of those who use computer media. Fulk et al. (1990, p. 125) argue that social information is "more influential for individuals who have less experience and knowledge" of a particular communication technology. In general, those with greater experience and skill in using CMC systems are more likely to be influenced by other factors (such as media features) that reduce the overall significance of social influence in predicting media behavior. Media experience is thus seen as modifying the impact of social influence processes in both the production of flaming behaviors and the interpretation of those behaviors as flaming.

This proposition seems warranted given the literature on flaming. Those with extensive experience in using CMC systems are likely to be more aware of proper "e-mail etiquette" (Goode & Johnson, 1991) than novice users and thus less likely to start a "flame war" inadvertently. Experienced users are also likely to have encountered a range of flaming behaviors, from a "mild scorch" to a "roaring blaze." This experience may temper their tolerance levels for hostile messages, influencing the interpretation of what constitutes a salient incident of flaming. Experienced users develop skills in "flame management," such as clearly delineating flaming content with the phrases FLAME ON and FLAME OFF (Sproull & Kiesler, 1991), or using pictographs or emoticons (symbolic icons made with punctuation marks) to indicate a facetious tone (Blackman & Clevenger, 1990; Miller, 1992).

Novice users may start flames by simply revealing their ignorance of CMC norms, such as typing in ALL CAPS (the electronic equivalent of shouting), failing to use descriptive message headers, posting personal messages to public forums, or sending "listserver" commands (such as "signoff," a command intended to be interpreted by a computer program) to a widely distributed electronic mail discussion list. Novice users may also fail to recognize attempts by experienced users to modify aggressive arguments (such as using IMHO before a comment, which is a common abbreviation for "in my humble opinion"), possibly contributing to an evaluation of messages as flames that were intended by the sender to be only mildly assertive.

The proposition that media experience influences the behavior and interpretation of flaming demands further research. As with social influence, the degree of experience one has with CMC systems is a potentially significant predictor of flaming and how flaming messages are interpreted. The social influence model also suggests additional factors that contribute to flaming. Those factors influencing the behavior of flaming are considered next, followed by those that influence the interpretation of flaming.

## OTHER FACTORS INFLUENCING THE BEHAVIOR OF FLAMING

In addition to social influence and media experience, the model suggests three additional factors that influence the behavior of flaming. These factors are media evaluations, task evaluations, and situational factors.

### Media Evaluations

How people evaluate the computer as a communication medium is likely to influence the behavior of flaming. Research has shown there are differences in the way people evaluate CMC's appropriateness for socioemotional communication (Rice & Love, 1987). Those who feel the medium is inadequate or inappropriate for the expression of emotions would seem to be less likely to craft flaming messages than those who may be more comfortable in expressing emotions in this manner. Flaming may also be related to anxiety or feelings of frustration in learning to use CMC systems (Siegel et al., 1986). Someone who evaluates a CMC system as difficult to use may take out her or his frustrations in belligerent messages to anonymous others on a computer network. Flaming may arise from conflicting evaluations of the CMC system being used and the most appropriate ways to use it.

## Task Evaluation

In some organizations, CMC systems are regarded as important channels for serious work: E-mail may be replacing the memo as the preferred method of internal communication. Flaming is officially discouraged in some organizations as an inappropriate waste of resources (see Foulger, 1990, for a description of the antiflaming policies at IBM). Other organizations may have a much "looser" attitude toward nontask use of CMC, even encouraging socioemotional communication in the desire to increase organizational camaraderie (Sproull & Kiesler, 1991). Flaming behavior may vary in both quantity and quality in these two task evaluation contexts. An explanation of flaming should thus account for how users view the purpose of a particular CMC medium or transaction.

## Situational Factors

As mentioned earlier, time may be a significant situational factor in flaming, especially in asynchronous CMC. Flaming may be influenced by the length of discussions, which may occur over days or weeks. The number of messages received in a given unit of time, the time between messages, and the time of day a message is read may be situational factors related to flaming. Location of CMC use may be another significant situational factor. CMC users may access communication networks in a variety of places: at the office, at home, on the road. Flaming behavior may be less common in messages originating in "serious" locations, such as an office, than in more casual settings. Situations also vary in the degree of privacy offered; flaming as behavior may be influenced by the presence of other people during a CMC interaction. There is some evidence that the mere presence of others influences CMC behavior (Robinson-Stavely & Cooper, 1990). Flaming within a geographically separate group may be of a different caliber and hold different consequences than flaming within a co-present group communicating with the aid of group decision-making software.

To summarize, the social influence model suggests that the behavior of flaming is a function of the two central factors of social influence and media experience. In addition, media evaluations, task evaluations, and situational factors contribute to the behavior of flaming. Although some evidence from previous research has been cited in support of these propositions, there exists a need for further research to explore how these factors work together. Such an effort could help bridge together some of the seemingly contradictory strands of previous research, which has primarily focused on the behavioral dimension of flaming. Perhaps an even more important research opportunity is an investigation into the factors that contribute to the interpretation of flaming, an area that has largely been ignored by previous research.

## OTHER FACTORS INFLUENCING THE INTERPRETATION OF FLAMING

The social influence model holds that flaming is more than just behavior; it also incorporates the interpretation of behavior. Why do some people consider a message to be a roaring flame, whereas others consider the same message to be a harmless chide? The model suggests that, as with the behavior of flaming, social influence and media experience are important factors. The model goes on to identify two additional factors influencing the interpretation of flaming: media features and the prior use of other media.

### Media Features

The characteristics of CMC systems may influence how individuals interpret messages received through such systems. Users read messages on a variety of hardware and software configurations, from large mainframe systems to portable personal digital assistants. The interpretation of flaming may differ between those who have a user-friendly electronic mail program with a graphical interface and those who read messages on systems that have painfully slow display rates or that lack message filtering capabilities. Some systems even have sophisticated "kill" commands to screen out messages from specific individuals or messages with objectionable words. Flaming may be influenced by the degree to which users are aware of (and make use of) these and other media features that enable "flame management" strategies.

### Prior Use of Other Media

Just as previous experience with flaming can influence how one interprets flaming, how people react to and make use of other media can influence evaluations of behavior in CMC contexts. The interpretation of flaming may be influenced by previous experiences with flaming-like behavior in other media, such as complaint letters, prank phone calls, and televised debates. How one interprets these similar behaviors in other media is likely to influence how one interprets flaming as it is encountered in computer media. People also bring to a flaming situation different expectations of the advantages and disadvantages of media use, based largely on previous experience. There is evidence that preusage expectations of media use influence media evaluations (Rice, Grant, Schmitz, &

Torobin, 1990). Thus, behavior patterns based on prior use of other media may contribute to a set of interpretive rules that aid in the sense making of flaming behaviors. Because individuals vary in the media experiences they bring to the CMC context, taking account of these diverse experiences can contribute to a more complete explanation of how people interpret flaming.

In summary, the social influence model holds that the interpretation of flaming is a function of social influence, media experience, media features, and prior use of other media. It should be stressed that this proposition, as with the rest of the model, is offered more for its heuristic value than its predictive value. The model is suggested as a framework for integrating previous research and for developing research questions to guide future research. Some of those questions, as well as some of the limitations of this model, are considered in the conclusion to this chapter.


CONCLUSION


The social influence model of flaming developed here seeks to provide a more complete understanding of flaming than previous efforts. Rather than limit the explanation of flaming to the influence of technological constraints on those who use technology, this model acknowledges the influence of humans on human behavior and in the negotiation of what that behavior means. The model allows the integration of many of the characteristics of flaming previously identified by research as well as suggesting some intriguing questions for future investigation.

For example, why is flaming more common in some CMC settings than others? To what extend do users frequently exposed to flaming develop a tolerance for it? What fire-fighting strategies do users develop for putting out flames? Are group norms really less influential in CMC, or can group norms be more influential? Rather than promote a lack of social context, could CMC systems in some settings actually increase awareness of the social context? Is flaming the result of a lack of "information richness," or the result of too much of a different kind of richness, an emotional intensity that cannot be attributed to the technology alone, but to the social environment in which the technology is used?

Indeed, could it be that, as Goodwin (1994) suggested, "flames are the friction born of minds rubbing too closely together?" (p. 69). As Goodwin put it: "The problem of flaming is not that we don't understand each other. It's that we understand each other all too well. We're mainlining each other's thoughts" (p. 69). As provocative as this idea may seem, it nevertheless strikes a resonant chord with many who have experienced flaming directly. For those who have been burned in a flame war, flaming is more than a technologically caused psychological neurosis—it is also clearly a social phenomenon, reflecting rational purpose, human conflict, and subjective interpretation. The model developed in this chapter acknowledges this social dimension of flaming in a way previous theories have not, and, by so doing, arguably provides a more complete perspective for understanding flaming.

Of course, the model of flaming outlined here is not without its weaknesses. The Fulk et al. (1990) model focused more on media choice than on media behaviors once that choice was made; the evidence remains limited for concluding that the extension of the model in the directions suggested here are warranted. Although the social influence model can account for many diverse strands in previous research, the model essentially remains untested. Furthermore, this model is less parsimonious than other theories that have been employed to account for flaming. The more comprehensive explanation for flaming offered by this model may necessitate complicated and perhaps impractical research designs in order to test its propositions fully.

Is it worth the effort? Is flaming a phenomenon that warrants the serious attention of scholars of communication? Or is flaming simply part of a passing phase in the development of computer-mediated communication? The jury is still out. Some believe flaming is an antisocial effect of CMC and thus provides an intriguing dependent variable for assessing the negative impact of computer technology on human communication. For others, flaming offers a unique opportunity to advance our understanding of conflict and interpretive sense making from within an environment that allows relatively unobtrusive observation (Rice et al., 1990). But for many flaming is simply not a big deal. Flaming happens. It is part of life on the electronic frontier.

As with previous frontiers, law-abiding citizens will eventually displace the outlaws. What has been learned about flaming in the past decade of research could thus be of little consequence in the future, as cyberspace becomes a more civilized place. This is particularly likely if claims about flaming continue to be based on the shifting sands of technological characteristics, claims that could easily wash away as the technology changes and as the application of that technology becomes more sophisticated. If scholarship on flaming is to have lasting value, researchers should move toward examining flaming not simply as an effect of communication technology, but as a reflection of the social negotiation of meaning through communication media.

## REFERENCES

Anderson, J.A., & Meyer, T.P. (1988). *Mediated communication: A social action perspective.* Newbury Park, CA: Sage.

Anderson, J.F., & Walther, J.B. (1992, May). *Relational tone in computer-mediated communication: A meta-analysis of past research.* Paper presented at the International Communication Association, Miami, FL.

Baldwin, C., & Holmes, M.E. (1992, May). *Social presence and verbal immediacy: A linguistic critique of media determinism.* Paper presented at the International Communication Association, Miami, FL.

Bales, R.F. (1950). A set of categories for the analysis of small group interaction. *American Sociology Review, 15,* 257-263.

Baron, N.S. (1984). Computer mediated communication as a force in language change. *Visible Language, 18,* 118-141.

Blackman, B.I., & Clevenger, T., Jr. (1990, November). *The promises, possibilities and pragmatics of using pictograph surrogates in on-line messaging: Implications for managing the adoption of computer-mediated communication technology.* Paper presented at the Speech Communication Association, Chicago, IL.

Brown, E. (1984, January). Fear and lurking on CB simulator. *PC World,* pp. 182-191.

Campbell, D.T., & Fiske, D.W. (1959). Convergent and discriminant validation by the multitrait-multimethod matrix. *Psychological Bulletin, 56,* 81-105.

Compton, D.C., White, K., & DeWine, S. (1991). Techno-sense: Making sense of computer-mediated communication systems. *Journal of Business Communication, 28,* 23-43.

Culnan, M.J., & Markus, M.L. (1987). Information technologies. In F. M. Jablin, L. L. Putnam, K.J. Roberts, & L.W. Porter (Eds.), *Handbook of organizational communication: An interdisciplinary perspective* (pp. 420-443). Newbury Park, CA: Sage.

Daft, R.L., & Lengel, R.H. (1986). Organizational information requirements, media richness, and structural design. *Management Science, 32,* 554-571.

Dery, M. (1993). Flame wars. *South Atlantic Quarterly, 92,* 559-568.

Dorwick, K. (1993, April). *Beyond politeness: Flaming and the realm of the violent.* Paper presented at the Conference on College Composition and Communication, San Diego, CA.

Eckholm, E. (1984, October 2). Emotional outbursts punctuate conversations by computer. *New York Times,* pp. C1, C5.

Festinger, L., Pepitone, A., & Newcomb, T. (1952). Some consequences of deindividuation in a group. *Journal of Abnormal and Social Psychology, 47,* 382-389.

Foulger, D.A. (1990). *Medium as process: The structure, use, and practice of computer conferencing on IBM's IBM PC computer conferencing facility.* Unpublished doctoral dissertation, Temple University, Philadelphia.

Fulk, J., Schmitz, J., & Steinfield, C.W. (1990). A social influence model of technology use. In J. Fulk & C. Steinfield (Eds.), *Organizations and communication technology* (pp. 117-140). Newbury Park, CA: Sage.

Fulk, J., Steinfield, C.W., Schmitz, J., & Power, J.G. (1987). A social information processing model of media use in organizations. *Communication Research, 14,* 529-552.

Goode, J., & Johnson, M. (1991, November). Putting out the flames: The etiquette and law of e-mail. *Online,* pp. 61-65.

Goodwin, M. (1994, April). ASCII is too intimate. *Wired,* pp. 69-70.

Hawisher, G.E. (1992). Electronic meetings of the mind: Research, electronic conferences, and composition studies. In G. E. Hawisher & P. LeBlanc (Eds.), *Re-imagining computers and composition: Teaching and research in the virtual age* (pp. 81-101). Portsmouth, NH: Boynton/Cook.

Hiltz, S.R., Johnson, K., & Turoff, M. (1986). Experiments in group decision making: Communication process and outcome in face-to-face versus computerized conferences. *Human Communication Research, 13,* 225-252.

Holmes, M.E., & Berquist, C. (1990, November). *Gender display in synchronous computer-mediated discourse: A case of channel constraints and opportunities.* Paper presented at the Speech Communication Association, Chicago, IL.

Judd, C.M., Smith, E.R., & Kidder, L.H. (1991). *Research methods in social relations.* Fort Worth, TX: Holt Rinehart and Winston.

Kiesler, S., Siegel, J., & McGuire, T.W. (1984). Social psychological aspects of computer-mediated communication. *American Psychologist, 39,* 1123-1134.

Kiesler, S., Zubrow, D., Moses, A.M., & Geller, V. (1985). Affect in computer-mediated communication: An experiment in synchronous terminal-to-terminal discussion. *Human Computer Interaction, 1,* 77-104.

Lea, M., O'Shea, T., Fung, P., & Spears, R. (1992). "Flaming" in computer-mediated communication: Observations, explanations, implications. In M. Lea (Ed.), *Contexts of computer-mediated communication* (pp. 89-112). London: Harvester-Wheatsheaf.

Lea, M., & Spears, R. (1991). Computer-mediated communication, de-individuation and group decision-making. *International Journal of Man-Machine Studies, 34,* 283-301.

Leeds-Hurwitz, W. (1992). Social approaches to interpersonal communication. *Communication Theory, 2,* 131-139.

Miller, M.W. (1992, September 15). A story of the type that turns heads in computer circles: Digital smiley faces are used in e-mail conversations by the lateral-minded. *Wall Street Journal,* pp. A1, A11.

Rice, R.E. (1984). Mediated group communication. In R.E. Rice & Associates (Eds.), *The new media: Communication, research and technology* (pp. 129-154). Beverly Hills, CA: Sage.

Rice, R.E., Grant, A.E., Schmitz, J., & Torobin, J. (1990). Individual and network influences on the adoption and perceived outcomes of electronic messaging. *Social Networks, 12,* 27-55.

Rice, R.E., & Love, G. (1987). Electronic emotion: Socioemotional content in a computer-mediated communication network. *Communication Research, 14,* 85-108.

Rice, R.E., & Steinfield, C. (1994). New forms of organizational communication via electronic mail and voice messaging. In J.H. Andriessen & R. Roe (Eds.), *Telematics and work* (pp. 109-137). Hillsdale, NJ: Erlbaum.

Robinson-Stavely, K., & Cooper, J. (1990). Mere presence, gender, and reactions to computers: Studying human-computer interaction in the social context. *Journal of Experimental Social Psychology, 26,* 168-183.

Romiszowski, A.J., & deHaas, J.A. (1989). Computer mediated communication for instruction: Using e-mail as a seminar. *Educational Technology, 29*(10), 7-14.

Roth, P.A. (1987). *Meaning and method in the social sciences: A case for methodological pluralism.* Ithaca, NY: Cornell University Press.

Salancik, G.R., & Pfeffer, J. (1978). A social information processing approach to job attitudes and task design. *Administrative Science Quarterly, 23,* 224-253.

Selfe, C.L., & Meyer, P.R. (1991). Testing claims for on-line conferences. *Written Communication, 8,* 162-192.

Short, J., Williams, E., & Christie, B. (1976). *The social psychology of telecommunications.* New York: Wiley.

Siegel, J., Dubrovsky, V., Kiesler, S., & McGuire, T.W. (1986). Group processes in computer-mediated communication. *Organizational Behavior and Human Decision Processes, 37,* 157-187.

Spears, R., Lea, M., & Lee, S. (1990). De-individuation and group polarization in computer-mediated communication. *British Journal of Social Psychology, 29,* 121-134.

Spitzer, M. (1986). Writing style in computer conferences. *IEEE Transactions on Professional Communications, PC 29*(1), 19-22.

Sproull, L., & Kiesler, S. (1986). Reducing social context cues: Electronic mail in organizational communication. *Management Science, 32,* 1492-1512.

Sproull, L., & Kiesler, S. (1991). *Connections: New ways of working in the networked organization.* Cambridge, MA: MIT Press.

Steele, G., Woods, D., Finkel, R., Crispin, M., Stallman, R., & Goodfellow, G. (1983). *The hackers dictionary.* New York: Harper & Row.

Steinfield, C.W. (1986). Computer-mediated communication in an organizational setting: Explaining task-related and socioemotional uses. In M. L. McLaughlin (Ed.), *Communication yearbook* (Vol. 9, pp. 777-804). Newbury Park, CA: Sage.

Steinfield, C.W., & Fulk, J. (1990). The theory imperative. In J. Fulk & C. W. Steinfield (Eds.), *Organizations and communication technology* (pp. 13-25). Newbury Park, CA: Sage.

Stewart, D. (1991, September). Flame throwers: Why the heated bursts on your computer network? *Omni,* p. 26.

Thompsen, P.A. (1994). An episode of flaming: A creative narrative. *ETC.: A Review of General Semantics, 51,* 51-72.

Thompsen, P.A., & Ahn, D.-K. (1992). To be or not to be: An exploration of E-Prime, copula deletion and flaming in electronic mail. *ETC.: A Review of General Semantics, 49,* 146-164.

Thompsen, P.A., & Foulger, D.A. (1993, May). *Effects of pictographs and quoting on flaming in computer media.* Paper presented at the International Communication Association, Washington, DC.

Turkle, S. (1984). *The second self: Computers and the human spirit.* New York: Simon and Schuster.

Walther, J.B. (1992). Interpersonal effects in computer-mediated interaction. *Communication Research, 19,* 52-90.

Walther, J.B., & Burgoon, J.K. (1992). Relational communication in computer-mediated interaction. *Human Communication Research, 19,* 50-88.

Weisband, S.P. (1992). Group discussion and first advocacy effects in computer-mediated and face-to-face decision making groups. *Organizational Behavior and Human Decision Processes, 53,* 352-380.

Williams, F., Rice, R.E., & Rogers, E.M. (1988). *Research methods and the new media.* New York: Free Press.

Zimbardo, P.G. (1969). The human choice: Individuation, reason, and order versus deindividuation, impulse, and chaos. In W.J. Arnold & D. Levine (Eds.), *Nebraska symposium on motivation: 1969* (pp. 237-307). Lincoln: University of Nebraska.

**21**

# The Information
# Arms Race

## Douglas Rushkoff

*Some have characterized cyberculture as offering an opportunity for increased freedom and openness, and evidence for this can be found on the Internet. On the other hand, with the rise of the World Wide Web, business interests have increasingly taken control of cyberspace, placing increasingly more emphasis on e-commerce, e-shopping, Web-based advertising, and content to lure in hits from potential consumers. In this chapter, Douglas Rushkoff characterizes this process as a form of information warfare, involving forms of pseudocommunication and propaganda. Placing the current cyberscene in the context of the history of cultural imperialism, he argues that similar forces are at work today as the Internet becomes increasingly more co-opted and commercialized. For more on the economics of cyberspace outside of this section of the book, see James Beniger's essay on control in Chapter 2, Neil Kleinman's arguments about copyright in Chapter 4, and Ron Jacobson's summary of cyberspace issues in Chapter 9; also note the arguments concerning social class presented by Frank Dance in Chapter 10, and Paul Lippert in Chapter 18.*

In any information war, we human beings lose by definition. For the moment communication becomes information, it is no longer alive. As living beings, when we accept a role in the InfoWar, we also lose the home field advantage—the defensive capability offered any indigenous population.

When we are fooled into believing the battle over information is, in fact, a battle over our reality, we have already lost the war.


## COMMUNICATION ONLY OCCURS BETWEEN EQUALS

Television broadcasting is not communication. Neither are radio news, magazines, or even this little chapter. These are all one-way distribution of content. However vital, realistic, or engaging a movie or book, it is not interactive or participatory in any real sense. Unless we can have just as much of an effect on the director, writer, producer, or journalist as he has on us, we are not involved in a communication. We are merely the recipients of programming.

Even the so-called "interactive" media, like computer games and most Web sites, simply allow for the user to experience a simulation of free choice. The creator of the simulation is no longer present. If a player creates a sequence of moves that have never been played before, or a reader moves through an interactive story along a path that has never been followed before, this still does not count as communication. It is merely a unique and personalized experience of essentially dead data. Multimedia CD-Roms are not interactive, because the user is not interacting with anyone.

This is not so terrible in itself. Stories, movies, and video games are all great storage media. The enduring values of many indigenous cultures are passed down from generation to generation through myths and stories. The artist, philosopher, and scientist alike have published their findings in one form or another for the consumption of others. For centuries, we have willingly submitted to the performances and writings of great thinkers, and have been enriched as result. They are what allow for a cumulative human experience over time, greater than any single life span.

But we should not confuse such experiences with communication. However lifelike it may feel, unless we are in a position to influence the presenter as much as he can influence us, we are not involved in a living exchange. In other words, to be aroused by pornographic tape is not to make love.

For like lovemaking, communication is a living exchange between equal partners. No matter how much our world's nihilists might like to deny it, there is an energy inherent to such exchanges: a living space of interaction. And this is the zone where change—and all its inherent dangers—can occur.

Just as lovemaking presents the possibility of new genetic combinations, communication initiates the process of cultural mutation. When equals are communicating, nothing is fixed. Honest participation means everything is up for grabs.

## INFORMATION WANTS TO BE PRESERVED

The so-called "communications departments" of most major universities would have us believe otherwise. The study of mass media has little to do with mass participation in the design of cultural values. Students do not learn how to foster the living interaction between a society's members. There are few courses in promoting media literacy, or creating USENET groups to solve problems collectively.

Today, communications is the science of influence. Mass communication is the study of how governments and corporations can influence their populations and customers—the so-called "masses." The tools they employ are rhetoric, the ancient art of influence (Aristotle, 1954), and information, the modern science of control (Wiener, 1967; see also Chomsky, 1991; Crossen, 1994; Kelly, 1998; Schwartz & Leydon, 1997; Simpson, 1994; Stauber & Rampton, 1995).

But wherever real communication is occurring, there is life. Like the new buds on a tree, the places where communication takes place are the most effective leverage points in a culture from which to monitor and direct new growth. Those hoping to direct or, as is most often the case, stunt the development of cultural change, focus on these points. By imitating the qualities we associate with living communication, and then broadcasting fixed information in its place, the mass media manipulator peddles the worldview of his sponsors.

## ANTHROPOLOGY AND RELIGION[1]

Most anthropology is carried out in service of a nation or corporation. The anthropologist is the research half of the "R & D" for cultural manipulation. Historically, the anthropologist is sent to a new territory ripe for commercial, religious, or political colonization. He looks for the gaps, or inconsistencies in the culture's mythology, so that these "soft spots" may be hardened with strong, imported data.

For example, 16th-century Christian missionaries to the New World first studied the indigenous people in order to appraise their pantheistic belief system, as well as gain their trust. They observed local rituals to learn about particular beliefs associated with each god. Then they converted people by associating local Gods with the closest corresponding Catholic saints or deities. The native god for animals, the people were taught, is really just St. Francis. The drinking of chicken's blood is really just a version of the communion. And so on, until a local, hybridized version of Christianity evolved.

---

[1]For more on the ideas presented in this section, see Carlisle (1993), Chomsky (1989), Cialdini (1993), Watson (1978; which is excerpted at Psywar Terror Tactics Web site, http://www.parascope.com).

In the 1500s, Franciscan brothers studied the language and religion of the people of Tenochtitlán before choosing to build the hilltop basilica of the Virgin of Guadalupe on the site of an Aztec temple dedicated to the earth goddess Tonatzin. In its new incarnation, the mountaintop church became an homage to Mary, who is pictured stepping on the stars and moon, the symbols of her pagan predecessor. She overlooks what is now called Mexico City. These missions were not generally sponsored by the church, but by the monarchy. As a result, the visiting missionary served the dual-role of converter and intelligence gatherer. Ultimately, both functions simply prepared the target population for its inevitable co-option by force.

This is the two-millennium-old process by which Christianity absorbed the rituals and beliefs of the peoples it converted. The Christmas tree began as a solstice ritual practiced by Germans to light the darkest night of the year. Smart missionaries of the time realized that this was the superstitious ritual developed to address the people's fear of the darkness of winter. The missionaries did a fairly advanced job of cultural analysis for the time, keying in on the local people's doubt in the rejuvenation of the coming spring season. The tannenbaum exposed their deepest fear—and most fertile ground for conversion.

By identifying the tree with the rood and the birth of Christ, the missionaries augmented the pagan ritual, and redirected the sense of hope that the ritual fostered away from pagan forces and towards their own messiah. They filled a living ritual with dead information.

Similarly, churches and cathedrals were most often placed on local pagan "power spots" and lay lines—not because the priests believed that these locations offered any magical leverage, but because the people believed they did. What better way to get people into your church than to build it on the same spot where they already did their praying? Ironically, the "black masses" that were conducted illicitly by pagans on church altars were not meant as a statement against Christianity at all. The unconverted people were merely attempting to carry out their pre-Christian ceremonies in the locations where they believed they would work.

In the years preceding World War II, anthropologists studied the cultures of the South Seas so they could more easily be turned to the "allies" cause against the Japanese once these territories were to become a war zone. Whether or not these well-meaning cultural researchers knew it, the governments funding them had more than pure science in mind when they chose which expeditions to fund.

After World War II, Air Force Brigadier General Edward G. Lansdale emerged as the pre-eminent "counterinsurgency" strategist for the CIA. Over a period of three decades, he developed a wide range of intelligence and propaganda theories that were employed and refined in the field. His principle strategy was first to engage in qualitative anthropological research to discover a target audience's underlying belief systems, and then exploit these beliefs mercilessly in the pursuit of military gains.

For example, in the 1950s as part of his counterinsurgency campaign against the Huk rebels of the Philippines, Lansdale began by conducting research into local superstitions. He learned that the Huk battleground was believed to be inhabited by an "asuang," or vampire figure. To capitalize on this mythology, his "psywar" units would follow Huk patrols and then quietly ambush the last man on the trail. They would kill the soldier by means of two punctures on the neck, drain him of his blood, and then leave him to found the next morning. On encountering the victim, the Huks in the area would retreat for fear of further vampire attacks.

Such information campaigns depend on concretizing living myth with fixed data. They invariably mine the most fertile cultural soil for inherent inconsistencies, and then replace them with symbols that can be more easily controlled.

This is the same process by which today's target marketers research and co-opt new cultural strains. Even the language of marketing, in which new populations are called "targets" reveals the warlike precision and hostility with which these marketers attack their new prospects.

When a public relations person reduces a group of human beings to a target market, he has effectively removed himself from the equation. Feedback and user surveys do not put us in communication with anyone, they simply make us the subjects of scrutiny and the victims of an eventual attack. He is the lone gunman at the top of the tower, intentionally isolated so as to get a better shot. When the gun goes off, we panic down in the plaza. Someone is out to get us.

The reticence of the Generation formerly known as "X" to belong to anything at all can be traced directly to the corrosive effects of target marketing on our society. In fact, the "slacker" ethic was little more than reaction to the segmentation of a culture based on demographic leanings. No sooner do young people find a new style of music, clothing, or attitude, than marketers seize on it as a trend to be exploited. The kids rush from style to style, but only stay until they sense the target marketer's sites closing in on them. Then they rush to find something different, and maintain their anomalous behavior until it is recognized and tagged.

When "GenX" adopted the anti-chic aesthetic of thrift-store grunge, for example, it was in an effort to find a style that could not be so easily identified and exploited. Grunge was so self-consciously lowbrow and depressed that it seemed, at first, impervious to the hype and glamour applied so swiftly to trends of the past. But sure enough, grunge anthems found their way onto the soundtracks of television commercials, and Dodge Neon's were hawked by kids in flannel shirts saying "whatever." The seminal grunge group Nirvana's lead singer Kurt Cobain's superstardom and eventual shotgun suicide bore witness to the futility of giving chase to the target marketers. Symbolically—at least for his fans—Cobain set his rifle's sites on himself rather than be subjected to the crosshairs of someone else's. Then the kids moved on to other genres.

## ADVERTISING AS INFO-WAR

The development of advertising throughout this century can best be understood as the process by which marketers find ways to attack our sense of well-being. Although advertising may have begun as a way to publicize a new brand or invention, the surfeit of "stuff" with little or no qualitative difference from its competition forced advertisers to find ways of distinguishing their products from their competitors'.

Advertising quickly became about creating needs rather than fulfilling them. Commercials took the form of coercive teaching stories. We are presented with a character with whom we identify. The character is put into jeopardy, and we experience vicarious tension along with him. Only the storyteller holds the key to our release.

Imagine a man in his office. The boss tells him his report is late. His wife calls to tell him their son is in trouble. His co-worker is scheming to get him fired. What is he to do? He opens his desk drawer: Inside is a bottle of Brand X Aspirin. He takes the pills and we watch as a psychedelic array of color fills his body. Whether or not we really believe that the aspirin could solve his problems—or cure his headache—we must accept the sponsor's solution if we want to be relieved from tension.

This simple form of programming has been used since Aristotle's day. Create a character, put him in danger, and then choose the method by which he will be saved. The remedy can be Athena or a new brand of sport shoe. The audience must submit.

Because television is not a communicator's medium but the programmer's (why do you think they call the stuff on TV "programming" anyway?) it depends on a passive, captive audience. There is no room for interaction, or the programmer's advantage will be lost.

This is why the remote control has wreaked such havoc on traditional coercive advertising. Although it does not allow for feedback, it does allow for escape. Regular television viewers, feeling the rising and uncomfortable tension of a coercive story, would have to walk all the way up to their television sets to change the channel. Their brains make the calculation of how many calories of effort this would cost, and instruct them to sit and bear the momentary anxiety.

A person armed with a remote control, on the other hand, can escape the dilemma with almost no effort at all. One simple click and the viewer is free. The less reverence the viewer feels for the television image, the less hesitation to click away. Video games help in this regard. The television tube's pixels, which used to be the exclusive province of the programmer, can now be manipulated by the user. Simply moving Super Mario across the screen changes our relationship to the television image forever. The tube is now a playground. It can be changed.

The viewer armed with a remote control becomes an armchair postmodernist, deconstructing images as he or she sees fit. The shorter the viewer's attention span, the less compelled the viewer feels to sit through coercive or tension-inducing media. In fact, attention deficit disorder—an ailment for which millions of parents are now giving their children medication—may just be a reaction to relentless programming. If everywhere you look someone is attempting to program you, you will quickly learn not to look anywhere for too long.

The most skilled viewers have become amateur media semioticians. They maintain an ironic distance from the media they watch so as not to fall under the programmer's influence. Young people watch shows like *Melrose Place* in groups, constantly talking back to the screen. They protect one another from absorption by the image.

Watching television skillfully means watching for the coercive techniques. Watching television with ironic distance means not to watch television at all, but rather to watch "the television." The new entertainment is a form of media study: What are they going to try next? Viewers remain alive and thinking by refusing to surrender to any of the stories they see.

Unfortunately, it did not take advertisers long to develop a new set of coercive techniques for their postmodern audience. The state of ironic detachment that young people employ to remain immune to the programming spell is now their greatest liability.

New advertising intentionally appeals to this postmodern sensibility. "Wink" advertising acknowledges its viewers' intelligence. These commercials readily admit they are manipulative, as if this nod to their own coercive intentions somehow immunizes the audience from their effects. The object of the game, for the audience, is to be "in" on the joke.

Sprite commercials satirize the values espoused by "cool" bands like Coke and Pepsi, then go on to insist that "image is nothing, thirst is everything." A brand of shoes called "Simple" ran a magazine ad with the copy: "advertisement: blah blah blah . . . name of company."

By letting the audience in on the inanity of the marketing process, such companies hope to be rewarded by the thankful viewer. Energizer batteries launched a television campaign where a "fake" commercial for another product would be interrupted by their famous pink Energizer bunny marching through the screen. The audience was rescued from the bad commercial by the battery company's tiny mascot. The message: The Energizer Bunny can keep on going, even in a world of relentless hype.

Of course the marketers haven't really surrendered at all. What's really going on here is a new style of marketing through exclusivity. Advertisers know that their media-savvy viewership prides itself on being able to deconstruct and understand the coercive tactics of television commercials. By winking at the audience, the advertiser is acknowledging that there's someone special out there—someone smart enough not to be fooled by the traditional tricks of the influence professional. "If you're smart enough to see our wink and get the joke, then you're smart enough to know to buy our product."

Where this sort of advertising gets most dangerous is when there's really no joke at all. Diesel Jeans recently launched a billboard campaign with images designed to provoke a "wink" response, even though no amount of semiotic analysis would allow its audience to "get" the joke. In one print ad, they showed a stylish couple, dressed in Diesel clothing, in a fake billboard advertisement for a brand of ice cream. The advertisement-within-the-advertisement was placed in a busy district of North Korea.

What does this advertisement mean, and why was it placed amongst bicycling North Koreans? Who knows? The meta-advertisement attacks hip viewers. They must pretend that they understand what's going on if they want to maintain their sense of ironic detachment. The moment they lie to themselves in order to turn to the page, they have actually admitted defeat. They have been beaten at their own game by the advertiser, who has been re-established as the more powerful force in the information war.

## THE CO-OPTION OF CYBERSPACE

The Internet posed an even greater threat to culture's programmers than channel zappers. For the first time, here was a mass media that no longer favored broadcasters.

A true communications medium from the start, the Internet was as much about sending as receiving. The early Internet was a text-only technology. Users would send e-mail, join in live chats, or participate in asynchronous discussions on bulletin boards and USENET groups. For those lucky enough to have engaged in this style of contact, there was a sense of liberation.

The early Internet spurred utopian visions because it was the first time that real people had the opportunity to disseminate their ideas globally. The Internet was less about the information itself than contact. Networked together through wires and computers, the Internet community—and it really was a community—was a living cultural experiment.

To some, it was as if the human race were hardwiring its members together into a single, global brain. People talked about the Internet as if it were the realization of the Gaia Hypothesis—the notion that all living things are part of the same, big organism (Lovelock, 1987). Many believed that the fledgling communications infrastructure would allow for the beginning of global communication and cooperation on a scale unimagined before.

Even if these dreams were a bit more fantastic than the reality of an Internet society, they indicated the underlying experience essential to this interconnectivity. The interactive communications infrastructure was merely the housing for a collective project in mutual understanding. It was not about information at all, but relationships. We were not interacting with data, but with one another.

This is why the Internet seemed so "sexy." It was not that pornography was available online. It felt and looked sexy because people and their ideas could co-mingle and mutate. A scientist sharing his new research would be challenged and provoked. A philosopher posing a new idea would be forced to defend it. Nothing was safe, and nothing was sacred—except, perhaps, the idea that everyone shared an equal opportunity to give voice to his or her opinions.

As more people turned off their TVs and migrated online, the question for influence professionals became clear: How do we turn this communications nightmare into a traditional, dead, and controllable mass medium?

Their great trick was to replace communication with information. The works of futurists like Alvin Toffler (1980) were twisted to proclaim that we were on the cusp of the Information Age, forever confusing a revolution in communication with an expansion of the propaganda machine. No, the Internet was not a medium for interpersonal exchange, but data retrieval. And it was tricky and dangerous to use. *Wired* magazine's hip graphics and buzzword-laden text convinced newcomers to the world of "hi-technology" that the Internet was a complex and imposing realm. Without proper instruction (from the likes of *Wired* editors), we would surely get lost out there.

Now that the Internet was seen as a dangerous zone of information, best traveled with the advice of experts, it wasn't long before the World Wide Web became the preferred navigational tool. Unlike bulletin boards or chat rooms, the Web is—for the most part—a read-only medium. It is flat and opaque. You can't see through it to the activities of others. We don't socialize with anyone when we visit a web site; we read text and look at pictures. This is not interactivity. It is an "interactive-style" activity. There's nothing participatory about it.

Instead of forging a whole new world, the World Wide Web gives us a new window on the same old world. The Web is a repository for information. It is dead. Although you and I are as free to publish our works on the Web as Coke is to publish its advertising or The Gap is to sell its jeans, we have given up something much more precious once we surrender the immediacy of a living communications exchange. Only by killing its communicative function could the Web's developers turn the Internet into a shopping mall.

The current direction of Internet technology promises a further calcification of its interactive abilities. Amped up processing speed and modem baud rates do nothing for communication. They do, however, allow for the development of an increasingly TV-like Internet.

The ultimate objective of today's communication industry is to provide us with broadcast-quality television images on our computers. The only space left for interactivity will be our freedom to watch a particular movie "on demand" or, better, to use the computer mouse to click on an object or article of clothing we might like to buy.

## PROMOTING THE FIXED REALITY

Once we have reduced the living exchanges that these new media promise to one side or other in an information war, we have given up the only advantage we really have: to evolve unpredictably.

The enemy of the coercer is change. Coercion and influence are simply the pushing of a fixed point of view. In this sense, the coercer is promoting death. The messy fertility of a living system is the information coercer's greatest obstacle. But it is also our greatest strength as a developing culture.

Finally, the conflict between "them and us" is fictional. The culture war is just a battle between those who see the need for change, and those would hope to prevent it. Those in power, obviously, seek to preserve the status quo. The only time they feel the need to make an adjustment is when they are hoping to absorb a unique new population, or when the populations already under their control have grown immune to the current styles of influence.

And, to be sure, the preservation of certain status quo values is crucial to the maintenance of organized society. Just as there are certain genes in the body with no function other than to resist mutation, there are institutions in our society that work very hard to resist change.

Because the chief agents of change are interaction and communication, these will be the activities that the enemies of evolution will want to keep in check. But when an overwhelming proportion of our world community seeks a referendum on the human project, we must not allow our efforts to be derailed by those who would prevent such a movement by any means necessary.

More importantly, we cannot let ourselves be fooled into thinking that simply having the right to select our data with the click of a computer mouse instead of a TV remote means we have won the Information Arms Race.

## REFERENCES

Aristotle. (1954). *Rhetoric* (W. Rhys Roberts, Trans.). New York: The Modern Library.

Carlisle, J. (1993, Spring). Public relationships: Hill & Knowlton, Robert Gray, and the CIA. *Covert Action Quarterly.*

Chomsky, N. (1989). *Necessary illusions: Thought control in democratic societies.* Boston: South End Press.

Chomsky, N. (1991). *Media control: The spectacular achievements of propaganda.* Westfield, NJ: Open Magazine Pamphlet Series.

Cialdini, R. B. (1993). *Influence: The psychology of persuasion.* New York: William Morrow.

Crossen, C. (1994). *Tainted truth: The manipulation of fact in America.* New York: Simon & Schuster.

Kelly, K. (1998). *New rules for the new economy*. New York: Viking.

Lovelock, J.E. (1987). *Gaia: A new look at life on earth*. New York: Oxford University Press.

Schwartz, P., & Leydon, P. (1997, July). The long boom. *Wired.*

Simpson, C. (1994). *Science of coercion: Communication research and psychological warfare, 1945-1960*. New York: Oxford University Press.

Stauber, J., & Rampton, S. (1995). *Toxic sludge is good for you!: Lies, damn lies, and the public relations industry*. Monroe, ME: Common Courage Press.

Toffler, A. (1980). *The third wave*. New York: Morrow.

Watson, P. (1978). *War on the mind: The military uses and abuses of psychology*. New York: Basic Books.

✧✧✧ **22**

# Cybertime[*]

## Lance Strate

*Throughout this volume we have focused on the concept of cyberspace as a site of human interaction, an electronic "place" made possible by computers and computer networks. But the concept of time is just as integral to understanding a given context, situation, scene, or environment as that of space. Moreover, time is a key element in the formation of cultures, communities, identities, and meanings, as Lance Strate notes in this last chapter. Thus, he introduces and examines the idea of cybertime both as an alternative, and as a complement to the concept of cyberspace. Strate argues that the computer functions both as a clock—keeping, measuring, and producing time both for the outside world and its own internal microworld—and as a medium—generating "virtual time" through stories, games, and audiovisual presentation. He also points to the ways in which computing and computer-mediated communication, as activities, involve a variety of temporal experiences. Outside of this section of the book, other views of time are implicit in Herbert Zettl's aesthetics of VR in Chapter 5, in the ecological approach employed by Sue Barnes in Chapter 14, and in Camille Paglia's essay on online publishing in Chapter 16. Also see James R. Beniger's views on cyberspace and control in Chapter 3, and Jay David Bolter's discussion of the self in Chapter 7; an alternative to the opposition between time and space can be found in Paul Lippert's focus on the concrete and the abstract in Chapter 18.*

---

[*]I would like to thank John M. Phelan, Edward Wachtel, Gary Gumpert, Raymond Gozzi, Jr., Ron Jacobson, and Stephanie Gibson, for their input and feedback. My only regret is that I was not able to implement more fully their suggestions.

You no longer have to be an Albert Einstein (1954) to know that space and time are interdependent and inseparable, two aspects of the singular phenomenon of physical reality. Nor do you still have to be a Kenneth Burke (1945), Harold Innis (1951), or Edward T. Hall (1959, 1984) to know that the same is true of social reality. And so, it follows quite clearly that the cyberspace that is associated with computing and computer-mediated communication has a counterpart: *cybertime.* But whereas the concept of cyberspace has proven to be both popular and powerful, the idea of cybertime has been all but ignored. Consequently, we tend to stress the similarities between computer technology and more traditional notions of physical place; we view computer media as a *where*, not a *when*. Along the same lines, there is a tendency to focus on computer technology's convergence with and subsumption by telecommunications and telematics and on cyberspace as the byproduct of the electronic transmission of messages and data over distance rather than over time. This imbalance not only hinders our attempts to assess the impact of computer media, but also influences political and economic decision making, as politicians, government officials, and the communications industry are guided by transportation and spatial metaphors of information superhighways and infrastructures. Moreover, whereas the emphasis on computer-mediated communication points us in the direction of cyberspace, as our focus shifts to computer-mediated *culture*, to the long-term construction of communities, psyches, and shared systems of signification, we need to consider the concept of cybertime.

This is not to say that the concept of time has been entirely ignored in discussions of computer technology, but the discussion has been fragmentary and diffused. My intent, therefore, is to begin the exploration of cybertime in a more systematic manner. There has been a long history of discussion and contention concerning the nature of time in general and our relationship to it (see, e.g., Whitrow, 1980, 1988), and this chapter samples some of the ideas and arguments concerning time that are relevant to the study of computer media.[1] Cybertime itself represents the intersection of several different phenomena. First, there is the computer's time-telling function—how it constructs an internal sense of time and measures the passage of time in the outside world, in order to coordinate actions and events. Second, there is the computer's representational function—how, as a medium, it conveys a sense of dramatic, fictional, or symbolic time, as well as a sense of past, present, and future. Third, there is our own subjective experience of time as we interact with and through computer media—how computing constitutes a human activity and an event that influences our perception of time and our sense of self and community.

---

[1]The literature on time is vast, transcending field, discipline, and specialization, and I make no claims to providing a comprehensive review or survey of this topic, let alone resolving any of the long-standing debates associated with it.

## MEASURING TIME: THE COMPUTER AS CLOCK

Typically, the origins of the computer are traced back to devices that aid in numerical calculation such as the abacus or to machines that perform a control function such as Jacquard's automatic loom (Kidwell & Ceruzzi, 1994; Sternberg, 1991); as a revolutionary technological innovation, comparisons have also been made to the steam engine (Toffler, 1981) and to the Gutenberg printing press (Provenzo, 1986). Often overlooked, however, is the computer's close kinship with the mechanical clock developed during the late Middle Ages. J. David Bolter (1984), one of the few to make this connection, argues that the computer is an extension

> of the clock rather than the steam engine. The clock provided information more conveniently and eventually more accurately than the sundial had done before, but it did not intrude physically upon life except by ringing the hour. . . . Like early computers, early clocks were expensive and delicate, and it required a major corporate effort to acquire one. As clocks became common, however, they became not merely useful but unavoidable. Men and women began to work, eat, and sleep by the clock, and as soon as they decided to regulate their actions by this arbitrary measurer of time, the clock was transformed from an expression of civic pride into a necessity of urban life. The computer too has changed from a luxury to a necessity for modern business and government. (p. 38)

Computers and clocks are both devices that manufacture no physical products, but instead produce pure information; the arbitrariness of the uniform hours and minutes produced by the clock means that, like the computer, the clock is a technology of simulation.[2] Moreover, as Lewis Mumford (1963) makes clear, the clock's main function is to coordinate and synchronize activities and events. It is an early technology of control, a forerunner of cybernetics and computing (Beniger, 1986; Weizenbaum, 1976; Wiener, 1967). Clocks are also early forms of automata, self-operating machines, and therefore ancestors of the modern von Neumann computer (Bolter, 1984; Levy, 1992); thus, both the clock and the computer have provided metaphors for the body, the mind, and the universe.

Beyond parallels and pedigree, the electronic computer actually functions as a clock, which is essential to its ability to carry out instructions and manipulate data: "The central processor of the computer contains within it an electronic clock, whose extremely rapid pulses determine when one operation has ended and another is to begin" (Bolter, 1984, p. 38). The clock's frequency (number of cycles per second, measured by the million in megahertz) determines the computer's processing speed, and it is not unusual for computers to incorporate additional clocks to perform other functions (Wyant & Hammerstron,

---

[2]In fact, I would suggest that clock time fits quite nicely into Baudrillard's (1983) concept of hyperreality. This, of course, calls into question the exclusive association of simulation with the postmodern, as opposed to earlier eras.

1994). Like dedicated timepieces, the computer clock can be used to measure duration, determine the present point in time, and even provide alerts along the lines of an alarm clock. The function of the clock is to tell the time of the outside world, but whereas traditional timepieces only measure time's passage and are not seen as creating time out of the whole cloth, the central processor does generate time for the computer's internal world. This electronic heartbeat *is* time insofar as the computer's microworld is concerned. Cybertime therefore corresponds to Sir Isaac Newton's (1934)[3] notion of time: "Absolute, true and mathematical time, of itself, and from its own nature, flows equably without regard to anything external" (p. 6). Although absolute time fits most people's intuitions about the nature of time, it is generally accepted among scientists and philosophers that time does not exist independently of action, motion, and event, but is in fact generated by physical change (hence, time's relativity in relation to speed). Of course, the computer exists in this same physical universe and draws energy from the outside world, but otherwise, the microworld is a closed system, and the computer makes absolute time manifest internally.

Cybertime is absolute time, and it is digital time. By this I refer to something more than digital clocks and watches, although they themselves are not without significance. Introduced at the end of the 1960s, digital timepieces along with electronic calculators signaled the beginning of an ongoing consumer electronics boom; again, computer genealogies typically include the calculator, but slight the digital clock (e.g., Kidwell & Ceruzzi, 1994). And, like calculators, the new timepieces generated a degree of controversy insofar as they short-circuited long-standing methods of "figuring" (in this case due to their mode of representing time). One of the objections to the digital display of time is that the traditional clockface provides a context that includes every possible time of day, out of which we calculate the "correct" time. The digital display, on the other hand, is decontextualized time, presenting only the present moment, which only needs to be read. Thus, the clockface's time provides a sense of past and future, so that we reckon the time as so many minutes before or after the hour; the digital display is entirely present-centered, representing the time as nothing more than a discrete quantity. These differences in display, and the underlying sense of time implied by them, represent significant differences in worldview and ideology, as Jeremy Rifkin, author of *Time Wars* (1987), makes clear:

> A digital timepiece displays numbers in a vacuum—time unbound to either a circadian reference or the past and future. By eliminating the circle, the digital watch helps eliminate the notion that time is cyclical and related to the larger rhythms of the earth and solar system. . . .The digital watch is a fitting metaphor for a society in which the time orientation is becoming increasingly separated from the ecological rhythms of the planet and in which the expediency of the

---

[3] I acknowledge that use of the APA editorial style in this manner generates a temporal anomaly, admit that I take a certain perverse pleasure in it, and apologize for any discomfort it may cause.

moment takes precedence over a sense of historical reflection and future projection. (p. 121)

However significant, the debate over display only scratches the surface of the computer's digitization of time. For internally, within the microworld of the computer's central processor, its sense of time is digital as well. Human time is generally analogic, that is, we tend to think of time as continuous and, therefore, infinitely divisible. We may watch the clock, counting the seconds and minutes as they tick by, noting the chimes marking the hour, but we generally see this as a byproduct of the clock's mechanics, not time's true nature; we perceive time as flowing seamlessly, rather than hiccuping periodically. Cybertime, in contrast, is based on a series of separate and distinct electronic pulses; just as is the case with the microworld's absolute time, these electronic pulses do not simply mark time—they are what passes for time in cyberspace (Bolter, 1984). Cybertime is therefore based on indivisible units, making manifest the concept of the chronon, the shortest unit of time. The notion that time, like matter, is made up of atoms was popular among intellectuals during the Middle Ages (Whitrow, 1980, 1988), its best known exponent being the 12th-century philosopher Moses Maimonides (1963), who wrote:

> Time is composed of instants. . . . There are many units of time that, because of the shortness of their duration, are not divisible. The division of time ends with the instants that are not divisible. For example, an hour consists of sixty minutes, a minute of sixty seconds, and a second of sixty thirds. And thus this division of time ends up accordingly with parts constituting, for instance, tenths or something even briefer, which cannot in any respect be separated in their turn into parts and are not subject to division. (p. 196)

The concept of temporal atomicity was consistent with the highly religious worldview that prevailed during the medieval period within Jewish, Islamic, and Christian cultures. As G.J. Whitrow (1988) explains, the "atomistic view of time was associated with a drastically contingent and acausal concept of the world, its existence at one instant not implying its existence at any subsequent instant" (p. 79). Rather than assuming an automatic continuity from event to event, this view required the continuous active intervention of God to keep time moving. There is more than a passing similarity here between the God of Abraham and the god of the machine; even with surge protectors, anyone working with computers for any length of time is aware of the uncertain temporal continuity of their microworlds. A momentary discontinuity in the flow of electricity and the computer may freeze—time stops! Thus, the computer's digital time has something in common with theistic time or sacred time.

In the modern era the best-known proponent of temporal atomicity was Descartes, also for theological reasons (Whitrow, 1980). What is of particular significance is that whereas Descartes's deductive approach looked backward to medieval theology for its support, his dream of a reality based entirely on mathematics comes the closest to being realized in the form of the computer's microworld. Apart from the concept of the chronon, the quantification of time that resulted from the clocking of discrete hours, minutes, and seconds led to the commodification of time (Mumford, 1963) and the uniquely Western notion that "time is money" (Lakoff & Johnson, 1980). The division of time into multiple uniform units facilitates the pricing of time and, therefore, the buying and selling of time, a key foundation of the industrial revolution and modern capitalism. It follows that the computer's digital time, and its further easing of temporal commodification, may well form the basis of postmodern or late capitalism (Jameson, 1991).

Digital time is not just a quantitative measurement of time, but rather a quantitative concept of time—time as a sequence of numbers. As Bolter (1984) puts it: "An ordinary clock produces only a series of identical seconds, minutes, and hours: a computer transforms seconds or microseconds or nanoseconds into information" (pp. 102-103). Anything that takes the form of information can be processed by the computer, subjected to statistical and symbolic manipulation. Digital time is entirely arbitrary, completely divorced from natural rhythms and human perceptions, therefore, entirely controllable and malleable.

Cybertime is absolute time, digital time, and it is quicktime. An emphasis on speed is consistent with what Innis (1951) refers to as space-biased societies; societies such as our own in which the emphasis is on communication over distance, territorial expansion, and the extension of centralized control (also see Beniger, 1986). Furthermore, space-biased cultures are present-centered, neglecting tradition and history, unconcerned with maintaining continuity between past and future. Increased speed enhances our ability to transmit messages over space and thereby control territory, while spotlighting the immediate and the ephemeral (Postman, 1985). From a somewhat different perspective, Alvin and Heidi Toffler (1993) state: "'third wave' societies—with economies based on information, communications and technology—run at hyper-speeds" (p. 17). And Paul Virilio (1986, 1991) argues that speed is the fundamental property of postmodern culture; in the age of relativity, the speed of light is the only constant. The electron has set the pace for a century and a half, since the introduction of telegraphy. To the electronic media's instantaneous transmission of information, the computer in turn has contributed the processing of information at electric speed. And it has given us a way of measuring the instantaneity of electronic technology. As Bolter (1984) puts it, "anyone who works with the computer is introduced to a second temporal world, a world of nanoseconds (billionths of a second)" (p. 100). The nanosecond represents cybertime's chronon, its indivisible temporal atom. The speed of the nanosecond's passage renders it essentially subliminal, as Rifkin (1987) makes clear:

> Though it is possible to conceive theoretically of a nanosecond, and even to manipulate time at that speed of duration, *it is not possible to experience it*. This marks a radical turning point in the way human beings relate to time. Never before

has time been organized at a speed beyond the realm of consciousness. . . . The new "computime" represents the final abstraction of time and its complete separation from human experience and the rhythms of nature. (pp. 23-24)

Rifkin (1987) sees this "new nanosecond culture" (p. 19) as an outgrowth of our emphasis on efficiency and centralization, our space bias; "bigger is better" leads to "faster is better." We have come to expect the instantaneous, so that it no longer excites us; we see no need to comment on how fast our messages are delivered through electronic mail, but it becomes quite natural to refer to preelectronic mail (the kind that the post office delivers) as *snail mail.* And we no longer find it very evocative to speak of jet speed, but we become quite conversant in jet lag. When sitting at a computer terminal, delays of a few seconds seem interminable and five minutes an eternity. Hyperspeed breeds impatience, haste, and intolerance, both online and in the real world. The instantaneity of electronic speed is commonly said to annihilate distance, leaving us with "no sense of place" as Joshua Meyrowitz (1985) puts it. But it also annihilates duration, leaving us with no sense of time—if cyberspace is a "nonspace" (Gibson, 1984, p. 51), cybertime is a nontime. Time as well as space breaks down as we approach the speed of light, so that the computer's quicktime is often associated with timelessness and hyperspeed with the break down of historicism (see, e.g., Critical Arts Ensemble, 1994; Rifkin, 1987; Rushkoff, 1994).

Internally, the fact that cybertime is absolute, digital, and quick makes possible a high level of synchronization; externally, the computer's hyperspeed makes it a powerful technology of control. The tendency to place computers in command of events, activities, and procedures has been well documented and subject to intense criticism (see Bolter, 1984; Roszak, 1994; Weizenbaum, 1976). The computer further extends the use of clocking, introduced in the 19th century to control labor and production (Beniger, 1986; Lubar, 1993). There is no question that here we find the totalitarian potential of computing, as well as its affinity with capitalism. And yet, at the same time, the computer's ability to control and coordinate in the interests of speed and efficiency have allowed for more flexible notions of time. The computer introduces the idea of *time-sharing,* initially a process by which mainframe computers are able to accommodate multiple users. Moving at hyperspeed, the computer is able to move back and forth among different users and programs, fulfilling a command here, a line of a program there, balancing a variety of tasks so quickly that the user is barely aware of the computer's divided attention. The introduction of time-sharing to mainframe computers made interactive programming via video terminals possible and led to the first electronic mail systems; a variation of time-sharing among different computers linked in networks made more sophisticated forms of computer-mediated communication, such as the Usenet news and discussion groups possible (Rheingold, 1993; see also Gelernter's, 1991, discussion of "tuple space"). Elsewhere, the term *time-sharing* as well as the general principle by which it works has been adopted by the travel industry to create more flexible vacation options. Many businesses have adopted the related idea of *flex time* as an alternative to traditional 9-to-5 job hours (although this tends to be a smokescreen for downgrading jobs from full time to part time), and in financial markets various forms of programmed trading rely on similar principles (Perkinson, 1996). Thus, the computer's extreme synchronization results in a more elastic form of time, replacing what Hall (1984) refers to as monochronic time, a linear, one-thing-at-a-time sense of the temporal. Cybertime is therefore polychronic time, which involves many things simultaneously; polychronic time is characteristic of many non-Western cultures and, as Marshall McLuhan (1964) argues, of electronic cultures.

In order to survive, every society requires a degree of synchronization from its members. For most of the history of our species, the rhythms of nature such as the sunrise and sunset, new moon and full moon, equinox and solstice, were sufficient for this purpose. When temporal technologies such as the calendar and the clock were introduced, however, they by and large served to further control and coordinate the actions of human beings (Mumford, 1963). The town clock, with its elevated clock face and its far-reaching chimes, established a local area of synchronized time that served the needs of most Western societies from the 14th through to the 19th century. The invention of the telegraph made it possible to extend this area from the local to the regional in the form of time zones (Beniger, 1986; Carey, 1989). Since that time, the many forms of telecommunications that have been developed, as well as the mass production of increasingly more accurate clocks and watches, have further enhanced coordinated action and procedures.

There is a certain irony, then, to the fact that whereas our technologies are highly synchronized in their use of time, our societies are still largely working with a 19th-century system of time keeping. We all may be wearing extraordinarily accurate watches, but the times that they are set to may differ by as much as 10 or 15 minutes. If past trends are any indication, this lack of synchronization will become intolerable, especially for a nanosecond culture; remedies have already begun to appear in the form of broadcast-controlled timepieces and VCR clocks. We can therefore look forward to the integration of computers and computer networks into one great global clock. The cyberspatial infrastructure would most probably be joined with a superstructure of orbital satellites; contemporary satellites such as the United State's Navstar already broadcast the time to the millionth of a second (Raley, 1994). The centralization of time keeping and its instantaneous dissemination through the global matrix seem to be the next logical developments, especially given the increasing rate of global hyperspeed transactions and the shift to a 24-hour society. I believe that we will eventually find ourselves referring more and more often to Greenwich mean time, global time, or simply Internet time, rather than our regional time, and that new timepieces will be widely adopted that are capable of receiving broadcast time signals (perhaps in conjunction with cellular communications products), thereby maintaining synchronization with the world clock. In a sense, absolute time would be established on a global level, or we might say that a "global microworld" would be established; when the world becomes contained within a cyberspatial network, cybertime will become the world's time. Although this would further separate clock time and natural time, the obsolescence of regional time zones may allow local time to resurface, resulting in the proliferation of heterogeneous time zones on one level, even while time is homogenized on another; of course, the internal time of the individual computer would be the most local time of all.

Thus far, the concept of cybertime has been contrasted with our conceptions regarding real time. Real time is relative and formed by physical change, whereas cybertime is absolute and independent of its microworld. Real time is continuous and infinitely divisible, whereas cybertime is digital and atomistic. Real time is tied to the rhythms of nature and human perception, whereas cybertime is quicktime, based on the hyperspeed of the nanosecond. Also, in modern, literate, Western cultures, real time is monochronic, whereas cybertime is highly polychronic, involving extraordinarily complex forms of synchronization. It would be incorrect, however, to place cybertime in antonymic opposition to real time; insofar as the computer functions as a traditional clock, measuring the time of the outside world, cybertime encompasses real time as one of its temporal modes. In fact, the term *real time* refers both to the time of the physical universe and human perception and also to the *interface* between the computer's present and the present of the physical world. When the two coincide and remain synchronized, the computer is said to be functioning in real time. The concept of real time is therefore connected to the microworld's ability to become attuned to the outside world (an ability that computer technology shares with other media). The interface is not monodirectional, however, so that real time also refers to the ability to synchronize that outside world's activities to cybertime's digital drumbeat.

## REPRESENTING TIME: THE COMPUTER AS MEDIUM

In addition to its ability to measure and display time, the computer also functions as a medium, meaning that it can represent time symbolically, communicate a sense of time that is not necessarily *the* time, and thereby produce virtual time. *Virtual time* here refers to a virtual reality's internally generated sense of time and may be used in reference to both computer-generated virtual worlds and the illusion of reality created by all forms of media.[4] Different media may generate

---

[4]This notion of "virtual time" is distinct from Jean Piaget's, which refers to a conceptual time involving the imagination, and Suzanne Langer's, which refers to symbolic form— both are discussed by Edward Wachtel (1980) in his research on perception. They are not unrelated, however, as virtual reality is a conceptual, symbolic, and imaginary "reality" given perceptual (if not actual) existence.

different types of virtual time, but the computer is a "metamedium" (Pimentel & Teixeira, 1993, p. 10), capable of incorporating all existing media. Cybertime is therefore what Hall (1984) refers to as *metatime*: "All those things that philosophers, anthropologists, psychologists, and others have said and written about time: the innumerable theories, discussions, and preoccupations concerning the nature of time" (p. 27). It is a concept of time that includes all other concepts and representations of time, such as the timeline, calendar, and clock face; game time, in which each move in a game represents a unit of time, independent of how long it takes to make the move; narrative time, in which the idea of time is conveyed through verbal description; dramatic time, in which the time represented through performance may move faster or slower than the corresponding clock time; and ritual or sacred time, in which the everyday sense of time is suspended, and the participants are plunged into an eternal present or archetypical moment from the past (Eliade, 1959, 1974; Kirk, 1974).

As audiovisual media, including current and projected forms of virtual reality technology, computers can deal with a wide variety of temporal formats: There is real time that may be transmitted, along the lines of live television, and delayed time that is recorded; a one-to-one time scale may be used so that playback occurs at the same rate as the original event, or the recording may be replayed in fast motion or slow motion, and the rate itself may be varied; motion itself may be frozen, as in photographs or when freeze frame is employed, and motion may be played back in reverse; the recording may be otherwise distorted through editing, cutting, or mixing it with other material to fill out the event (Robinett, 1992; Zettl, 1990). In all these ways, computers can generate a sense of virtual time, the illusion that the sense of time that is presented or represented is truly real time. Additionally, the perception of time may be mediated by the perception of space, specifically the scale of the environment. Hall (1984) discusses the experiments of Alton De Long, in which subjects were supplied with dollhouse-like models and asked to imagine themselves engaged in activities within them. The results indicate that as the scale of the environment decreases, individuals increase the rate at which they interact, process information, and perceive time's passage; thus, in an environment one-twelfth the size of reality, five minutes feels like an hour. These experiments were completed without the benefit of virtual reality (VR) technology, but are clearly relevant to VR and related notions such as telepresence.

Ultimately, what makes cybertime's virtuality distinctive is the great variety of modes by which time can be represented, the unprecedented possibilities for combining the different modes in various ways, the enhanced potential for controlling and manipulating those modes on the part of the user (both as source and receiver), and the enhanced potential for immersion in those modes through VR technology. Cybertime's digitality is the key here, for when time is composed of discrete units of information, it becomes highly malleable, a property that holds true for all digital modes of expression (Lanham, 1993). The combined properties of control and flexibility exhibited here appear contradictory, but are reconciled through computing's ability to achieve complex forms of synchronization. And whereas the computer's virtual time includes natural and traditional temporal modes, it also undermines these older representations by making them part of a large collection of alternatives. Along the same lines, the computer undermines our traditional conceptions of dimensionality.

The idea of dimension is associated with the quantification of attributes, a concept clearly compatible with computing. The attribute of dimension can itself be measured, so that we commonly refer to the three-dimensional space that we live in, to the two-dimensional representations of that space on screen, canvas, or paper, and to the one-dimensional lines we use to form boundaries and maintain order. Dimensionality is a gauge of complexity and a measure of freedom: Movement in three spatial dimensions, for example, is more complex and affords a greater degree of freedom than movement in two. The concept of dimensionality can be applied to any set of attributes. Thus, Herbert Marcuse's (1964) "one-dimensional man" is an individual who is shielded from the complexities of the world and consequently subject to a loss of freedom. We might conclude, then, that our fundamental social and intellectual conflicts are conflicts between one-dimensionality and multidimensionality (see also Atkin, 1981). From McLuhan's (1962, 1964) point of view, the one-dimensional individual, mindset, and society that Marcuse describes is the product of the *linearity* of alphabetic literacy and typography and the resultant mechanical and industrial technologies;[5] in contrast, both oral and electronic cultures are described as multisensory and therefore multidimensional.

The idea of dimensionality also provides a common ground for time and space. By adding time as a fourth coordinate to the spatial dimensions of length, width, and height, we are able to integrate time and space into the unified concept of spacetime. Thus space and time are represented as mathematical coordinates occupying a form of logical space. It is for this reason that time is commonly referred to as the fourth dimension in popular culture. This designation is a misnomer, however, as Rudy Rucker (1984) explains:

> Nobody goes around saying width is *the* second dimension and height is *the* third dimension. Instead we just say that height and width are space dimensions. Rather than saying time is *the* fourth dimension, it is more natural to say that time is just one of the higher dimensions. (p. 139)

In the place of time, we could use some other quality—color, for example—as our fourth dimension. Or we might imagine a fourth spatial dimension, referred to as hyperspace, and including four-dimensional objects such as hypercubes; although impossible to visualize, four-dimensional space can be represented mathematically, especially with the aid of computing.

---

[5]See Jacques Ellul's (1968) study of propaganda for a discussion of the intimate relationship between propaganda and literacy, which in this context serves as the "missing link" between Marcuse and McLuhan.

Alluding to this hyperspace, the terms *hypertext* and *hypermedia* refer to a multidimensional network of verbal and audiovisual items. Thus, hypertext theorists such as Bolter (1991) and George Landow (1992) see in electronic writing the potential to break away from the constraints of one-dimensional linear text and the tyranny of the two-dimensional page. The multidimensionality of hypertext transforms the notion of text from an object held by the reader into an environment through which the reader navigates. Time can be represented in this format just as easily as space, so that the reader may explore a hypertextual network that links representations of different moments or eras. As Bolter (1991) points out, hypertext and hypermedia make available "an electronic space in which the text can comprise a network of diverging, converging, and parallel times" (p. 139). Hypertext has the potential to provide a sense of time that is less fixed and more complex than traditional linear storytelling. Although much of the critical attention has been directed to hypertext, and the ways in which it differs from traditional literature, this same potential is present in a variety of computer software, from word processors and spreadsheets to games and VR simulations (see, e.g., Novak, 1991; Woolley, 1992).

What is significant about these new forms is not that they include the higher dimension of time; after all, time is represented in narrative and dramatic forms such as oral storytelling, novels, and television. Time itself, however, tends to be presented as one-dimensional and generally linear in these older forms, whereas computer software is relatively more open to multidimensional temporal modes. Thus, it becomes feasible to represent and to navigate through parallel timelines (as noted above), or timelines that exist at an angle to each other (MacBeath, 1993), or two separate time dimensions that move in opposite directions from each other (Whitrow, 1980). A computer-mediated narrative can easily present both objective time and the corresponding sense of subjective time held by a human agent, which Zettl (1990) sees as equivalent to the horizontal and vertical dimensions of space. Multiple dimensions of subjective time could be represented if more than one character is involved. Multidimensional time can of course be imagined and discussed without the aid of computing, but this technology makes it possible to simulate it, experiment, and play with it in an unprecedented manner.

Multidimensionality is not the only alternative to one-dimensionality, however. The notion of the fractional dimension, developed through the application of computer power, represents a new way to measure complexity, the complexity of the irregular and the chaotic (Gleick, 1987). The fractal geometry that this idea generated has become a mainstay of motion picture special effects and video games and is essential for the creation of effective VR programming (Hayward & Wollen, 1993). Beyond the visual, fractal mathematics allow computers to model and simulate all manner of systems that otherwise behave unpredictably over time, such as economic trends and meteorological patterns. Thus, they contribute to a more realistic depiction of temporal phenomena as they are better able to capture the randomness and chaos of the real world.

Fractal time itself is a more irregular idea of time, closer to human experience than the uniform rate of clock time. Thus, a computer simulation might vary the tempo of time: "Within a region of cyberspace, time itself may pulse, now passing faster, now slower" (Novak, 1991, p. 240).

Although computers deal with the extreme complexity of higher dimensions and fractals, they do so by reducing phenomena down to a state of extreme simplicity, in the form of binary code. This code represents phenomena through combinations of two possible states, be they zero or one, on or off, or yes or no; like a point in geometry, the mathematical concept of the binary unit or bit has no dimensions (although the space in which a bit of information is stored in memory or on a disk has dimension). The function of a bit of information according to Norbert Wiener (1967), founder of the field of cybernetics, is to reduce uncertainty, possibilities, choice; the ultimate goal is to reduce the degree of freedom to zero. And although there are clear distinctions between human and technological systems, the two interface, overlap, and are influenced by each other, as Wiener makes clear. Here, then, we can see the totalitarian implications of the computer traced to its zero-dimensional code; what Baudrillard (1983) would consider its DNA. There is, of course, a great sense of security associated with the elimination of degrees of freedom, a key point for Marcuse (1964), and individuals who become immersed in computing also derive pleasure from the lack of ambiguity characteristic of the microworlds they create and explore; they may also come to expect the same of the real world (Levy, 1984; Roszak, 1994; Turkle, 1984, 1986). The point, however, is that the zero-dimensional is an alternative to the one-dimensional. Zero-dimensional time would correspond to the frozen time of the photograph or freeze frame and to the experience of timelessness or the "eternal now" associated with sacred time.

Ultimately, whether computing eliminates dimensionality or expands it depends on how the technology is used, the choices that are made. Underlying those choices, however, is a more basic and general effect of computing—its undermining of traditional notions of dimensionality, of the one-dimensional, the three-dimensional, and the four dimensions of spacetime. Whether we are moving into unimaginably high numbers of dimensions, dealing with fractional dimensions, or reducing phenomenon down to zero dimensions, the notion of dimensionality itself has been made multidimensional. In the microworld, it is possible to move easily from one form of dimensionality to another, placing us in the realm of the *metadimensional*. Cybertime is not characterized by any fixed dimensionality, but rather is open to a wide variety of dimensional modes, to metadimensionality; this is consistent with the idea that cybertime is a form of metatime.

Dimensionality, along with digitality, are ways of representing and conceptualizing time through mathematics, and hence tend to be somewhat abstract. Although the metaphor of time as money relies on the quantification of time, currency and commodity make for more concrete comparisons than number alone. Even more concrete is the use of space to make time more accessible and user-friendly. We attempt to grasp the temporal by spatializing it through the linear metaphor of the timeline, the two-dimensional graph metaphor of the calendar page, or the circular metaphor of the traditional clockface. Even the concept of spacetime subordinates time to space by turning time into a fourth *spatial* dimension. The tendency to spatialize time can be seen as another manifestation of Western culture's space bias. And although it is clearly rooted in modern, typographic culture's emphasis on linearity, electronic media such as the computer are associated with nonlinear forms of spatialization. The flowchart, the fundamental diagramming of computer programming, with its nonlinear, tree-like structure (Bolter, 1984), is a highly spatialized representation of events unfolding in time and has become a key image in contemporary culture (e.g., in recent television commercials). This same idea of programming structure, applied to electronic writing, yields the medium of hypertext; thus, there is a tendency to spatialize time in hypermedia. The dimension of time may be represented by travel from node to node, but it may be absent from the individual nodes themselves; each textual item would tend to present time as fixed and frozen. In this respect, the criticism of well-known software designer Brenda Laurel (1993) is noteworthy, as she discusses the quality of reversibility in computing:

> What if I failed to save a copy of my spreadsheet before I monkeyed around with a scenario that turned out to be disastrous? What if that scenario altered a significant amount of my data? The theory of hypertext suggests one solution, where various stages of a "document" . . . can be saved and linked to the current version. This solution is unsatisfactory in that it is likely . . . to create a bewildering proliferation of documents. I don't really want to page back through versions of my work; I want to turn back the clock. The dimension of change is best represented through time, not fixed states. A simple chrono-scrollbar would suffice. Yes, the implementation is hard, but the hardest part is probably visualizing the appropriate representation in the first place. (pp. 114-115)

Here Laurel (1993) is able to overcome the space bias of computer software and contemporary culture, in general, and suggest an alternative interface that better represents the temporal dimension. Her preferred metaphor is that of the theater and the experience of dramatic events and actions unfolding through time, rather than the spatial metaphor of hypertext and hypermedia and the idea of navigation through spaces or worlds. Hypertext theorists do not entirely ignore time; for example, Bolter (1991) points out that "the computer makes possible a kind of historical atlas in which invasions and battles, colonization, and the growth of populations and cities are shown in time as well as space" (p. 81). Still, in hypermedia and in software in general, spatialization is the norm. Although less explicitly time-based, Arthur Kroker (1993) and Steven Jones's (1993) criticisms of virtual reality are related to Laurel's point. Both Kroker and Jones note that discussions of virtual reality tend to focus on the visual aspect and downplay the creation of acoustic virtual reality. Although the visual can register change over time, it also can give us the impression of frozen time, of the timeless. Thus visual VR simulations (at present) often present us with spaces to explore, and although the exploration takes place over time, the environment explored does not change over time—it is a frozen space. The acoustic, on the other hand, can only exist in time: "All sensation takes place in time, but sound has a special relationship to time unlike that of other fields that register in human sensation. Sound only exists when it is going out of existence" (Ong, 1982, pp. 31-32). Sound therefore gives us the impression of temporal continuity and never implies timelessness. Thus, media with a strong aural component (including drama) function as representations of time itself, independent of spatial metaphors.

The spatialization of time in the form of discrete, unconnected, and decontextualized units or moments, as is possible in hypermedia, is also a characteristic of the postmodern condition, as described by Fredric Jameson (1991):

> Different moments in historical or existential time are here simply filed in different places; the attempt to combine them even locally does not slide up and down a temporal scale . . . but jumps back and forth across a game board that we conceptualize in terms of distance.
>
> Thus the movement from one generic classification to another is radically discontinuous, like switching channels on a cable television set; and indeed it seems appropriate to characterize the strings of items and the compartments of genres of their typologization as so many "channels" into which the new reality is organized. (p. 373)

The connection between temporal discontinuity and television's flow is made more explicitly and clearly by Neil Postman (1985), whereas Susan Sontag (1977) traces it further back to the innovation of photography. The key point is that the audiovisual media, while continuing to represent time in a spatial format, have dispensed with print media's emphasis on linearity and continuity; we are therefore left with historical moments lacking a coherent relationship. In this way history, a form of knowledge, is transformed into nostalgia, a set of commodities (such as images and styles removed from a continuous historical context) to be bought and sold. This tendency affects computing and is in turn affected by the computer, in whose memory banks commodified historical information may be deposited or withdrawn. To the extent that cybertime takes the form of nonlinear, spatialized time, computing favors the dissolution of history as a narrative form. At the same time, computer technologies are revolutionizing the way we look at the past by the expansion of our capacity for record keeping; for information storage, processing, and retrieval; and for the preservation of audiovisual material. Alvin Toffler (1981) provides an enthusiastic look at the possibilities:

> Today we are about to jump to a whole new stage of social memory. The radical de-massification of the media, the invention of new media, the mapping of the earth by satellite, the monitoring of hospital patients by electronic sensors, the computerization of corporate files—all mean we are recording the activities of

the civilization in fine-grain detail. . . . We shall before long have the closest thing to a civilization with total recall. Third Wave civilization will have at its disposal more information, and more finely organized information, about itself than could have been imagined even a quarter-century ago. (pp. 176-177)

There certainly is much to be said for enhancing our social memory, our ability to retain and access historical information. But there is also much that is disturbing about this vision of "total recall," as Theodore Roszak (1994) argues: "Most of what will fill that social memory will be the dross of everyday life: every phone call, every check passed, every credit card purchase, every traffic citation, every airline ticket. Of what use is this to a healthy culture and a vital political life? Obviously none" (p. 211).

As Michael Benedikt (1991) points out (without irony), cyberspace is the realm of the "permanently ephemeral" (p. 11). And as Postman (1985, 1992) argues, decontextualized information is irrelevant, leaving us only with information overload; data do not substitute for history. Like Roszak (1994), Kroker (1993) rejects the idea that more information storage is better, and that "memory" is an appropriate metaphor for that computer function:

The computer has no memory, if by memory we mean the presence of political judgment and aesthetic reflection. Perfectly recalling everything in the cold language of data, it is incapable of the act of forgetting so necessary for mediating politics and history. In this case, computer memory is always cynical, always about the actual disappearance of embodied memory and the vanishing of aesthetic judgment. (p. 31)

Beyond the problem of information glut, there are very legitimate fears concerning the loss of privacy, fears that our every move leaves behind a trail of electronically recorded transactions. These permanent electronic trails make us vulnerable to anyone with the resources to gather and process the information (Gandy, 1993; Roszak, 1994). Thus, total recall becomes totalitarian recall. We are in the process of becoming a surveillance society, each of us subject to the computer's "panoptic sort" (Gandy, 1993), largely for the benefit of corporations and government. What makes this even more problematic is that these digital cybertime trails are in no way composed of indexical signs; the trail is left in binary code that is arbitrary and therefore easily altered; in the microworld, memory is virtual. And although this may in some instances serve to delegitimize computer memory, more often it seems to breed a sense of fatalistic, bureaucratic indifference. Consider how hard it is to correct a mistake in your credit history, or to convince a company that its computer records are erroneous. Both accidental and purposive manipulations of records and evidence are simple to carry out in a digital medium, and such tampering is undetectable, presenting us with the possibility of Orwellian history—history that is contingent on the needs and whims of those in control of the (operating) system. To the extent that individuals are aware of this, it also serves to remind us that all histories are socially constructed. This form of multidimensional time—a branching, hypertextual past made up of alternate histories and unconnected moments— parallels the postmodern breakdown of objectivism.

Given the hyperspeed of computing technology, surveillance can occur in real time. Total recall becomes total see-all. Thus, David Gelernter (1991) argues that some time in the near future the following scenario will become commonplace:

> You will look into a computer screen and see reality. Some part of your world— the town you live in, the company you work for, your school system, the city hospital—will hang there in a sharp color image, abstract but recognizable, moving subtly in a thousand places. This Mirror World you are looking at is fed by a steady rush of new data pouring in through cables. It is infiltrated by your own software creatures, doing your business. (p. 1)

Like Toffler (1981), Gelernter is enthusiastic about computer power and its potential to revolutionize such activities as news gathering, traffic control, hospital organization, and the political process. It is therefore difficult to decide which is more frightening: the implementation of the system that he describes, or Gelernter's seeming obliviousness to the threat it poses to freedom and privacy. Moreover, he misses the irony of installing *mirror worlds* in a culture characterized by rampant narcissism (Lasch, 1979). Mirror worlds, as symbolic representations or maps of the present (and the past), also represent the computer's potential to both control and contain the outside world through hyperspeed surveillance and information processing and the ability to respond immediately.

Moreover, computer-mediated control is extended into the future. Computer programs are plans for future actions to be taken by the computer, consisting of instructions that are to be carried out at some point in the future. Although flexibility may be included in the program, computers "lock future events into a predetermined course in a way schedules cannot" (Rifkin, 1987, p. 115). (One of the consequences of programming the future was the stock market crash of 1987.) Aside from actually determining the future, computer models are used to forecast the future (Warner & Buzbee, 1994; Rifkin, 1987). The danger here is not just from erroneous models and predictions, but from the possibility of self-fulfilling prophecies (e.g., a computer projection of a stock market crash might easily make investors nervous enough to cause one). In other words, the boundary between forecasting and programming is permeable; both are forms of representation, and prophecy has always been as much if not more about persuasion than prediction. Ultimately, the future becomes a simulation, one that may or may not be modeled on physical reality:

> The age of progress is about to give way to the age of simulation. The new simulated vision of the future incorporates the Promethean appetites of the former age while rejecting the restraints that have shackled it to historical consciousness. . . . The

future is no longer viewed as something that unfolds in strict linear fashion along a historical plane. Rather, it is something that is continually being reprogrammed to suit the transitory needs of each emergent reality. . . . The new future image conceives of reality as a vast reservoir of information to be fashioned into simulated experiences. (Rifkin, 1987, pp. 171-172)

Virtual time yields virtual futures, hypertextual, multidimensional futures. In some ways, the prospect appears liberating, opening possibilities for change. In other ways, it trivializes the future, making it "permanently ephemeral," replacing notions of fate and progress, evolution and revolution, with game playing. The future as a reality to be prepared for is replaced by the future as a virtual reality, a timeless state that is experienced in the present. Thus, the future is brought under the control of the present. The simulation may be played out from past to present to future, repeatedly, but it exists in the present. Even if multiple futures are simulated, they are futures that are always-already manifest in the programming. Along the same lines, the forecast is an attempt to bring knowledge of the future into the present, thereby processing the future as information. Given that knowledge, we can then act to control that future; and with or without the forecast, the program creates a predetermined future: "In the computer age, temporal power will be defined as having access to and control over raw data extracted from past experience, and being able to effectively program future realities" (Rifkin, 1987, p. 197). Total recall becomes total see-all becomes total be-all and end-all.

Gary Gumpert (1987) explains how magnetic tape produces ambiguity in the perception of the present, the now, as it becomes impossible to tell whether a broadcast is live or recorded. The computer's digital recordings, programmed simulations, hyperspeed surveillance, and virtual realities extend this ambiguity to include the future as well. In cybertime, we see the distinction between past, present, and future begin to breakdown as the three tenses become indistinguishable and essentially interchangeable. In some ways, cybertime makes manifest the argument put forth by St. Augustine (1961) in the fifth century:

> It is abundantly clear that neither the future nor the past exist, and therefore it is not strictly correct to say that there are three times, past, present, and future. It might be correct to say that there are three times, a present of past things, a present of present things, and a present of future things. Some such different times do exist in the mind, but nowhere else that I can see. The present of past things is memory; the present of present things is direct perception; and the present of future things is expectation. (p. 269)

St. Augustine (1961) suggests that only the present is objectively real, whereas past and future exist solely in the mind; as the computer is an extension of the mind, it likewise creates "a present of past things and future things." In cybertime, past and future collapse into the present, contributing to the almost mystical sense of timelessness sometimes associated with cyberspace (e.g., Rushkoff, 1994); this is also consistent with the spatialized, decontextualized, and commodified time discussed by postmodernists. Moreover, the computer's treatment of past and future matches the physicist's concept of spacetime, in which time is simply another set of coordinates to be graphed; the spacetime model spatializes time, making it static and fixed. In human terms, what cyberspacetime implies is a technological version of Calvinism, a fatalistic concept of a predetermined future; it is exactly this point of view that Kurt Vonnegut satirizes in *Slaughterhouse Five*, as it suggests that change is impossible and that any efforts to influence the future or avert disaster are futile. This present-centered concept of time is zero-dimensional time, time reduced to absolute certainty. But cyberspacetime also implies the other extreme, that time is infinitely malleable, that we ourselves can anticipate and predetermine the future. The problem then is hubris and isolation from the natural time world. Both extremes undermine traditional notions of the past and the future.

## EXPERIENCING TIME: COMPUTING AS ACTIVITY AND EVENT

Human interaction with and through computer media includes our use and experience of time or cyberchronemics. For example, it is commonly noted that electronic mail and computer conferencing are asynchronous forms of interaction: Participants need not transmit and receive at the same point in time. This flexibility combined with the speed of electronic transmission makes e-mail a highly efficient mode of interpersonal communication (Sproull & Kiesler, 1991). Used for networked group communication, the asynchronous character of e-mail eliminates many time-related cues, such as how long a particular task takes to complete, or when it is due. This may result in a deregulation of behavior, a loss of control over the group's output, and even an increase in the time it takes to complete a task, but it also allows for increased creativity, participation, and satisfaction. Although asynchronous communication all but guarantees that the e-mail messages we receive were composed at some point in the past, there is a tendency to experience them as if they were being communicated in the present. This sense of immediacy can also be present when reading other people's electronic discussions in the archives of bulletin boards, listservs, and so on, as Dery (1993) notes:

> on-line conversations exhibit a curious half-life; as the reader scrolls down-screen, scanning the lively back-and-forth of a discussion that may go back weeks, months, or even years, he experiences the puns, philippics, true confessions, rambling dissertations, and Generation X-er one-liners as if they were taking place in real time—which, for the reader watching them flow past on his screen, they are. (p. 561)

As noted earlier, in cybertime distinctions between past, present, and future fade, and our sense of time's passage becomes distorted. Waiting for only a few seconds seems to drag on forever, whereas time truly flies when engaged in computing. Immersed in the microworld, time seems to slow down relative to the outside world; it is almost as if Einstein's theory of relativity and the fact that the faster the speed, the slower the relative rate that time passes, applies to "travelers" along the hyperspeed infobahn. And as Rifkin (1987) relates:

> The really good video game players are able to block out both clock time and their own subjective time and descend completely into the time world of the game. It is a common experience for video game junkies to spend hours on end in front of the console without any sense whatsoever of the passage of clock time. According to Craig Brod, one of the growing number of psychologists specializing in computer-related distress, "those who live with computer workers invariably complain that disputes over time are a major source of friction."

> Long-term computer users often suffer from the constant jolt back and forth between two time worlds. As they become more enmeshed in the new time world of the computer, they become less and less able to readjust to the temporal norms and standards of traditional clock culture. They become victims of a new form of temporal schizophrenia, caught between two distinctly different temporal orientations. (p. 25)

These other experiences of time, or experiences of other time, suggest a comparison between cybertime and Mircea Eliade's (1959, 1974) concept of sacred time:

> The computer has an infinity of times in potential, ready to be actualized. Flashy splinters of time, speedy batches of time, dumb loops, programs that open up like fans according to the number of frames you assign them. Michaux speaks of "a time that has a crowd of moments". . . . Paul Virilio of "an intensive time . . . (that) . . . is not complete any more, but indefinitely fractionated in as many instants, instantaneities as the techniques of communication allow it". . . . The computer is also home to "real time," 30 frames per second, a time that fits exactly Eliade's definition of sacred time. "Religious man lives in two kinds of time, of which, the more important, sacred time, appears under the paradoxical aspect of a circular time, reversible and recoverable, a sort of eternal present that is periodically reintegrated by means of rites." "Real time" too is an eternal present of symbols, reversible and recoverable, an ontological time that never gets exhausted and that can be reintegrated at any time. Eliade's sacred time is nonhistorical. It is the time that "floweth not," that does not participate in profane duration. (Stenger, 1991, p. 55)

As metatime, cybertime would include the concept of sacred time. And although entry into cyberspace is not generally viewed as a religious experience, there is a sense in which this electronic environment is a mythical landscape, a magical realm in which incantation has efficacy, in which objects exhibit intelligence, resurrection is a matter of course (e.g., in games), and a sense of total control is possible (Davis, 1993; Hayward & Wollen, 1993; Rheingold, 1993). It is in this sense that Douglas Rushkoff (1994) refers to "man's leap out of history altogether and into the timeless dimension of Cyberia" (p. 4). The term *Cyberia* is a variation of cyberspace, but he uses it to include New Age mysticism, psychedelic drug culture, and raving, as well. The connections are not unreasonable: "Virtual reality is the closest simulation to what a world free of time, location, or even a personal identity might look like. Psychedelics and VR are both ways of creating a new, nonlinear reality where self-expression is a community event" (p. 58). It is no wonder, then, that Timothy Leary is a VR booster. Rushkoff describes virtual environments as a form of sacred space and virtual time as a form of sacred time, a mystical, Zen-like experience. It is interesting to note that this promises both the elimination of time, timelessness (zero-dimensional time), as well as its infinite expansion in nonlinear form. The sense of temporal dislocation in cybertime is a key characteristic of the experience of computing, whether it is compared to religious epiphany, drug-induced hallucination, or the dream state.

Cybertime is in some ways a form of sacred time, a mythic time or dreamtime (Kirk, 1974). And although it has become commonplace to compare the experiencing of audiovisual media to the act of dreaming, no other media provide the same sense of active personal presence as the computer; no other media allow us to construct and encounter other versions of ourselves: dream selves. As a number of scholars have pointed out, computer-mediated communication has led to a great deal of play and experimentation with multiple roles, personalities, and identities (Rheingold, 1993; Sproull, & Kiesler, 1991; Stone, 1991). Cyberspace is implicated in the fragmenting, saturating, or populating of the self (Gergen, 1991) and the decentering of the subject (Poster, 1990). We find ourselves dealing with a multitude of dream selves. Other meanings take hold here as well: Our dream selves are ideal versions of ourselves, fantasy selves; one day, through VR technology, they will also provide us with our ideal body images (Rheingold, 1991). In the psychoanalytic literature, there is a clear connection between the notion of the double, the shadow, the mirror image, and the condition of narcissism (Rank, 1971); thus, virtual doubles feed into our culture of narcissism (Lasch, 1979). Our cyberselves are digital creatures, made not of flesh and blood, but of data and information. They are unaffected by time, suffering neither from age nor injury, essentially immortal (Novak, 1991); the double, in psychoanalysis, may also signify death or its denial (Rank, 1971). Although our physical selves are subject to the ravages of time, our dream-self doubles are the masters of cybertime.

The double is sometimes seen as a threat, a frightening image of ourselves, or a doppelgänger intent on taking our place (Rank, 1971). One such double produced in cyberspace is the shadow left behind electronically and processed through the panoptic sort, through surveillance and the gathering of information about us; it is the double we encounter, for example, in a credit report (Gandy, 1993). This meeting with our data doubles cannot help but be disturbing, as it reflects the effort to reduce us down to a zero-dimensional state, to boil all of our individual qualities and histories down to a yes-or-no answer. In the face of this changeling, we often try to assert the integrity of our individuality, to express our outrage over this violation of our privacy, and, especially if our doppelgänger is a poor reflection of ourselves, to object to its inaccuracy. This generally provides mixed results, and it seems that the only logical course of resistance in a surveillance society is through the time-honored method of aliasing. With privacy eliminated by the panoptic sort, the only place we can hide is behind a multitude of masks; through the generation of doubles we may use the system against itself, creating information glut or *spamming* the data gatherers.

Much of our online doubling is not a matter of choice, however. When viewed spatially, it is reasonable to conclude that the self becomes more divided as more time is spent in communicating with greater numbers of people (Gergen, 1991). As time is subdivided into nanoseconds, and the time it takes to complete tasks such as the sending and receiving of messages decreases, our communication commitments increase, and we are pulled in more and more different directions. Because the past does not fade in cybertime, neither do past relationships, nor past versions of ourselves that remain current in e-mail, listserv, and bulletin board archives. This form of cybernetic cloning seems to promote identity diffusion, multiple personality disorders, and schizophrenic behavior. As we spend more and more of our time in cyberspace, experiencing cybertime, we may simply have to suffer this condition gladly and learn to cope with it somehow, or we may be able to use it to forge a more integrated, metadimensional sense of self. We will certainly have increased opportunities to encounter our own unconscious through our cyberspace doubles. The immediate and improvisational nature of computer-mediated communications allows for more of a direct tap into the unconscious mind than the more careful process of face-to-face public communication and the deliberate composing of written messages. Through flaming, we encounter our id or shadow; through experimentation with online gender reversal, our anima or animus. Doubles and dream selves are deeply connected to the unconscious.

Sherry Turkle (1984, 1986) refers to the computer itself as "the second self" because we tend to use it as a Rorschach test, projecting ourselves onto the technology. As our relationship with the technology has evolved from communicating with computers to communicating within them, the computer becomes the place where our second selves dwell, a dreamscape. Thus, our encounter with cyberspace may, over time, perform a therapeutic function akin to psychoanalysis. Moreover, according to Walter Ong (1982), there is less of a barrier between the conscious and unconscious mind in oral cultures than in literate ones. Writing and print allow us to explore the conscious mind self-consciously, but at the price of repressing the unconscious. The electronic media, and especially computer media, have unstopped the bottle of the unconscious, and what comes out will not be easy to deal with. The immediate effect seems to be a certain fragmenting or fractalizing of the self. Over time, however, a new synthesis between the conscious and the unconscious may well emerge, a more integrated mindset of the sort that Carl Jung (1971) was concerned with. As Ong (1982) puts it, "human consciousness evolves" (p. 178), and a new consciousness may therefore emerge through a synthesis between our physical selves and the dream selves we generate in cybertime.

In addition to consciousness, the computer joins with other media in altering our sense of community. In referring to these new forms of affiliation, Gary Gumpert (1987) speaks of media communities, Kenneth Gergen (1991) discusses symbolic communities, and Howard Rheingold (1993) uses the term virtual communities. Communities, it must be remembered, are something more than just a gathering or a group. Community ties can only emerge over time; they are not so much a matter of spatial proximity as they are a function of patience, growth, and continuity. Traditional communities, villages, and tribes tend to be stable and singular associations. Clearly, this notion of community is being undermined by our new technologies, as individuals and groups are connected into global networks, electronic tribes dispersed through cyberspace. The unique characteristics of cybertime make it possible to maintain multiple associations, to change group membership frequently and without difficulty, and to develop fairly strong ties in short periods of time. This more fluid arrangement yields a kind of liquid tribalism. Tribalism at hyperspeed is amorphous and constantly changing, multiple and overlapping. This is not the homogenous global village, but rather a dense web of interconnected tribal networks, multidimensional and fractalized. The microworld is indeed a *small world,* one in which the real world's *six degrees of separation* (see Milgram, 1974) approaches zero. Of course, we will be increasingly open to the panoptic sort as well. As Kroker and Weinstein (1994) put it: "You will pay for information with information; indeed, you will be information" (p. 11). What they are implying is that we will become our own liquid assets. But our own value will be based on gregariousness; on the number of relationships, associations, and networks we are a part of; on the number of doubles we have in play; on our ability to navigate the networks at hyperspeed, on our nomadic power (Critical Arts Ensemble, 1994). Print-mediated culture may have fostered individualism (McLuhan, 1962, 1964), but computer-mediated culture promotes networking, tribal associations, and various forms of virtual (and possibly global) communities.

The network is usually seen as a spatial concept, but we must remember that time too is a network of relations among different events. Cybertime is networked time and also a network of different concepts of time. As metatime, it has a certain liberating potential. But it also threatens us with overload and a loss of coherence, with the breakdown of the signifying chain, the connection of signifier to signified and of one sign to another needed to generate meaning; this is the schizophrenic breakdown associated with the postmodern condition (Jameson, 1991). Cybertime does not eliminate, but rather subsumes one-dimensional time, clock and calendar time, and the sense of historical time that has taken us so long to develop. We need not lose touch with the one-dimensional, but instead can use it as an anchor to a more stable and coherent sense of time. What is needed is a balance between these tendencies and a balance that also includes the zero-dimensional tendencies of cybertime. Timelessness is a much sought after experience, but it should not come at the expense of history and tradition, and certainly not at the expense of the future. The ways in which we use and experience time are, after all, the key to cultural survival.

## REFERENCES

Atkin, R. (1981). *Multidimensional man.* New York: Penguin.

Augustine, St. (1961). *Confessions* (R.S. Pine-Coffin, Trans.). New York: Penguin.

Baudrillard, J. (1983). *Simulations* (P. Foss, P. Patton, & P. Beitchman, Trans.). New York: Semiotext(e).

Benedikt, M. (Ed.). (1991). *Cyberspace: First steps.* Cambridge, MA: MIT Press.

Beniger, J.R. (1986). *The control revolution: Technological and economic origins of the information society.* Cambridge, MA: Harvard University Press.

Bolter, J.D. (1984). *Turing's man: Western culture in the computer age.* Chapel Hill: University of North Carolina Press.

Bolter, J.D. (1991). *Writing space: The computer, hypertext, and the history of writing.* Hillsdale, NJ: Erlbaum.

Burke, K. (1945). *A grammar of motives.* Berkeley: University of California Press.

Critical Arts Ensemble. (1994). *The electronic disturbance.* Brooklyn: Autonomedia.

Carey, J.W. (1989). *Communication as culture: Essays on media and society.* Boston: Unwin Hyman.

Davis, E. (1993). Techgnosis: Magic, memory, and the angels of information. *The South Atlantic Quarterly, 92*(4), 585-616.

Dery, M. (Ed.). (1993). Flame wars: The discourse of cyberculture [Special issue]. *The South Atlantic Quarterly, 92*(4).

Einstein, A. (1954). *Relativity, the special and the general theory: A popular exposition* (rev. ed.; R.W. Lawson, Trans.). London: Methuen.

Eliade, M. (1959). *The sacred and the profane* (W. Trask, Trans.). New York: Harvest/HBJ Books.

Eliade, M. (1974). *The myth of the eternal return or, cosmos and history* (W. Trask, Trans.). Princeton, NJ: Princeton University Press.

Ellul, J. (1968). *Propaganda: The formation of men's attitudes* (K. Kellen & J. Lerner, Trans.). New York: Alfred A. Knopf.

Gandy, O.H., Jr. (1993). *The panoptic sort: A political economy of personal information.* Boulder, CO: Westview.

Gelernter, D. (1991). *Mirror worlds or the day software puts the universe in a shoebox . . . How it will happen and what it will mean.* New York: Oxford University Press.

Gergen, K.J. (1991). *The saturated self: Dilemmas of identity in contemporary life.* New York: Basic Books.

Gibson, W. (1984). *Neuromancer.* New York: Ace Books.

Gleick, J. (1987). *Chaos: Making a new science.* New York: Viking Penguin.

Gumpert, G. (1987). *Talking tombstones and other tales of the media age.* New York: Oxford University Press.

Hall, E.T. (1959). *The silent language.* New York: Doubleday.

Hall, E.T. (1984). *The dance of life: The other dimension of time.* Garden City, NY: Anchor.

Hayward, P., & Wollen, T. (Eds.). (1993). *Future visions: New technologies of the screen.* London: British Film Institute.

Innis, H. A. (1951). *The bias of communication.* Toronto: University of Toronto Press.

Jameson, F. (1991). *Postmodernism, or, the cultural logic of late capitalism.* Durham, NC: Duke University Press.

Jones, S. (1993). A sense of space: Virtual reality, authenticity, and the oral. *Critical Studies in Mass Communication, 10*(3), 238-252.

Jung, C.G. (1971). *The portable Jung* (R.F.C. Hull, Trans.). New York: Viking.

Kidwell, P.A., & Ceruzzi, P.E. (1994). *Landmarks in digital computing.* Washington, DC: Smithsonian Institution Press.

Kirk, G.S. (1974). *The nature of Greek myths.* New York: Penguin.

Kroker, A. (1993). *Spasm: Virtual reality, android music, and electric flesh.* New York: St. Martin's Press.

Kroker, A., & Weinstein, M.A. (1994). *Data trash: The theory of the virtual class.* New York: St. Martin's Press.

Lakoff, G., & Johnson, M. (1980). *Metaphors we live by.* Chicago: University of Chicago Press.

Landow, G.P. (1992). *Hypertext: The convergence of contemporary critical theory and technology.* Baltimore: John Hopkins University Press.

Lanham, R.A. (1993). *The electronic word: Democracy, technology, and the arts.* Chicago: University of Chicago Press.

Lasch, C. (1979). *The culture of narcissism: American life in an age of diminishing expectations.* New York: Norton.

Laurel, B. (1993). *Computers as theatre.* Reading, MA: Addison Wesley.

Levy, S. (1984). *Hackers: Heroes of the computer revolution.* New York: Dell.

Levy, S. (1992). *Artificial life: A report from the frontier where computers meet biology.* New York: Random House.

Lubar, S. (1993). *Infoculture: The Smithsonian book of information age inventions.* Boston: Houghton Mifflin.

MacBeath, M. (1993). Time's square. In R. Le Poidevin & M. MacBeath (Eds.), *The philosophy of time* (pp. 183-202). New York: Oxford University Press.

Maimonides, M. (1963). *The guide of the perplexed* (Vol. 1, S. Pines, Trans.). Chicago: University of Chicago Press.

Marcuse, H. (1964). *One-dimensional man: Studies in the ideology of advanced industrial society.* Boston: Beacon Press.

McLuhan, M. (1962). *The Gutenberg galaxy.* Toronto: University of Toronto Press.

McLuhan, M. (1964). *Understanding media: The extensions of man.* New York: Mentor Books.

Meyrowitz, J. (1985). *No sense of place.* New York: Oxford University Press.

Milgram, S. (1974). The small-world problem. In J.B. Maas (Ed.), *Readings in psychology today* (3rd ed., pp. 324-330). Del Mar, CA: CRM Books.

Mumford, L. (1963). *Technics and civilization.* New York: Harcourt Brace Jovanovich.

Newton, I. (1934). *Newton's principia* (A. Motte, Trans., F. Cajori, Ed.). Berkeley: University of California Press.

Novak, M. (1991). Liquid architectures in cyberspace. In M. Benedikt (Ed.), *Cyberspace: First steps* (pp. 225-254). Cambridge, MA: MIT Press.

Ong, W.J. (1982). *Orality and literacy: The technologizing of the word.* New York: Methuen.

Perkinson, H. (1996). *No safety in numbers: How the computer quantified everything and made people risk-aversive.* Cresskill, NJ: Hampton Press.

Pimentel, K., & Teixeira, K. (1993). *Virtual reality: Through the new looking glass.* New York: Intel/Windcrest/McGraw-Hill.

Poster, M. (1990). *The mode of information.* Chicago: University of Chicago Press.

Postman, N. (1985). *Amusing ourselves to death.* New York: Viking.

Postman, N. (1992). *Technopoly: The surrender of culture to technology.* New York: Alfred A. Knopf.

Provenzo, E.F., Jr. (1986). *Beyond the Gutenberg galaxy.* New York: Teachers College Press.

Raley, J. (1994). Global positioning systems. In A. Grant (Ed.), *Communication technology update* (3rd ed., pp. 302-313). Boston: Butterworth-Heinemann.

Rank, O. (1971). *The double: A psychoanalytic study* (H. Tucker, Jr., Trans.). New York: New American Library.

Rheingold, H. (1991). *Virtual reality.* New York: Touchstone.

Rheingold, H. (1993). *The virtual community: Homesteading on the electronic frontier.* Reading, MA: Addison Wesley.

Rifkin, J. (1987). *Time wars: The primary conflict in human history.* New York: Touchstone.

Robinett, W. (1992). Synthetic experience: A proposed taxonomy. *Presence: Teleoperators and Virtual Environments, 1*(2), 229-247.

Roszak, T. (1994). *The cult of information: A neo-Luddite treatise on high-tech, artificial intelligence, and the true art of thinking* (2nd ed.). Berkeley: The University of California Press.

Rucker, R. (1984). *The fourth dimension: A guided tour of the higher universes.* Boston: Houghton Mifflin.

Rushkoff, D. (1994). *Cyberia: Life in the trenches of hyperspace.* New York: HarperCollins.

Sontag, S. (1977). *On photography.* New York: Farrar, Strauss and Giroux.

Sproull, L., & Kiesler, S. (1991). *Connections: New ways of working in the networked organization.* Cambridge, MA: The MIT Press.

Stenger, N. (1991). Mind is a leaking rainbow. In M. Benedikt (Ed.), *Cyberspace: First steps* (pp. 49-58). Cambridge, MA: MIT Press.

Sternberg, J. (1991). The abacus: The earliest digital computer and its cultural implications. *New Dimensions in Communications: Proceedings of the 48th Annual New York State Speech Communication Association Convention, 4,* 69-71.

Stone, A.R. (1991). Will the real body please stand up? Boundary stories about virtual cultures. In M. Benedikt (Ed.), *Cyberspace: First steps* (pp. 81-118). Cambridge, MA: MIT Press.

Toffler, A. (1981). *The third wave.* New York: Bantam.

Toffler, A., & Toffler, H. (1993, October 31). Societies at hyper-speed. *The New York Times,* Section 4, p. 17.

Turkle, S. (1984). *The second self: Computers and the human spirit.* New York: Simon and Schuster.

Turkle, S. (1986). Computer as Rorschach. In G. Gumpert & R. Cathcart (Eds.), *Inter/media: Interpersonal communication in a media world* (3rd ed., pp. 439-459). New York: Oxford University Press.

Virilio, P. (1986). *Speed and politics: An essay on dromology* (M. Polizzotti, Trans.). New York: Semiotext(e).

Virilio, P. (1991). *The lost dimension* (D. Moshenberg, Trans.). New York: Semiotext(e).

Wachtel, E. (1980). *Visions of order: The influence of technology on space conception.* Unpublished doctoral dissertation, New York University, New York City.

Warner, T.T., & Buzbee, B. (1994). The future of weather and climate prediction. In C.A. Pickover (Ed.), *Visions of the future: Art, technology and computing in the twenty-first century* (pp. 43-52). New York: St. Martin's Press.

Weizenbaum, J. (1976). *Computer power and human reason.* San Francisco: Freeman.

Whitrow, G.J. (1980). *The natural philosophy of time* (2nd ed.). Oxford: Oxford University Press.

Whitrow, G.J. (1988). *Time in history: Views of time from prehistory to the present day.* Oxford: Oxford University Press.

Wiener, N. (1967). *The human use of human beings: Cybernetics and society.* Boston, MA: Avon.

Woolley, B. (1992). *Virtual worlds: A journey in hype and hyperreality.* Oxford: Blackwell.

Wyant, G., & Hammerstron, T. (1994). *How microprocessors work.* Emeryville, CA: Ziff-Davis Press.

Zettl, H. (1990). *Sight sound motion: Applied media aesthetics* (2nd ed.). Belmont, CA: Wadsworth.

# Epilogue: Cyberspace, Shmyberspace

## Neil Postman

*Throughout this volume we have maintained that cyberspace is a phenomenon that needs to be taken seriously and analyzed critically. Some have written in praise of cyberspace, computers, electronic media, and the information society. Others raise critical questions about their uses, effects, and the policies surrounding them. But for the most part we have taken for granted the presence of electronic technologies and their continued evolution. It is for this reason that we have given the last word to Neil Postman. In the epilogue to this volume, he raises the most basic question of all—Do we actually need cyberspace technologies? Is there a problem that cyberspace is needed to solve? Postman suggests that the difficulties contemporary information technologies were meant to address were, in fact, resolved in the 19th century. Thus, we suffer from too much information and from empty simulations that take the place of genuine experience. Far from a dismissal, Postman reminds us that in fulfilling new functions, older, more important, ones may be ignored; in creating new forms, more traditional and satisfying ones may be forgotten; and that in generating new codes and meanings, we may become lost in a Babel-like state of incoherence. Even if you do not agree with Postman's argument, you might take him up on his challenge to justify cyberspace on the basis of genuine human needs.*

"We feel that even when all possible scientific problems have been answered,
the problems of life remain completely untouched."
—Ludwig Wittgenstein

Here is a problem that people faced in the 19th century. It was only one among many, but it was taken quite seriously: A message could travel only as fast as a human being could travel—about 35 miles per hour (on a train). Nineteenth-century people also worried about another communication problem: Language, either spoken or written, was very nearly the only form messages could take. And they also worried about this one: Most people did not have access to the increasing volume of information that science, commerce, medicine, and other fields of knowledge were generating.

When human beings are presented with problems, they often embark on creative efforts to solve them. This is exactly what happened in the 19th century. The problem, taken as a whole, was this: How can we get more information to more people, fast, and in diverse forms? The good news is that beginning with the invention of telegraphy and photography in the 1840s, and for 100 years afterward, *we solved the problem.* For those who are unfamiliar with the 19th century, here are some of the inventions that contributed to the solution: telegraphy, photography, the rotary press, the transatlantic cable, the electric light, radio, movies, the x-ray, the penny press, the modern magazine, and the advertising agency. Of course, in the first half of the 20th century, we added some important inventions so that once and for all we need not worry about information scarcity or the limitations of space, time, and form.

From millions of sources all over the globe, through every possible channel and medium—lightwaves, airwaves, ticker tapes, computer banks, telephone wires, television cables, satellites, printing presses—information pours in. Behind it, in every imaginable form of storage—on paper, videocassette and audiotape, on disks, film, and silicon chips—is an even greater volume of information waiting to be retrieved. Yes, we solved the problem in spectacular fashion. But in doing so we created a new problem never experienced before: information glut, information incoherence, information meaninglessness. To put it bluntly, information has become a form of garbage, not only incapable of answering the most fundamental human questions, but barely useful in providing direction to the solution of even mundane problems. What has happened is that the tie between information and human purpose has been severed. Information is now a commodity that is bought and sold; it comes indiscriminately, directed at no one in particular, in enormous volume, at high speeds, disconnected from theory, meaning, and purpose.

Several prescient people saw the problem coming and warned us to prepare for it. Among them were Martin Heidegger, Aldous Huxley, Lewis Mumford, Harold Innis, Jacques Ellul, and Marshall McLuhan. But none expressed the dangers more eloquently and precisely than Edna St. Vincent Millay. In her wonderful poem, "Huntsman, What Quarry," she wrote:

Upon this gifted age, in its dark hour,
Falls from the sky a meteoric shower
Of facts . . . they lie unquestioned, uncombined.
Wisdom enough to leech us of our ill
Is daily spun; but there exists no loom
To weave it into fabric . . .

No loom to weave it into fabric. This is the problem we have to confront, and with as much intelligence and energy as we can muster. Why, then, do we tarry so long in addressing it? Well, for one thing, there is the matter of plain denial. I refer to those who are encased in a 19th-century mentality and do not, therefore, acknowledge that we have solved the problem of information scarcity. To understand their outlook we may use the example of the automobile. The automobile was the solution to the problem of how to increase speed and mobility, of how to shrink distance, of how to collapse time. This it accomplished quite well, but in so doing created other problems, including poisoning the air, choking our cities, and dispersing families. To those who are burdened by a sense of denial, the answer to these newly created problems is to add cruise control, electric windows, and telephones to our cars. But such innovations are trivial; they do not, in fact, enhance the basic contribution of cars, and they distract us from confronting the most urgent problems created by cars.

This is the sort of outlook we may associate with people who are enthusiastic about virtual reality machines. Finding themselves insufficiently stimulated by real reality, they seek a solution by escaping from it, exciting themselves through a technologically simulated experience. The same may be said for those immersing themselves in e-mail and other forms of computer-mediated communication. Finding themselves short on real friendships, perhaps even afraid to make them, they seek a solution in simulated friendships, pathetically surfing the net to locate a kindred spirit, who like spirits everywhere will have no material existence. And the same may be said for those who spend uncountable hours watching television so that they may escape from the terrifying prospect of formulating an unpackaged original thought. All these souls have this in common: They refuse to acknowledge what their real problem is—respectively, boringness, friendlessness, thoughtlessness.

You will think, at this point, that I do not like such people and have no sympathy for them. But this is not so. Who among us has not been faced with these problems? Who among us has not tried to weave a fabric to our lives by employing some ridiculous simulation, a momentary distraction, a pretense at living? My point is the same one Wittgenstein made about science (in the quote at the beginning of this essay): Technology does not touch life's deepest problems. We may think it will, as so many thought in the 19th century, when the aim of technological development was to reduce ignorance, superstition, and suffering. And to some extent, they were right to hope so. And to some extent, technology did address those problems. But the technology celebrated now is just cruise control and electric windows.

The engineers, computer gurus, and corporate visionaries who claim to speak for the future are, in fact, addressing problems that have already been solved. It is time for us to give up the notion that we may find solutions to our emptiness through technology. We must now turn to our poets, playwrights, composers, theologians, and artists, who, alone, can create or restore the narratives that will give a meaningful pattern to our lives. They are our weavers who can liberate us from cyberspace and put us back in the world.

# Author Index

◇◇◇◇

# Subject Index